REBELS & YANKEES
THE
COMMANDERS
OF THE CIVIL WAR

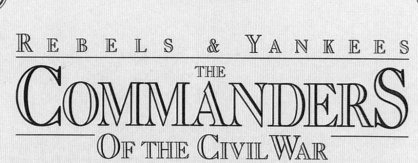

REBELS & YANKEES
THE
COMMANDERS
OF THE CIVIL WAR

An account of the lives of the commissioned officers during America's war of secession.
Including a remarkable collection of photographs of historical and personal memorabilia

WILLIAM C. DAVIS
TECHNICAL ADVISOR: RUSS A. PRITCHARD

PUBLISHED BY
SALAMANDER BOOKS LIMITED
LONDON

A SALAMANDER BOOK

Published by Salamander Books Ltd
8 Blenheim Court, Brewery Road
London N7 9NT
United Kingdom

© Salamander Books Ltd 1990, 1999

ISBN 1 58209 100 5

CREDITS

Editor: Tony Hall
Designer: Mark Holt
Indexer: David Linton
Color artwork: Jeff Burn © Salamander Books Ltd
Line artwork: Kevin Jones Associates,
Geoff Denney Associates
© Salamander Books Ltd
Color photography: Don Eiler, Richmond, Virginia
© Salamander Books Ltd
Filmset: SX Composing Ltd, England
Color reproduction: Bantam Litho Ltd, England
Reprinted 1999 in China

ACKNOWLEDGMENTS

In the preparation of this book we received the
generous assistance and advice from militaria
collectors and museum directors and staff in the
United States. Without the help of the individuals
and organizations listed below, this record of Civil
War militaria could not have been assembled. We
would also like to extend a very special thanks to
Russ A. Pritchard, whose work and support have been
invaluable to the success of this project.

INSTITUTIONAL COLLECTIONS

**The Civil War Library and Museum, Philadelphia,
Pennsylvania**
Russ A. Pritchard, Director

**The Museum of The Confederacy, Richmond,
Virginia**
Howard O. Hendricks, Curator of Collections
Malinda S. Collier, Registrar
Rebecca Ansell Rose, Curatorial Assistant
Corrine P. Hudgins, Photographic Assistant
Guy R. Swanson, Curator of Manuscripts and Archives
Eleanor G. Lewis, Curatorial Intern
Harry G. Gaydos, Curatorial Intern

Virginia Historical Society, Richmond, Virginia
Linda Leazer, Assistant Curator/Registrar, Museum
Services

Virginia Military Institute, Lexington, Virginia
Keith E. Gibson, Executive Director

West Point Museum, West Point, New York
Michael E. Moss, Director
Robert W. Fisch, Curator of Arms
Michael J. McAfee, Curator of Uniforms and Military
History

PRIVATE COLLECTIONS

Gary Leister, Sunbury, Pennsylvania
William Le Pard, Ardmore, Pennsylvania
C. Paul Loane, Merchantville, New Jersey
Russ A. Pritchard, Wayne, Pennsylvania
Mort Sork, Gladwyne, Pennsylvania
David Stewart, New Hope, Pennsylvania
Donald R. Tharpe, Midland, Virginia
Don Troiani, Southbury, Connecticut
Bob Walter, Arlington Heights, Illinois

CONTENTS

INTRODUCTION

Leadership is a quality still indefinable after thousands of years of study. No one can predict with certainty who will or will not make an able commander in war or a capable statesman in peace. Events themselves so often bring out the qualities lying dormant within the individual that any attempt to foresee in advance, or to explain afterward, the emergence of a great leader is almost futile.

Certainly it was so in the American Civil War. Out of a nation torn in two, and out of a pre-war military that was practically non-existent, tens of thousands of leaders, from the mightiest generals to the most obscure lieutenants, virtually appeared out of the crowd.

Where they came from and why, how they learned – and at times failed to learn – the skills necessary to lead men into the inferno of the battlefield, and how they dealt with the sudden power and responsibility given them, have been largely overlooked. In the preoccupation with the great individual commanders – and with the less than great – attention has drifted away from the officers of the war as a whole, both North and South.

And that is too bad. For when simple men are called forward by great events, sometimes remarkable things happen. Tens of thousands of these young men – and many who were not so young – put aside their civilian lives, their educations, loves, and all their other hopes and dreams of the future, to set forth on the great adventure of their generation. Indeed, it was *the* event of their century. To stay out of it would have been unthinkable for most, and impossible for many.

Yet mere participation hardly guaranteed that a man would rise to command. That required something else entirely. For some it was influence; for others it would be money. Many more found their path to leadership in personal popularity, back-slapping, glad-handing, and drink-buying. But, as the incompetents and the politicians were sifted out by time and the battlefield, men rose to lead through experience and competence.

Indeed, it is one of the ironies of the conflict that by 1864 and 1865 the quality of the enlisted men was generally considered to be inferior to that of the 1861 volunteers, because by that time both North and South were resorting to conscription to fill the gaps in the ranks left by the loss in battle of the men who were patriotic enough to enlist early in the war. At the same time, the quality of many of the officers had actually improved, because only trial and experience could take even the bravest and most patriotic of men and turn them into first rate leaders. It was for this reason, perhaps, that the best lower level officers were available just at the time they were needed. The only trouble was, the best men were also the most likely to have fallen in battle. As new regiments were formed to replace those mustered out or reduced by combat, experienced men could be found to come forward and act as the vitally important company and regimental officers. The tests that identified and separated those born to command from those born to be led were to confront these men all across the battle-scarred landscape of civil war America. Battle certainly acted as a great arbiter of competence. But there were other, more subtle, yet equally taxing challenges that the would-be officer had to meet and overcome during his time in uniform. Learning the rules and the ways of any army or a navy. Discovering how to command obedience from unruly volunteer soldiers in camp so that they would obey when their lives depended upon it in the field. Facing the debilitating and demoralizing prospect of imprisonment if captured. And for a few, learning not just how to be leaders, but how to be generals, when the full weight of command both practical and moral would settle upon a single man's shoulders.

How these men of North and South bore this weight, and how they came to handle the responsibility entrusted to them, is a story little-told in all the memoirs and post-war accounts. For those seem only to portray scene after scene of stirring command and bravery, as if that was all there was to leadership in the Civil War. There was a great deal more, in fact, as tens of thousands of American men were to discover when the momentum of events propelled them and their country toward those first shots at Fort Sumter.

In their thousands they served, the young men like Lieutenant J.B. Neill, Company C, 153rd New York. He could represent here the quiet moments of them all . . . the pipe, the shade, and the peaceful time between the storms of battle.

CHAPTER ONE
THE "OLD ARMY"

Americans are rarely prepared for their wars when they erupt, and the Civil War was no exception. A tiny army, scattered over thousands of miles, was ill-prepared to defend the Union. In the South, the new Confederacy faced a situation that was little better. Enormous demands would, therefore, be placed upon the few trained and able men ready to assume the responsibility of command.

IN THE late spring of 1861, in the infant western city of Los Angeles, a sad group of old friends gathered for the last time. They met at the home of Captain Winfield Scott Hancock and his wife Ada to bid farewell to half a dozen of their number who were about to embark upon the overland journey to the new Confederacy. All had resigned their commissions in the United States Army and were preparing to don a different uniform, one that meant they might have to fight against their old friends in blue who were seeing them off at midnight on that day, June 16.

Leader of the traveling party was Albert Sidney Johnston, colonel and brevet brigadier general, until recently commander of the Department of the Pacific. He had resigned back in May, hoping to stay out of the coming war entirely and become instead a farmer in southern California. When that failed, he thought to go to Texas to try again and, ostensibly, this was why he was leaving in company with the others. There was no question, however, about his companions' intent. Lewis Armistead, George Pickett, Richard B. Garnett, and the others were going to take commissions in the Confederate Army. Despite his peaceful hopes, Johnston would too, and in only a few weeks.

At the end of the evening, as tears began to well in the eyes of all present, Johnston asked his wife to "sing me one or two of the old songs you used to sing." She obliged, treating the company to "Mary of Argyle" and "Kathleen Mavourneen". She sang sadly, saying that in her heart she feared all cause for singing was gone. All around her the old friends put on brave smiles that covered, all-too-imperfectly, what Ada Hancock felt were "hearts that were filled with sadness over the sundering of life-long ties, and doubts as to the result of their sacrifice."

Finally Armistead, a North Carolinian, could contain himself no longer. He wept openly. The tears spread throughout the gathering. It was time to go. Armistead gave Ada a small satchel with some personal effects, asking her to open it only in the event of his death, and then to send the contents to his family. To Hancock he gave his new, unworn major's uniform, commenting that "he might sometime need it." Then, in farewell, he stood before Hancock, put his hands on his shoulders, looked him squarely in the eyes, and spoke through his tears. "Hancock, goodbye", he said. "You can never know what this has cost me." Praying that he might be struck dead rather than have to fight his old friends, he and the others rode off into the warm California night.[1]

It was a scene oft-repeated from ocean to ocean in the small 16,000-man United States Army – in what, after the outbreak of civil war would ever-after be called, fondly, the "Old Army". It was an odd fondness, for it grew out of years of service in an under-funded, often ill-equipped corps that demanded loneliness, hardship, Job-like patience, and almost unrelenting self-sacrifice from its officers. No wonder the years of isolated duty at frontier outposts, the incredibly slow advancement for junior officers and the oppression of superannuated old commanders, and all the other frustrations of a seemingly unappreciated service, tended to forge a bond among those who endured it all. Theirs was a very small world. When the war broke out, there were only 1,098 serving officers in the entire Old Army. Inevitably their social and family ties became exaggerated, especially in outposts where there might not be more than half a dozen officers with whom to associate. While not everyone might have felt as desolated as Armistead, still when the war came, the destruction of the small world that had been all they knew cost them all.[2]

"I always found them the same," a British visitor wrote of the American officers he met in 1852: "gentlemen-like and agreeable."[3] It is remarkable, considering what they endured. They were soldiers in a nation that had never liked armies and always maintained a suspicion of a professional military. The overwhelming majority of them had been educated at public expense at the United States Military Academy, leading to a dual resentment, from taxpayers who objected to the cost, and from would-be volunteer officers who found their aspirations stunted or eclipsed by a super-abundance of West Point graduates.

The Old Army had always been small, rarely more than 10,000 of all ranks, and frequently less since the War of 1812. That alone severely limited the chances for advancement of any young officer hoping to find promotion. Worse, the Military

Part of the panoply and splendor of peacetime soldiering, the Guthrie Grays of Cincinnati, Ohio, in the 1850s. Their officers were truly gentlemen, the cream of local society for whom a commission was a badge of social standing.

Academy yearly turned out more graduates than there were vacancies to fill, especially in peacetime. Since the country had enjoyed decades of peace, interrupted only by war with Mexico and an occasional Indian conflict, vacancies through casualties were few. Instead, graduates accepted brevet – essentially honorary – rank, and a place on a waiting list. The final, and worst contributor to making that list a long one was the complete absence of a mandated retirement policy. An officer could remain in service as long as he chose and so long as he seemed relatively healthy. When Colonel John Walbach, commanding the 4th Artillery, died in his command in 1857, he was ninety-three years old and had been continuously in the service since 1799. The 4th Infantry was led by Colonel William Whistler in 1861. He had been in the army since 1801, and had taken command of the regiment some sixteen years before, when his aged predecessor died of exertion on the field after giving the regiment its first field drill in a number of years.[4]

In fact, the "fogeyism" in the army's upper levels was so bad that half of the colonels commanding regiments in 1823 were still in command two decades later. When the war broke out in 1861, the army's commissary general, George Gibson, had been in the same post since 1818, and stayed there until his death on September 29, 1861. Indeed, half of the chiefs of the War Department's bureaus when Fort Sumter was fired upon had been in office since before the Mexican War.[5] More telling than this was the fact that at the time of secession there were only four line officers of general rank in the army, and only one of them, William S. Harney, was under the age of seventy! On average they had spent forty-seven years in the service, and Winfield Scott, aged

Above: A typical pre-war officer, with the servant that military regulations allowed for him. Colonel Joseph Plympton would not recognize the kind of warfare that lay in store for Old Army men in 1861.

Below: Aged, infirm, so corpulent he could not mount a horse or take the field, old Lieutenant General Winfield Scott had to make way for a whole new breed of officer in the wake of secession.

seventy-four, had been in uniform since 1808. The oldest, Brigadier General John E. Wool, was seventy-seven when war broke out.

No wonder then that one official estimate provided to the secretary of war speculated that a new West Point graduate would wait eight years to make first lieutenant, another ten years to receive a captain's bars, and two decades more after that to become a major. Twenty more years would see him promoted lieutenant colonel and then, finally, colonel . . . after almost sixty years in uniform. An 1842 graduate of the Military Academy, fresh from his education and training, proud of his new uniform and anxious to serve and get ahead, could expect to wait into the next century before he got to command a regiment, if he lasted. No wonder that an outfit like the 4th Artillery was called "the immortal Regiment" – not for its heroic deeds, but from the fact that most of its lieutenants – junior officers – were already gray-haired![6]

Even for those officers who could handle the stultifying effects of years without a promotion, the concomitant problem of inadequate income often proved too much to bear. Just four years before the outbreak of the war, a second lieutenant's pay of $300 per year was exactly what it had been in 1812, forty-five years earlier. In the earlier years of the century the only way to get more pay was to obtain promotion – hardly a glowing prospect. Later on, special allowances for clothing and victuals and other amenities had the effect of increasing income even without promotion, but still almost every officer began to look after a few years at the attractions of more remunerative civilian employment. The rate of resignations among lieutenants and captains, as a result, was continually high, providing the only steady source of vacancies for new West Point graduates, and leading to an actual shortage of junior officers in some regiments. In fact some infantry companies were left with no officers to command them. In the year 1836, just over 18 percent of the officers in the Old Army resigned. Of the 117 who left, 97 were West Point men, and all but seven were junior officers. Low pay and no advancement had been simply too much for them, and only the war with Mexico in the late 1840s would bring some of them back into uniform.[7]

This effect of the hardship of military service put the lie to an old canard that West Point only educated the sons of the wealthy and influential. To be sure, many officers did come from well-established old families with good political ties to the Senators and Congressmen who gave the appointments. But for every Robert E. Lee whose family name and connections assured him an appointment, there were a dozen others who went because they could not afford any other education, because they really wanted to be soldiers, or because they had no choice. Hiram Ulysses Grant went because his father made him go, and while at the academy saw his name changed forever to Ulysses S. Grant. Another who would be known by a different name, Thomas J. Jackson of Virginia, went there because the education was free. By the 1840s, most claimed that their families were in "reduced circumstances", though just prior to the Civil War the number of cadets who admitted to independent wealth went up sharply, indicating perhaps that the growing sectional crisis was attracting the sons of the planters in the South who would soon have to fight to keep their wealth.[8]

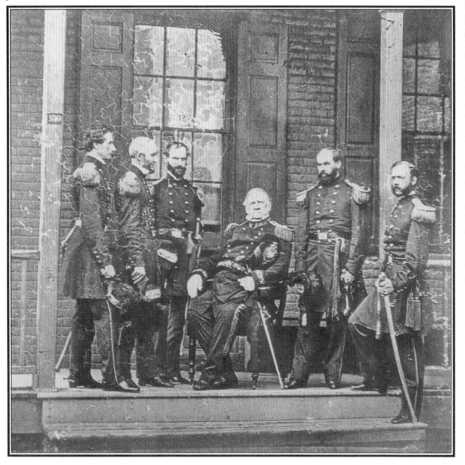

Captain 1st Dragoons, 1858

The pre-war Old Army was always a pitifully small organization. At about 16,000 men in 1860, it was hardly larger than it had been thirty years before. Only a handful of infantry, cavalry, and artillery units made up its ranks. One of the newer regiments was the 1st Dragoons, created in 1834 as the Regiment of Mounted Dragoons, one of its officers then being later Confederate President Jefferson Davis. As the 1st Dragoons, it served on until the outbreak of war, being essentially a cavalry regiment. Based in California, the unit saw constant action against Indians in the Far West. This captain wears the typical dragoon officer's uniform of dark blue blouse, sky blue trousers, and the so-called "Jeff Davis" or Hardee hat. A heavy .44 caliber Colt pistol and a heavy dragoon saber complete his arms. The old regiment soon disappeared as newer cavalry tactics of fighting dismounted essentially pre-empted the dragoon's role.

Regular Infantry Regiment

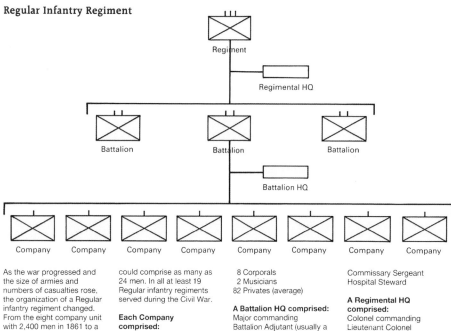

As the war progressed and the size of armies and numbers of casualties rose, the organization of a Regular infantry regiment changed. From the eight company unit with 2,400 men in 1861 to a ten company unit with 1,000 men in 1865. Other changes included the phasing-out of the regimental band which could comprise as many as 24 men. In all at least 19 Regular infantry regiments served during the Civil War.

Each Company comprised:
Captain commanding
First Lieutenant
Second Lieutenant
    4 Sergeants
8 Corporals
2 Musicians
82 Privates (average)

A Battalion HQ comprised:
Major commanding
Battalion Adjutant (usually a lieutenant)
Battalion Quartermaster (usually a lieutenant)
Sergeant Major

Commissary Sergeant
Hospital Steward

A Regimental HQ comprised:
Colonel commanding
Lieutenant Colonel
Regimental Adjutant
Regimental Quartermaster
Drum Major
    2 Senior Musicians

Whatever their family background, by the time of the Civil War the West Point men dominated the officer corps of the Old Army. In 1861, out of the 1,098 commissioned officers in uniform, 744 were Military Academy graduates.[9] Naturally enough, most were from the classes that finished their schooling after the Mexican War, but again, the absence of any retirement policy allowed for a number of septuagenarians as well. All of the general officers in service had been born before the Military Academy was founded in 1802, and none of them had attended. Of the roughly 350 non-West Point graduates who were officers in 1861, almost all had received special appointments from civilian life, or else had originally been elected or appointed leaders of state volunteer regiments raised during the Mexican and earlier conflicts. Such men, if they performed well, were often commissioned into the Regular Army after their volunteer units had mustered out. Thus it was that the commanding general of the army, Major General Winfield Scott, had been appointed by President Jefferson in 1808. The other generals, William Harney, David E. Twiggs, and John E. Wool, had all been similarly commissioned, and all but Harney were veterans of the War of 1812.[10] Ironically, not one of the men in command of the Old Army had ever had so much as a single day of professional military training.

Regular Cavalry Regiment

At the close of 1860 there were only five mounted regiments in the Regular Army, all of which were posted on the frontier. These were the 1st and 2nd Cavalry, the 1st and 2nd Dragoons, and the Regiment of Mounted Riflemen. This situation, together with the belief that it would take at least two years to train volunteers cavalry regiments for combat led in part to the ascendancy of Rebel cavalry in the first years of the war.

The organization of these regiments was based on the battalion. Three battalions per regiment was the norm though the number was reduced in wartime to two, (as shown here). The battalion itself was phased out after 1862.

Each Company comprised:
Captain commanding
First Lieutenant
Second Lieutenant
First Sergeant

Quartermaster Sergeant
4 Sergeants
8 Corporals
2 Farriers
2 Musicians
1 Wagoner
1 Saddler
72 Privates (average)

Each Squadron of two Companies comprised:
46 Officers and NCOs
144 Privates (average)

Battalion Staff comprised:
Major commanding
Battalion Adjutant
Battalion Quartermaster
Sergeant Major
Quartermaster Sergeant
Commissary Steward
Hospital Steward
Saddler Sergeant
Veterinary Sergeant

Regimental Staff comprised:
Colonel commanding
Lieutenant Colonel
Regimental Adjutant
Regimental Quartermaster
2 Buglers

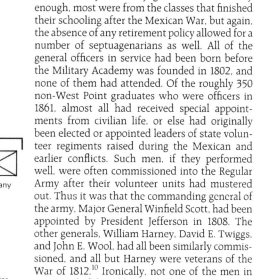

Regimental Organizations of the Old Army: Infantry, Cavalry and Artillery

The whole idea behind the organization of the Regular Army, and the Union and Confederate volunteer units modeled upon it, was orderliness and systematic use of the men and *materiel* at hand. While such organization in the abstract or on paper always worked well, in practical application in the field real units rarely matched the preferred regulations. An infantry regiment in the Old Army was larger than the new volunteer outfits, however, numbering more than 2,400 men in three battalions of eight companies each, with 807 men per battalion at the maximum. As the armies grew to great proportions with the coming of the war, manageability called for smaller-sized units, bringing the infantry regiment down to 1,000 men in ten companies. The Old Army cavalry regiment's organization carried into the Civil War volunteer forces almost unchanged. A regiment numbered 8-12 companies in either case, with around 100 men per company, and companies usually combined into no more than two battalions.

It was in the artillery, however, that the Old Army and the new volunteer services differed most dramatically. Pre-1861 artillery regiments numbered 12 'companies', each constituted of six guns and being in all respects the same as the 'batteries' in the Civil War volunteer armies. Companies were managed by two-gun sections containing about 50 men, and an entire artillery regiment could thus number in excess of 1,800 men at full strength. This cumbersome organization persisted in the Regulars during the war, but was quickly supplanted in the volunteer army by the battery system that was simpler and more efficient.

Regular Artillery Regiment

The smallest artillery unit in a regiment was the section. This comprised two guns each with team and limber. The battery of three sections held six caissons and limbers in reserve together with a field forge and battery wagon.

Artillery rarely fought as a regiment but were usually farmed out in batteries to brigades, divisions and corps.

Each Company comprised:
Captain commanding
First Lieutenant
Second Lieutenant
First Sergeant
Quartermaster Sergeant

4 Sergeants
8 Corporals
2 Musicians (until 1862)
2 Artificers
1 Wagoner
122 Privates (average number)

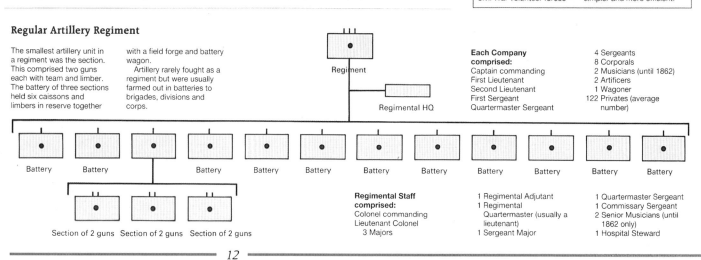

Regimental Staff comprised:
Colonel commanding
Lieutenant Colonel
3 Majors

1 Regimental Adjutant
1 Regimental Quartermaster (usually a lieutenant)
1 Sergeant Major

1 Quartermaster Sergeant
1 Commissary Sergeant
2 Senior Musicians (until 1862 only)
1 Hospital Steward

Whatever they knew they had learned on the field of battle.

But there were a host of other, younger officers in 1861 who had learned their trade more systematically, though unlike Scott and the other generals, these younger men for the most part had more military education than military experience, thanks to years of relative peace. The overwhelming majority, in fact, had never led in the field or in combat anything more than a company of less than 100 men, and there were less than two dozen in uniform who had ever commanded a regiment. In the four years that followed 1861, however, many of these inexperienced officers would be leading brigades, corps, and even armies. Men whose biggest prewar command in action might have been a squad, would find themselves leading tens of thousands.

Their names were little known outside the Old Army at the time, but they would be heard from in the war between the states. Gouverneur K. Warren finished second in the class of 1850 and eleven years later was only a first lieutenant teaching mathematics at the Military Academy. First Lieutenant Alexander McD. McCook, 3rd Infantry, class of 1852, was teaching infantry tactics at the academy. From the same class came George Crook, now a first lieutenant in the 4th Infantry serving in Californian outpost. James B.

Above: A pre-war photograph of a man destined to achieve greatness as a Confederate. James Ewell Brown Stuart was obscure as a cavalry lieutenant – as Lee's Jeb Stuart, he became immortal.

Above: Pre-war friends like Lieutenant Philip H. Sheridan, center, with George Crook at left and John Nugen on the right, went to war together in 1861. Crook became a leading subordinate of Sheridan's.

Below: When the call for volunteers went out, scenes like this were repeated all across the divided nation, with recruits here mustering in faraway Empire, Colorado, forming Company G, 1st Colorado.

McPherson graduated first in the class of 1853 and went into the elite corps of Engineers, but he was still only a lieutenant when war broke out. Philip H. Sheridan ranked thirty-fourth in McPherson's class and the two were good friends, but he had never gotten a single promotion and was still a junior lieutenant in Crook's regiment. Sheridan's classmate John Bell Hood of Kentucky was a lieutenant in the 2nd Cavalry. Oliver O. Howard finished fourth in the 1854 class, but 1861 found him still a lieutenant teaching mathematics at West Point with Warren. Wesley Merritt, class of 1860, was in the 2nd Dragoons, while James E. B. Stuart, known to friends as "Jeb", served as a lieutenant in the 1st Cavalry out in Colorado. Four of these obscure officers would command armies in the war just starting, and the rest would lead army corps. A few of them would become immortal by their deeds.[11]

Considering the frustrations they endured and the life they led in the Old Army, it is little short of amazing that these men were still in uniform when the war came. As one officer observed, civilian life could look very alluring to men who, naturally enough, would prefer that they "not be dragged into the wilderness to be either stationed there separate from their families, or fighting the Indians in unhealthy climates, where nothing can be gained but everything lost – health, reputation, money."[12] With all of the territory gained from Mexico or acquired by treaty with other nations, the frontier of the United States had practically doubled in the fifteen years prior to 1861. The demands that put upon an army were enormous. It had to man and hold 138 posts and garrisons, almost three times the number prior to the war with Mexico. Yet the army itself grew by substantially less than half. As a result, at least thirty of the frontier posts were held by fewer than 100 men each. That meant long, lonely, isolated duty, with little chance of furloughs, and nowhere to go even if leave was obtained.

There were inevitable consequences of such a life. With little to do in their off-duty time, officers turned to drinking and gambling, quarreling with each other, fighting bureaucratic battles with higher authorities, and sometimes even dueling. In 1852 an officer of the 4th Infantry observed that every day all of the officers in his regiment except two were drunk, and the commander liked to pile furniture in the center of a room and set fire to it when inebriated.[13]

Typically, an officer's quarters might be a bare room with no furniture, he having to provide it all for himself. At best he would have a cot, a table and one or two chairs, and perhaps a shelf for possessions provided for him. Anything else he had to buy out of his own pocket. If he were fortunate enough to be stationed at one of the eastern forts or garrisons, the officer could at least look forward to the opportunity to visit New York or Baltimore or Charleston, and other civilized centers of activity and entertainment. If less fortunate, as most fresh officers were, a man would find himself posted to Arkansas or Colorado, or the Pacific northwest, where the overriding experience was monotony. An officer in Arkansas felt himself "buried in oblivion", and another concluded after eleven years of frontier duty that, "no amount of money could induce me to remain in such a state of isolation from society."[14]

Many found solace and company in religion, though the majority ignored any kind of formal church attendance. Churches did not exist near many outposts, and few garrisons were large enough to merit their own army chaplain. Most often the officers simply had informal prayer meetings in their own quarters. Meanwhile, many found other ways to use their abundant free time. Intemperance was epidemic in some regiments, to the point that some officers literally drank themselves to death, while others got drunk at their funerals. Even though much exaggerated in later years, the problems of young Captain U.S. Grant were typical of many who found the isolation from friends and family so depressing that it could turn otherwise sober men to the bottle. Grant resigned his commission in 1854 after his drinking to while away lonely months on the Pacific coast got him in trouble.

The mixture of a very small circle of associates in close quarters, over long periods of time, with the frustrations of almost universally stalled careers, added to the widespread abuse of alcohol, inevitably led to an unusually exaggerated tendency to disputatiousness among the officers. While a man usually made his closest lifelong friends during his Old Army days, he also made his most implacable and despised enemies.

Officers quarreled over rank and seniority, over leaves and furloughs, over the few white women of marriageable age in their vicinity, over politics and religion and gambling. They often argued with neighbouring civilians. Courts-martial were common occurrences as officers pressed charges against one another, providing one of the frontier service's chief forms of entertainment. Many an officer like Jefferson Davis and Thomas J. Jackson became so disillusioned and disgusted over the quarreling that they resigned. Those who stayed in the army not infrequently turned to violence. Dueling was officially outlawed in the military, but that did not stop a host of challenges being issued and accepted, and duels being fought. In 1845 Lieutenant P. G. T. Beauregard challenged a fellow officer over a minor matter of supply. John C. Frémont did the same during the Mexican War, and as late as 1856 a bloodless meeting between brother officers took place in the Wyoming territory.[15]

Personal Memorabilia of General Thomas Jonathan Jackson

1 Confederate forage cap worn during the war
2 Handmade embroidered scarf presented by an admirer
3 Cased Adams revolver with accoutrements
4 Leather case for 5
5 Field glasses
6 Forage cap worn by General Jackson
7 A Lefaucheaux Brevete revolver presented to the general by his officers
8 A pair of epaulettes worn on dress occasions at V.M.I.
9 Pair of gold spurs presented to General Jackson by the ladies of Baltimore, Maryland
10–12 Packets of five Le Mat revolver cartridges
13 Leather gauntlet worn by Jackson on the night of his mortal wounding, May 2, 1863, Chancellorsville, Va
14 A pair of silver spurs worn during the war
15 Leather haversack
16 Gold watch carried by General Jackson at Chancellorsville
17 Spur worn at the time of his wounding
18 Jackson's sword: a U.S. Model 1850
19 The black waterproof worn by General Jackson at the moment of his wounding

Artifacts courtesy of: The Museum of the Confederacy, Richmond, Va: 1, 2, 3, 4, 5, 7, 8, 9, 13, 14, 15, 17, 18; Virginia Historical Society, Richmond, Va: 10, 11, 12, 16; The Virginia Military Institute, Lexington, Va: 6, 19

In the end, the contentiousness escalated to a point where the most insignificant matters could lead to an argument. Such a situation, especially when combined with a temperament that might already be disputatious, could lead to ridiculous results. Legendary in the Old Army was the story later recalled by Grant of one of the most contentious of all officers, Braxton Bragg. While holding the position of quartermaster at his post, Bragg was also temporarily in command of his company. In the latter role, he submitted a requisition to himself as quartermaster, but acting as quartermaster he refused it. As acting company commander he protested, but again wearing his hat as quartermaster he refused to change his original rejection of the requisition. When word of this got out, one officer declared, "My God, Mr. Bragg, you have quarrelled with every other officer in the army, and now you are quarrelling with yourself!"[16] It was a story that gained even more currency during the Civil War, when Bragg continued to fight more with his own officers than with his enemy.

No one summed up the hard side of Old Army service better than Captain John W. Phelps of the 4th Artillery. After two promotions in twenty-three years of service, and after one miserable posting after another, he declared in 1859 that "I am suffocating, physically, morally and intellectually – in every way." "Fairly, gasping for fresh outside air", he said he felt like a brother officer who a few days before begged, only half in jest, "to be taken out and hung for the sake of variety." Phelps resigned his commission just weeks before John Brown's raid on Harpers Ferry, Virginia, electrified the nation and helped set the states on the road to disunion. Eighteen months after his resignation, with the country going to war, Phelps was given a commission of brigadier general and more than enough to do that monotony was never a problem for him again.[17]

Phelps represented a type, a resource for both sides of trained officers that in 1861 was to be of great importance in supplementing the corps of currently serving commanders. Indeed, officers who had resigned their commissions and returned to private life probably had a greater

Above: News of the coming of the war reached Old Army men in a host of places. It came to U.S. Grant here in Galena, Illinois, where he scratched out a living in the leather business at Grant & Perkins.

Below: Word of hostilities found a number of men and officers already under arms awaiting an opportunity, as with the Kentucky State Guard, shown here in Louisville in 1860, and packed with Rebs.

impact on the war than any other class, chiefly because many of the commanders of the major armies, especially for the Union, were men who were out of uniform when Fort Sumter was fired upon. U.S. Grant was failing almost as badly in private business in 1861 as he had as an officer. The war was literally his salvation, and he was delighted to accept the colonelcy of an obscure Illinois regiment in 1861, hardly suspecting that he would end the war as general-in-chief of all Union armies. His chief lieutenant in the war, William T. Sherman, had also resigned from the army, leaving in 1853 after thirteen years' service. He, too, failed in business and the law, and in 1861 was running a streetcar company in St. Louis when war came and the government offered him the command of the 13th United States Infantry. George B. McClellan spent eleven years in uniform before resigning his captaincy to become a railroad manager. Then overnight he became a major general of Ohio volunteers after Fort Sumter. Thomas J. Jackson, after resigning in a huff in 1852, taught young cadets at the Virginia Military Institute and was regarded as an eccentric fanatic nicknamed "Tom Fool". When war came, he found himself a Confederate brigadier by June 1861, and a month later the holder of a rather less derogatory nickname, "Stonewall". These are only the most outstanding. Literally scores of others of lesser note were out in the land working as planters and farmers, lawyers, businessmen and politicians; a tremendous potential reserve of experience and ability, good and bad. The armies that were to be formed in the aftermath of secession would depend heavily upon them.

Some of these men shared a common role with yet a third potential source of leaders for the coming war, many of them men without West Point or other formal military training. Every state North and South boasted numerous publicly and privately supported militia organizations,

Below: Many had left the Old Army, like Thomas J. Jackson, shown here in his Mexican War uniform as a first lieutenant. A simple instructor at the Virginia Military Institute, he little expected greatness.

founded for a variety of reasons ranging from fraternalism to an enthusiasm for drill competitions, to a rising militarism in the face of the sectional friction. While a number of West Pointers did take prominent positions in such organizations, most notably Simon Buckner, who resigned in 1855 from the army and in 1861 was adjutant general of the Kentucky State Guard, most of the militia officers were drawn from local men in private life. As a result, their training and ability varied dramatically.

Best known of them all was probably E. Elmer Ellsworth, leader of the Chicago Zouaves, a spectacularly skilled volunteer company that he

raised before the war and led in exhibitions and competitions throughout the North. Coming to Washington with his friend and newly-elected president Abraham Lincoln, he soon organized another company, the New York Fire Zouaves, so-called because many of its members were firemen. Ellsworth had no formal military training at all, and was a prime example of the dilettante officer whose enthusiasm for things military sprang from a love of the show and finery. His record inspired many others. That is not to say that he was not a brave and patriotic young man, for he became, in fact, the first Union officer to die in the war, being shot dead by a secessionist in

Alexandria, Virginia, on May 24, 1861, as he tried to take down a Confederate flag. Ellsworth's lasting contribution to the war came from his unit continuing in service as the 11th New York.

North and South there were a number of other such young men, and older ones as well. Frequently, men with good political connections achieved high positions in their pre-war state militias, and these, too, provided a limited source of potential officers. While few might have any practical field experience with an army, they did at least know much of the inner workings of a military organization and how to administer one, almost as important to a leader as ability to lead in battle. Alpheus S. Williams was president of Michigan's state militia board with the rank of brigadier, and readily in place for transfer into the Union's volunteer army. In Tennessee, Benjamin Franklin Cheatham served as major general of state militia before the war, making it only natural that he would be commissioned a brigadier in the Confederate service as soon as Tennessee seceded. And elsewhere down the line, as private military organizations offered their services to one side or the other, company officers were accepted and commissioned wholesale. The South was blessed to get the services of New Orleans' famed Washington Artillery and the Washington Light Infantry of Charleston. Lincoln, by the same token, readily extended commissions to the leaders of the civilian military companies in the North.

The same was occasionally the case with the officers at the private military academies. Many Northern states had such institutions, and almost all of the Southern states possessed them, such as the Virginia Military Institute, the Citadel at Charleston and the State Seminary of Learning and Military Academy in Louisiana. When war came, of course, many of the instructors and academy officers immediately volunteered. Thus Thomas J. Jackson left V.M.I. to take a commission as colonel for the Confederacy. Others who did not leave their schools could still be called upon from time to time for emergency services with their state forces, as throughout the war when the cadets and cadet officers of V.M.I. did

Above: The special crack drill units and fraternal regiments and companies already existing helped greatly in the initial enlisting. Ellsworth's Zouaves in 1860: E. Elmer Ellsworth is second left.

Below: The Washington Light Infantry of Charleston, South Carolina, were right on hand for the opening guns at Fort Sumter. Later, as the 25th South Carolina, they would spend the war defending home.

duty training troops. And, of course, the graduates of these private and state academies, whether recent or past, were a source of potential officers second only to the West Pointers and serving Old Army men for desirability.

Finally there remained the largest single source of leaders, and the most difficult to tap predictably. Out in the great multitude of private citizens, among the bankers, cotton brokers, lawyers and doctors, farmers, store clerks, and even simple day laborers, there lay an undoubted reservoir of raw, native talent. There were brave men who could rise to leadership, win the trust and respect of their men, the approval of their superiors, and use it all to help win battles. But

finding these officers-to-be would be the most costly and time-consuming search of all, for they could only be found through trial and error, by testing and retesting, the way a dairyman let his cow's milk sit and waited for the cream to rise to the top. There was cream out there in the millions of untried young men of America. By 1861 the time had come for it to rise.

Yet before anyone could rise, decisions had to be made. There was an old story told of a Kentuckian, later a Confederate officer, who before the war said he was for the Union. If it failed, then he was for the South, and beyond that for Kentucky. If Kentucky fell apart, he would stand by his home county, even his home town if need be.

And should his own town be torn apart, then his loyalty would go to his side of the street.[18] All of these men, young and old, had to choose their sides of the street in 1860-1861. For most there was never a question where their allegiance lay. But for many others, especially those with family ties on the other side, or worst of all the men of the Old Army, men who had served the Stars and Stripes so long that to fight against it was just as heart-breaking as the thought of fighting against their native states and people, the decisions came very hard.

"No act of my life cost me more bitter pangs than mailing my resignation as a captain in the United States Army," lamented Henry Heth of

Uniform and Personal Belongings of Major General George G. Meade

1 Buff silk general officer's sash
2 Case for *3*
3 Meade's binoculars
4 Wool frock coat with shoulder strap insignia denoting the rank of major general
5 Officer's slouch hat with the insignia of major general. This hat was worn by Meade during the Battle of Gettysburg
6 Pair of officer's leather boots

7 High grade general officer's sword belt of red morocco leather featuring gold bullion embroidery
8 High grade eagle head officer's spurs
9 Model 1839 topographical engineer officer's saber and scabbard made by N.P. Ames, Springfield, Massachusetts
10 Attachment straps for eagle head spurs, *8*

11 Coin silver forks made by Filley and Mead, from a mess set used by Meade during the Mexican and Civil Wars
12 Coin silver tea spoons from Meade's mess set
13 Coin silver table spoons from Meade's mess set
14 Major general's forage cap, worn by Meade during the 1864 campaigns
15 Major general's dress epaulettes

Artifacts courtesy of: The Civil War Library and Museum, Philadelphia, Pa

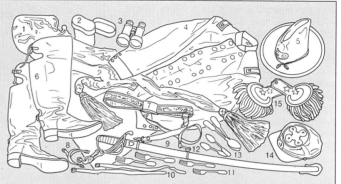

Virginia, "separating myself from those I loved, bidding adieu to my splendid company, my pride, and the finest regiment in the army.[19] It was a commonly held and expressed emotion. Not infrequently, other friends in the Old Army attempted to persuade Southern men not to go South. When Lieutenant Edward Porter Alexander reported for duty in San Francisco to his close friend Lieutenant James B. McPherson, there was no question that the Georgian Alexander intended to leave the army. He talked with McPherson telling him of his intention and asking him to accept his resignation.

"Aleck if you must go," said his friend, "I will do all I can to facilitate your going. But don't go." He promised that Alexander would be able to remain on the Pacific coast, far from the war, honorably continuing his service without having to fight against his own people.

"Now this is not going to be any 90 days or six months affair", McPherson continued. If Alexander went South, with his training he would certainly wind up in the front lines. "God only knows what may happen to you individually," he said, "but for your *cause* there can be but one possible result. It must be lost." McPherson tried to explain how Alexander's promotion would be rapid as other officers were drawn away to the war. He even suggested that the Georgian could make good investments in the expanding land business in San Francisco.

"In short, remaining here you have every opportunity for professional reputation, for promotion, and for wealth," McPherson concluded. "Going home you have every personal risk to run and in a cause foredoomed to failure."

Alexander was deeply impressed by McPherson's words. "A crisis in my life was at hand", he

Above: With war a fact, Old Army men were suddenly much in demand, and men like Captain George G. Meade of the topographical engineers found speedy promotion in the volunteer services.

Below: All of a sudden, those pre-war gatherings of state and local militia, like this August 1860 Kentucky State Guard muster at Louisville, were looked to as sources of officers to lead new units.

recalled later. He was utterly helpless to avert it, however. "Mac," he cried, "my people are going to war, and war for their *liberty*. If I don't come and bear my part they will believe me a coward – and I will feel that I am occupying the position of one. I must go and stand my chances."

"So I wrote my resignation of my beautiful position in the Engineer Corps", Alexander remembered. McPherson gave him a leave of absence to return to the East to await its acceptance, and then as his last gesture of friendship, helped arrange Alexander's passage home at a reduced steamship rate. The two never met again. Alexander would serve with the Confederates in Virginia, from First Manassas all the way to Appomattox; McPherson, during the Atlanta campaign in the summer of 1864, would be the only Union army commander to be killed in the field.[20]

The only Confederate army commander to be killed, Kentuckian Albert Sidney Johnston, had faced the same dilemma as Alexander, and only came to the same conclusion after painful deliberation. He had been a nationalist all his life. A West Point graduate in 1826, ranking eighth in his class, he gave distinguished service in the Black Hawk War of 1832, then resigned and joined the Texan revolutionaries in 1836, becoming their senior brigadier. He led a Texas regiment in the war with Mexico, and then re-entered the Old Army in 1849 and had risen to the brevet rank of brigadier general by 1861. The blood in his veins was as red, white, and blue as that of any other officer in the army. As a result, unlike Alexander, he hoped that he could simply stay out of the coming civil war by remaining in California and resigning from the army. But the old ties to Texas began to pull at him. While he

resisted all attempts by Southern sympathizers to get him to turn over public property to them while he was still in command at San Francisco, refusing to dishonor the uniform he still wore, once he resigned and went to Los Angeles to take up farming he could no longer turn a cold ear to the entreaties from Texas. He had resigned rather than have to bear arms against the Lone Star State. At the same time, men in Washington were trying to hold up acceptance of his resignation as they tried to persuade him to withdraw it, and promised that he would receive an important command in the volunteer army being formed.

Thus pulled and torn from both sides at once, Johnston in the end decided that he had to follow his heart into the Confederacy. "It seems like fate," he told a friend, "that Texas has made me a Rebel twice."[21]

Yet in the minds of many, most tragic of all was the decision faced by Robert Edward Lee. His had been a distinguished, yet typically frustrating, Old Army career. Graduating second in the West Point class of 1829, Lee came of an honored old Virginia family, served his trying time on frontier posts before the Mexican War, but emerging from that conflict with a considerable reputation. Yet by 1861, after thirty-two years in the army, he was a colonel in the 1st Cavalry, with nowhere to go until some of the older generals died or retired. Then came the outbreak of the war. With all of the line generals too old for active service, senior men like Lee and Johnston were the ones Lincoln would have to turn to for the command of his armies. On April 18, 1861, Lee was called to a meeting in Washington, where an emissary of Lincoln's told him that the President wanted to know if Lee would take the command of the major army to be raised in the East.

Above: The choices facing Old Army men as war approached called for agonizing decisions; as they did for young Lieutenant E. Porter Alexander of Georgia, shown here as a cadet at West Point c. 1857.

Below: The scene of conflict that forced choices on everyone was here at Charleston, South Carolina, where decades of controversy and posturing finally came to a crisis and plunged the nation into war.

Few men have ever had to face such an agonizing test of ambition against loyalty. Lincoln was offering what Lee had sought all his professional life, the capstone to any military man's career, and one offered to precious few. But just the day before, Lee's beloved Virginia had voted to secede. Inevitably the commonwealth would join with the new Confederacy, and just as inevitably, any Union army seeking to put down the rebellion in the East would make Virginia a battle-ground.

"I declined the offer," Lee wrote later, "stating, as candidly and courteously as I could, that though opposed to secession and deprecating war, I could take no part in an invasion of the Southern States." As soon as the interview concluded, Lee went to the office of his mentor, friend, and commanding general, Winfield Scott, and expressed his intention to resign. Two days later he sent in his resignation. He apologised to Scott for not bringing it in person and for taking two days to make himself write it. It had been, he confessed, a "struggle to separate myself from a service to which I have devoted all the best years of my life." "Save in defense of my native state," he concluded, "I never desire again to draw my sword." The next day a message came from Virginia's governor asking Lee to come to Richmond to discuss the state's defense. Inevitably, Lee would be drawn into the war.[22]

Not all of the anguish of torn loyalties fell to the lot of Southern-born men in the Old Army. Many a Yankee found himself caught between conflicting emotions. John C. Pemberton of Pennsylvania was a West Pointer who served twenty-four years in the military. But he had married a Virginia girl in 1848, and the ties to an adopted family were great enough to persuade him to cast

his lot with the Confederacy. Franklin Gardner was a New Yorker who finished at the Military Academy in Grant's class, and was a lieutenant colonel in 1861 when he resigned to go South, following political principles rather than geographical loyalties. Two years later Pemberton and Gardner would command, and lose in siege, the two main Confederate bastions on the Mississippi: Vicksburg and Port Hudson. Both would be accused of treason to the South due to their Northern birth. Both were innocent.

And there were loyal Union men of Southern birth who faced equal heartache. Stephen Hurlbut was born in Charleston and lived for thirty years in South Carolina, but when war came he became a Yankee brigadier. Even more dramatic is the story of William Terrill of Virginia. A West Pointer, he stayed with the Union and rose from captain in the 5th Artillery to be a brigadier general in 1862. His brother James was a brigadier general in the Confederate Army. Both brothers would be killed in the war. Equally heart-rending was the choice faced by another Virginian, George H. Thomas, who served as a major in the 2nd Cavalry before the war, his commanders including Albert Sidney Johnston and Robert E. Lee. In January 1861 he had applied for the position of commandant of cadets at the Virginia Military Institute, perhaps hoping to stay out of the coming war, and feeling as did a few at that time that Virginia might not secede, and her sons not be called on to fight the Union. However, he

Auburn Guards Officer, Alabama Volunteer Militia, 1861

Easily the most colorful of all the units coming into the Confederate Army were the local militia and privately raised outfits that took arms for the South in 1861. With no prescribed uniformity, they arrived in uniforms of almost every color of the rainbow – green, red, buff, brown, gray, and most frequently of all, blue.

Among the most colorful were the Auburn Guards of the Alabama Volunteer Militia. Their blue trousers and short jackets were glorious, covered with bright brass buttons, set off by a white crossbelt, epaulettes, white gloves and facings, red sash, and a gleaming black leather Pattern 1851 Albert shako topped by a red and white feather pom-pom. The rigors of campaigning played havoc with such outfits, and these beautiful uniforms did not last long in the field. As they wore out, they were steadily replaced by Confederate regulation gray or butternut.

went through some kind of political or emotional epiphany that spring, and in the end turned down the offer of a high command from Virginia's governor in the days before Fort Sumter. Within a few months he was a Federal brigadier, and would finish the war as commander of one of the two major armies that defeated the Rebellion. His family in Virginia never spoke to him again. His portrait still hung in the family home, but his sisters turned it to face the wall.[23]

So there was more than enough anguish over choices to go around in the continent in 1861. If any place was to symbolize it best, however, one needed to look no further than the small garrison of Old Army men out in the middle of Charleston Harbor in Fort Sumter. Almost to a man they were career military men, mostly West Pointers, put in the most awkward spot of all. Their commander, Major Robert Anderson, was a Kentuckian, married to a Georgia woman, and a personal proponent of slavery and state rights. Yet he had been given the trust of this command by the army that had been his life. All he had to do was turn it over bloodlessly to the Confederates who were ringing him with batteries, and he would be a Southern hero. Lieutenant R. K. Meade of Anderson's garrison was a Virginian, a young officer with a bright future before him. Even more than Anderson, he sided with the South. How would he behave if the Confederates opened fire on Sumter? Many in both nations expected them to do as another Southern-born officer in a position of trust had done. Old David E. Twiggs of Georgia was seventy, and one of only four general officers of the line in the Old Army. He commanded the Department of Texas in 1860, and early in 1861 he listened to his Southern loyalties. He turned over his command to the state forces of Texas, along with all of his stores and armaments and men. It was an act of clear treason, for he had not bothered to resign his commission first, and for it he was vilified in the North and even in some quarters of the South, and almost universally throughout the Old Army. It was an act without honor.[24]

But Anderson and Meade were different sorts of men. When the guns opened up on Fort Sumter on April 12, 1861, both did what almost every Old Army officer could be counted upon to do . . . his duty. Indeed, while some suspected Meade in particular, he actively joined in helping man the few cannon that returned the fire of the Confederates commanded (by now General) P. G. T. Beauregard. As for Anderson, he manfully held out until the wooden portion of his fort was in flames, and his supplies were running out. Only then did he capitulate. All of Sumter's defenders were later given a hero's welcome when they returned to the North. Anderson became a brigadier and served the Union cause faithfully until his broken health forced him to leave active duty in 1863. And Lieutenant Meade soon resigned his commission, but took one in the Confederate army instead. Having more than honorably fulfilled his duty to his first country, he would soon give his life for his second.

Those old friendships that were broken, some forever, by the coming of the war would remain among the most heart-rending of its casualties. They all had to choose their own way. "How strange it is," wrote new Confederate Brigadier General Braxton Bragg to his old friend Captain Henry J. Hunt, who would one day be a Yankee brigadier responsible for all of the artillery of the Army of the Potomac.

Above: Symbolic of the years-long friendships that the war tore apart, was that between Braxton Bragg and William T. Sherman. Bragg, above, became the most controversial Rebel general of the war.

Above: Pierre G.T. Beauregard served barely more than a few days as superintendent at the Military Academy before his state's secession forced him out of the Old Army, ending a bright career.

"We have been united in our views of almost all subjects, public and private", continued Bragg. "We still have, I trust, a personal regard for each other, which will continue whatever course our sense of duty may dictate, yet in one short year after exchanging at your house assurances of friendship, here we are, face to face, with arms in our hands, with every prospect of a bloody collision. How strange."[25]

How strange, indeed, lending all the more poignancy to that little dinner party in far off Los Angeles on June 16, 1861. Though they never spoke together in peace again, Hancock and some of his friends would meet once more in a strange way. On July 3, 1863, at Gettysburg, Pennsylvania, when General Robert E. Lee launched the biggest infantry assault of his army's career, he hurled it at the center of a fortified Union line commanded by Major General Winfield Scott Hancock and his II Corps. Leaders in the assault were Major General George Pickett and Brigadier Generals Lewis A. Armistead and Richard B. Garnett. Garnett fell amid a storm of bullets and smoke and was never seen again. Armistead, his hat atop his sword so his men could see him, actually penetrated the Union line and had laid his hand on one of Hancock's cannon before he took a mortal wound from the Federal line. His last request before death was to see Hancock, one it was not possible to grant for Hancock himself had just received a near-mortal wound from Armistead's attacking Confederates.[26]

References

1 Ada Hancock, *Reminiscences of Winfield Scott Hancock* (New York, 1887), pp.69-70; Charles P. Roland, *Albert Sidney Johnston, Soldier of Three Republics* (Austin, Tex., 1964), p.252.
2 E. B. Long, *The Civil Day by Day* (New York, 1971), p.709.
3 Edward M. Coffman, *The Old Army* (New York, 1986), p.102.
4 Ibid., pp.49, 99.
5 Frank J. Welcher, *The Union Army 1861-1865: Organization and Operations: Volume I, The Eastern Theater* (Bloomington, Ind., 1989), pp.2-4.
6 Coffman, *Old Army*, p.49.
7 Ibid., pp.50, 52.
8 Ibid., pp.47-8.
9 *Register of Graduates and Former Cadets, United States Military Academy* (New York, 1948), pp.386-8.
10 Ezra J. Warner, *Generals in Blue* (Baton Rouge, 1964), pp.209, 430, 573-4; Ezra J. Warner, *Generals in Gray* (Baton Rouge, 1959), p.312.
11 George W. Cullom, *Biographical Register of the Officers and Graduates of the U.S. Military Academy* (Boston, 1891), III, pp.254, 323, 329, 333, 356, 362, 369, 375, 509.
12 Coffman, *Old Army*, p.54.
13 Ibid., p.63.
14 Ibid., p.81.
15 Ibid., pp.70-1.
16 U.S. Grant, *Personal Memoirs* (New York, 1885), II, pp.86-7.
17 Coffman, *Old Army*, p.67; William H. Powell, comp., *List of Officers of the Army of the United States from 1779 to 1900* (New York, 1900), p.529.
18 William C. Davis, *The Orphan Brigade* (New York, 1980), p.1.
19 James L. Morrison, ed., *The Memoirs of Henry Heth* (Westport, Conn., 1974), p.149.
20 Gary W. Gallagher, ed., *Fighting for the Confederacy, The Personal Recollections of General Edward Porter Alexander* (Chapel Hill, N.C., 1989), pp.23-5.
21 Roland, *Johnston*, pp.250-2.
22 Douglas Southall Freeman, *R. E. Lee* (New York, 1934), I, pp.436-7, 441, 447.
23 Warner, *Generals in Blue*, pp.496, 500-1.
24 Warner, *Generals in Gray*, p.312.
25 Coffman, *Old Army*, p.96.
26 Hancock, *Hancock*, p.70.

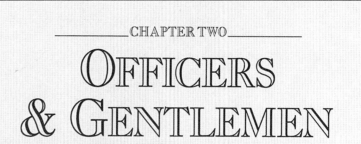

CHAPTER TWO

OFFICERS & GENTLEMEN

In the rush to arms after the firing on Fort Sumter, tens of thousands of raw new recruits had to be turned into soldiers quickly. There was not enough time. The armies, barely more than organized mobs, were impelled to their first clash at Bull Run in July 1861. The confused and uncontrolled fighting on both sides proved that leadership in this war would not be easily gained, and would have to be prized when found.

WHILE NO precisely accurate tally exists, it is clear that at least 5,085 separate regiments, battalions, companies, legions, and batteries saw service in the American Civil War. While no accurate tally exists of the total number of officers who served in those units, on staff duty, and in the departments and bureaus that provided support services, obviously the number had to be enormous. A workable estimate would be about 140,000 individuals who at varying times served as commissioned officers during the course of the war. Many more held unofficial rank in informal guerrilla commands and in some of the local home guard units that were never absorbed into the formal Union or Confederate services. Due to the high rate of battlefield attrition among officers, the actual figure might be higher by several thousand. Far more important, however, is the fact that a nation with little military tradition found itself, in a comparatively short span of time, facing the task of finding this many men who were or could be made into leaders. It was a tall order indeed.

Certainly there was no dearth of men who thought they had the stuff of leadership, and even before the guns sounded in Charleston harbor, both Union and Confederate governments were bombarded with applications for commissions from former and serving officers, militia commanders, influential politicians and private citizens, adventurous foreigners, and even a few ladies. Almost everyone, it seemed, fancied himself a potential Alexander.

To their credit, and quite logically, both governments turned first to the professionals, to current and former officers of the Old Army, and especially those with West Point training. Both sides knew that such men would not be enough, but they could form the nucleus of experienced leaders around whom a much larger officer corps could form, as volunteer commanders were added to the army. And from the outset, the high level vacancies created in the new regiments and brigades were chiefly to be filled by these professionals. Thus it was no surprise that many of the more esteemed Old Army officers found themselves wooed by both sides in what at times almost amounted to a bidding war in which the prize was not money, but rank. Simon Buckner of Kentucky was offered brigadier generalcies by both Lincoln and Davis in the summer of 1861. He sided with the latter. Another Kentuckian, Ben Hardin Helm, was offered first a major's commission in the Union Army, then took the colonelcy of a new Confederate infantry regiment. Robert E. Lee, of course, had reportedly been offered command of the Union Army by Winfield Scott but took the command of Confederate Virginia's state troops instead. Even as he was resigning his commission to go to the South, Albert Sidney Johnston was wooed by Washington to remain in the Federal service, to no avail.

Once the men of the Old Army had made their choice of whether or not to serve, and for which side, there remained for most the sometimes daunting task of simply getting to their respective armies. The 1,000-odd officers were scattered all across the continent, with more than a third of them in the far West, some of them more than a thousand miles from their destinations. Further, for many there was a gnawing uncertainty for families that were back in the East, as well as a personal anxiety, especially on the part of Southern-born officers. With news traveling very slowly, many officers who determined to cast their fortunes with their native states did not know for weeks whether or not their states had seceded. The only 'rapid' communication came by way of the famed Pony Express, which sent its riders from the westernmost telegraph line at Fort Kearny, on the Platte River in the Nebraska Territory, on to the Pacific coast.

On "pony day", as they called it, the officers and men in the frontier garrisons assembled at the post trader's store or perhaps company headquarters at the appointed hour for the rider to arrive. Captain John Gibbon, 4th Artillery, joined others at Camp Floyd in the Utah Territory, looking anxiously across the level sagebrush plain to see the tell-tale streamer of dust in the distance

They could look pretty raw, these new-born leaders of men. Colonel William Wilson, at center, commanded his Wilson's Zouaves with little or no formal training, and never looked entirely comfortable in his buttons and braid.

raised by the rider's pounding hooves. If the express was late, officers climbed atop the store for a better view, all ears cocked for the magical cry "here he comes". As the news from the East became more and more dire prior to the firing on Fort Sumter, the faces on pony day were the more anxious. When the first news of the outbreak of hostilities did arrive, Gibbon noted how all within hearing of the officer reading the dispatch were "serious and thoughtful".[2]

For men of the South, when news of their native states' secession came through, or for those who had decided to take Confederate service in any case, the sometime pain of the decision was at least compensated for by the immediate control they could take of their own destiny. A simple letter of resignation, once posted, freed them of any sense of further obligation or necessity to wait around. They were free to make their way to the Confederacy, saying farewell to their remaining brothers of the Old Army who had to wait where they were for orders to come.

Thus it was that Albert Sidney Johnston made his journey all the way from Los Angeles to Richmond, Virginia, the Confederate capital after May 1861. While he may have equivocated about simply staying out of the war altogether, once his adopted state of Texas seceded he knew he had to go. After the tearful party at the Hancock home on June 16, he joined with the others in a daunting trek across the southwest by horseback that took them to Fort Yuma, then along the Gila River, south on the Rio Santa Cruz to Tucson, then due east to Picacho on the Rio Grande. It was more than 800 miles, on foot and horseback, and in the worst of the summer, when daytime temperatures could rise above 120°F in the deserts. It

Above: One of a host of old Regular Army officers who had to face the toughest choice of their lives was Lieutenant Ambrose Powell Hill. He would give up this uniform to become a Rebel giant.

Below: Such officers as the little Old Army had were spread out over scores of frontier posts like Fort Marcy at Santa Fe, New Mexico Territory. Just getting them to the war would be a daunting task.

took more than a month for the trip, and once in Texas it took Johnston another month to reach New Orleans, and another week, perhaps, to get to Richmond. In the end, he had covered more than 2,000 miles in two and a half months to reach the capital. He went straight to the executive mansion, only to learn that President Jefferson Davis, his old friend, was upstairs ill. But Davis was awake, and he heard the traveler's boots in the hall below. "That is Sidney Johnston's step", the President exclaimed. "Bring him up." In less than a week, Johnston was a full general and the second ranking officer in the entire Confederate army.[3]

Literally dozens of other officers preceded or followed Johnston in the exodus of Old Army men to the Confederacy. While few others traveled so far or through such danger and hardship, still each had his story. James Longstreet of South Carolina was a major and paymaster of the post at Albuquerque, New Mexico Territory, when the war came. Here, too, the men stood atop the quartermaster's office roof to look for the dust raised by a coming mail wagon. When the tragic news arrived, and Longstreet and others made their choice to "go South", many of their old friends who remained loyal to the Union rode out on the trail with them a few miles, "which only made the last farewell more trying" for Longstreet. They rode across the territory to the Texas line, stopping in El Paso to find everyone singing "Dixie" and "The Bonnie Blue Flag". Even then he had another 500 miles to travel before he could take trains on to Richmond. Ironically, his chief traveling companions were two Yankees heading home, and for whom he provided protection. Once in Richmond, Longstreet applied at the Confederate war department on June 29 for an

assignment in the pay department, having as he said "given up all aspirations of military honor." Two days later he found himself commissioned a brigadier general with orders to go to Manassas. In time the would-be paymaster became what Robert E. Lee called "my old War Horse", the longest serving and most dependable of the corps commanders of the Army of Northern Virginia.[4]

An officer whose Civil War career would be intricately linked with Longstreet's had a considerably different experience in reaching the Confederacy, and clearly a different strategy about his resignation. Lieutenant Edward Porter Alexander of Georgia knew that his resignation was inevitable the moment Georgia seceded. He was stationed in far away Washington Territory, however, and shortly expected orders for his company to return to the East. However, he decided to wait until the army had ordered and moved him back before he turned in his resignation. The expected orders came, and he and his family embarked aboard a steamer bound for San Francisco, whence he would take passage on another ship to Panama, cross the isthmus by rail, then board another steamer to Washington.

But once in San Francisco, Alexander's plans were totally upset by that same harbinger of bad news that had set so many on their way east, the Pony Express. Orders arrived canceling his trip to the East, and instead assigning him to Alcatraz Island in the bay. "I was very sorry for this," he recalled, "because it precipitated my resignation & compelled me to pay my own expenses for the journey." In short, Alexander had hoped to stay in the United States service long enough for it to pay to get him home so that he might then resign and join the Confederacy.[5]

Like many others, Alexander made the trip home by ship. So did Hancock, though his was a different destination and destiny. For all of them

First Lieutenant, 9th New York Infantry

A first lieutenant of the 9th New York Infantry, one of the more colorful zouave regiments. Most zouave outfits, in fact, uniformed their officers in fairly standard Union Army dress, reserving the flamboyant short jackets and other zouave trappings for the men in the ranks. Side arms were almost universally the same, however.

Almost every Union officer carried a Colt Model 1860 "Army" pistol in .44 caliber. The field officer's sword showed more variation, some being Army issue, such as the 1850 staff and field officer's saber carried here. Others were brought from home or specially purchased. Particularly favored were sabers from the Ames company of Chicopee, Massachusetts. Zouave outfits caused no little confusion on the battlefield, because those of both sides shared many similarities, especially the blue color of their jackets and the use of shoulder straps by officers.

who chose that route, there was nearly as much excitement, and danger as for those who went overland. For some the peril was more imagined than real. Rumors abounded of events in the East, but there was little hard information. When Hancock procured an American newspaper in Panama, he had to read it aloud to everyone in the cabin, so starved were they for war news. More unsettling were the stories of Confederate warships prowling the sea lanes hoping to intercept ships from California that might be carrying gold. When his ship was almost home, steaming off the North Carolina coast, an unidentified vessel did approach, and Hancock hastily organized some of the passengers for defense, while other Old Army friends bound for the Confederacy looked on in amusement. Alexander, too, encountered the rumors of Rebel warships, but on his vessel there were so few Unionists that no defense could be organized. In the event, no threat appeared, but they were almost lost in a severe storm, and after that two crewmen were killed in accidents.[6]

Even these dangers might have seemed as nothing compared to the frustration of the loyal officers who did not resign, and as a result had to sit at their posts awaiting news and hoping for orders to report to the East. It would have been unnatural for these men, most of whom had only known peacetime service with its boredom and glacial rate of advancement, not to be anxious to participate in the excitement in Virginia and elsewhere. There careers could be made, promotion won, and real experience gained. After the news of Fort Sumter, said Gibbon, "days and weeks now dragged their slow length along and all eyes were turned eagerly eastward for more news, while orders for our recall to the States were anxiously awaited." Every succeeding pony day brought more news, none of it good for the Union, and produced more and more excitement and frustration among the men. They were torn between anger at what was happening to their country, and fear that the war would end too soon for them to participate. When finally Gibbon's orders arrived, he was directed to march 1,200 miles to Fort Leavenworth in Kansas. Stores

Above: The fastest way to a big promotion was to leave the Old Army and take a volunteer commission. Ambrose Burnside (center) was a West Point graduate who had left the Army in 1853 to go into business. He

and supplies that could not be carried with his marching column were sold locally, and all excess arms and ammunition were destroyed. On July 27 they started on their two months' dusty march, and four days later were startled to see a Pony Express rider hastily hand a slip of paper to an officer as he raced past. All gathered to hear the man read an account of the battle of July 21 along Bull Run, near Manassas, Virginia, the war's first major engagement. He read of the initial success of Irvin McDowell's Union army as it pushed back the Rebels commanded by Beauregard and Joseph E. Johnston. When the reader paused for breath, one disgusted listener muttered, "Great

became a leading figure in the Rhode Island militia and at the outbreak of war became colonel of the 1st Rhode Island Infantry. He is seen here with members of his staff in 1861 in a camp outside Washington D.C.

God, the thing will be over before we get there." But then the reader went on, told of the Confederate counterattacks, the timely arrival of reinforcements, and the ultimate rout of McDowell's army. "Good God," muttered the same incredulous listener, "there will be no government when we get there."[7]

Once Gibbon's column reached Fort Leavenworth, more personally tragic news began to reach the Old Army men. Few were touched by it as Gibbon, when he opened two months' worth of mail. He learned that his three brothers were all entering the Confederate service, following their allegiance to North Carolina, which had seceded. He never saw or spoke to them again until after the war. When he finally reached Washington, he met the same sight that confronted so many of his brother officers. The army and the country were in disarray. "Everywhere were troops, camps, baggage-wagons, the sound of martial music, and saddest of all, the constant boom of distant guns which told the story of our distracted country."[8]

George Crook felt the same way as that muttering officer on the plains when, ordered to come east, he reached Panama and heard the news of what later became known as First Bull Run. "We all felt that the war would be over," he recalled, "and a bluer set of people could not well have been found."[9] It was almost as frustrating for some officers who did not have to make a long journey to reach the armies. Lieutenant Cyrus Comstock, on the faculty at West Point, had to sit idly by and watch other officers ordered to the gathering army at Washington, while he sat and continued teaching his classes. Officer after

Left: When the new volunteer officers had their commissions and their regiments, the time came to lead them to the Front. Well-wishers here are seeing the 1st Minnesota off to the war.

Above: In the early days there were parades everywhere. When Burnside's 1st Rhode Island left Providence for Washington D.C. in April 1861, much of the city turned out to send them off to battle with a cheer.

Below: Far out to the west the scenes were less formal. At Cairo, Illinois, an obscure colonel, once disgraced, and not yet uniformed, stands before a post at center, ready to take command: U.S. Grant.

officer left before him. A new class was graduated in May 1861, and almost every new lieutenant would be going to war. "We who are still here expect to be sent any day", he wrote hopefully, but by late June he was still seeing others from his faculty and members of his own graduating class getting promotions and assignments. In July he went to Washington on his own to seek a field assignment, but returned dejectedly to West Point "as a fixture". At last on July 26 his orders came, and a man who would become one of U.S. Grant's most trusted and effective staff members two years later finally got to go to war.[10]

For a number of officers, even those already in the Regular Army, personal politicking had to be resorted to in order to get a field assignment. Never in any other conflict in American history was personal influence – local, financial, family, and other connections – to play so large a role in determining who was to receive a commission. Never before or afterward did the ingenuity or persistence of the prospective officer himself have so much to do with his success in getting a place – often more to do with it, in fact, than any training or experience he might have had.

When George Crook finally reached Washington, he had been given a captaincy in the 14th Infantry, a new Regular Army regiment. But all around him he was seeing others being made colonels and even generals in the volunteer armies being raised. Since the War Department apparently intended to fight the war chiefly with volunteers enlisted for ninety days' service – and later for three years or the duration of the war – rather than by expanding the Regular Army, it was obvious that advancement in the few Regular units would be little faster than before the war. Thus the overwhelming majority of officers like Crook sought appointments from the governors of their home states. Crook first went to Washington hoping to see President Abraham Lincoln. He went in company with Brigadier General Robert C. Schenck, a fellow Ohioian, who had never had a day of military service in his life. But he had been an influential campaigner for Lincoln's election, and his brigadier's star was his reward. Now he sought to use his political influence on behalf of Crook. Lincoln told them that in a cabinet meeting the day before, it had been agreed to allow 100 Regular officers to take volunteer commissions, but when Schenck suggested one for Crook, Lincoln gave an excuse that he probably had to use hundreds of times in the months ahead. He never interfered with the running of any branch of the government, he said, any more than he would try to mend a watch. Should he "put his foot into it", as he said, it might never run again. So he referred them to the adjutant general's office. There Crook was told that to get a volunteer commission he would have to have a state governor make application for him. At once he telegraphed the governor of Ohio, and a few weeks later he found himself in Columbus, the state capital, taking command of the 36th Ohio Infantry as Colonel Crook.[11] It was a routine to be repeated again and again both North and South.

Yet with barely 1,100 actual serving officers in uniform when the war broke out, and with 300 of those resigning to go South, demand for leaders clearly outstripped supply. Even counting West Pointers who had left the service and might be brought back, such as Grant and Sherman, that only offered another potential 200 or so for the Union, and even fewer for the Confederacy.

Lincoln's initial call for 75,000 volunteers after the fall of Fort Sumter would alone require at least 2,500 officers, easily double the number of trained men currently in uniform or in retirement. Obviously he and Jefferson Davis would both have to lean heavily on state militia officers, private military school faculty and graduates, and even politicians who, if nothing more, knew how to run election campaigns and might just be trainable for military campaigns as well. In the end, both governments utilised a host of means in choosing officers. The rule of the day was that there were *no* strict rules of procedure. What was policy was simply whatever means succeeded in getting a man a commission.[12]

G. Moxley Sorrel was a Georgian with no military experience other than his being a private in the Georgia Hussars, a Savannah militia company. His company offered itself to the Confederate service after Fort Sumter, but Davis was so besieged with similar offers that he could not arm and equip all the volunteers, and many companies were put off. Sorrel determined to get into the war any way he could, and so went on his own to Richmond to "seek employment." Even with the influence of a brother in the surgeon general's department, Sorrel could get nothing in the way of an appointment, and consequently went to visit his father's farm in Fauquier County, just ten miles from the army being built by Beau-

regard near Manassas. Sorrel's father had just days before met Beauregard's adjutant, Colonel Thomas Jordan, an acquaintance from years earlier. "This was my opportunity", said the young man. He went to Jordan to plead his case. Nothing happened, and Jordan kept him waiting as the days led up to July 21 and the First Battle of Bull Run. That morning, awakened by the sound of the guns, Sorrel was delighted to be handed a note from the adjutant ordering him to report to a new brigadier, James Longstreet, as an aide with the rank of captain. Incredibly, young Sorrel got his commission and his first taste of battle on the very same day, though Longstreet's brigade was left out of almost all the fighting, and Sorrel's first

Confederate Headgear and Epaulettes

1. 1858 Hardee hat of Colonel Francis S. Bartow, of the 7th and 8th Georgia Regiments
2. 1858 Hardee hat of Capt. Paul Hamilton with N.C. palmetto insignia and officer's hat cord
3. Rubberized rain hat of Col. Bradflute Warwick, 4th Texas
4. Full dress beaver skin chapeau of Capt. A.J. Grayson, Co. B (F), 45th Virginia Infantry
5. Civilian slouch hat of Lt. John Selden, 2nd Co. Richmond Howitzers
6. Forage cap of Henry Carter Lee, A.N.V. Cavalry Corps
7. Forage cap of Capt. Benjamin Chase, Co. B, 22nd Virginia
8. Forage cap belonging to Lt. Gen. Simon Bolivar Buckner
9. Wool headwarmer of Maj. Robert B. Taylor, 6th Virginia Infantry
10. Cotton havelock of W.H. Kirkpatrick of Georgia
11. Non-regulation cap of Capt. David L. Smoot, Alexander Artillery, Va
12. Forage cap of Brig. Gen. George Wythe Randolph
13. Colonel's epaulettes of Brig. Gen. Alexander Galt Taliaferro
14. Captain's epaulettes of Maj. Gen. H.D. Clayton
15. Captain's epaulettes of Capt. James K. Lee, Co.B, 1st Virginia Inf

Artifacts courtesy of: The Museum of the Confederacy, Richmond, Va

impressions of his commander were drawn from seeing him throw his hat on the ground, stamp his feet, and curse the luck of being left out of the fight. Sorrel would be at Longstreet's right hand for nearly three years, then would himself become a brigadier.[13]

For others, the high rank seemed to come from nowhere, with almost no effort at all. Walter P. Lane had no formal military training, but was a veteran of the Texan war for independence, the Mexican War, and a host of Indian campaigns. When the war came he joined a Texas cavalry company as a private. When the company was joined with others to form the 3rd Texas Cavalry, and officially mustered in, the men set about electing their own officers. Lane found himself made lieutenant colonel, "a big stride for a private to make." In the end he would be one of the very last generals appointed before the Confederacy collapsed.[14]

Alpheus S. Williams of Michigan was a major in a large company of state militia when the war commenced, and was almost immediately made brigadier general of state volunteers. Such a militia rank, however, carried no weight in the rapidly-growing United States volunteer service, for generals could only be commissioned by Washington. He went to the Capital and met Lincoln, Secretary of War Simon Cameron, and a host of other influential men. "I have the promise of an appointment" he wrote home in July. In a few weeks he had his generalship, and was already politicking to get command of just the right brigade.[15]

The whole subject of such politically motivated appointments would be a sore one for both Lincoln and Davis. In the Union Army especially, literally hundreds of commissions would go to men with no military experience or ability at all. Lincoln's was a coalition government, his majority made up not only of fellow Republicans, but also of so-called "War Democrats", men who put commitment to saving the Union above party loyalties. The latter were specially important, for their influence could deliver votes to sustain the

Union Officers' Headgear and Insignia

1 Standard infantry officer's McDowell pattern forage cap with infantry insignia
2 Slouch hat with badge of the 2nd Corps, 1st Division
3 Patent havelock cap or 'whipple hat', with battery insignia. The unit name is stencilled in black on the front of the hat
4 Forage cap with 10th Corps insignia
5 Chasseur's pattern cap

with regimental insignia
6 Staff officer's forage cap
7 Chasseur's pattern cap with regimental insignia
8 Forage cap with regimental insignia, and patent air vent in the crown
9 and 10 Hardee hat regimental and national insignia
11 Colonel's shoulder straps
12 Second Lieutenant's

shoulder straps
13 First Lieutenant's shoulder strap insignia
14 Captain's shoulder straps
15 Lieutenant Colonel's shoulder strap insignia
16 Colonel's shoulder straps
17 and 18 Hardee hat regimental and national insignia

Artifacts courtesy of: G. Paul Loane Collection: 1-8; The Civil War Library and Museum, Philadelphia, Pa: 9-18

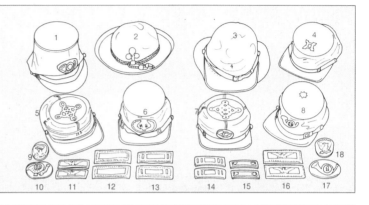

Above: Ever-ambitious, the politicians turned out for commissions, North and South. Benjamin F. Butler of Massachusetts became one of the Union's senior generals, and one of its worst.

Left: One of the exceptional "political" generals was a Kentuckian, John C. Breckinridge. Once vice president of the U.S., he cast his lot with the South, rising to corps command, and finally to secretary of war.

Above: Fortunately for North and South, many states already had active militia units ready to go straight into the volunteer service. The 7th New York State Militia stood among the best trained.

administration. Consequently, from among their number several men immediately achieved high command.

The very first major general of volunteers appointed by Lincoln was Benjamin F. Butler of Massachusetts. He had opposed Lincoln's election in 1860, but immediately supported the war effort after Fort Sumter, and was so influential that Lincoln had to give him a high command. As a result, Butler outranked for a time every other general in the army except Winfield Scott and George B. McClellan. Failing ever to demonstrate any real command ability, he was an obstacle to every subsequent general-in-chief until Grant finally removed him in 1865. Equally troublesome to Grant was John A. McClernand, a Democrat from Illinois made brigadier and later major general. In the same way, twelve members of Ohio's influential McCook family, all of them brothers or cousins of a former law partner of Lincoln's second secretary of war, Edwin M. Stanton, became Union officers. Six of them became generals.[16] Nathaniel Banks of Massachusetts, a thoroughgoing incompetent militarily, was made a major general the same way as Butler, and then

for four years lost almost every engagement he fought, often in command of actual armies. So useful were his services in raising troops and money for the war effort, however, that Lincoln felt justified in retaining him.

Jefferson Davis, too, had his problems with political generals and other officers. To his credit, and perhaps reflecting his own experience in the Old Army, and later as President Franklin Pierce's secretary of war in the 1850s, his judgments were somewhat better than Lincoln's and he issued commissions to politicians and influence holders more sparingly. Bombarded incessantly in the early years of the war for appointments, Davis, despite his protestations of making decisions solely upon individual merit, handed out quite a number of places to old friends, the sons of friends, and prominent state and local politicians. Indeed, the power to appoint generals he reserved exclusively to himself throughout the war, and only two career politicians ever achieved high rank from him, Howell Cobb of Georgia, and John C. Breckinridge of Kentucky. Cobb had been a Congressman, Speaker of the House, Secretary of the Treasury, and in 1861 a close contender for

President of the Confederacy. Though he had no military experience, happily he turned out to be a good field officer. Breckinridge, former Vice President of the United States and Lincoln's chief opponent in the election of 1860, proved even better, becoming one of the premier volunteer generals of the Confederacy.

But for every good political appointee, at whatever level, there were two or three who proved worthless. The war tended to weed out most of them, either by dismissal as with Butler, or resignation, as with McClernand. A marginally more reliable source of commanders North and South would be the men who led pre-existing militia companies. As it happened, they often tended to be prominent in local public affairs as well, thus affording to Lincoln and Davis a double advantage. Many of the units, such as the North Santee Mounted Rifles of South Carolina, formed themselves when the sectional controversy heated up in the final months of 1860. Arthur Manigault was elected captain of the unit, and when Confederates started building batteries ringing Fort Sumter, Manigault became an aide on Beauregard's staff and oversaw much of the construction. From there it was only a short step to the colonelcy of the 10th South Carolina Infantry, and thereafter a distinguished combat career that led to a general's stars. Though not a true professional with formal training, Manigault's exposure to militia training and command gave him at least enough background when opportunity afforded to best display his leadership abilities.[17] Far more remarkable would be John B. Gordon of Georgia. With no military experience at all, he was elected captain of the "Raccoon Roughs", which later became a part of the 6th Alabama Infantry. Four years later Gordon would be a major general and commander of a corps in Lee's army.[18]

The genesis of Gordon's career illustrates the manner by which the overwhelming majority of officers were chosen, North and South, especially early in the war. In a nation that was fiercely democratic, that did not entirely trust the professional military, and that always vocally lauded the ability and judgment of the 'common man', volunteer regiments both North and South had the long-held tradition of electing their officers. Practice varied from unit to unit, but typically the men in each company of infantry or cavalry would choose among themselves their captain and two lieutenants. If one man had been especially important in raising the company, or if as was often the case he had paid to arm and equip the company out of his own pocket, then almost certainly he was elected the captain. The captains, in turn, voted from among their number to choose a major, a lieutenant colonel, and a colonel to command the regiment. Again, a man signally responsible for recruiting several of the companies might expect the colonelcy, or else the governor of the state might have indicated a preference, for the governor in the end had to issue the actual commissions. In many cases, men of new regiments purposely left their colonelcies vacant to give the governor a chance to exercise his best judgment.

Inevitably in many regiments the electioneering took on a carnival atmosphere when more than one candidate sought a commission or if there was no clear favorite from the start. Liquor and other inducements could flow freely, along with promises of rapid promotion for the lower ranks. Sometimes even money changed hands. "Our election has not yet come off," wrote a new Johnny Reb, "and to one who like myself is not a candidate it is a time replete with feelings of disgust and contempt." Everywhere he turned, he found his favor courted, and himself hugged and coddled by would-be officers. "I never dreamed before that I was half as popular, fine-looking, and talented as I found out I am during the past few days."[19]

Highhanded methods were commonplace. One Yankee colonel simply called a regiment together, informed them that he had had their *acting* officers mustered in as permanent, "not knowing of any objection" on their part, and then asked the men to ratify his act. "No one *daring* to object," complained one soldier, the colonel was sustained. "This is called an election!" he decried. "What a farce!"[20] Another disgruntled man in the 3rd North Carolina told how his company's first

Right: The young men in the enlisted ranks who were to be commanded by the new officers, men like this boy of the 6th Wisconsin Infantry of the Iron Brigade, often recoiled at their electioneering.

lieutenant pushed through the election of a second lieutenant. "Men, there are two candidates for office, and there is but one of them worth a damn," he bellowed, "and I nominate him." Directing that all in favor of electing his nominee should come to the position of shoulder arms, the lieutenant then ordered the entire host to "company, shoulder arms!" Declaring the election unanimous, he turned the company over to its new lieutenant to dismiss.[21]

If the men of a company or regiment found they did not care for their officers once elected, there was nothing they could do about it until the regiment's term of service expired. Early in the war most units enlisted for twelve months'

service, expecting the conflict to be short. When the war continued, and their enlistments expired, most regiments re-enlisted for three years or the duration of the war, and now they elected officers again. Thanks to having had a year's experience in observing themselves and their officers in action, the men made decidedly better selections the second time around.

When men found that they could not abide the original choices made, little but mutiny could help them, and that was dangerous. When the 4th New Jersey formed, one company fought against the captain somehow imposed upon it and tried to elect its own candidate, but the result was a poisoned atmosphere in the company that

spread to much of the rest of the regiment.[22] One Mississippi company called the Madison Guards rebelled and disbanded in displeasure at the regimental officers elected, and not infrequently the disappointed aspirants for commissions themselves left the service immediately.[23]

Ironically, some who did not seek office and yet found themselves elected company officers, considered leaving the service too, only out of terror. Notified of his selection as lieutenant of his North Carolina company, Walter Lenoir quailed. "Oh! that I could but once have gone to school for two or three months as a diligent student of the company and battalion drills", he lamented in his diary.[24] It did not help that most of the company

Union Zouave and Rifle Officers' Uniforms and Equipment

1. Rifle officer's Hardee hat insignia of the 8th New York Regiment (German Rifles)
2. Rifle officer's hat insignia
3. Frock coat belonging to Lt. Col. Frederick Mears, 1st U.S. Sharpshooters
4. Hat insignia of Colonel Augustus Funk, 39th New York, (also known as the Garibaldi Guard)
5 and 6 Colonel Funk's epaulette numerical designation
7. Colonel Funk's shoulder strap insignia
8. Officer's sword belt
9. Non-regulation officer's sword, a German manufactured import
10. Officer's false boot tops
11. Trousers of aide-de-camp W. H. Mallory, 5th New York Regiment (known as Duryee's Zouaves)
12. Mallory's forage cap
13. A non-regulation Bartholomae's Patent Water Filtration Canteen
14. Forage cap of Lieutenant Colonel William Fowler, 146th New York Regiment
15. Short jacket of Lieutenant Colonel Fowler
16. Smith and Wesson No. 2 Army rimfire revolver, taking a .32 caliber cartridge

Artifacts courtesy of: Don Troiani Collection: 1, 4, 5-10, 11-16, 11, 12, 13, 14, 15, 16; Gary Leister Collection: 2, 3

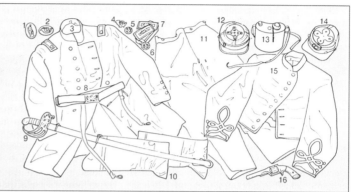

officers elected had long been known to the other members of the company either as friends, business associates, childhood playmates, or even brothers and cousins. "It was a trying ordeal for the officers", wrote one Texan, when they had suddenly to exercise authority and arbitrary control over young men they had known on an equal footing since youth.[25] The brother or friend long accustomed to cuffing the ears or touseling the hair of a fellow, could find it very difficult to salute and obey him without a smirk or question just because he had been made an officer.

But an overwhelmingly greater obstacle for thousands of the newly elected regimental officers was their utter ignorance of what an officer was supposed to do. The strutting about in bright buttons, sash and sword and gleaming boots, came easily enough, but the business of command was as good as a foreign language to them, and some of it, in fact, was foreign, many of the drill evolutions being called by French rather than English names. Unfortunately, in all the rush to go to war, neither side made any provision to give officer training to the newly elected or appointed leaders. Whatever hasty education the new officers received was strictly of an ersatz and informal variety. Some regiments – usually those with an experienced Regular Army colonel appointed to command – set up their own schools to train men in the manual of arms, drill evolutions, and the duties and deportment expected of an officer. With no system or uniformity, however, the students often learned nothing more than the weaknesses and prejudices of their teachers.

It would have helped immeasurably in the Union Army if the remaining Old Army officers had been parceled out evenly over the new volunteer units. Certainly it would have made hundreds of lieutenants and captains delighted to become colonels of their own regiments. Had such been done, then these professionals could have overseen training their own officers, as those Regulars who took volunteer commands often did. But Washington decided to keep the Regular Army units intact, with as many of their officers as possible, expecting them to be the stiff backbone needed to keep volunteer outfits in line in battle, a largely needless function as it turned out. Here, at least, the Confederacy fared better, for having no pre-established regular army of its own, all former Regular officers who joined the cause could be put in charge of volunteers.[26]

Some states like Michigan did establish camps of instruction, and sent their officers to them first before the enlisted men followed. More often than not, however, fresh officers and men were both simply dumped into the maelstrom of camp life and training and left to learn and fend for themselves. The results were usually comical and not infrequently tragic.

For starters, the officers, especially at the company level, were often hardly more educated than their own illiterate men. Drill maneuvers of the simplest kind could not be performed because the men did not know the meaning of the words, and because frequently enough there were enlisted men who literally did not know right from left. One ingenious officer devised the system of tying hay to the left feet of his men, and straw to the right. Then, instead of commanding them to march "left, right, left" and so on, which many could not understand, he simply called orders for "hayfoot, strawfoot." The technique was a success and achieved a wide usage in both armies.[27]

Worse still, many men given sudden power were not able to grasp fully the difference between the use and abuse of it. Early in 1862, the lieutenant of Company E, 4th Kentucky, abused and mistreated one of his privates. Only the intercession of now General Breckinridge brought a remedy. On another occasion that spring, a different officer ordered a private to

Above: Europeans, whether trained or not, were the delight of the volunteer regiments. Hosts of them became officers, as with Colonel Frederick D'Utassy at center, commanding the "Garibaldi Guard".

Below: A popular officer might even find himself honored with his name in boughs in a company arbor, as Company A of the 30th Pennsylvania did for Captain M. Hooton, at left center leaning on his sword.

Second Lieutenant, The Washington Artillery

The pre-war militia and private units that came into the Confederate service rarely adopted the national uniform regulations entirely, and the Confederate government never made any real concerted attempt to enforce them. In the hard-pressed Rebel service, any uniform, even one with improper insignia, was better than none at all.

The Washington Artillery of New Orleans enjoyed a long and distinguished history, and probably sent the best trained private officers into the Southern armies. This Second Lieutenant shows some of the distinctive Washington Artillery uniform features – blue tunic, shoulder strap indications of rank rather than collar insignia, and the crossed cannon at the neck. The red kepi would also call attention to them on the field. They served all through the war, and with distinction. Its success was such that the unit stayed in existence even after Appomattox.

sweep out the officer's tent. When the private refused, he was put in the guardhouse until Breckinridge learned of it and ordered the officer to apologize to him and sweep out his own tent. Occasionally the men themselves turned the tables on abusive commanders. When a North Carolina captain put one of his men in the guard house, other soldiers got even by catching the captain when he was drunk. "We put him in the Sh-t House," wrote the offended private, "so we are even." And in 1863, the men of the 55th Georgia deposed their colonel and rode him about camp on a rail until he promised better behavior and was allowed to resume command.[28]

There was a great deal of routine involved in being an officer – making out reports, inspections, roll calls, promulgating general orders from headquarters, specifying guard details, and more. Throughout many of the volunteer regiments, there would always be complaints of these and other functions not being performed in a routine and timely fashion. Throughout the war there would be repeated complaints of laxity made by army inspectors. The Confederates attempted to do something about it by instituting competency examinations in 1862, but they were ever haphazard, and the simple needs for more officers in a hurry due to the attrition of disease and the battlefield always placed untried and untrained men in hundreds of vacancies every month.

The inevitable result of such inexperience was embarrassingly evident in the early months of the war. At drill especially, most regiments were like unto the mute leading the deaf. Infantrymen at bayonet drill stuck each other in the back when orders were garbled. Cavalrymen inflicted more saber wounds upon themselves and their horses than they ever later visited upon their enemies. There were a number of accepted drill manuals available, especially *Rifle and Infantry Tactics* by William J. Hardee, now a general in the Confederate Army. But others with conflicting ideas were also used, and it wasn't until 1862 that the War Department in Washington issued a new standard manual by Silas Casey. Even then, the manual was massive, in three volumes, and far too much for a volunteer officer to master in the brief time allowed before and between campaigns. In the end, if an officer learned to march his men forward in good formation, could make it turn right or left, about face, break into squads or

Below: The bearded young men, standing uneasily at attention in some Pennsylvania or Ohio Street surrounded by Mennonite girls, were the raw stuff with which the new officers had to work.

Below: The bearded young men, standing uneasily at attention in some Pennsylvania or Ohio Street surrounded by Mennonite girls, were the raw stuff with which the new officers had to work.

companies and reform them again, and run them through the manual of arms for loading and firing and advancing into battle, he knew about as much as he needed. In only a very few units was there sufficient expertise among the officers to achieve high proficiency at drill and parade.

Some of these new officers, it seemed, could not even count. The adjutant of the First Kentucky Brigade, Breckinridge's first command, had to be reprimanded when he detailed more men from the 5th Kentucky for camp and police duties than the regiment actually mustered. A Pennsylvanian complained of "a total lack of system about our regiment." Everything was late, there was little or no anticipation of the needs of the future, and good managers in the form of officers seemed to be in dire want. "We can only be justly

Above: In those raw volunteer regiments, officers, non-com's, and enlisted men mixed democratically with each other, as with the 12th New York at Camp Anderson in 1861. Barriers, however, would emerge.

called a mob & one not fit to face the enemy."[29]

The results of all this inexperience were nowhere more evident than on the drill field. Trying to keep the men in proper step while putting them through ill-understood maneuvers with orders often mispronounced, all amid choking dust and under the eye of superiors, could be an inordinately difficult task. A man in the 14th New Hampshire told of the preening officers "who had been cramming Casey for a fortnight", vainly trying to make it all work on the parade ground. "That the men got into a snarl, a tangle, a double and twisted, inextricable tactical knot, is tame delineation", he wrote. "The drill caused a great deal of serious reflection."[30]

Men in the ranks coughed so much that officers' commands could not be heard. If a rabbit jumped out of its nest in front of the tramping men, all discipline could dissolve as the boys took off after the potential meal. Orders passed down the ranks became garbled. When a Rebel major sent back word for the men at the rear of his column to close up at the double-quick, it finally reached the stragglers as "double quick back there." Suiting action to word, the rear of the column promptly turned around and marched off at high speed in the opposite direction, leaving the major in command lying on his back, kicking his feet into the air, and swearing "benedictions of an unusual kind for a Presbyterian elder."[31]

It did not help that many amateur officers felt free to choose their own particular set of drill instructions. When time came for battalion drill of more than one company at a time, and one captain had trained with Hardee and another with Casey or Winfield Scott's old manual, the result could be chaos. More than one officer simply skirted the whole issue by abandoning military jargon and telling the men plainly what he wanted them to do. Seeing his command approaching a mud hole, and not knowing the proper commands to have the men march around it, one finally shouted, "Boys! Break up, scoot the hole, and git together on t'other side." In the end, one Tennessee colonel used three commands:

Above: When all the training worked as it should, an officer could look with pride at a splendid unit like this smart New York regiment on parade at Fort Pulaski near Savannah, Georgia.

"Form line", "Forward march", and "Fix bayonets". Colonel Robert Preston of the 28th Virginia apparently saw nothing incongruous about ordering his men: "Fall in Twenty-eighth, fall in! If you don't fall in, I will march the regiment off and leave every one of you behind!"[32]

Not infrequently the men in the ranks were openly disrespectful or laughed at the expense of an inexperienced and confused officer. "Drill is aching funny", wrote a New Hampshire boy. "Mistakes are corrected by making still worse mistakes. The men in the ranks grin, giggle and snicker, and now and then break out into a coarse, country hee-haw." When an inordinately youthful lieutenant rode in front of his men for the first time, wags shouted from the rear, "And a little child shall lead them", to peals of laughter. The laughs turned to groans the next day when the lieutenant published an order for a twenty-mile practice march. "And a little child shall lead them!" it read, "on a damned big horse!"[33]

Indeed, as insubordinate and disrespectful as many of the enlisted men could be toward a novice officer, the position of company and even regimental commander could be anything but pleasant. "My post is no sinecure", lamented a Mississippi captain. "My hands are full – perfectly full. I have no hope of being a popular Capt. I am only trying to make a good one." The good ones were appreciated in time by their men, and respected. For the rest, the common soldier North or South had little use. "I wish to God one half of our officers were knocked in the head by slinging them Against A part of those still Left", declared one Yank. Another proclaimed late in the conflict that "had it not been for officers this war would have Ended long ago." Confederates could be just as critical. While one declared his colonel "an ignoramus fit for nothing higher than the cultivation of corn," another Reb from Florida achieved even greater heights of invective, pronouncing his officers "not fit to tote guts to a Bear."[34]

No wonder that many officers could not take the pressure of their new job, nor the disapproval of their men, and chose to resign. The rapid for-

Below: If the training did not go well, at least an officer could hope to muster out soon in the 90-days outfits. The 1st Michigan, an excellent regiment, returns to Detroit after 1st Bull Run, in 1861.

mation of the armies, and their launching into active campaigning with barely a few weeks for training, quickly separated those who could stand the frustrations from those who could not. While the Regular Army officers, whichever side they chose, knew what they were getting into when it came to training and leading men, the unskilled volunteer officers who were to form the overwhelming majority of this war's leaders had no alternative but to learn by doing, and it was a hard school of experience that awaited them in America's bloodiest war. There were many who might have agreed with one officer from Texas who found he could not take the strain, and resigned. "If he had to associate with devils," he had said, "he would wait till he went to hell, where he could select his own company."[35]

References

1 Warner, *Generals in Gray*, pp.38, 132; Roland, *Johnston*, pp.249-50.
2 John Gibbon, *Personal Recollections of the Civil War* (New York, 1928), p.3.
3 Roland, *Johnston*, pp.252-60.
4 James Longstreet, *From Manassas to Appomattox* (Philadelphia, 1896), pp.29-33.
5 Gallagher, *Alexander*, pp.22-3.
6 Hancock, *Hancock*, pp.73-5; Gallagher, *Alexander*, pp.30-1.
7 Gibbon, *Recollections*, pp.5-7.
8 Ibid., pp.9-10.
9 Martin F. Schmitt, ed., *General George Crook, His Autobiography* (Norman, Okla., 1960), p.83.
10 Merlin E. Sumner, ed., *The Diary of Cyrus B. Comstock* (Dayton, Ohio, 1987), pp.230-5.
11 Schmitt, *Crook*, pp.83-5.
12 Coffman, *Old Army*, p.92.
13 G. Moxley Sorrel, *Recollections of a Confederate Staff Officer* (New York, 1905), pp.21-6.
14 Walter P. Lane, *The Adventures and Recollections of General Walter P. Lane* (Austin, Texas, 1970), p.83.
15 Milo M. Quaife, ed., *From the Cannon's Mouth: The Civil War Letters of General Alpheus S. Williams* (Detroit, 1959), pp.16-8.
16 Mark M. Boatner, *The Civil War Dictionary* (New York, 1959), p.526.
17 R. Lockwood Tower, ed., *A Carolinian Goes to War: The Civil War Narrative of Arthur Middleton Manigault* (Columbia, S.C., 1983), pp.9-10.
18 John B. Gordon, *Reminiscences of the Civil War* (New York, 1904), pp.4, 26.
19 Bell I. Wiley, *The Life of Johnny Reb* (Indianapolis, 1943), p.20.
20 Bell I. Wiley, *The Life of Billy Yank* (Indianapolis, 1952), p.24
21 James I. Robertson, Jr., *Soldiers Blue and Gray* (Columbia, S.C., 1988), p.13.
22 James I. Robertson, Jr., ed., *The Civil War Letters of General Robert A. McAllister* (New Brunswick, N.J., 1965), p.30.
23 Wiley, *Johnny Reb*, p.20.
24 Robertson, *Soldiers*, p.51.
25 Ibid., p.51.
26 Wiley, *Billy Yank*, pp.25-6.
27 Robertson, *Soldiers*, p.49.
28 Davis, *Orphan Brigade*, pp.54-5; Wiley, *Johnny Reb*, p.242.
29 Ibid., p.54; Wiley, *Billy Yank*, p.26.
30 Francis H. Buffum, *A History of the Fourteenth Regiment, New Hampshire Volunteers* (Boston, 1882), p.45.
31 Robertson, *Soldiers*, p.52.
32 Robertson, *Soldiers*, pp.50-1.
33 Ibid., p.49.
34 Ibid., p.51; Bell I. Wiley, *The Common Soldier of the Civil War* (New York, 1973), pp.87-8.
35 Robertson, *Soldiers*, p.53.

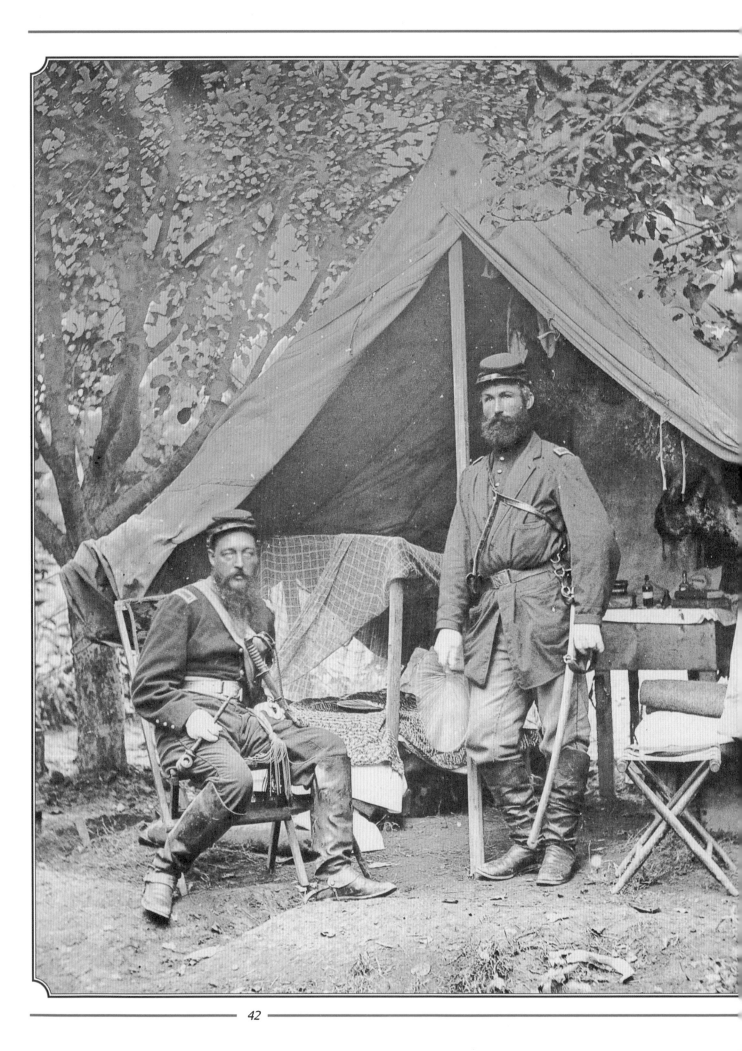

CHAPTER THREE

UNDER THE MARQUEE

With the trauma of their first battle behind them, North and South marched on through 1861 – a bloodless time of "phony war" – and then into the maelstrom of 1862. They met at Forts Henry and Donelson, then at Shiloh, Pea Ridge, Corinth, and Vicksburg in the West, and all along the Virginia Peninsula and in the Shenandoah in the East. Great names began to emerge – Jackson, Grant, and Lee. Bloody battles like Antietam were to provide the greatest challenge yet to the quality of leadership on both sides.

"A CAPTAIN does not only his own, but all the thinking of the company", lamented an officer of the 125th New York. "A captain has as much to do as – in fact, he is practically – the father of ninety children. Men in camp, sensible men, lose all their good judgment and almost their good sense; they become peurile, and come to the captain on a multitude of silly, childish matters."[1]

In other words, this new business of being an officer and a gentleman in an army of volunteers was no picnic. Even the Old Army men were ill-prepared for it – indeed, they may have been even less prepared for it than the men who were commissioned out of civil life, for the Regulars were accustomed to Regular enlisted men who did not question orders, who recognized and respected the chain of command. This new army of volunteers, imbued with the old Jacksonian spirit of individuality, was a different thing altogether. An officer did not command the regard of his men by divine right. He had to earn it.

This situation was always difficult because from the very outset the officer had a number of marks against him in the men's eyes. He was paid more. He received a much better allowance of rations, or pay allowances that enabled him to buy better food than his men. Whereas most of them – infantry anyhow – had to walk, the average officer was mounted. The officer did not have to obey the same restrictions to camp that applied to the men. He lived in a larger and better furnished tent or winter quarters, and the frequent rules against drinking and gambling did not necessarily apply to him. However much the enlisted men may have liked a man when they first elected him to company or regimental office, sooner or later at least some came to resent the markedly different status of a man who was, in their eyes after all, no better than they were. Only years of service in the field, tempered by performance in battle and a demonstrated concern for the welfare of the men in the ranks, would eventually win for an officer the approbation of the men he commanded.

Certainly the men in command did live a different life. "It seems queer, though, and almost magical", wrote the new brigadier Alpheus S. Williams when he joined his brigade in October 1861. The officers' encampment was on a lovely hillside, eight or ten tents being for Williams and his staff and escort. Nearby were the tents for the officers' servants, and even the horses were sheltered in woods under the shade of a tent fly. "Altogether it is a delightful spot," he concluded, "especially towards sundown when the bands of the regiments strike up for the evening parades and the hillsides in front are covered with moving bodies of troops and the bugle calls from the neighboring brigades float up the valleys and are echoed along the hillside."[2]

Even then, Williams could complain of hardship . . . of a sort. When he and his three wagons of impedimenta reached the camp, no one offered assistance. Of himself, a captain, two lieutenants, and three servants, only Williams and the captain had ever pitched a tent. Still they got their tents erected, then settled down and opened their mess chest to a dinner of broiled ham and soda biscuits, lamenting that they could not find fresh meat or bread. At the same time, most of the men in the ranks were sleeping crammed into crowded circular tents that held a dozen packed in like spoons, and eating salt pork or pickled beef and hardtack. No wonder many of the men commenced the war with an immediate resentment of their leaders.[3]

It was much the same all across the country in the early days of the war. Even in the Confederacy, where in time supplies would be so tight that the officers lived little better than the men, at first there was an abundance of everything. The men of Charleston's Washington Light Infantry went to the front taking their black servants and valets with them, lived in crisp white canvas tents with spacious accommodation, and dined from

The camp life of the average officer could be almost as humdrum as that of his men, though surely most never looked so bored and bemused as the sorrowful Lieutenant John W. Fox at left. Army life could not have been as dreary as that.

hampers sent by family and friends and filled with cakes and cheeses, fresh coffee and tobacco, champagne and beer and wine, and the finest of smoked meats. Often they had their own musicians to serenade them. The Washington Artillery of New Orleans went to war in bright awning striped marquees, set up on raised wooden floorboards to get them out of the mud and dust. They had real chairs and tables, lanterns, cots with mattresses, even sheets and table service. In 1861 the officers of a single company could pose proudly for a photographer in front of a tent brimming with more equipment than a whole regiment of officers would have by war's end. They came with squirrel rifles for sport, fresh changes of uniform, even havelocks hanging down from the back of their hats to keep the sun from their necks. War might be hell, but it need not be unduly uncomfortable.[4]

Below: For many, the mere fact of going to war hardly offered a reasonable excuse to give up the comforts of home. Officers of South Carolina's Washington Light Infantry took comfort to war.

The daily routine in these officers' quarters varied considerably from regiment to regiment, army to army. For Williams and his staff it began with reveille at sunrise, after which his servant William served all of the officers good strong coffee. An hour later he served breakfast. By 8 a.m., the morning reports of men present for duty, absent without leave, on sick call, and so forth, began to arrive from the several regiments in his brigade, all of them prepared by officers who had to arise earlier than Williams and awaken their men for roll call. The morning reports out of the way, the lieutenants and their sergeants began making out copies of the day's orders for the regiments, filling out leaves and furlough papers, requisitions for quartermaster or commissary stores. Then orders would come down from division for Williams' officers to copy and distribute through his regiments.

Right: Colonel Henry Hoffman of the 23rd New York offers a fair look into the average commander's field quarters. A table, a cot, a few necessities, and little more made up his furnishings.

Once he had seen and approved a consolidated report of those present for duty for his entire brigade, Williams mounted his horse to start his daily rounds of his command, usually not returning until noon or later for a meal before remounting and continuing his inspections. "In this way the days seem short," he wrote home, "and by eight or nine o'clock we are all in bed."[5] To his wife he would complain that "according to the custom of the army I am obliged to live and travel in considerable state." A guard was detailed for him every day by each of his regiments in turn, every time he came or went turning out to present arms. A mounted orderly followed him everywhere, and whenever he approached the camps of one of his regiments, shouts of "The Brigadier General" would result in a guard of a hundred or more rolling out. He had to ride past and review them, repeating the same performance with each regiment. "I go through this process at least once a day", he complained.

More onerous were all the petty details to which he had to attend, or which he oversaw his subordinate officers in attending. He even had a special clerk detailed to help with the paperwork. All issues from the quartermaster's or the commissary's stores required his approval. His signature appeared on every leave and furlough, every order for a court-martial, and all reports. "In short, everything for 5,000 men has to pass under my supervision." And at that, he believed that he had streamlined the process from what many other brigade and regimental commanders went through, so much so that he still found time to visit each of his regiments daily, look in on the condition of the camps and hospitals and kitchens, and attend personally to the special reports turned in each day by field officers designated to review all the complaints and suggestions that needed acting upon within the command. To get everything done satisfactorily, he frequently stayed up late on the nights when the moon allowed a few extra hours.[6]

The tasks were much the same for all officers of all grades, the differences lying mostly in degrees of responsibility, and in the amount of help available. A general could have a staff of up to half a dozen to assist him, many of them volunteer aides. A captain or lowly lieutenant in an infantry company might have only a sergeant-major, and perhaps an enlisted man detailed as clerk or orderly. It could be even less in the South, where not only the nation was new, but also the army, and all the million little details of military regimen had to be, as it were, reinvented. In consequence, many Confederate officers simply never had time to learn some of the finer points of standard officer behavior.

First Lieutenant, 2nd Rhode Island Infantry

This first lieutenant of the 2nd Rhode Island Infantry shows the distinctive early war uniform of this state's first 90-days regiments. The pleated blouse with the full skirt, and the rolled collar, would be very little seen after 1861, and future Rhode Island outfits opted for the more traditional Union Army uniform. Again, like most infantry officers, he carries the .44 caliber Colt "New Model Army" pistol, a powerful percussion weapon though not terribly accurate. Just firing it required a man with fortitude, for its recoil was substantial.

Reflecting the tradition that still bound the army, an officer carried his pistol in a holster that required drawing it with the left hand, freeing the right for drawing the saber, despite the fact that bullets inflicted hundreds of wounds for every edged weapon wound. Tradition died hard. The sword being carried here is a Model 1850 foot officer's sword.

Even the poor volunteer officer who tried his best to master his sudden new 'craft' faced considerable obstacles, not the least of which were the frequently contemptuous Regulars who often commanded the regiments or otherwise oversaw the training of new company commanders. There was nothing worse, wrote Yankee Thomas W. Higginson, than the experience of having "some young regular army lieutenant ride up to your tent at an hour's notice, and leisurely devote a day to probing every weak spot in your command – to stand by while he smells at every camp-kettle, detects every delinquent gun-sling, ferrets out old shoes from behind mess-bunks, spies out every tent pole not labelled with the sergeant's name, asks to see the cash balance of each company fund, and perplexes your best captain on forming from two ranks into one by the left flank." Yet Higginson and others had to admit that, unpleasant as they were, these inspections "are the salvation of an army." They were the fulcrum with which a regiment could be lifted by training into a first-class unit. "So long as no inspecting officer needs twice to remind you of the same thing, you have no need to blush", Higginson continued. "He may be the most conceited little poppinjay who ever strutted in uniform; no matter; it is more for your interest to learn than for his to teach."[7]

A few senior commanders recognized that this teaching was especially important for volunteer officers, and that special schools of instruction were needed. These were sporadically operated, however, depending chiefly upon the whim of the individual camp commander. Some form of system was introduced on July 22, 1861, when the Congress in Washington enacted a bill in response to the chaos at Bull Run, making provision

Above: In the photographer's studio the new officers posed stiffly in their pristine military finery; like this staff officer, probably in the medical service, his buttons and bullion gleaming brightly.

Below: Yet when they were in the field, the officers could sometimes be less self-conscious, simply holding a pose that was nothing more than what they did naturally day in and day out.

for the establishment of a military commission in every department, charged with examining all volunteer officers to adjudge their competency. The act showed some immediate salutary effects, for many officers who knew themselves unequal to their commissions resigned rather than go before the examining boards and suffer the possible humiliation of dismissal. A man who did not appear for his scheduled examination automatically failed. By November 1861, for every officer discharged by the boards, nearly three others resigned voluntarily.

Of course the new system had its faults, not the least being that since it was created by politicians, it suffered from political influences that hampered its full and impartial operation. The overwhelming majority of officers being dismissed or forced into resignation were from the lower grades; very few colonels and no generals were affected. Though they could be no better schooled or able than the lieutenants and captains, the men with high rank had connections that the examining boards did not want to offend.[8]

Occasionally more drastic measures were necessary to deal with inept or insubordinate volunteer officers, as when General George B. McClellan had perhaps a score of them from one regiment sent to the prison at Fort Jefferson in the Dry Tortugas to labor until they changed their ways.[9] But by and large the examining boards accomplished much of what they were intended to do. A side effect was that governors and others raising regiments showed more discretion in their appointments, rather than risk having their appointees later discharged by the boards. Thus, generally with plodding pace, the organization and discipline of the volunteer officers and their

men gradually improved. And as officers were re-moved by discharge or battle, the soldiers slowly acquired much better judgment in voting for their replacements. Making things easier, the War Department began to print instructions on the forms and blanks that some services required officers to fill out. In the ordnance service, for instance, these instructions were "so simple and so minute that it seems as if, henceforward, the most negligent volunteer officer could never make another error." Of course they did, just the same.[10]

And no examining board or set of instructions could protect either Union or Confederacy from the relentless operation of the seniority system. The higher an officer's rank from the beginning, the less his chances of being dismissed for incompetency or removed from command thanks to wounds or death. And when such a man, a colonel or a general, did leave the service, the system dictated that someone of high seniority replace him. In short, many of the inept early-commissioned leading officers could not be displaced by any means. "Beneath the shadow of their notorious incompetency all minor evils may lurk undetected", complained a lower officer. "To crown all, they are, in many cases, sincere and well meaning men, utterly obtuse as to their own deficiencies, and manifesting all the Christian virtues except that of resignation."[11]

It did not help that among many of the volunteer regiments, men and officers chose not to recognize that a difference existed between them. When Major General Richard Taylor inspected a new Texas cavalry regiment joining the Confederacy, he at first thought them well disciplined since their camp was so quiet. Then when he got to the center of the group of men, he

Below: Brigadier General John Martindale sits beneath the tree, surrounded by his staff officers in June 1862. Frequently the less able an officer, the more time he found for being photographed.

Top: The more entrenched a general became, the larger his staff grew. Major General Alfred Pleasonton commanded the cavalry of the Army of the Potomac, not well, but with a hefty military "family".

Above: Life in the field for Confederate leaders differed little from that of their foes, except that in the Rebel army it could be hard to tell officers from enlisted men, as here at Pensacola in 1861.

discovered that their silence was due to their intent concentration on their colonel whom he found seated beneath some trees on a blanket, "dealing the fascinating game of monte." Only grudgingly did the colonel stop playing cards and start playing commander. "Officers and men addressed each other as Tom, Dick, or Harry," lamented Taylor, "and had no more conception of military gradations than of the celestial hierarchy of the poets."[12]

When they did learn to recognize those gradations of rank, men and officers in each army knew them by different insignia. By regulation, and almost without fail, all Union officers wore their insignia of rank on rectangular shoulder straps rimmed with gold bullion, worn one on each shoulder of their dark blue uniform blouse or tunic. A second lieutenant, the lowest form of officer, wore plain shoulder straps that were blank inside the bullion border. A first lieutenant was recognized by a single gold bar at each end of the strap. A captain wore a pair of bars at each end. A major showed a gold oak leaf front and back on his strap, and a lieutenant colonel the same, except that his leaf was silver. A full colonel had a single silver eagle in the center. Among the grades of general, a brigadier wore a single gold star in the center of his epaulette, a major general wore two, a lieutenant general three. Only U.S. Grant wore three stars during the war, and

Union Rank Insignia

In the Civil War the Union service used exactly the same insignia of rank for officers that have obtained in the U.S. down to the present day. It was simple and easy to recognize. Better yet, despite the branch of service, the insignia remained the same, the only difference being the color of the background facings, namely blue for infantry, yellow for cavalry, and red for artillery.

Of course, of the rankings shown here, two were unique to the war, each being held by only one officer, U.S. Grant. lieutenant general and general or general-in-chief, were given only to him, though Winfield Scott at the beginning of the war did hold a lieutenant generalcy by brevet. Indeed, the archaic system of brevets caused confusion even in this simple system of insignia, for officers were entitled to wear the signs of their brevet rank, despite their actual rank.

Second Lieutenant

Colonel

First Lieutenant

Brigadier General

Captain

Major General

Major

Lieutenant General/General-in-Chief

Lieutenant Colonel

Full General – U.S. Grant after 1866

Confederate Rank Insignia

Uniform insignia for Confederate officers was less precise than that of their foes, largely because the Rebel Congress authorized new grades of commissions without getting around to specifying suitable markings. Thus any one of four grades of general officer – brigadier, major, lieutenant, or full general – all wore the same sleeve and collar insignia. Worse, as with Robert E. Lee and Joseph E. Johnston and others, high ranking generals sometimes wore the insignia of colonels for no apparent reason. At least the Confederates did not further complicate matters by resorting to the cumbersome brevet system. Striping on their kepis was also officially specified for rank, but many generals and lesser officers eschewed the kepi in favor of the more practical slouch or round brimmed hat. Branch facing colors were the same as those used in the Union service.

shortly afterward he was given a fourth.

Officer insignia in the Confederate Army was entirely different, and probably made so solely for the sake of the difference, and perhaps to avoid confusion early in the war since several regiments in the South wore blue uniforms.

All badges of rank in the Confederacy were ordered by regulation to be worn on the front sides of the stand-up collar on the officer's blouse. A second lieutenant wore a single horizontal gold stripe on either side; a first lieutenant two stripes, one above the other; and a captain three. For a major, a single five-pointed star replaced the bars. A lieutenant colonel wore two stars on either side of his collar, and a colonel three stars. Thereafter, however, it got a bit confusing, for even though the Confederate Congress eventually authorized four grades of general – brigadier, major, lieutenant, and full general – it never amended its original specifications for insignia when only the brigadier grade existed. Thus, all generals of all grades were to wear three stars, one larger one flanked by two smaller, encased in a gold wreath. Further, the Confederate law specified distinctive – yet imprecise – cap and sleeve markings. Lieutenants of both grades were to wear gold braid or "frogging" one wale (ridge of cloth) in width. For a captain it was two wales wide, and the same for a major. A lieutenant colonel and a colonel both wore three wales of

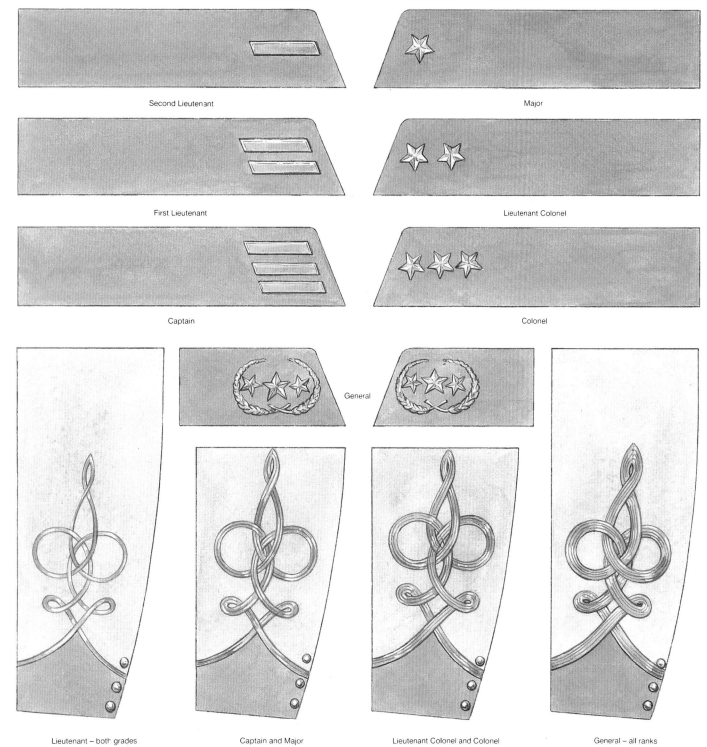

Second Lieutenant

Major

First Lieutenant

Lieutenant Colonel

Captain

Colonel

General

Lieutenant – both grades

Captain and Major

Lieutenant Colonel and Colonel

General – all ranks

braid, and all ranks of general four. Each officer's uniform kepi, a short cap with a brim in front, was to carry vertical side stripes in number corresponding to the sleeve braid. It was a more complex insignia system than the Federals, and less precise. Worse, a combination of scarcity of materials and/or seamstresses, and the idiosyncratic nature of the officers themselves, meant that regulations were honored almost as much in the breach as in the observance of the law. Many former U.S. officers simply continued to wear their Old Army uniforms, as did Thomas J. Jackson for a time. Many more, uniformed by their states before Confederate regulations were established, wore shoulder straps, or epaulettes and collar insignia. The sleeve braid never saw light of day on a majority of Southern leaders, and neither did the kepis, full brimmed slouch hats being more practical for field service. And even among the highest ranking officers observance was lax. Robert E. Lee and Joseph E. Johnston, both full generals, never got around to encircling the three stars on their collars with wreaths, and only Johnston wore the sleeve braid. Had not their men recognized them by sight, these army commanders might have been mistaken for colonels.[13]

North and South, there were also arrangements of buttons to denote rank, but these were often misleading, for men who won promotion frequently did not bother to rearrange their buttons. Also, in the Union Army the practice of awarding brevets might entitle a man who was only a major to wear the insignia of his brevet rank, which could be colonel or even brigadier. It was not all quite as complex as Taylor's reference to the "celestial hierarchy of the poets", but to men entirely new to military etiquette, it could certainly be confusing.

Perhaps the frequent disinclination to recognize the differences in rank sprang in part from many of the volunteers' initial refusal to admit an obligation to pay attention to officers. Here was

the new officer's chief hurdle. Most of his men believed, as one soldier put it, that enlisted men were the equals of their leaders, "and not a few . . . the superiors." One Yankee volunteer general found his men completely ignorant of "the proper deference due superior officers", and it was worse in the more individualistic Confederacy, where one observer noted that it took years to teach the privates "to give unquestioning obedience to officers because they were such."[14]

As a result, initially many inexperienced officers tried to deal with their men by staying their friends, by assiduously denying their own different status. "Gentlemen of the Banks County

Above: While uniform regulations pretty specifically stated what an officer was to wear, idiosyncracies were the rule, as with the flamboyant medal and civilian dress of Colonel James Mulligan.

Guards," one Georgia captain suggested, "will you please halt." A firmer hand than that would be needed for real effective command, but it took the green officers many months in camp and field to acquire the self-confidence to take such a hand with the men.[15] Less wise were those who sought from the outset to control their men by the imposition of bullying or flagrant exercise of rank. "Tell a soldier that he must not do a certain thing or go to a certain place," wrote a Rebel Texan, "and he will immediately want to know the reason why and begin to investigate." Consequently, in the training of these volunteers, the officers had to exercise considerable judgment of how far they could be pushed before they would push back. Lieutenant Colonel John Beatty went past that line with his 3rd Ohio. When he approved court-martial sentences for men who broke camp rules, he was vilified in the unit. Insubordination broke out, and a mutiny ensued after he punished a soldier for drunkenness. Only by dint of staring them down did he prevent open rebellion, but later he lost them again when the ineffectual colonel of the regiment went back on a promise to resign rather than have Beatty press charges against him. The men liked the loose – indeed, non-existent – rule of the colonel, and when he decided not to resign 225 of the men in the ranks signed a petition that called for resignation from Beatty instead. Only by unyielding steadfastness did Beatty manage to hold onto his command.[16]

Even when they did not actually mutiny or rebel, the men knew of ways to show their lack of approval of their officers, and especially of men with inflated egos. Not a few swell-headed bluebloods from Massachusetts or South Carolina

Below: When the cold weather came, the officers, like their men, went into winter quarters. Some, like these log and tent shelters at Fort Brady, Virginia, became virtual cities, with street names.

openly showed a disdain for the common men in the ranks. Colonel Charles S. Wainwright of New York was not at all embarrassed to denounce the indiscriminate mixing of the social classes in the army, and the inclination of privates to "hobnob" with their betters. Seeing so much in the army that took place on "a purely democratic footing" was disgusting to him. Some Massachusetts units even dismissed officers for fraternizing too much with the private soldiers, and in the Confederate army soldiers often complained of the officers setting themselves above and apart. "The officers above the rank of captain knew but little of the hardships of war from personal experience", complained a Virginian. "They had their black cooks. . . . The regimental wagons carried the officers' clothes, and they were never half-naked, lousy, or dirty. They never had to sleep upon the bare ground. . .; the officers were never unshod or felt the torture of stone-bruise."[17]

Consequently, the men struck back however they could. In Virginia, one regiment put on black-face minstrel shows in which the most ludicrous characters were clearly recognizable as parodies of unpopular officers. A major in the 20th New York was taken by a group of his men and tossed into the air repeatedly from a tent fly. A stuffy New York captain of the 9th Infantry found his men openly derisive. They shouted insults and taunts at him when he tried to form them for parade, hanged and burned him in effigy, and drew rude caricatures of him on the walls of his own tent. Finally he was virtually a prisoner in his own quarters, fearful to venture out lest the baiting continue. In the end he resigned. "Nothing," said one soldier, "was more keenly relished than a joke on an officer."[18]

Even a less aristocratic and otherwise well-liked officer had to be wary not to allow momentary harshness or a loss of temper or demeanor to poison his relations with his men. When a Massachusetts officer thoughtlessly whistled for his

Above: Just what sort of "Fun & Fury" the "5 Drons" anticipated is uncertain, but obviously these officers are well equipped to entertain themselves with a host of diversions during the long idle winter months.

Below: Largely because they had to perform the meaner chores in camp, like this soldier at the wash tub, the enlisted men relished getting even with an officer by making him the butt of a joke.

young drummer to come to him, the boy belligerently replied that he was not a pet and would not come when whistled at. If the men in a company or a regiment decided that they did not respect an officer, they could affront him either by refusing to salute when he passed or, just as often, by offering in mockery exaggerated responses to his orders. Even more galling to an officer was the occasional barracks 'lawyer' who found in the army regulations a weapon to use against him. When a Virginia lieutenant ordered his company to dig a trench, he himself returned to the comfort of camp. After a time, so did many of his men, arguing that they had worked as hard as the men on either side of them. The lieutenant found that

John Casler was the ringleader, and immediately started cursing him to his face. "You must not curse me," Casler retorted, "or I will report you to headquarters." In the end the officer apologized for his intemperance. "An officer can punish a private," Casler well knew, "but he dare not curse him. That was one advantage a private had over an officer."[19]

Even in obeying orders without rebellion, an unpopular officer could find his men a torment. One man gave a sentry orders so exhaustively complete and minute that the sentry felt his intelligence had been insulted. Instead of protesting, he simply carried out his orders as given – exhaustively and minutely, to the point that the

offending officer was forced, by literal interpretation of the instructions, to dismount himself in the center of a stream.[20]

Not many of the soldiers appreciated the fact that a lot of the volunteer officers themselves were painfully aware of their ignorance and lack of experience. The more conscientious ones did their best to study or otherwise learn quickly what they needed to know. Colonel Roger Hanson sat up for several nights in late 1861, studying in his tent with his brigade drillmaster, as the teacher instructed him in the latest regimental and brigade drill by moving kernels of corn around on a table. Many a young man like Lieutenant Samuel Craig would go off alone into a field

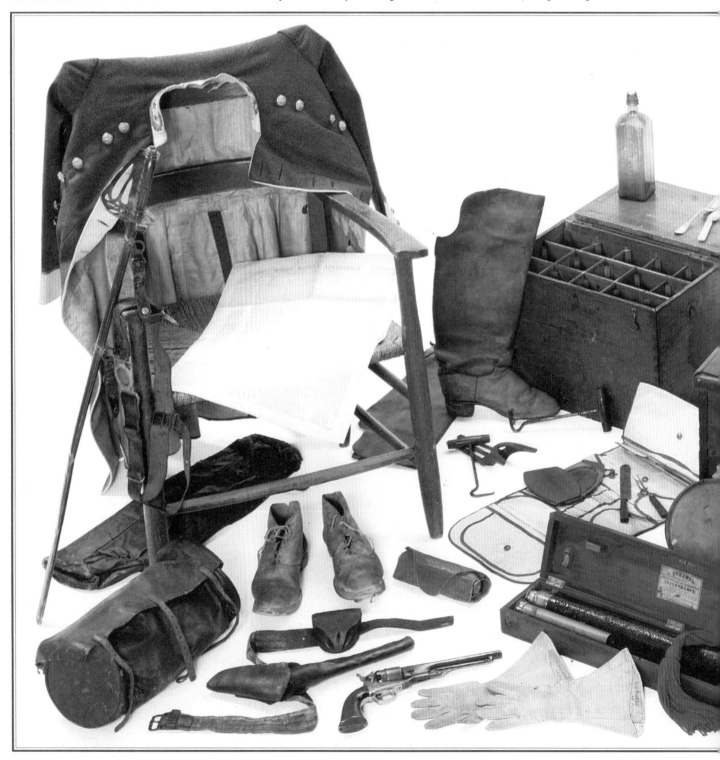

Confederate Officers' Camp Equipment

1 Frock coat of Brig. Gen. James Connor
2 Connor's English Model 1822 infantry sword
3 Camp chair used by Robert E. Lee, 1863
4 Boots of J.T. McKenna
5 Bourbon whisky bottle
6 Walnut wine chest
7 Ammunition box
8 Wooden trunk of Gen. Joseph E. Johnston
9-10 Saddle roll and valise
11 Leather brogans

12 Leather dressing case
13 Belt and plate of Capt. William A. Wright
14 Colt 1860 Army revolver of Dr. H. H. McGuire
15-17 Boot pullers
18 Dressing case of Maj. Gen. Robert Ransom Jr.
19 Field glass of Gen. P.G.T. Beauregard
20 Cavalry gauntlets
21 Officer's sash
22 Hat of Capt. John M. Hudgins, 30th Va. Inf.
23 Confederate tobacco

24 Carved dogwood pipe
25 Shaving glass of Brig. Gen. Henry A. Wise
26 Velvet housewife of Col. Nathan Davis
27 Wooden inkwell of Gov. John Gary Evans, S.C.
28 Evans' pen
29 Pearl handled dagger
30 Bone handled knife
31 Field desk of Gen. J.E.B. Stuart
32 Walnut chest of Lt. Gen. Richard S. Ewell
33 Wooden cane

Artifacts courtesy of: The Museum of the Confederacy, Richmond, Va.

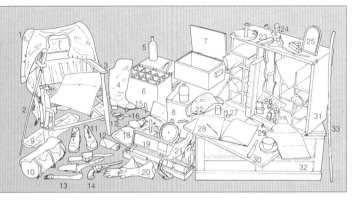

or deep wood, and there read from Casey or Hardee the necessary commands to drill the men, shouting the orders at the mute trees. A few even wrote their required orders on small pieces of paper, then read from them – perhaps concealing them by their saddle, when drilling on parade. Unfortunately for the colonel of the 5th Wisconsin, when he did this his horse spooked at noise from the band, and all his notes fluttered to the ground. Parade had to halt while he picked them up and got them resorted into proper order.[21]

Besides learning what to say to the men when on parade, every officer had to wrestle with the question of his own personal deportment and the example he set. Forbidden by regulations from excessive drinking or gambling, or other vices, and liable to punishment if guilty, the private soldiers would not long tolerate similar behavior in officers. Certainly the same temptations that lure a private or non-commissioned officer could work upon the spirit of one of his commanders. "Temptation was around me in a thousand forms", wrote a Mississippi lieutenant. "In none of these things did I indulge."[22]

Drunkenness, especially, outraged the men, not because of insobriety itself, but because an officer could get away with it without punishment often as not, while that same officer might very well impose harsh sentences on the men in the ranks caught drinking. A man of the 10th Confederate Cavalry wrote of seeing his colonel "always drunk when he can get whiskey", and in the 61st Illinois one lieutenant was damned by a soldier as a "mean, pucelanamous, low bread, nigerdly, unprinculed drinking sot." When a captain with too much liquor in him became insulting and berated and harrassed a guard who had challenged him at the picket line, a number of other soldiers came to the rescue and collectively yanked the inebriate from his horse, beat him thoroughly, and sent him afoot back to his camp.[23]

An officer also had to be careful not to fall into other habits of his men, or to become even a passive participant in their vices, for fear it would give them a weapon to use against him. In every army there were orders prohibiting foraging in

Right: For the officer, release from the pressures of command came at his mess table with his fellow leaders, like these officers of the 16th United States Infantry at Brandy Station, Virginia.

neighboring farmyards, and officers were duty bound to enforce both the regulations and punishments. However, when part of the booty from such stealthy expeditions was mysteriously left beside or inside a company officer's tent, all too often he was not too diligent about finding the offenders. Instead, officers and men evolved a little bit of play acting in which the officer regularly made stirring and ferocious speeches before the men denouncing such infractions and promising the direst of penalties if any were caught transgressing. But the men well knew he was saying it only as a matter of form, and kept right on with their mischief. An Ohio colonel who found his men robbing haystacks fumed at the men, then rode away and told others met along the way that they would have to hurry if they

Above: The real test of the new officer's grasp of his task came on the parade ground, where he had to take from 100 to 1,000 men and mold them to his bidding, like the 34th Massachusetts here in 1862.

wanted to get any hay. The colonel of the 14th Wisconsin near Vicksburg, Mississippi, spoke his warnings so hyperbolically that none of his men could mistake his real intent. "Boys, you have heard the orders", he shouted. "Now I don't want to see a d----d man touch any of them sheep we just passed, and these hogs, I don't want to see any one touch them. Break ranks!" Quickly the men went to work, and later that day the colonel himself discovered a fine ham in his tent.[24]

Many officers simply turned a blind eye,

Above: Unlike their men, the officers were not supposed to forage for themselves. Yet foraging expeditions like this one leaving Camp Griffin, Virginia, in 1862, served officers and enlisted alike.

rationalizing their men's behaviour by considering the poor rations the government furnished them, and the undoubted fact that the war was all the enemy's fault anyhow, and enemy civilians should pay the price with his livestock and fence rails. And worse, a few commissioned men actually participated in the transgressions. An Ohio lieutenant helped some of his men steal hogs, and was later caught eating a rib by his major. His incredible explanation was that "it rained pieces of fresh pork this morning." Yet the

major, smilingly it must be assumed, accepted the excuse, and later accepted a nice chunk of pork from the lieutenant.[25]

The point was, however, that sooner or later an officer who joined with the men or condoned their depredations tended to lose their respect. Certainly he lost whatever healthy quotient of fear or awe there might have been that gave him an edge in exacting obedience from them when it really mattered. And such a man also lost the respect of his fellow commanders, for though it was a very large army, North or South, it was still a rather small and closed society in which nothing stayed secret for long. "The men talked about the officers, and the officers talked about each other," wrote a New Yorker, "in a manner that led strangers to believe that like Ishmael of old,

'Every man's hand turned against his neighbor, and his neighbor's hand against him'."[26]

In short, while precious few officers were figuratively placed on a pedestal by admiring men, every man with a commission had the eyes of hundreds – sometimes thousands – turned toward him, many of them ever-ready to find fault or spot an infraction. As the war continued into its later years, this seems to have increased rather than abated, perhaps because both men and officers were jaded from the seemingly endless toils and hardships. Then, too, in both Union and Confederate armies, the individual quality and character of both leaders and led actually declined rather than improved. The most motivated and patriotic men had enlisted in the first two years. By 1864 and later both sides were resorting to conscription to fill the ranks, and the men the draft brought in were more often than not those who could not be enlisted into the war by any other means. Thus such men in the ranks would be even more than usually inclined to be malcontents. So would the officers they elected from their number, and if they had experienced veteran officers assigned to them instead, such men were very liable to be pretty disdainful of what they had to work with after years of leading much better soldiers. Late in the war many on both sides detected a diminution of "the friendly feeling of cordial comradeship between the enlisted men and their officers," wrote one, "which was one of the distinguishing characteristics of the volunteer troops."[27]

Below: Many officers and men of the Union believed that the civilians of the South should be made to pay for the war. This seems so among these men of General Sherman's army; in winter camp among cannabalised homes.

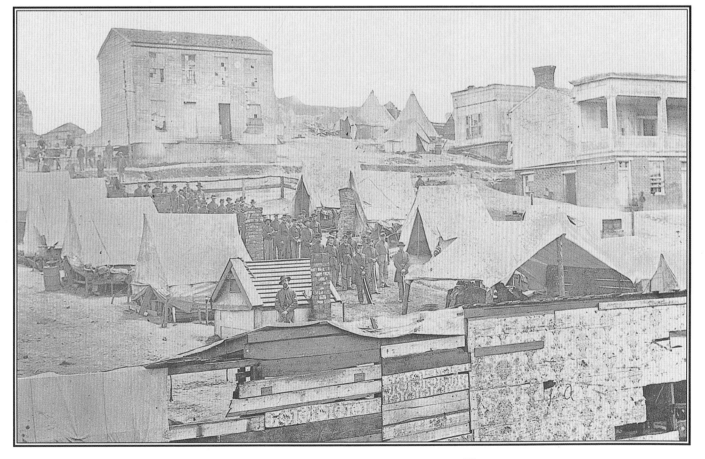

Of course, it took years of experience for even a very perceptive officer to fully grasp all that he was expected to do, and all that he could accomplish, which was usually less than was expected. And so very much depended upon the men themselves that, quite likely, no two regiments would have responded in the same way to the same leaders. Purest accident could also have a massive effect. One instance of bravery on the battlefield, or a single act of cowardice in a career of heroics, or even a small incident of charity or brutishness on the march, could mark an officer's relations with his men for the rest of the war.

After the first few months in camp, army life took on a routine a bit more relaxed than the days of initial training. In the Confederate Army of Tennessee in north Georgia in the early months of 1864, the officers saw that their men had breakfast first before drilling them for ninety minutes at regimental or company evolutions. Then after lunch and time taken for details and camp policing, another ninety minutes of drill by battalion and brigade, with occasionally a drill of an entire division or even corps. On Sundays brigade commanders inspected their men, and looked over all equipment and impedimenta, including wagons and ambulances, animal harness, even blacksmiths' forges. "Having little else to do," wrote one Rebel officer, "all our time was devoted to such duties as tended to improve the men as soldiers, and added to the efficiency of the army." It was good for all concerned, for Brigadier General Arthur M. Manigault observed, even at this late date, that "soldiers are proverbially careless, and officers of our army, those of the line particularly, were scarcely any more careful than their men." Unlike many officers, North and South, Manigault made his command engage in daily target practice, something that, unimaginably, was never taught to recruits with any system or science.[28]

Most armies devoted more time than usual to drill and other such matters when in winter quarters. Since the armies could only campaign seriously in the spring, summer, and fall, the cold

Union Officers' Camp Equipment

1 and 2 Silver goblet and tray
3 Brass traveling candlestick
4 Ledger
5 Tin document tube
6 Newspaper
7 Military forms
8 Silver pitcher with tray
9 Ceramic cup
10 Sand shaker
11 Quill pen and ink
12 *Carte-de-visite*
13 Military documents
14 Ledger
15 Silver personal box
16 Field desk
17 and 18 Ledgers
19 Map
20 Glass decanter from *28*
21 Silver Goblet
22 Newspapers
23 U.S. Army blanket
24 Traveling/folding writing desk
25 Officer's frock coat
26 Officer's silk sash
27 Model 1850 foot officer's sword together with scabbard
28 Traveling liquor case
29 Hand mirror
30 and 31 Straight razor and case
32 Field chest
33 Military manuals
34 Officer's high boots
35 Folding camp chair
36 Binoculars and case
37 Newspaper
38 Patent cast-iron camp stove, made in Philadelphia
39 Tin coffee cup
40 Tin coffee boiler

Artifacts courtesy of: The Civil War Library and Museum: Philadelphia, Pa

months of the year they stayed stationary, usually building semi-permanent quarters of logs and tents combined. Officers, too, lived in such dwellings, and many found a cosy sort of comfort in them. "You probably think living in tents in the winter is a killing thing", Alpheus Williams wrote home in February 1863. "But it is vastly more pleasant and comfortable than you in a warm house imagine." Of course, he did have to stoke his little stove constantly to keep off the cold, but still he was not uncomfortable. Certainly he did not complain. Instead, he lamented, "think of my poor 600 men on picket out in front, and the thousands around so poorly sheltered." Williams was a beloved officer, thanks to his concern for his men.[29]

Across the lines, the routine of officer life took on much the same aspect, though one feature of Confederate officers was the number of them – especially colonels and generals – who had their wives and even children with them when not on active campaign. The wife of Colonel and later General John B. Gordon was a frequent sight in the camps of the II Corps, and a frequent annoyance to his commander General Jubal A. Early. Yet Early had to admit, as he did publicly to Mrs. Gordon, that "General Gordon is a better soldier when you are close by him than when you are away, and so hereafter, when I issue orders that officers' wives must go to the rear, you may know that you are excepted."[30] The wives of men like Breckinridge, Joseph E. Johnston, and many others were frequently with the armies, providing not only comfort to their husbands, but also serving as nurses and comforters for the wounded, writing letters for illiterate soldiers, and simply bringing to men away from home a little genteel feminine company. The other thing that a Southern officer could expect that few Yankee counterparts endured was a good snowballing in winter. For some reason Johnny Rebs

Above: Still, some of the amenities of home could be brought to the camps, and one such was an officer's wife. Many were the wives and sweethearts who came to winter quarters to brighten camp life.

felt this a peculiar right of theirs. "All distinctions were levelled," wrote a Georgia colonel, "and the higher the officer the more snow balling he received." Occasionally it got a little out of hand, and captains came out with black eyes and missing teeth.[31]

On the other hand, there was one unique experience that only Northern officers would have in this war – leading black troops. It is one of the great ironies of the Civil War that the Negro, and especially the slave, was the *sine qua non* of the conflict. Without slavery, there would have been no war. Yet once the conflict had commenced, blacks – slave or free – had almost nothing to do with it for at least the first two years. Very few Yankees went to war to end slavery, and very few Southern men went to war to protect the institution. To the former the idea of emancipation and freedom for the Negro was an abstraction, while to the latter the continuation of slavery hardly mattered because only one in a thousand Confederates ever owned a slave or had any personal stake in perpetuating slavery. The fact is that a host of motivations sent these men out to be officers and gentlemen – adventure and glory-seeking, misplaced nineteenth century romanticism, boredom, even embarrassment at staying behind while so many others went to war. But only a very small portion of Union officers were fighting for abolition or emancipation or for anything connected with the Negro. They went to war chiefly out of patriotism, to defend the Union and remove the stain on the national banners left there by what they saw as the treasonable rebellion of the South. By the same token, Southern

Below: Some officers had a special challenge: to train and lead men who had never been trusted with weapons before . . . blacks. Leading Negro regiments was the route to advancement for many a white officer.

Above: At first this vast reservoir of manpower was viewed indifferently by North and South. Yet in time each would realize that in the black soldier there lay a tremendous resource.

Below: Organized in Nashville in 1864, Battery A of the 2nd U.S. Colored Artillery was only one of scores of units forged out of the uneasy blending of black enlisted men and white officers.

men became Confederate officers not to defend slavery or the shadow-issue of state rights, nor even for the most part because of any sense of Southern nationalism. They donned their uniforms and led men into battle simply to protect their homeland, which, in their eyes, was being invaded by a hostile foe bent on conquest. On both sides, interest in or concern for the slaves did not enter into more than a tiny fraction of the decisions to become an officer.

Even Lincoln's Emancipation Proclamation of January 1, 1863, was more a move to make the Union cause a holy war for freedom for all than a real involvement of the nation's blacks in the contest. But that involvement was bound to come, for no sooner had the war begun than prominent abolitionists in the North began to clamor for free blacks to be allowed to go to war to fight for their brethren's freedom. At first the raising of Negro regiments was such a politically dangerous issue that the Lincoln government would not entertain the idea. Knowing that if black soldiers were enlisted they would, of course, not be integrated into white regiments, Negro leaders even proposed that "efficient and accomplished" white officers be selected to command them. Still Lincoln would not dare act. But by late 1862, with losses in his armies mounting, and with tens of thousands of runaway Southern slaves coming into Yankee lines for refuge, something had to be done. That fall, while he was issuing his preliminary Emancipation Proclamation, he quietly authorized the raising of a single black regiment in Union occupied territory in South Carolina. From that modest start, eventually more than 186,000 Negroes would take service for the Union.[32]

An adverse reaction from many was immediate. "A decided majority of our Officers of all grades have no sympathy with your policy", a Wisconsin commander told Lincoln. "They hate the Negro more than they love the Union." Nevertheless, enlistments went at a brisk pace in the new Bureau of Colored Troops, and that emphasized the immediate need for officers to train and lead them.

Eventually some 7,000 whites would become officers of the regiments officially designated United States Colored Troops – generally shortened to U.S.C.T. They came from a variety of motivations. At first, the government and the Bureau assiduously sought out men who felt committed to black freedom and who actually wanted to help blacks work and fight for abolition. They wanted men who would be proud to lead Negro soldiers, men who were helping to make a grand social and moral statement. A number of able and experienced non-commissioned officers from white volunteer regiments were so selected, and for a time it appeared to some that the caliber of leaders in the U.S.C.T. would be better than in the white regiments, because influence and ambition could not get a commission out of the examining boards, only intelligence and ability. Unfortunately, such men were not a sufficient source for all that were needed. Eventually, far more men came to the U.S.C.T. regiments for the opportunity to obtain high promotion and better pay, or simply because they saw it as a quicker way of winning the war. In many white regiments, a sergeant might never rise to a commission, but by taking a commission in a black unit he had a much brighter future. "I would drill a company of alligators for a hundred and twenty a month", one man admitted, while others sought the commissions because an officer – unlike an enlisted man – could resign at will. Becoming an officer in a U.S.C.T. unit, thus, was a faster way out of the army altogether.[33]

However he obtained that commission, the white officer in a black unit faced some very special challenges. Almost all had to overcome their own prejudice toward Negroes, their attitude that blacks were essentially children, and that former slaves would not fight. A few officers actually viewed their men as victims, defrauding them of pay, and others berated them, and even sexually assaulted the wives or sweethearts who were near camp. Indeed, there were many tests of character faced by such officers that would not have presented themselves in white outfits. Then, too, the officers also had to cope with the derision and prejudice of fellow officers in the regular volunteers. This especially, helped lead to the resignation of many U.S.C.T. leaders. Fortunately, more remained however.

In many regiments, a genuine bond grew between men and officers. Perhaps it arose from the special nature of their service, under the eyes of

Second Lieutenant, The Sumter Light Guard

The Sumter Light Guard of South Carolina, like so many of the Confederate volunteer outfits, came to war with its own arms and uniforms. Unlike the Washington Artillery, however, it adapted its specifications to be compatible with Confederate regulations. This first lieutenant wears the single collar bar of his rank, and the corresponding cuff facing, though without the long curling lace generally seen. The "cadet gray" color of the uniform is right within regulations, as is the red sash. Only the absence of a stripe on the trouser legs is really in substantial variance from regulations.

Often it was only when the uniforms of such volunteer units wore out, that regulation replacements from Richmond saw them properly uniformed according to official regulation. Even then, officers throughout the Rebel service were doomed to haphazard attire.

the world, in which each had to prove himself worthy of his place. Colored regiments were often more difficult to manage than others, and training and discipline required special patience. More patience was required when in proximity to white regiments, for many would not conceal animosity and prejudice. Fights were a constant problem, and insults hurled at the Negroes a daily occurrence. But now and then a U.S.C.T. regiment did so well that it won the approval, if not the respect, of fellow white soldiers. When his black regiment peformed ably at drill, a colonel wrote proudly that "even the N.Y. Cavalry in the street forgot to say 'Nigger'." It was a small victory.[34]

When it came to battle, the black regiments did well enough to win commendation, and by war's end a few dozen blacks themselves became officers, the highest being Major Martin Delaney of the 104th U.S.C.T. Perhaps it was seeing this that led the South to the greatest irony of the war.

On March 23, 1865, the Confederacy authorized raising black units with white officers to lead them. The promise was that freedom would be granted to any slaves who enlisted, and surprisingly there was some small measure of enthusiasm for the plan. At one military hospital, sixty out of seventy-two slaves said they would volunteer should their masters agree. The press in Virginia, North Carolina, Georgia, and elsewhere, endorsed the desperate last-minute measure, and in Richmond itself the work of raising a Negro unit actually got under way.

By March 27 there were thirty-five recruits drilling daily, fully uniformed and equipped, under their new white officers Major Thomas P. Turner and Lieutenant Virginius Bossieux. Moreover, a dozen of the recruits were not slaves at all, but free blacks apparently fighting for their native state. General Lee, especially, endorsed the idea, hoping that the full quota of 75,000 slaves could be enlisted, creating virtually a new army.

But unfortunately for Lee, the experiment was too late for the Confederacy and too soon for Southern society. Richmond fell ten days after the enabling legislation passed, and the Confederate Negro units being raised never saw action. Indeed, the only violence they did experience came when they drilled on Cary and Twenty-first Streets in Richmond. Crowds of citizens gathered on the sidewalks and jeered and spat at both the black soldiers and the white officers who led them.[34]

Above: Difficult as it was for them to stand out from their fellows, some blacks excelled, winning praise and recognition. Martin R. Delaney rose higher than all, eventually becoming a major.

Below: The United States Colored Troops produced a remarkable synergy – white officers and black enlisted men, who might otherwise have been forgettable, forged a new chapter in race relations.

References

1 Robertson. *Soldiers*, p.122.
2 Quaife, *Williams*, p.18.
3 *Ibid.*, p.18.
4 William C. Davis, ed., *Touched by Fire* (Boston, 1985), I, pp. 186-7.
5 Quaife, *Williams*, p.20.
6 *Ibid.*, pp. 22-3.
7 Thomas W. Higginson, "Regular and Volunteer Officers", *Atlantic Monthly*, XIV (September 1864), p.353.
8 Fred A. Shannon, *The Organization and Administration of the Union Army 1861-1865* (Gloucester, Mass., 1965) I, pp.186-7.
9 George B. McClellan, *McClellan's Own Story* (New York, 1886), p.99.
10 Higginson, "Officers", pp.354-5.
11 *Ibid.*, p.354.
12 Richard Taylor, *Destruction and Reconstruction* (New York, 1879), p.126.
13 George B. Davis, et al., comps., *Atlas to Accompany the Official Records of the Union and Confederate Armies* (Washington, 1891-1895), Plate CLXXII.
14 Gerald F. Linderman, *Embattled Courage: The Experience of Combat in the American Civil War* (New York, 1987), pp.37-9.
15 *Ibid.*, p.40.
16 Robertson, *Soldiers*, p.124; Linderman, *Courage*, p.41.
17 Linderman, *Courage*, pp.229-230.
18 *Ibid.*, pp.48-50.
19 *Ibid.*, p.51; John O. Casler, *Four Years in the Stonewall Brigade* (Dayton, Ohio, 1971), p.193.
20 Linderman, *Courage*, p.54.
21 Davis, *Orphan Brigade*, p.50; Robertson, *Soldiers*, p.127.
22 Linderman, *Courage*, p.122.
23 Robertson, *Soldiers*, pp.126, 129.
24 Linderman, *Courage*, pp. 188-9.
25 *Ibid.*, p.190.
26 Robertson, *Soldiers*, p.128.
27 Linderman, *Courage*, p.230.
28 Tower, *Manigault*, pp.163-4.
29 Quaife, *Williams*, pp.165-6.
30 Gordon, *Reminiscences*, p.319.
31 Wiley, *Johnny Reb*, pp.63-5.
32 Joseph T. Glatthaar, *The March to the Sea and Beyond* (New York, 1985), pp.3, 10.
33 *Ibid.*, pp.10, 39-41.
34 *Ibid.*, pp.279-80; Robert F. Durden, *The Gray and the Black* (Baton Rouge, La., 1972), pp.268, 270, 274-5.

CHAPTER FOUR

THE TEST OF LEADERSHIP

By the end of 1862, the test of battle had been applied all across America, and the men who led and those who followed could look down into their souls and see what courage was. At Fredericksburg the bumbling of a commander almost shattered his army. The bumbling of another lost a Rebel chance to take Kentucky, then the same general lost middle Tennessee at Stones River. Experience could identify incompetence, but it would not always weed it out.

"OH, EVERYONE is brave enough," wrote one Federal speaking of the officers in his army; "it is the head that is needed." How right he was. In all the preparation, sometimes amounting to months of training and campaigning before a unit saw its first action, it was the intelligence of their leaders that accomplished or failed to accomplish their preparation for battle. And when finally an officer led his men into the fight, for all that personal courage was a necessity, still more requisite was a cool head and the ability to think under the severest kind of pressure man can experience. Many a brave soldier got himself and his men killed through bold foolishness. The commander who knew when to temper his courage with discretion, who knew how to control his men by means other than mere personal example, who knew how to control himself, was the one who achieved the greatest goals with the means available to him.[1]

Much had to do with simply knowing how to control the men, whether on the march or before going into battle. Mere use of the authority of rank was rarely effective, for the simple fact was that most of the volunteers never equated rank with the right to command, and they always felt at liberty to question the directives of an officer if they did not agree. Thus the martinet had a difficult and often insurmountable task before him. Simply stated, the men would never yield. If they could not stymie him one way, they would find another. In the worst extremity, if their claims be believed, they threatened to, and perhaps did, exact their revenge in battle.

"Many a wearer of shoulder-straps was to be shot by his own men in the first engagement", wrote a Massachusetts boy speaking of the expressed intentions of comrades in the ranks. However, once under fire, most men found themselves occupied pretty much full-time by the enemy, so the threats may have been hollow. Still, many enlisted men believed that such things had happened, and the stories were told and retold, and no doubt magnified, in hushed tones around the campfires. "Such officers," said one man referring to a martinet he had seen, "received a stray ball occasionally on the field of battle." Indeed, some claimed to know officers who were afraid to go into battle at all, and not from fear of the enemy. If it actually happened, no one can say with certainty. It is known, however, that General Charles Winder, a regulation-bound Confederate stickler who repeatedly meted out humiliating punishments to his men for minor infractions, was so hated and despised by his private soldiers that they "spotted" him. In other words, he was marked for death in their next battle. "The next fight," wrote one Virginia private, "would be the last for Winder." Indeed it was, though he fell to a Yankee cannon ball before his own men could shoot him, if in fact they really intended to do so.[2]

Undoubtedly some officers were killed by their own men. But for the most part such extreme means were not necessary. They could get an offending commander's attention much more effectively by less violent means. Many were the companies that staged mock funerals in camp, with the officers they disliked hanged in effigy before being placed in a gaudy coffin covered with dire records of his offenses. Seeing how his men felt about him, many a tyrannical commander either changed his ways or else resigned before the mock coffin had to be exchanged for a real one.[3] When such means did not achieve success, the men could go farther, as when they fired a volley through the tent of Rebel General Allison Nelson out in Arkansas in 1862. Firing just above his head, their volley had the desired effect, and he quickly loosened his oppressive rule.

At the same time, an officer dared not be too easy or lenient with his men, else he could not command their respect, and only hope that they would obey important commands without question. Consequently, the leader had to walk a fine line between being sufficiently detached and

In the last measure, the test came on the battlefield, and there the officers of North and South proved themselves, as here in the trenches around Atlanta, where the Confederacy lived or died by the leadership of its armies.

authoritarian to remind the men that he was different, while at the same time not assuming to be so self-important that the men still did not think of him as one of them. He had to understand and to some degree empathize with their problems – even if he could do little to remedy complaints, he had to appear to sympathize with them. He had to be very reluctant to criticize their faults openly, and show a lot of discretion in doling out reprimands or punishment when required. He had to be able to read his men to anticipate how they would accept his actions, and most of all, he had to fall back upon cold and final military law only as a last resort. That was a lot to expect even from Regulars who were accustomed to command. When it had to come from civilians-turned-officers, more often than not it sprang from basic instinct for leadership rather than training.[4]

The trick was to instill a little bit of fear along with respect, and it came more often in isolated gestures than from the daily regimen or drill. On the march men were generally under orders not to fire their weapons, nor even to have them loaded. When one man shot down a buzzard, his lieutenant immediately and profanely reprimanded him in front of his company. Later during a halt, the officer returned and apologized to the offender for losing his control. Thus he had achieved two ends. His initial outburst showed that there was fire in the man, and that similar infractions in the future might elicit the same response. His apology showed him to be a man of good heart and fair play, and won him the admiration of his men. Another time, when he found his sentries asleep, instead of upbraiding them, he simply concealed their rifles, then woke them with shouts that the enemy was coming. Their consternation, confusion, and finally embarrassment at not being able to find their rifles at a seemingly critical moment, were enough to teach them a lesson. A Confederate captain from Alabama, en route to Virginia, found one of his men drunk in a barroom and refusing to go any farther with his company. A regular barracks lawyer, the private pointed out that the company had not yet been officially mustered into service, and therefore the captain could not compel him to do anything. Wisely the captain agreed, then pointed out that the soldier was wearing an Alabama state uniform, the property of the state. Even if the soldier was not under the captain's orders, the uniform was. "That uniform is going to Virginia with me and the Company," he declared. "I will have that uniform stripped from you at once and turn you loose in the streets without it." Given the prospect of being abandoned in the nude in a strange city, the drunk speedily gave in and went on to Virginia.[5]

Second Lieutenant, 5th New York Infantry

This second lieutenant of the 5th New York Infantry, otherwise popularly known as Duryee's Zouaves, represents one of the more colorful of the Union regiments. His bright red kepi and trousers differ distinctly from the regulation. Otherwise there is nothing unusual in his outfit yet he stands out just enough to be worthy of note.

Indeed, his commander Colonel Abram Duryee was a flamboyant type, exactly the kind to organize and lead one of the dramatic zouave regiments. Often their hallmark was intensively precise drill and *élan*. Unfortunately for Duryee's men, in battle their red pants made them standout targets for Confederate sharpshooters.

By the later years of the war, the zouave craze died out as most of the new volunteer regiments went to war in government issue uniforms with little or no variation.

The purpose of mastering this kind of human psychology was all, in the end, directed to making the enlisted man a part of a team, his company, regiment, and ultimately his army, and all to prepare him to be his most effective when he went into battle. This was one of the things that many enlisted men never understood; that all of the boring routine was designed, not just to keep him occupied, but to condition him to immediate response to an order when his own and the lives of his companions might depend upon it.

However much success at it the officers might think they were having when the armies were in winter quarters or field camp, they could quickly discover that the men would behave differently when on the march or heading toward the enemy. Whether 100 men or 100,000, they were easier to control in the confines of an encampment where sentries and provosts could keep an eye on them. But string them out over miles and miles of dusty country roads, marching past wells when they were thirsty or well-stocked farmhouses and barns when hungry, and the men proved almost impossible to control. Every farmer's fence rails looked like excellent firewood, and henhouses and cornfields appeared to be there for the taking. Many Confederates, specifically ordered not to take farmers' hogs, simply decided to call the hogs bears instead, and then gleefully boasted of the abundance of wild "bears" they shot and ate on the march.

Straggling – lagging behind the rest of the company by not maintaining the rate of march – was epidemic in both armies. Officers of every rank had constantly to ride along their lines urging the men to keep up. The two most frequently heard words out of the mouth of Confederate General Thomas J. "Stonewall" Jackson were "close up,

Above: To take these raw, undisciplined young men and boys and mold from them a formidable weapon of war, required herculean efforts from men no more accustomed to lead than they were to follow.

Below: When they did their task well, men like the officers seated amidst these turbaned members of the 114th Pennsylvania Infantry, could take extraordinary pride in the units they had built.

close up", as he pushed his infantry forward. Sometimes a frustrated commander even drew his saber and smacked the laggard on the head or shoulders to force them forward, though not without risk. One officer made ready to strike a slow soldier with the flat of his blade, and was told "put up your sword or I'll shoot you."[6]

As busy as he was when his command lay in camp, an officer's duties seemed to multiply tenfold when the army was on the march. Often no more than two or three days' notice were given from army high command. The officers had to see that the prescribed number of rations were issued for the march, cooked if necessary before leaving, the ordered rounds of ammunition passed out, any defective or missing weapons and equipment replaced, and the men carefully inspected one last time to weed out those who could not stand the march. The officer supervised the breaking down of the encampment, the storing of impedimenta not being taken on the march, saw that the company wagons – if there were any – were in shape to haul tents and heavy baggage, and looked to the condition of the horses and mules. A week's worth of inspections, it seemed, had to be accomplished in a single day. Moreover, there were constant demands from higher authorities for daily – even hourly – status reports, mostly to soothe the nerves of anxious regimental and brigade commanders who fidgeted before the final jump-off of the campaign. The last evening before the march began, the company and regimental officers had to circulate through all their encampments, calming the anxieties of the enlisted men, perhaps exchanging stories and jests with them, maintaining quiet so that sleep – for those who could – might come early.

The day of the march the whole column might be up at 3 a.m., not because commanders really expected to march at that hour, but because the larger an army, the longer it took to get it moving. If the column were only a few regiments, it might get going with relative dispatch. If it were an army of 50,000 or more, then it would move in several columns from four or five different

Above: When the time came to take the field, the winter quarters had to come down, and the officers made it their business to harden their men for the weeks or even months of marching ahead.

Left: By the time they were on the campaign trail, all the finery and posing of an officer like this one of a New York regiment counted for nothing. It was his mettle as a man that measured him.

general encampments, using parallel roads when possible rather than stringing itself out endlessly on a single road. Even then, a single column of a division or a corps might stretch out for miles, with any event along the way that caused a delay – a narrow bridge, a halt for water, men breaking ranks to pick berries by the roadside – being transmitted back down the line and exaggerated. Thus the march was often a series of fits and starts, with the officers all the while riding or walking along the line trying to keep the men from bunching up, leaving the column, or simply stopping when tired. Whereas a single man could easily walk twenty miles a day, a marching column of any size could rarely achieve half that. This was why officers really needed horses. In battle, almost everyone moved afoot. But on the march a commander had to ride back and forth almost constantly to maintain some sort of control. Enlisted men resentful of walking while their company commanders rode might have thought differently at the end of a ten or twelve hour day spent constantly in the saddle.

Matters became more tense for everyone as the column approached the intended scene of action, especially if the battle was already under way and the men had heard the boom of the cannon for hours, and the rattle of rifle fire as they neared the conflict. Then, too, the wounded coming to the rear, the demoralized or cowardly who skulked away from the field, the riderless crazed animals, and the other scenes of carnage, all could conspire to dishearten the soldier, especially men going into their first fight. Thus with every step

Above: It was the men who knew how to lead who got their regiments through the test of battle and brought them home again, like the 7th Vermont here on the streets of Brattleboro . . . home at last.

Below: Undeniably there were those men who led from the pure joy of it, whose example in battle infused others with their spirit. Until Chancellorsville, General Joseph Hooker was such a man.

towards the battlefield, the challenge to maintaining discipline and order became greater.

Those final hours before the fight, when officers and men alike knew that they were about to launch themselves into the inferno, could be either the most difficult of all or – oddly – the easiest, for many men achieved a kind of peace and calm before battle, especially the veterans. It was now that the individual strengths and personalities of the company and regimental officers revealed themselves most fully. The mar-

tinets stayed in their tents or busied themselves with issuing orders and even punishments, right up to the last minute. The officers who understood leadership more perceptively walked among their men, encouraging them, comforting those with the inevitable premonitions of death, and attempting to assure all that each would do his duty, not show the white feather, help achieve a victory, and emerge unscathed from the fight. The officer knew, of course, that for many his words were hollow or meaningless, but still it

often helped the men to hear his reassurances just the same.

Sometimes they made speeches or issued more formal pre-battle orders that sought to arouse the patriotic fervor of their commands. The exhortations could vary as widely as the literacy and background of the officers themselves. Some were quite brief. "You love your country, you are brave men, and you came out here to fight for her", a New Hampshire major told his men. "Now go in! Forward!" Others indulged in overly lengthy and florid addresses that traced the history of the political differences leading to the present war, reviled the foe for his exclusive role in bringing on the contest, and promised the men an easy and speedy victory if they would only do their duty. "Your general will lead you confidently to the combat," Albert Sidney Johnston declared on April 5, 1862, before the Battle of Shiloh, "assured of success." In fact, they lost the battle, and he lost his life.[7]

And, for reasons known only to themselves, a very few officers took the opposite approach, perhaps thinking that the worse the picture they painted of what lay ahead, the more the men would be relieved if it turned out to be not so bad. "They are strongly fortified," said a colonel to his men. "They have more men and more cannon than we have. They will cut us to pieces. Marching to attack such an enemy, so entrenched and so armed, is marching to a butcher shop rather than to a battle. There is bloody work ahead. Many of you boys will go out who will never come back again." With talk like that no wonder his men were so dissatisfied with him that he was forced to resign.[8]

In the last minutes before the fight, the officers felt exactly the same emotions as their enlisted men. Tension. Dry mouth and throat. Sweaty palms. A hollow or empty feeling in the pit of the stomach. Enhanced senses of hearing and smell. A faintly electric quavering that ran from shoulder to shoulder through the center of the chest, sometimes causing a brief quiver or shake. The feelings that men of all times have felt in all

Confederate Infantry Officers' Uniforms and Equipment

1. Uniform frock coat of Col. Lawrence Massillon Keitt; killed Cold Harbor 1864
2. Forage cap of Col. W.J. Clark, N.C. troops
3. Uniform frock coat of Col. Ellison Capers
4. Capers' overcoat
5. Gray felt officer's hat
6. Uniform frock coat of Capt. Charles S. Fleming, 2nd Florida; killed 1864
7. Leech and Rigdon foot officer's sword

8. Sash of Capt. William A. Oliver, 9th Va. Cav.
9. Haversack of Sgt. A.H. Bayly
10. Sword belt
11. Boyle, Gamble & Co., sword
12. Two-piece C.S. plate
13. Officer's sword
14. Fleming's silk sash
15. Keitt's trousers
16. Slouch hat of First Lt. W. James Kinchloe
17. Sash of Col. James B.

Martin; killed 1861
18. Tin drum canteen of Capt. W.K. Bachman
19. Wooden canteen
20. Officer's haversack
21. Haversack of O. Jennings Wise, Richmond Light Infantry Blues
22-26. Effects from Wise's haversack
27-28. Uniform jacket and vest of Adjutant Joseph V. Bidgood

Artifacts courtesy of: The Museum of the Confederacy, Richmond, Va: 1-4, 6-11, 14-19, 21-28; Virginia Historical Society, Richmond, Va: 5, 12, 13, 20

wars. If the officer was more fortunate than his men in these moments, it was only because they had little to do but wait, while he could be busy with last minute duties and arrangements right up to the firing of the first gun.

The actual place of an officer in battle in the Civil War varied widely, chiefly according to rank by regulations, but more by temperament of the individual officer. While army rules did not so specify, most professional and volunteer generals in time came to understand that their presence was most important behind the lines, not to save them from danger, but to have them where they could stay in touch with all of their units and maintain some control over their part of the battle. It was difficult to do, of course, for men of that era, regardless of rank, felt it unmanly to stay in safety when the fighting was going on. But it was foolhardy for generals to risk going into battle. Johnston did it at Shiloh, personally leading a balky regiment into the fight, and taking a mortal wound in the offing. He felt that the personal example of the cool and collected commander leading his men to the foe would have a calming effect on his unblooded volunteers in this, their first action. Indeed it did, but it may have cost the Confederacy the battle. Men like U.S. Grant and R.E. Lee, who were every bit as brave, knew where they belonged and stayed there. Grant never tried to take personal part in the actual fighting, and Lee apparently only attempted to do so once or twice in the desperate days of 1864, and then his men wisely refused to risk him. "Lee to the rear", they shouted, and he obeyed. For every fighting battleline general like Nathan Bedford Forrest who survived the maelstrom, at least two others fell in the fight, causing a continual drain of experienced officers at the highest levels of command. In Lee's Army of Northern Virginia, the losses of generals in battle practically crippled his command system after Gettysburg.

Corps and brigade commanders, too, belonged at the rear, and sometimes stayed there. Only the regimental colonels really had any business going

Union Infantry Officers' Uniforms and Equipment

1 Officer's slouch hat of First Lt. John A. Beall 94th Ohio Infantry
2 and 3 Officer's slouch hat insignia of 24th Michigan Infantry
4 Captain's insignia
5 Officer's cotton shirt
6 Housewife
7 Forage cap of Lt. Col. Thomas Scott Martin
8 Forage cap of Colonel Charles P. Herring, 118th Pa. Inf.
9 Forage cap of Major E.C. Pierce
10 Smoking Pipe
11 Herring's insignia
12 Forage cap of Capt. Charles Burton
13 Officer's slouch hat
14 Model 1850 foot officer's sword
15 Beall's frock coat
16 Beall's vest
17 Monocular glass
18 Herring's short jacket
19 Frock coat of Colonel

Clarence C. Buell, 169th New York Infantry
20 Sword belt
21 Leather haversack
22 Beall's trousers
23 Brass spurs
24 Private purchase shoes
25 Herring's sash
26 Model 1850 sword
27 Herring's trousers
28 Buff gauntlets of Maj. Gen. Amos B. Eaton
29 Brass stencil
30 Officer's sash

Artifacts courtesy of: The Civil War Library and Museum, Philadelphia, Pa: 1, 8, 11, 15, 16, 20, 22, 25, 26, 27, 29; Don Troiani Collection: 2-7, 9, 10, 12-14, 17, 19, 23, 24, 28, 30

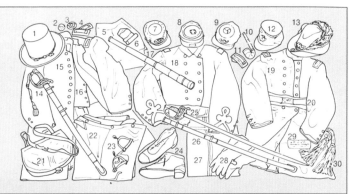

Above: The places that tried men's souls. The Peach Orchard at Shiloh became a butcher's yard. Leadership in the maelstrom of fire meant life or death for thousands, and here at Shiloh, officers were still learning.

Below: In the works around the Ponder House near Atlanta, much of the fate of the Confederacy lay. Leadership here was measured by inches of ground held, and by the lives of the men lost holding it.

into the fight with their men, and even they were better used by staying close to the battleline, but out of fire. It was the company captains and lieutenants, however, who truly belonged with their men. Whether charging on the attack, or standing to meet an enemy assault, the company officers had to be right there to inspire the men, hold them in line – with their swords and pistols if necessary – and rush in reserves to fill gaps in the line or transmit instructions from higher command. Years after the war, however much they may have revered their colonels and field officers, the men in the ranks most remembered the bravery – or the failings – of their immediate company officers. These were the leaders the men lived with, saw every day, came to know and respect – or despise – and trust. When his lieutenant or captain stood toe-to-toe with the enemy, the private knew he was in good hands. Let that officer quail or fail to share the risks of his men, and he had lost them. Thus it was that the losses among company officers in this war would be the greatest of any of the commissioned ranks. These captains and lieutenants had to pay a great price indeed for their little bits of gold braid, their shoulder straps or collar bars, and their $300 per year plus allowances.

Every officer, of course, carried side arms. He was entitled by regulations to a saber and a pistol, though the variety of both was wide. In the Union Army a standard field officer's saber was the

model 1840 cavalry or 1840 light artillery saber, or variations of one or the other, though many officers preferred to furnish their own blades from such makers as Ames of Chicopee, Massachusetts. More ceremonial than practical, the officers found – like the cavalrymen who were issued sabers – that it was most useful for spitting meat or hacking brush. Very few saber wounds were inflicted on an enemy in this war. In the main, the officer carried it overhead to signal the advance, or to show where he was, or else used it to persuade skulkers and cowards to return to the line. He may have treasured his sword as a symbol of his office, but he rarely trusted his life to it.

Far more useful was his pistol. It was no mere symbolic weapon, but one that allowed him to add his firepower to that of his men. Again, a host of varieties went into action in the hands of officers, but on both sides they most often came down to one of two types, either a .36 caliber or a .44. The larger bore was favored more by infantrymen, and the chief providers were Colt and Remington. Naval officers and many cavalrymen were issued the lighter .36 model, again usually a so-called Colt "Navy". Yet for often sentimental reasons, or because nothing else was available, many men carried sidearms that were clearly out of date. General Breckinridge went to war with a brace of single-shot H. Aston pistols that he had carried in the Mexican War.

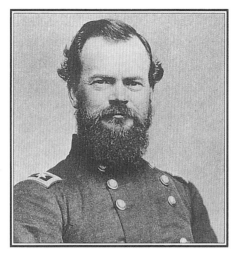

Above: Leadership had its risks. Only two army commanders in this war were to lose their lives in battle. One was General James B. McPherson, killed in the battles for Atlanta by an enlisted man.

Below: All of the formidable earthworks and fortifications ringing a besieged city like Atlanta had to be carefully planned, and it was officers who did it, supervising the efforts of men who followed.

Confederate General Joseph E. Johnston actually went into battle wearing the saber his father had carried as a hero of the Revolution. In the Southern armies, especially, where scarcity was the order of the day in all articles of equipment, an officer might wind up carrying anything from a rusty old flintlock to a shotgun. Pistols ranged from antiquated smoothbores to the exotic French-made Le Mat, with a revolving cylinder carrying eight .40 loads, and a separate barrel underneath that fired a single .18 gauge shotgun blast. A few officers even had to provide their own side arms because Richmond could not furnish them, and the confusion of dozens of different calibers and ammunition requirements made supplying these officers a headache that was never fully eased.

The test of those weapons, as of the officers themselves, came when the armies met in battle. If the regiment was taking a defensive position, the colonel might hold two of his ten companies in reserve, with himself or his lieutenant colonel in charge, while the remaining companies went to the line, standing pretty much in the open early in the war, and taking cover behind fences or downed trees, or other obstructions later in the conflict. Each captain stayed with his company, while the higher field officers moved from place to place, checking on positions, carrying fresh orders, and filling in if necessary for downed officers.

If, on the other hand, the regiment was to attack, then the colonel put the companies in line according to the wishes of his brigade commander. Perhaps the entire regiment went on the line, or maybe several companies were held back as a second wave, or as a reserve. Officers kept the men standing at attention, gave orders to load their weapons if it had not been done previously, dressed the ranks and exhorted the privates one last time to behave well, go in with a shout, fire their volleys only when ordered to do so, then charge with their bayonets.

Ironically, the bayonet was another weapon that inflicted almost negligible wounds in this war. The fact was, by the time one line closed with another, either the attacker or the defender was on the verge of breaking and withdrawing. Hand-to-hand combat as pictured in the paintings of the day was a rare occurrence, thus making the bayonet obsolete so far as causing casualties. But symbolically, the long, brightly polished, sharp blade had an intimidating effect on men who saw a whole line of them advancing toward them. As a result, the fear of the bayonet often accomplished far more than its actual use. How well Civil War commanders understood this psychological advantage to the weapon is arguable. Certainly they never stopped expecting their men to be well trained in the arcane exercise of bayonet thrust and parry, though not one soldier in a hundred ever had to do it for real.

By the time the first bullets started to whistle over their heads – all Civil War soldiers tended to fire high and waste inordinate amounts of ammunition – the tension was so great for both officers and men that the actual start of combat came almost as a relief. At least now their waiting was over. Indeed, some were so anxious to get into action and end the waiting that they ran to get to the battlefield. "We were repulsed the first charge," wrote an officer of the 59th Georgia, "because the men were so completely exhausted when they made it." They had run nearly a quarter mile to get into the fight.[8] Just before the Battle of Ball's Bluff, in October 1861, the men of

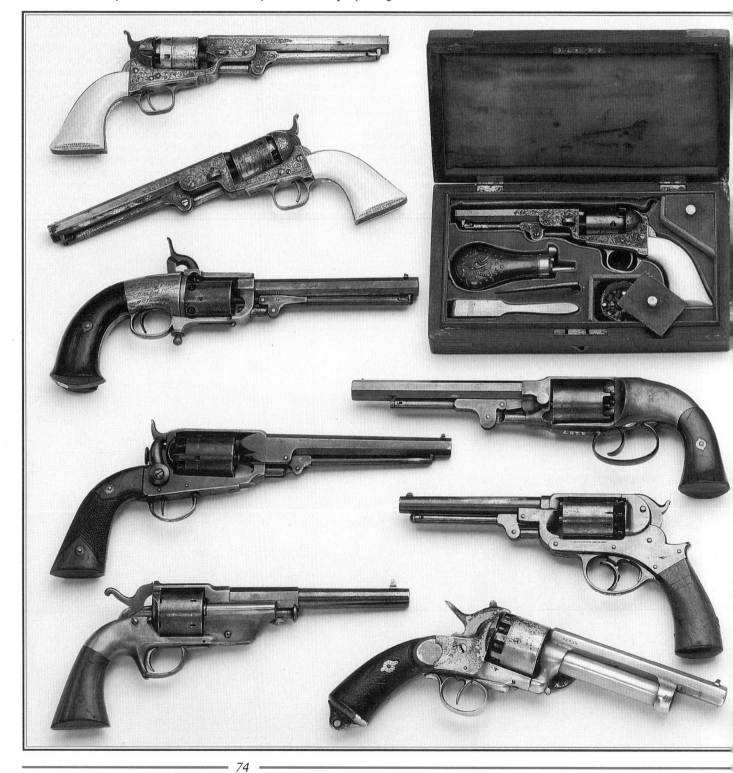

74

Union and Confederate Officers' Handguns

1 and 2 Pair of Colt Model 1851 Navy revolvers, .36 caliber; of Maj. Gen. John M. Schofield
3 Butterfield Percussion Army revolver, .41 cal
4 Colt Model 1849 Pocket revolver, engraved; of Captain J.N. Derby
5 Pettengill Army revolver, .44 caliber
6 Joslyn Army revolver, .44 caliber
7 Starr Model 1858 Navy revolver, .36 caliber
8 Allen and Wheelock Lipfire Army revolver, .44 caliber
9 Le Mat 2nd Model revolver, .41/.65 cal, of Capt. J.N. Maffatt of the Confederate Navy
10 Adams Patent revolver
11 Colt Model 1860 Army revolver, .44 caliber, engraved, of Maj. Gen. George B. McClellan
12 Whitney Navy revolver, .36 caliber, of Col. Julius W. Adams
13 Colt Model 1851 Navy revolver, .36 caliber
14 Savage-North Navy revolver, .36 caliber
15 Starr Model 1863 Army revolver, .44 caliber
16 Remington-Beals Army revolver, .44 caliber
17 Colt Model 1848 Army .44 revolver, 1st Model
18 Perrin and Company revolver, .45 caliber

Artifacts courtesy of: The Civil War Library and Museum: Philadelphia, Pa: 16; West Point Museum, West Point, N.Y.: 1, 2, 4-8, 10-15, 17, 18; Donald Tharpe Collection: 9; David Stewart Collection: 3

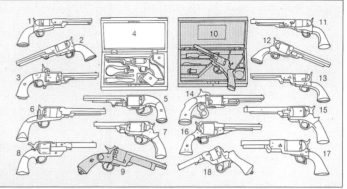

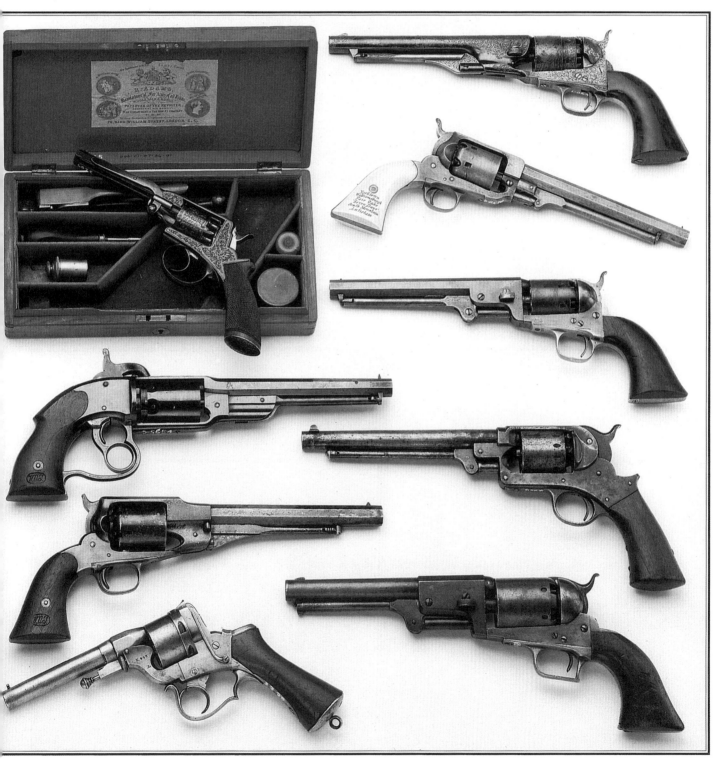

Alpheus Williams' brigade were "cheering all the way" as they approached what they thought would be their first fight, and Williams confided privately that they were in "excellent spirits, better, I confess, than I was."[9]

The battlefield quickly became a confusion. The thick, white smoke from the black powder weapons tended to hang low, like a fog over the ground. The more guns that fired, the sooner much of the field was obscured to vision unless the wind was brisk enough to blow it away. The electric booming of the cannon and the flat, low crackling of thousands of rifles made orders nearly impossible to hear. In time, men and officers often could neither hear nor see one another, and maintaining control of even a company – much less a regiment or a brigade – could be more a matter of chance than design. In the First Battle of Bull Run, one captain went into battle leading his company, and when the smoke cleared discovered that only two of them were still with him, but that along the way he had somehow picked up a surgeon, a staff clerk, three cavalrymen without their horses, a confused artilleryman, and one very bemused chaplain.[10]

With the first moment under fire, every officer had to face a basic question within himself. What sort of leader was he to be? Would he lead, or follow; be an example to the men by taking a leading part in the actual fighting, or play the less romantic but perhaps more effective role of a good behind-the-lines manager? The fact was that both officers and men in this war expected that the leaders would lead by example, that they had to show their own bravery not only to win the respect of their soldiers, but also to inspire them to emulate such conduct. And for most, this meant that the officer had to risk his life intentionally by exposing himself to enemy fire, often even in ways not risked by his men. To some it came instinctively as the battle-lust seized them; for others, it was a calculated pose.

In Kentucky, in 1862, Colonel John Beatty ordered his 3rd Ohio Infantry to take cover from a storm of Confederate artillery fire while he remained standing. He did it intentionally. The regiment had caused him a lot of trouble, been insubordinate and disrespectful. "Now," he found after his display of bravery, "they are, without exception, my fast friends."[11]

The gallant young Major John Pelham kept his Confederate artillerymen under cover from an enemy fire, while he not only exposed himself,

Above: Battle took the leaders from and to every point of the American compass. Here at the Matthews house on the Bull Run battlefield, the command of Yankee officers was first tested.

Below: One of the fighting regiments of the western theater of the war, the 22nd Ohio Infantry, poses at Corinth, Mississippi in 1862, mute testimony to the efforts of its officers to ready it for service.

Above: Dash and bravery knew no boundaries or place or preferment. An officer's courage was just as great, his blood just as red. Here at Petersburg in 1864, Yankee batteries brave the best that Lee has.

Below: The countryside lay stained with the fields of blood where leaders and led combined to leave a legacy of bravery and devotion, as here at Antietam, where the bloodiest day of the war took its toll.

but sat atop his horse for a better view of the battle unfolding, and all the while maintaining a perfect calm and composure. It won the hearts of his men, who would afterwards follow him anywhere.

The stories of such conspicuous bravery abound from both sides. Particularly affecting is that of Colonel John B. Gordon, commanding that same 6th Alabama that he had entered as a private. But now it was the spring of 1862, and he was leading it into its first real battle, at Seven Pines, Virginia. Early on the morning of May 31, the brigade of which they were a part hurled itself against Yankee breastworks. Gordon, to be seen by his men, rode his horse in the attack, his adjutant mounted beside him. The instant that Gordon spurred his animal over the enemy works, his adjutant fell dead at his side. Gordon reformed his men under fire and sent them forward in another charge to pursue the retiring Federals. Then his lieutenant colonel fell dead. The regiment's major, also riding, went forward with the line and took a fatal ball. Gordon was the only field officer left, and his soldiers later declared that they could hear Yankee gunners shouting, "Shoot that man on horseback." By this time six of his twelve companies had lost their officers as well, and their brigade commander had also fallen. "Still I had marvellously escaped", Gordon remarked. Then he passed his younger brother, lying shot through the lungs, it appeared fatally. But there was no time to stop, "no time for anything," said Gordon, "except to move on and fire on." Then his horse was killed under him, and Gordon had to slog on foot through a near swamp, to find that his regiment had become separated from the rest of the brigade.

"My field officers and adjutant were all dead", he later recalled. "Every horse ridden into the fight, my own among them, was dead. Fully one half of my line officers and half my men were dead or wounded." Men were fighting from water, knee- and hip-deep, moving against a solid line of blazing Yankee rifles, with reinforcements swelling the Federal number. Gordon sent a flanking force under one of his remaining captains to stall the reinforcements, only to lose that captain and most of his men. Finally, orders came for Gordon to withdraw. Gordon alone of the field officers was alive. Of the forty-four line officers, only thirteen were left, though one of them, Gordon's brother, did survive his wound. And of the few Alabamians in the enlisted ranks who came through the fight alive, few indeed were those who did not thereafter think of John

B. Gordon as a charmed god of war whom they would follow anywhere.[12]

Men like Gordon were often special cases for another reason. Men with wide military experience before the war often did not have to prove themselves overmuch. Volunteer officers like Gordon found themselves put more on their mettle to show themselves worthy of their rank. But those whose commissions came due to political influence or connections very frequently had to overcome considerable animosity on the part of their men and subordinate officers, and ostentatious bravery was frequently the quickest and surest means of achieving this. Breckinridge, who had never experienced a day of battle in his life

prior to Shiloh, exposed himself repeatedly wherever he went on that field. Struck by spent balls – bullets that had lost the force to penetrate or do more than inflict a bruise – and feeling more than one bullet pass through his clothing, the newly-created general from Kentucky seemed to dare death that day. Part of his behavior was simply bravery or imperviousness to danger, for he showed the same calm and unstudied indifference on every battlefield on which he fought. But also a measure of such behavior certainly came from the need to show his men, also in their first battle, that he deserved their respect and complete obedience.[13]

On the Union side Carl Schurz received a briga-

dier's commission solely because he was a vocal and influential German-American who could help rally thousands of his fellow countrymen to enlist. By "displaying courage in battle", he wrote, he was able to dispel the objections of his men. A Confederate officer from France, the Prince de Polignac, took a generalship, and was so resented by men who thought he got high rank thanks only to aristocratic birth, that the men dubbed him "Pole-cat" and openly ridiculed him. But when the time came and they saw him cool and brave under fire for the first time, they thereafter "got on famously".[14]

Moreover, once such a man did prove himself, it was still occasionally necessary to reinforce his

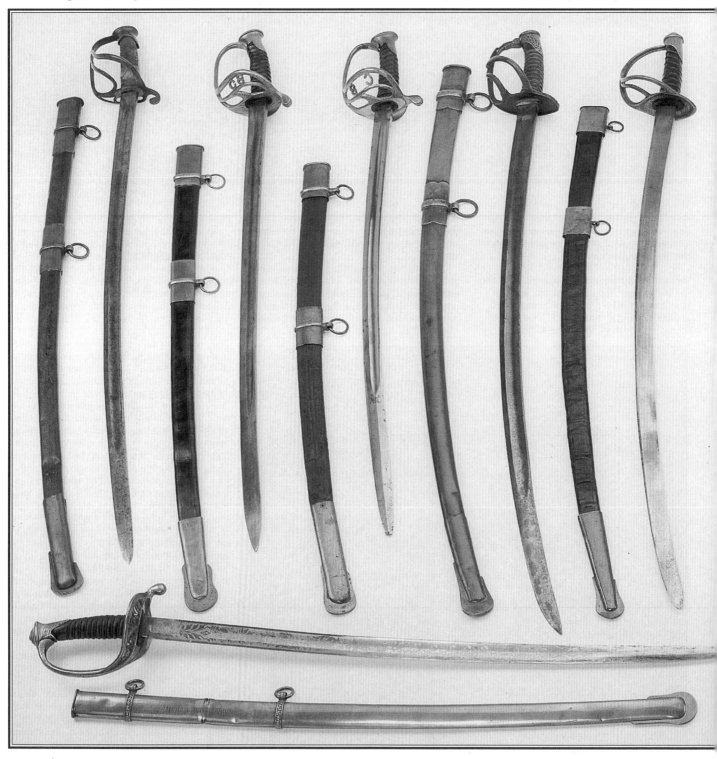

Confederate Officers' Edged Weapons

1 Boyle, Gamble and Company engineer officer's sword with brass mounted metal scabbard
2 Leech and Rigdon staff and field officer's sword, variant
3 Leech and Rigdon staff and field officer's sword
4 Thomas, Griswold and Company, cavalry officer's saber
5 Boyle, Gamble and Company, cavalry officer's saber. The blade is unusual in that it has no fuller (the groove cut into the blade to lighten it)
6 W.J. McElroy cavalry officer's saber
7 Dufilho staff and field officer's saber, with ivory handle and brass mounted german silver scabbard
8 Haiman lion pommel officer's saber
9 Haiman engineer officer's sword. The guard decoration features the silvered letters 'CSA'
10 E.J. Johnston and Company, foot officer's sword, made in Macon, Georgia
11 Thomas, Griswold and Company foot officer's sword, featuring an etched blade
12 Thomas, Griswold and Company engineer officer's sword, featuring engineer branch insignia in brass on guard

Artifacts courtesy of: Donald Tharpe Collection

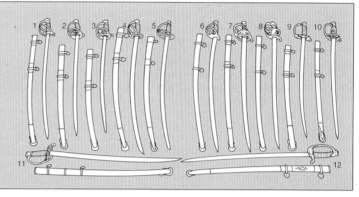

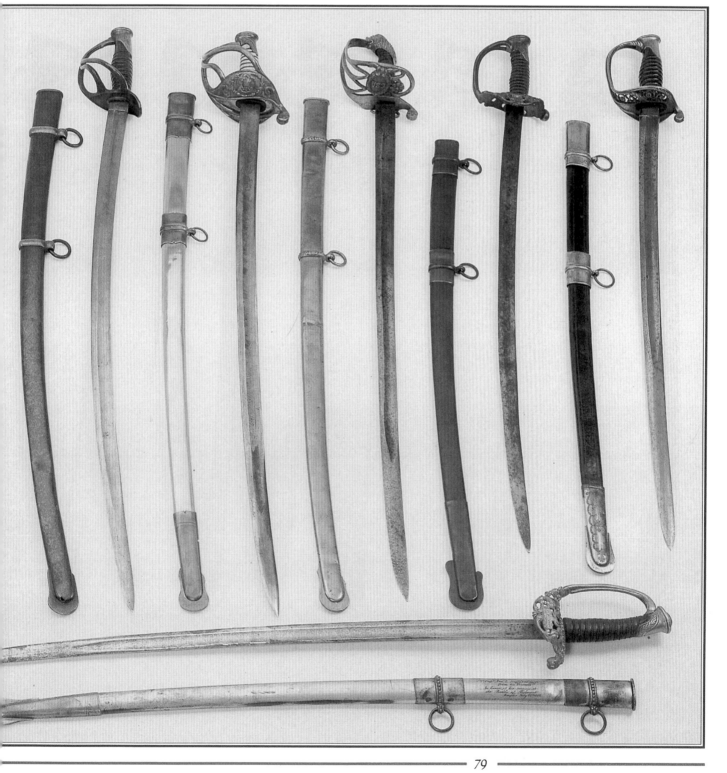

image as courageous and cool. Major General Richard Taylor received his Confederate commission for no discernible reason other than the fact that he had been Jefferson Davis' brother-in-law. As a result, he found himself much resented, even though he became a creditable battlefield commander. In 1863, in Louisiana, engaged in a sharp engagement, he saw his troops wavering and clearly in danger of giving way should the enemy attack. "It was absolutely necessary to give the men some *morale*", he concluded. Consequently, he mounted a breastwork in clear sight of the enemy, took out paper and tobacco, and coolly rolled a cigarette, lit it, and then walked back and forth atop the parapet casually enjoying his smoke. "These examples," he concluded, "gave confidence to the men, who began to expose themselves."[15]

Sometimes an officer even stood out to embarrass his men into doing likewise. General Daniel H. Hill once reprimanded a skirmisher for taking cover, then made the man stand beside him, under fire, and load his own rifle for Hill to fire back at the enemy. In time, such actions could have the effect of making the enlisted men ashamed to be cautious or take cover when their officers so brazenly showed themselves. It was a risky, and ultimately costly example to set, but it was what was expected by the private soldier who, seeing himself as intrinsically the equal of any officer, felt it undue to be asked to take any risks that an officer would not gladly share.[16]

Indeed, when their officers did not spontaneously exhibit such courage, the men in the ranks had their ways of testing, of drawing out whether a man was a hero or a coward, and woe to him if he proved the latter. Cowardice among themselves the men would tolerate occasionally, especially if a man had performed well in battle before. Everyone, they reasoned, could lose his nerve now and then. But for an officer to turn 'yellow' was the most public form of humiliation. He was not a face in the crowd like a private. Thus when an officer was truly conspicuous, the men never forgot.

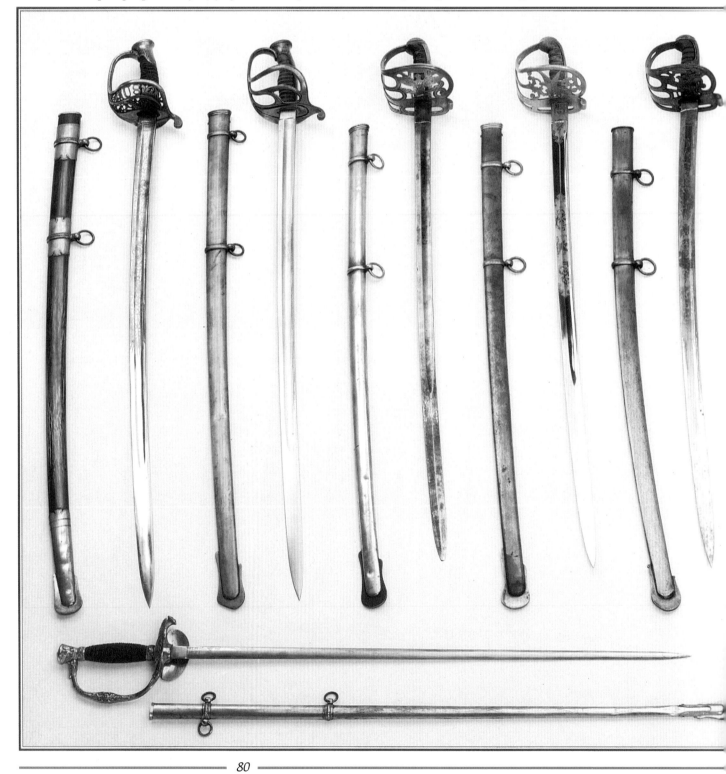

Union Officers' Edged Weapons

By the outbreak of the Civil War, swords were technically obsolete but continued to be regulation officer's equipment even to the lengths of being carried in the field. Edged weapons were badges of rank, and varying styles designated branches of service and an officer's grade.

1 Model 1850 staff and field officer's sword
2 Non-regulation, steel- hilted, imported officer's sword
3 Non-regulation, steel- hilted, imported officer's sword
4 Non-regulation, brass- hilted, imported officer's sword
5 Non-regulation, steel- hilted, imported officer's sword
6 Model 1840 regulation foot officer's sword, together with scabbard
7 Model 1850 foot officer's sword with brass mounted leather scabbard
8 Model 1850 foot officer's sword with all german silver scabbard
9 Model 1840 cavalry officer's saber
10 Model 1860 cavalry officer's saber
11 Model 1860 staff and field officer's sword
12 Model 1840 medical officer's sword, with scabbard

Artifacts courtesy of: The Civil War Library and Museum, Philadelphia, Pa

For the rest of their lives, the survivors of the 54th Massachusetts, a black regiment commanded by Colonel Robert G. Shaw, told of how they watched Shaw lead them in the attack on Fort Wagner, South Carolina, in the summer of 1863. In a nighttime assault, he led his men forward under orders not to fire a shot until they closed with the Confederates, emplaced behind a massively formidable sand and earthen fortress. Shaw led the regiment, walking at first. To begin with long-range artillery opened up on them, without effect. Shaw kept walking. Within 200 yards of Fort Wagner, the defenders opened fire, and men started to fall. Shaw drew his sword, raised it over his head, and rushed forward calling for a charge. All across the remaining sand he was in front of his regiment, and when they reached the fort's sandy rampart, he was perhaps the first to race up its steep slope into the enemy's rifles and cannon. The last the men ever saw of him was his silhouette against the starry sky, sword in hand, atop the parapet, before he fell dead inside. A leader did not have to give his life to inspire his men and win their confidence but, like Shaw, he had to risk that chance sooner or later.[17]

And should the officer show fear or cowardice, the men would not let him forget it. Indeed, few commanders who lost their nerves managed to stay in power for long. At Stones River, in January 1863, in Tennessee, Breckinridge caught Brigadier General Gideon J. Pillow hiding behind a tree when the brigade he had begged to command was going into battle. Pillow was one of Jefferson Davis' political appointees, and Breckinridge

rather publicly ordered him from his cover and out onto the field with his men. Pillow, who had also showed cowardice the previous February when he abandoned his command at Fort Donelson and escaped to safety while they were forced to surrender, would never hold a field command again.[18]

For all the cowards – and there were many – the number of the brave was one hundred fold, but somehow the stories of the timid or weak achieved inordinately wide currency just the same. Sometimes the men thought they could spot a coward even before their first battle, and looked especially askance at young officers who appeared foppish or overly concerned about rank and military etiquette. Virginians in 1862 noted such a young man, and sure enough, just as the next battle was commencing, he ran away, only returning several days later. The colonel of the regiment sarcastically asked the man how the battle had gone for him when he was eighty miles to the rear of it, then dismissed him.[19]

As they gained more experience, officers learned that the line between prudence and cowardice, between bravery and foolhardiness, was at best indistinct, but could be approached. After seeing more and more fellow leaders shot down as they exposed themselves carelessly, the surviving officers acquired some discretion. At Antietam in September 1862, a Confederate officer of the 21st Georgia did not hesitate to admit: "Did the officers take shelter? Yes, you bet they did! We had learned to conserve our strength and that at times 'discretion is the better part of valor'."[20] The men, too, came to see that

Above: With bravery at a premium, few officers could match the heroic devotion of Colonel Robert G. Shaw of the 54th Massachusetts, who died on the parapet of Fort Wagner setting a timeless example.

Below: The 127th Ohio at Delaware, Ohio, one of the thousands of unsung regiments that paid its price in the war, billable in blood. Only leadership kept this street from being empty at the war's close.

Captain, Rutledge's 1st Tennessee Light Artillery

Sometimes volunteer Confederate outfits combined their own regulations with those of their enemies in their uniforms. The officers of Rutledge's 1st Tennessee Light Artillery wore both collar insignia and shoulder straps or epaulettes, like this captain, each carrying badges of his rank. The style of his cuff facings is also different from prescribed design. In time, and thanks to the idiosyncratic nature of Confederate uniforms in general, men and fellow officers came to recognize and accept almost all such differences. Indeed, it made for a colorful variety in the command structure of a Rebel army.

Especially unusual in an artillery officer is the broad brimmed hat worn in the place of the customary kepi. Units from west of the Alleghenies generally showed more variation in hat and uniform styles. By war's end the only thing all had in common was tatters.

concern for their officers' safety was at times more important than gestures, hence when generals became dangerously exposed, the men sometimes took it in their own hands to reprimand them. Indeed, in 1864, when Lieutenant General Leonidas Polk was killed by an artillery shell while foolishly standing on an exposed hillside with other generals, there was less sadness than criticism expressed within the army.

The commanders also lost in time an odd feeling they had had early in the war that bravery was somehow its own protection. "The best officers and men are liable, by their greater gallantry, to be first disabled", complained Colonel Theodore Lyman of the Army of the Potomac, and he was right. Innumerable times in this war, commanding generals had to file reports in which they lamented that their best and bravest officers had fallen. It was soon a common belief, and often a correct one, that riflemen were instructed to aim first for the bravest of an enemy's officers, in the hope that bringing such men down would demoralize their command. It is certain that the men in the ranks discerned a decline in the quality of company and field commanders by 1863, when the bravest had fallen and were being replaced by men who, in addition to probably not being enthusiastic volunteers at the war's start, were also not of the stripe that could have gotten them chosen as officers at the outset. The most conspicuous tended to be replaced by the less conspicuous, by men who had devoted more time and effort to protecting themselves.[21]

Along with this gradually acquired sophistication in judging their officers, the men in the ranks also began to discern between those whose qualities included bravery but not good judgment. This was when the "everyone is brave enough; it is the head that is needed" lament was heard. When Lieutenant General John Bell Hood, one of the most ferocious division commanders in the Confederate army rose to the command of the Army of Tennessee, there were many who felt ill on the outlook. Hood had the heart of a lion, said one of his subordinates, but with it went "a

Wooden Head." He was "simply a brave, hard fighter", but that he possessed personal daring no longer seemed to guarantee to the men in the ranks that he was also smart enough to lead them well. As events were to prove; for at Franklin, Tennessee, late in the war, he almost destroyed his army through a number of senseless attacks. No wonder that afterward, to the tune of "The Yellow Rose of Texas", men of his army changed

the final lines to "the Gallant Hood of Texas played Hell in Tennessee."[22]

In time, too, many officers learned that so far as their careers were concerned, often there was little to gain by conspicuous bravery, for battlefield promotions were effectively non-existent. Grant is known to have made only two during the war, and in the Confederate service there were probably none, since Davis steadfastly held onto

Above: The price of heroism. Three Yankee officers show the cost in mangled bodies that they paid for their chance to lead, the toll they suffered in following their presumed destiny as leaders.

Below: Indeed, the cost in blood and flesh was staggering. Wounded men and officers at Savage Station in 1862 pay ample homage to the risks of taking men into battle. Only the brave need apply.

the exclusive authority to commission and endorse promotions. There were no medals to win in the Southern cause, though the Union did create the Medal of Honor in 1862. Unfortunately, the criteria for its award were always ambiguous. Extraordinary heroism could win one, but so could simply capturing or even picking up a Rebel battleflag. In the 27th Maine, 864 were issued as an inducement to re-enlist, though only 300 actually did so. The only man in history to be awarded the Medal twice was Lieutenant Thomas Custer, brother of General George A. Custer. In the last week of the war he twice captured Confederate flags from overpowered regiments, and received a Medal for each banner.

But of bravery, in the end, there was more than enough to go around, and chivalry, too, though many of the nonsensical old notions about glorious war dissolved in the blood-sodden fields of Virginia and Tennessee. It was just as brutal for an officer as for an enlisted man. The sight and stench of a battlefield after the fight did not distinguish between the eyes and nose of a private or a general. The disillusionment, depression, shame, guilt, and exhaustion that battle's aftermath imposed on almost everyone also struck the officers. They were not immune to the effects of what they saw; unlike their men, however, they were expected not to show it.

Like their men, however, they never lost their humanity. Out in Virginia's Shenandoah Valley in 1862, a Pennsylvania private had just drawn a bead on the dashing Confederate cavalryman, General Turner Ashby, Stonewall Jackson's right-hand man. Before the Yankee could pull the trigger on a certain shot, the colonel of his regiment knocked aside the private's rifle, thus saving the unsuspecting general. "Ashby is too brave to die in that way", said the colonel.[23]

Ashby would die in battle that same year anyhow, but an act of nobility by a foe preserved him for the South a little longer, and at the same time revealed a great deal about the kind of men who led soldiers North and South into the war. Those soldiers were well served by those they served.

Above: For a tragic many, the cost came not in blood, but in life. The funeral of Lieutenant Colonel George E. Marshall of the 40th Massachusetts, killed at Cold Harbor in 1864, could stand for thousands.

Below: And the rude headboards in this cemetery in Richmond, though raised over Confederates, symbolize the sacrifice of Blue and Gray on the altar of heroism. To lead was to court death.

References

1 Theodore H. Lyman, *Meade's Headquarters, 1863-1865* (Boston, 1922), p.139,
2 John D. Billings, *Hardtack and Coffee* (Boston, 1888), p.152; David H. Donald, ed., *Gone for a Soldier: The Civil War Memoirs of Private Alfred Bellard* (Boston, 1975), pp.187-8; Casler, *Four Years*, p.102.
3 Linderman, *Courage*, p.53.
4 *Ibid.*, p.56.
5 *Ibid.*, p.55.
6 *Ibid.*, p.51.
7 Robertson, *Soldiers*, pp.215-6.
8 *Ibid.*, p.219.
9 Quaife, *Williams*, p.24.
10 Robertson, *Soldiers*, p.219.
11 John Beatty, *Memoirs of a Volunteer, 1861-1863* (New York, 1946), pp.139-40.
12 Gordon, *Reminiscences*, pp.56-8.
13 William C. Davis, *Breckinridge: Statesman, Soldier, Symbol* (Baton Rouge, 1974), p.313.
14 Linderman, *Courage*, p.45.
15 Taylor, *Destruction and Reconstruction*, pp.130-1.
16 Linderman, *Courage*, p.46.
17 Peter Burchard, *One Gallant Rush* (New York, 1965), pp.137-8.
18 Davis, *Breckinridge*, pp.343-4.
19 Linderman, *Courage*, p.47.
20 James C. Nisbet, *Four Years on the Firing Line* (Chattanooga, 1914), p.154.
21 Linderman, *Courage*, p.158.
22 *Ibid.*, p.162.
23 *Ibid.*, p.70.

CHAPTER FIVE

THE ARMIES THEY LED

As 1863 dawned, the expectations of a quick war had been dashed on both sides in the mounting losses and the realization that no victory was in sight. By May, Grant was advancing toward Vicksburg, and in Virginia a Yankee army promised, yet again, to move "on to Richmond", but at Chancellorsville it was stopped cold by dash and bravery, and organization. Yet victories that cost lives like that of Stonewall Jackson were dearly bought.

IT IS CERTAINLY no surprise to discover that neither North nor South was prepared to wage a massive continental war in 1861. Besides the pitiful number of men actually under arms at the dawn of 1861, the military organization in Washington was barely more than adequate to handle the few thousand Regulars of the Old Army, while the new Confederate government, of course, did not even exist, and therefore, neither did any kind of military management. That both sides evolved, under the worst sort of circumstances, a complex military organization, and the equally complicated civil hierarchy to run it, is a testament to the ingenuity and resourcefulness – and occasional folly – of both Union and Confederacy.

The North, of course, started with a distinct advantage. Even though its War Department was not much compared to what it would be by 1865, still it was a lot more than Jefferson Davis had to start with when he took office. By contrast, on in-auguration day in 1861 Abraham Lincoln did at least find a functioning though antiquated military establishment. At its head sat a cabinet officer, the secretary of war, and here as so often political and military policy intertwined. One of Lincoln's first acts was to appoint a new secretary, and he chose Simon Cameron of Pennsylvania. The choice was an entirely political one, for Cameron had no military or administrative experience at all. But he was a powerful Republican who traded his influence in the election of 1860 for the promise of a cabinet post. He would last less than a year, when a combination of military reverses to Union arms, and the scandals over corruption in the War Department, led to his replacement on January 15, 1862, by Edwin McM. Stanton. Stanton, too, lacked military experience, but he had served as attorney general in the previous administration and, though a Democrat, was an able and effective administrator. Indeed, he proved to be the most effective of all Lincoln's cabinet ministers, and held his post for the balance of the war and beyond.

The secretary of war was not expected to be a master strategist. While different incumbents would see the office in varying ways, for the most part the secretary was the one responsible for implementing the policy of the civil leaders through military channels. He was much involved with raising new regiments, using the military to quell civil unrest when necessary, facilitating the transfer of large numbers of troops from one region to another via civilian railroad or other transportation, and, indeed, consulting with the president and top generals on broad military policy and objectives. Most of all he needed to be an able executive, and Stanton was superb.

Chief responsibility for grand strategy for the war effort rested at first with the commanding general, so long as Lincoln had confidence in him. Until November 1, 1861, that meant Lieutenant General Winfield Scott who, despite his age and more than twenty years in his position, was still a brilliant man. Too corpulent and infirm to mount a horse or take the field, he was a desk general, planning strategy and leaving it to the younger men to carry out. He it was who first conceived the plan that, effectively, was followed by the Union for four years to victory: controlling Southern shipping with a tight blockade, while seizing the Mississippi and its southern tributaries to split the Confederacy into pieces and squeezing them between river and ocean, the so-called "Anaconda Plan". By the end of 1861, however, Scott was maneuvered out of his office by the younger and immensely popular Major General George B. McClellan. In many ways the opposite of Scott, McClellan was a brilliant army administrator and a timid battlefield commander, yet his success in organizing and training the Army of the Potomac in 1861 was so great that Lincoln made him general-in-chief.

McClellan proved to be a great disappointment, though part of the problem was that no one had a clearly defined idea of what a commanding general was supposed to do. Fearing that his new responsibilities were interfering

Even the most tired and cynical old officer could not fail to feel a thrill of pride when he saw his army assembled in its tens of thousands, as here at Cumberland Landing, Virginia, in 1862, with the Army of the Potomac covering the plain.

with getting the Army of the Potomac into the country to fight, Lincoln relieved McClellan in March 1862 and returned him to the field. For four months Lincoln and Stanton ran the army themselves before calling on Major General Henry W. Halleck in July 1862. A noted military intellectual known as "Old Brains" in the Old Army, he had been a disappointment on the battlefield yet was known as a brilliant administrator. Unfortunately, he became, instead, a pettifogging bumbler whom Lincoln once called "little more than a first rate clerk". Now dubbed "Old Wooden Head" by subordinates, he shone only in imposing order and discipline in the military staff departments, but while he held his office, Lincoln and Stanton were forced to continue to act essentially as their own general-in-chief.[1]

When U.S. Grant was promoted to the reactivated military rank of lieutenant general on March 9, 1864, he became at once general-in-chief, and Halleck thereafter served as chief of staff, his responsibilities reduced into adapting Grant's and Stanton's decisions into the detailed orders necessary for an army with nearly a million men under arms. In a later time, an army of such size would not think of existing without a sophisticated top staff system in place, but in the Civil War, the organization to manage the huge armies always advanced several steps behind the growth of those armies.[2] Once Grant took command, Lincoln happily bowed out of military affairs almost entirely, having at last found the man he needed.

Primitive as army organization was in 1861, still there were a number of subordinate hierarchies within the War Department necessary to maintain the armies in the field. Each of them was

Above: The notion of a civilian as commander-in-chief was not an easy one for some military men to accept. Abraham Lincoln showed them what a civilian could do that they could not – lead a nation.

Above: For three years Lincoln looked for a general who could lead his armies to victory. Finally he found him in U.S. Grant; a man who failed as a civilian, but who led all others when in uniform.

stretched beyond its means in the early days, and often beyond the abilities of the officers who commanded them. For most of the war there were ten general staff departments or bureaus, each with specific – though often conflicting – functions, headed by independent officers rather than members of what would later become known as a general staff.

Probably more influential than any other department head was the adjutant general of the army. It was he who dealt most often and most intimately with the secretary of war, transmitting reports from field commanders, managing recruiting, assigning new officers to positions, and promulgating the directives of the president and secretary. He did not make any policy on his own, other than department policy, but the effectiveness with which Lincoln and Stanton's policy was carried out had much to do with the ability of the adjutant general. For the entire war period, fifty-seven-year-old Brigadier General Lorenzo Thomas held the post. He had been Scott's chief-of-staff for several years before the war, and perhaps for that reason he seemed a good choice for adjutant, but Stanton was never happy with him, and after 1863 sent him away from Washington on errands while Colonel E.D. Townsend did his job as acting adjutant general.[3]

Continuing the seeming policy of elevating the older officers to staff and department heads, perhaps to get them out of the field, Scott and Lincoln made Colonel Randolph B. Marcy inspector general, responsible for all kinds of inspections required throughout the army, from morale to desertion to military contractors. Happily, Marcy served well, won promotion to brigadier, and remained inspector general until 1881. Often closely involved with Marcy would be the judge-

Union Officers of Infantry, Artillery, and Cavalry

Officers in the Federal service enjoyed a luxury denied to their foes – they could almost always count on their uniforms measuring up to established regulations. Variations in colors and insignia were almost negligible, and usually owed more to the individual tastes of officers than to an inability of the War Department to supply the officers properly. The colonel of infantry at left illustrates well a completely uniformed commander who meets the regulations – proper buttons, proper gloves, proper kepi, etc.

Standing next to him is an equally completely outfitted officer of artillery, every color according to regulation. And standing next to him, at right, is a captain in the cavalry, equally correct in almost every detail. These are the men who led as they were most commonly seen and recognized by the men they led from Manassas to Appomattox.

advocate general who oversaw courts-martial and courts of inquiry. There were two incumbents, though elderly Joseph Holt of Kentucky held the post the longest, and was a civilian given a military commission solely to enable him to become judge-advocate general.

While the men in the ranks, and even officers so long as they stayed out of trouble, had little contact with or appreciation for these departments, the other bureaus of the War Department were vitally important indeed. The chief of the Ordnance Department had the responsibility for procuring and distributing all of the weapons issued to the men, from small arms to the heaviest cannon, along with appropriate ammunition and impedimenta. He bought some, and oversaw the manufacture of the rest. The first incumbent, Henry K. Craig, had been in the Old Army nearly fifty years when war erupted, and he resigned less than two weeks after Fort Sumter fell. His successors, James W. Ripley, George D. Ramsay, and Alexander B. Dyer, each had relatively short tenures. Ripley was sixty-eight when he took office, and Ramsay sixty-one. Only the younger, forty-six-year-old Dyer was up to the strains of the office, which he took over in September 1864 and where he continued until 1874.

If the men in the armies were to eat properly, they depended upon the competence of the Commissary General of Subsistence, who purchased and distributed all rations of any kind. The department was in the hands of George Gibson when the war began, he having held the post

Above: The center of all Union military activities was this almost collegiate-looking building in Washington, the War Department. Stanton ruled it like a lord, and from it came organization for victory. The expansion of the Union War Department during the course of the war revealed how essential increased organization and efficiency were to be as weapons against the rebellion. Bravery had to be matched by bureaucaracy.

since 1818. Colonel and later Brigadier General Joseph O. Taylor, brother of President Zachary Taylor and uncle of Confederate General Richard Taylor, succeeded Gibson at the age of sixty-five, and died in office, to be succeeded by Brigadier General Amos Eaton, the most effective of the lot, and the only one not born in the 1700s!

Hand in hand with the Commissary General went the work of the Quartermaster General and his department. Uniforms, camp equipment, horses and fodder, and everything else not already supplied by Subsistence or Ordnance, came through the Quartermaster General, and here, thankfully, a good, capable, young and healthy man was found almost from the start. When Sumter was fired upon, Brigadier General Joseph E. Johnston held the post, but he resigned and went south when Virginia seceded. An acting quartermaster filled in for a few weeks, and then the post was given to (later Brigadier General) Montgomery C. Meigs, arguably the most effective department head in the War Department. A career officer, amateur photographer, and brilliant engineer who oversaw the building of the new House and Senate wings in the 1850s, as well as the dome, on the Capitol, he handled the expenditure of over half a billion dollars on his own authority during the war, accounting for every cent spent. He was the only department head to be made a major general in honor of his services.

Less dramatic, though certainly indispensable to the welfare of the men, were the officers in charge of the Medical and Pay Departments.

Below: Military organizations also required laws. This is the tribunal that tried the Lincoln assassination conspirators. Judge Advocate General Joseph Holt is fourth from right. Officers often made partial jurers.

Above: Running a war meant more than finding men and weapons. It also meant feeding them. This small commissary tent with hanging beeves is only the tip end of the enormous subsistence system.

While four men held the post of surgeon general during the war, it was William Hammond who held it the longest, and made the greatest impact. He revitalized a somnambulent department, organized the first ambulance corps, brought young and skilled surgeons into the army, and also stepped on so many toes that he was ousted in 1864. The Pay Department also had four incumbents, none of them particularly distinguished, and none of whom rose above colonel. At least they were all honest in handling hundreds of millions of dollars in military payrolls.

Several departments concerned themselves with specific branches or functions of the armies in the field. The Corps of Engineers, under a chief engineer, was responsible for providing the officers and expertise for the construction of fortifications, bridges, roads and railroads, and the like. Elderly Brigadier General Joseph G. Totten, who had held the post of chief of engineers since 1838, continued to hold it until 1864, when sixty-six-year-old Brigadier General Richard Delafield succeeded him. Closely related was the Corps of Topographical Engineers, indeed so closely related that in 1863 it was abolished and merged into the Corps of Engineers, where its survey and map work was most useful anyhow. The newest staff department was the Provost Marshal's, established in 1862, and created to handle the apprehension of deserters, traitors, the institution and maintenance of punishment within the camps for infractions, and eventually the administration of conscription, or the draft. Two officers, neither very popular, held the office of provost marshal general.

Finally, in 1863, an informally designated signal officer was commissioned chief signal officer of the newly created Signal Corps. The first incumbent of this important post was Colonel Albert J. Myer, who along with Edward Porter Alexander invented the "wig-wag" system of signalling by flags before the war. He used observation balloons, the telegraph, and signal towers, to gather and transmit intelligence. He was transferred in 1863 and his department essentially phased out under his successors.[4]

All of this, in some instances moving haltingly and at a snail's pace, and in others with alacrity and skill, had to support the efforts of some two million men who wore the blue. Conservatism and a reluctance to accept change, always typical of entrenched military high command, was rife

Above: Surgeon General William A. Hammond made himself very unpopular with the military establishment, but with hundreds of thousands of casualties to handle, the medical department had to advance.

Below: Transportation took on whole new dimensions in this most mobile of wars to date, and the U.S. Military Railroad had to have its own Construction Corps to send the rails where the war was.

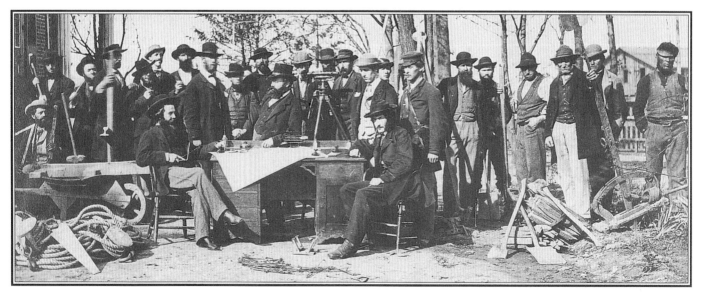

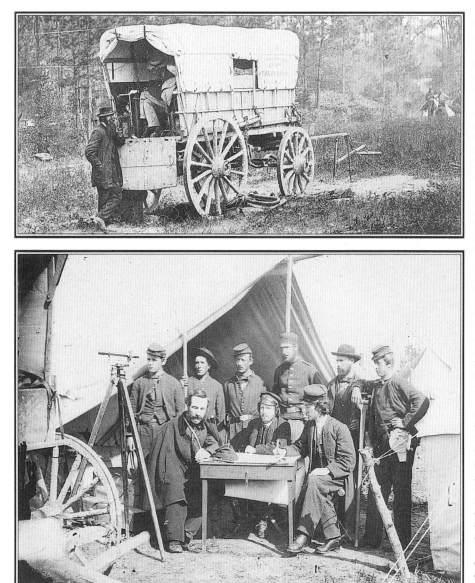

throughout the bureau chiefs. At Ordnance the adoption of repeating weapons, those using self-contained cartridges as opposed to more time-consuming cap and ball systems, improved rifled small arms and cannon, and almost everything else that later generations would look upon as an advance in the evolution of weaponry – were all resisted. In the Quartermaster's department, despite Meigs' extraordinary efforts, defective supplies and unsound horses for the cavalry were a constant problem. Indeed, to solve the latter, in 1863 a special Cavalry Bureau was established. Pay was often late, especially at more distant outposts. Maps, when there were any at all, proved insufficient thanks to the Federals' unfamiliarity with Southern terrain. Yet for all their shortcomings, their conservatism and obstructionism at times, the War Department bureaus more often than not accomplished what they were supposed to achieve. For the officers in charge it was about the least glamorous service a man could endure, sitting at a desk in Washington while the reputations and promotions were being won out in the field. But most of the incumbents were old Regular Army men, used to dull service with slow advancement and little emotional reward. The fact that many of them were too old to serve elsewhere in the service does not lessen the thanks they were due for enduring the tedium of department staff work.

The War Department itself was only the beginning of the total organization of the Union war effort, for somehow from that central point all the operations on the whole continent had to be overseen and managed. When the war began, it appeared that, if a short conflict, the existing geographical division of the army's command might suffice, but as the conflict escalated and more and more men went into the field to campaign for ever smaller sections of territory, it soon became evident that a more sophisticated territorial organization was needed.

At the very beginning of the war, there were only seven territorial divisions comprising the entire United States and its territories. The Department of the East included everything east

Top: Communications assumed an absolutely essential role for both armies. The telegraph put armies and capitals in almost instant touch with each other, allowing a coordination never before known in war.

Above: Topographical engineers at Camp Winfield Scott, near Yorktown, Virginia, in May 1862, made the surveys that helped commanders find their way through a terrain poorly mapped prior to the war.

Below: The Military Telegraph Construction Corps had to stay abreast of the advancing armies, to keep the singing wire supplying the latest intelligence to commanders. Without the wires the war could not have been fought.

of the Mississippi, from Canada to the Gulf of Mexico. Most of the old Louisiana Purchase, much of it still not organized into states, constituted the Department of the West, while the balance of the country was divided into departments that roughly coincided with their namesake states or territories: Texas, New Mexico, California, Utah, and Oregon. It was a peacetime organization designed mostly to cope with managing the Indians and furthering the gradual admission of western territories to statehood.

Secession quickly changed all that. Meeting the requirements of increased attention to affairs east of the Mississippi, the western departments began to expand and combine, while the old Department of the East became increasingly fragmented; into four departments by June 1861, six a year later, nine by June 1863, and eleven in June 1864, until the war's end. The more important military operations became in a region, the more attention it required, and territory was accordingly reduced to prevent distractions upon the commander of the military forces in that region. By war's end, the number of formal divisions was further subdivided into more than 60 departments, generally named for a river or geographical feature. These, too, evolved considerably as territory was won or lost, and as field operations shifted to other scenes. Some were as large as the huge Department of the Missouri, while others were nothing more than administrative jurisdictions as small as the Department of Key West. Within each department, its military forces, if they were large enough in size to merit being called an army, were given the same name as the department. Thus from the Department of the Potomac came the fabled Army of the Potomac, and from the Department of Tennessee the mighty Army of the Tennessee.[5]

The formation of those armies themselves also evolved. When the war commenced, there was no intent in Union military planning for any subdivision of an army larger than a brigade, usually constituted of four or five regiments and an artillery complement. But as the armies grew prior to

Union General Officers' Uniforms and Equipment

1 Frock coat of Maj. Gen. G. K. Warren
2 Warren's corps badge
3 Warren's forage cap
4 Shoulder strap of Maj. Gen. Mulholland
5 Mulholland's sash
6 Sherman's frock coat
7 Frock coat of Brig. Gen. C. P. Herring
8 Slouch hat of Maj. Gen. John Sedgwick
9 Frock coat of Maj. Gen. R. B. Potter

10 Model 1850 sword
11 General's sword belt
12 General Sherman's sash
13 and 14 Sash and belt of Gen. J. F. Reynolds
15 Sword belt of Maj. Gen. Robert Patterson
16 Sash of Brig. Gen. C. W. Cullom
17 Cased epaulettes
18 Shoulder straps of Brig. Gen. James Nagle
19 Gold pin of Maj. Gen. Robert Anderson

20 Gold pin of Maj. Gen. Philip H. Sheridan
21 Sheridan's saber
22 Sword of Maj. Gen. James B. McPherson
23 Sword of Maj. Gen. Winfield Scott
24 Militia sword of Maj. Gen. George H. Thomas
25 and 26 Thomas' dress chapeau and box
27 Sash of Maj. Gen. Truman Seymour
28 Boxed dress epaulettes

Artifacts courtesy of: The Civil War Library and Museum, Philadelphia, Pa: 4-7, 12-15, 18, 25, 26; West Point Museum, West Point, N.Y.: 1, 2, 3, 8, 10, 16, 17, 19, 20-24; Bob Walter Collection: 9

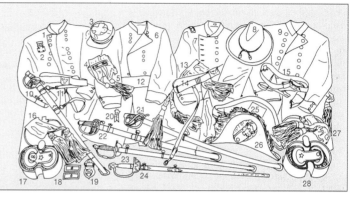

First Manassas, such an increasing number of brigades could become difficult for an army commander to handle, and so they were formed into divisions, each division to contain from two to four brigades. Still the armies grew bigger, so that by July 1862 it was necessary to formalize what a number of army commanders had already done informally on their own. Divisions were joined together to make army corps, usually consisting of between two to four divisions. They were numbered with Roman numerals from I through XXV, plus a Cavalry Corps. Other informal organizations appeared from time to time, as at the Battle of Fredericksburg in December 1862, when army commander Major General Ambrose Burnside consolidated his several corps into three "grand divisions". However, by war's end the standard descending order of organization throughout the Union Army was army, corps, division, brigade, regiment, and company. No specific regulations prescribed the exact rank of the commander of the larger groupings. Major generals always led the main armies, but in a smaller department a brigadier could command. Corps almost always had a major general at their head, but again brigadiers were seen occasionally. Many major generals also led divisions, mostly men with junior commissions, though a number of brigadiers also held such command. Brigades were exclusively the province of brigadiers and quite a few senior colonels, and, of course, regiments were led exclusively by colonels except in the case of a temporary absence from duty.

The chain of command was almost always clear to any officer. Especially important – particularly when viewed in comparison to the working of the Confederate command system – was the fact that a department commander reported directly to his military division commander, and the latter to the general-in-chief. Both Lincoln and Stanton were in the main very good about not circumventing the chain of command by sending orders directly to a lower level commander, and by-passing his superiors. It was the only sure way to prevent confusion and cross-purposes.

Throughout this whole increasingly sophisticated system, there really existed two kinds of army, not as separate field forces, but mixed together. There were the Regulars and there were the volunteers. While the Lincoln government looked primarily to volunteers from the states to swell its armies and fight the brunt of the war, the old career Regular service also saw some expansion. By war's end the Regular Army had grown to six regiments of cavalry, sixty batteries of artillery, one engineer battalion, and nineteen regiments of infantry.[6] Still, taken altogether, their

The Chain of Command of Blue and Gray

On both sides of the conflict there was a direct chain of command leading from the president, right down, link-by-link, to the lowliest private in the army.

Over all military forces lay the civil authority of the president. Reporting to him, through the War Department, was his general-in-chief if he had one. Below that officer were the several army commanders, almost always major generals. Then came the three, four, or more army corps, each led by a major general, each corps made up of about three divisions, led by major or brigadier generals. A division might have up to five brigades, each led by a colonel or a brigadier, and each brigade had four or more regiments. Colonels commanding regiments often divided them into battalions, under their majors, each battalion having half of the regiment's ten companies, each company led by a captain who commanded up to 100 privates and non-commissioned ranks.

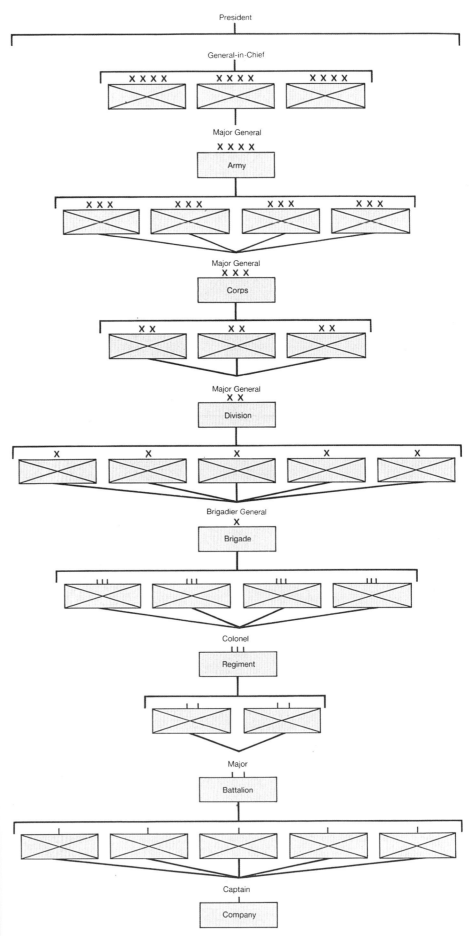

Company strength on average: 3 officers, 15 NCO's and 82 privates

numbers did not amount to much more than a good full-sized army corps. Rather than keep them all combined, however, the War Department parcelled them out among all of the field armies, occasionally in complete brigades, but more often mixed into brigades, the theory being that they would provide a professional, steadying influence on the volunteers. Many of the Regular units never even got into the war, being left out in garrisons on the western frontier to maintain order.

It must have been a frustrating service for many of the officers, as they saw former brother officers who had resigned to take volunteer commissions rise in rank. For the fact is that men who stayed in the Regulars during the war tended to experience the same glacial advancement as before the war. Of the 1,098 Regular officers serving at the start of the war, 767 remained loyal to the Union. Of their number, only 142 eventually became generals, and almost all of them did so by leading volunteers. Some 161 who were captains at the commencement of the war were still captains or majors at the end. By contrast, of the 102 Military Academy graduates who had left the service before the war, then enlisted in 1861, 51 – exactly half – became general officers. Perhaps the only consolation many of the unpromoted Regular officers would have – and they had to wait until after the war for it – was the fact that when the volunteer armies were disbanded in 1865 and 1866, almost all of the Regulars who had achieved high rank in the volunteers reverted to their pre-war rank, or perhaps a step or two above. Thus George Custer

Above: Here on State Street in New York City, sat a Union quartermaster's office, right next to a recruiting office. The quartermasters had to maintain offices in most Northern cities for purchasing.

Below: The Washington Arsenal in the Union capital shows a yard full of ordnance, representing a tiny fraction of the cannon that passed through the Ordnance Department's hands during the war.

finished the war a major general of volunteers, but a year later he was only a lieutenant colonel second in command of a cavalry regiment.[7]

Across the lines in the new Confederacy, a very similar and at the same time very different military command system appeared. It owed its peculiar organization to two overwhelming influences: the model of the old United States War Department prior to the conflict, and President Jefferson Davis. Indeed, no assessment of the Confederate army in any of its facets, particularly its officer corps, can fail to take into account the pervasive influence of the man who led the country.

Jefferson Davis, despite having been a distinguished senator and spokesman for Southern rights, always saw himself at his core as a military man. He attended West Point, served in the Old Army for several years, and then after resignation came back into the field in command of a Mississippi volunteer regiment during the Mexican War. At the Battle of Buena Vista he distinguished himself and his regiment, and contributed materially to the victory by an otherwise ill-advised formation in which he placed his men in an inverted "V". Fortunately, the Mexican cavalry that charged him was repulsed, and Davis became a hero. Then in 1853, when President Franklin Pierce took office, Davis became his secretary of war.

That moment of glory at Buena Vista never left Davis. Ever after he assumed that he knew and understood the management of an army in the field as well as or better than anyone else. When he took office as president of the Confederacy, consequently, he interfered far more than Lincoln did in the actual operations of his armies, leading one wag to quip that the Confederacy perished "because of a 'V'."

The irony is that, however much he denied it, Davis was at heart an administrator. Throughout the Civil War, all the while complaining that he dreaded paperwork, he immersed himself in it and actually made much more of it for himself than was necessary. Having served as secretary of war, he naturally felt that he knew how to set up his own War Department, and indeed he did pretty well. But then he proceeded to run it largely himself, instead of leaving the details to his cabinet secretaries. Davis had the sort of mind that could not delegate even the smallest detail, for fear that if left to someone else, it would not be well handled. As a result, he almost worked himself to death, suffering dreadful health and exhaustion during most of the war. Yet even at war's close, when most of his letters opened with an apology for lateness in replying because of the burden of all his correspondence, he would still repeatedly spend up to an entire afternoon personally penning remonstrances of fifteen pages or more lecturing some subordinate on fine points of military law, aimed always at pressing the conclusion that Davis was invariably correct. It is certain that no man in the Confederacy devoted himself more heart and soul to the cause, or made that cause and his own name more synonymous. Davis' loyalty and dedication are beyond question. Unfortunately for the fate of the South, his temperament, personality and character simply did not suit him to be a chief executive, and the reasons why are amply demonstrated in the makeup and management of his War Department.

It was an incredible challenge. Everything in the new Confederacy had to be created out of

Above: Even if Jefferson Davis had possessed the executive skills of Lincoln, which he did not, the task of organizing the Confederacy for victory would still have required a superhuman effort against the odds.

Below: Confederates had to make do whenever they could. During the first war winter, here at Manassas, they lived in their log cities better than in later years. Their War Department was always short of supplies.

nothing. Not surprisingly, one of the very first acts of the new Provisional Confederate Congress was to create a War Department. Indeed, it was done just three days after Davis' inauguration as President on February 18, 1861. In the initial legislation, just four bureaus or staff departments came into being, reflecting the most immediate and obvious needs of the army to come: Adjutant and Inspector General's Department, Quartermaster General's, Commissary General's, and a Medical Department. The secretary of war presided over all – theoretically. In actual practice, Davis ran it himself.[8]

As a result, whether by design or unconsciously, Davis repeatedly chose as cabinet ministers for the department men who had few skills, little reputation or experience, and poor health. Thus all were totally domitable, offering little or no resistance to his daily involvement in their responsibilities. Not surprisingly, he went through six war secretaries and four assistant secretaries, creating more turnover than in any other cabinet position. Leroy P. Walker served until September 1861, resigning largely due to poor health. Judah

Below: These four unknown Louisiana Confederate officers were probably photographed early in the war, when uniforms could still look this complete. Four years later they would be in tatters.

P. Benjamin, formerly attorney general and later to be secretary of state, filled in for seven months until George W. Randolph took over. He, too, left from poor health that would kill him five years hence, and also out of frustration at the president's high-handed meddling. Gustavus W. Smith filled in for a very few days, having previously suffered a nervous breakdown when he briefly commanded the Army of Northern Virginia. Then he was succeeded by James A. Seddon, who served for more than two years and suffered constantly from a frail constitution. Only the final incumbent, Major General John C. Breckinridge, enjoyed both good health and a reputation and stature that made it impossible for Davis to treat

him as a mere clerk as he had the others. But by the time Breckinridge took office in February 1865, the cause was lost.

In the staffing and initial operations of those first four departments, Davis showed a weakness for old cronies and ineffectual appointees that would plague the War Department throughout the war, As adjutant and inspector general, he appointed Samuel Cooper, who had held the same position in the Old Army until secession. That, alone, made him seem a logical choice. But he was sixty-three years old, had never held a field command, and was tired and weak-willed. A department employee, Robert Kean, head of the later established Bureau of War, characterized Cooper as ignorant and incompetent and kept in office solely thanks to Davis' preference for "accommodating, civil-spoken persons of small capacity." Though he was, in fact, the senior ranking general in the entire army, Cooper was regarded and treated by most subordinates as a mere cypher.[9]

Two men held the post of Quartermaster General. Colonel Abraham C. Myers was effective but fell out of favor with Davis, apparently over a remark attributed to his wife. In 1863 Davis replaced him with Brigadier General Alexander R. Lawton, who found the post so uncomfortable that he soon wanted to resign, but stayed on until the end of the war.[10]

Where Davis' weakness for old friends really hurt was in his appointment of Brigadier General Lucius B. Northrop to be commissary general. All aspects of feeding the armies came under his control, and Northrop early showed himself to be an incompetent. Worse, he had been on permanent sick leave from the Old Army since 1839! But he and Davis had been friends at West Point, and despite almost four years of clamour against Northrop, Davis refused to replace him until February 1865, when Breckinridge made Northrop's dismissal a condition of his accepting the cabinet post. Breckinridge – not Davis – then replaced Northrop with Brigadier General Isaac M. St. John, and in a matter of weeks the remaining

Confederate General Officers' Uniforms and Equipment

1 Frock coat of Brig. Gen. Paul Semmes
2 Frock coat of Maj. Gen. Joseph Wheeler
3 Frock coat of Lt. Gen. John Bell Hood
4 Frock coat of Maj. Gen. Frank Gardner
5 Frock coat of Lt. Gen. Simon Bolivar Buckner
6 Frock coat of Brig. Gen. George Wythe Randolph, Sec of War, C.S.A.
7 General's silk sash
8 Forage cap of Brig. Gen. Paul Semmes
9 Epaulettes of Maj. Gen. Joseph Wheeler
10 Hood's sword belt
11 Hood's silk sash
12 Forage cap
13 General's silk sash
14 Epaulettes of Brig. Gen. Carnot Posey, died 1863
15 Forage cap of Maj. Gen. John B. Magruder
16 Magruder's silk sash
17 Le Mat revolver
18 Field glass of Gen. Joseph E. Johnston
19 Savage Navy revolver of Maj. Gen. Wheeler
20 Hood's saber from Paris
21 Sword of Brig. Gen. Robert S. Garnett
22 Saber of Maj. Gen. Matthew C. Butler
23 Sword of Lt. Gen. Hood
24 Colt 1860 Army of Gen. J.E. Johnston
25 Johnston's spurs
26 Le Mat 1st Model revolver of Gen. P.G.T. Beauregard
27 Johnston's sash

Artifacts courtesy of: The Museum of the Confederacy, Richmond, Va

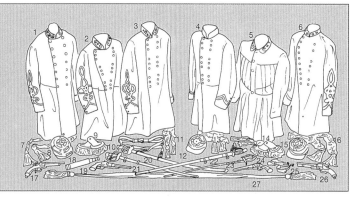

Left: Samuel Preston Moore acted as surgeon general of the Confederate Army. It was a frustrating task, with medicines, facilities, and trained personnel in constant short supply. Any achievement was a victory.

Above: Some of the Confederate wounded that Moore did not have to cope with were those captured in battle, like these convalescent Rebels, many missing limbs, at Camp Letterman at Gettysburg in 1863.

men in the field were being better supplied than they had in months, all too late of course.[11]

Only in the Medical Department did Davis make an initially happy choice. Surgeon General Samuel P. Moore served from July 1861 until the end of the war, supervising hospitals, medical officers, and acquisition of precious medical supplies. His performance, under terrible conditions, proved to be excellent.

Considering that Davis was essentially a regulation-bound kind of administrator, it is much to his credit that he demonstrated a willingness to evolve his War Department to suit changing needs. Thus when it was evident that functions required more than the existing departments, he expanded the War Department. In 1861 he created the Engineer Bureau, a Bureau of Ordnance and Ordnance Department, and a Bureau of Indian Affairs (the Confederacy had no Interior Department, where Indian matters would normally be handled). The next year there was even more growth, with the creation of the Signal Bureau, the Army Intelligence Office, the Bureau of Exchange, and the Bureau of Conscription. In 1863 there appeared the Niter and Mining Bureau and the Bureau of Foreign Supplies, and in 1864 the Office of the Commissary General of Prisoners was created.[12]

Each office, headed in all cases by an officer with the rank of colonel or brigadier, had its own very specific area of influence, and many were tailored to the peculiar needs of the Confederacy's strained and ill-equipped war effort. Indian Affairs, unlike the Federal bureau of the same name, was concerned not with keeping the Indians west of the Mississippi peaceful, but instead with attempting to persuade them to join the Confederate forces in the conflict; with some success it has to be said.

Contrary to the name it held, the Army Intelligence Office did not deal in confidential information, but rather acted as a kind of Red Cross, keeping track of sick and wounded and getting information to families of soldiers. It was the Signal Bureau that dealt with the clandestine;

one of its branches being the shadowy "Secret Service", its operations still only imperfectly known.[13]

The Bureaus of Exchange and Conscription both attacked the problem of manpower, though from different directions. Early in the war, and again toward the end, cartels went into effect providing for the exchange of prisoners of war. Such exchanges took place on a one-for-one basis based upon rank, a private being worth one private, a general worth one general, and so forth. A lieutenant might be worth several privates, and a general worth several lieutenants. The Bureau of Exchange was to handle all this, but when prisoner exchange was brought to a halt by the Federals in 1863, the bureau had little to do. Conscription, on the other hand, oversaw the drafting of men of military age under the several conscription acts passed in Richmond. Even more specialized was the function of Niter and Mining.

Reliant upon what it could make internally for much of its munitions, the War Department took over supervision of the mining of raw materials like lead for bullets, and niter for gunpowder. What could not be made domestically had to be brought in by the Bureau of Foreign Supplies through the blockade. And as the prisoner exchange system broke down and the number of imprisoned Federal prisoners continued to mount, a cabinet level bureau to feed and care for them came into being, though shortages prevented it being very effective.[14]

Borrowing from the organization he had known so well as Pierce's secretary of war, Davis

Below: The blockade runner *Old Dominion* being fitted out at Bristol, England, was one of a host of ships that the Confederates had to depend upon to get much needed supplies to a strapped war effort.

Confederate Officers of Cavalry, Infantry and Artillery

These were the men seen most often in the field in the armies of the Confederacy. With little or nothing particularly distinctive about their uniform dress, they were the average officers who made up the bulk of the officer corps.

The major of cavalry at left wears the so-called butternut colored uniform that became common when dies were too scarce to produce a uniform gray. At least his yellow facings match the regulations for his branch of service. Standing next to him is an infantry captain who also shows some ersatz in his dress. Uniform is the proper gray, but his hat is definitely a makeshift substitution.

Seated at right is a full colonel of artillery, and he, at least, has everything right. This was the rarity, and probably indicates that he was uniformed early in the war. For all of them, just staying clothed became a struggle, much less meeting regulations.

organized the Confederacy into a number of territorial commands, as did Lincoln. Like the Washington government, the Confederates also saw the number of departments grow in reaction to the course of military affairs. In the summer of 1861 they had only the Department of Texas, the Indian Territory (now Oklahoma), Department No. 1 encompassing chiefly Alabama, Department No. 2 containing both banks of the Mississippi from Tennessee nearly to Baton Rouge, and then a massive unnamed territory that embraced literally all of the rest of the Confederacy clear to the Atlantic. It was an ungainly organization to say the least, but with no enemy armies threatening anywhere except in northern Virginia, and the only western threat the control of the Mississippi, the lopsided organization briefly suited its purpose. Six months later there were eight departments, the borders between them badly blurred. By the summer of 1862 everything west of the great river had been redesignated the Trans-Mississippi Department, virtually a third of the Confederacy. Eighteen months later the Confederacy east of the river contained ten departments, those beyond the Appalachians grouped into a still larger Western Department. At the end of the war the departmental organization was bizarrely laid out, with the Department of Tennessee and Georgia commencing at Tallahassee, Florida, on the Gulf of Mexico, then extending several hundred miles north before turning west at the Tennessee line and continuing on to the Mississippi River. Though more than 600 miles long, with a dog-leg to the left at Tennessee, it was in places only 50 miles wide.[15]

As with the Union forces, the individual military command within each department constituted its "army". However, an unfortunate flaw in Davis' adherence to his department system was that each commander was an independent entity, responsible only to the War Department. Therefore, if a Yankee threat or invasion appeared in one department, the threatened commander could not require a neighboring commander to

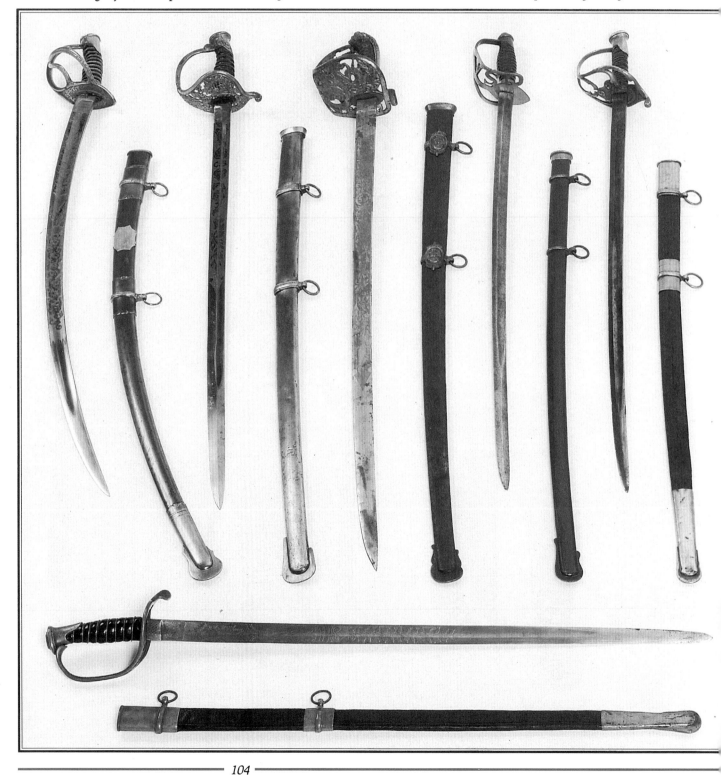

Confederate Officers' Edged Weapons

1 Cavalry saber of Gen. George W. Rains, made at the Memphis Novelty Works
2 Staff and field officer's saber made by Kraft, Goldsmith & Kraft
3 Kraft, Goldsmith & Kraft deluxe lion pommel saber carried by Col. William Lowther Jackson, 19th Virginia Cavalry
4 Confederate States Armory officer's sword

made by Louis Froelich in Kenansville, N.C.
5 College Hill foot officer's sword made in Nashville, Tennessee
6 College Hill staff and field officer's sword
7 Foot officer's sword belonging to George Sweet, made by Thomas Griswold
8 Louis Haiman and Brother foot officer's sword carried by Capt. Edgar

G. Dawson
9 Louis Haiman saber carried by Dawson Terrell Light Artillery
10 Saber of Brig. Gen. Archibald Gracie, Jr., killed at Petersburg, 1864; made by Louis Haiman and Brother
11 W.J. McElroy foot officer's sword made in Macon, Georgia
12 Saber of Gov. Letcher of Va

Artifacts courtesy of: The Museum of the Confederacy, Richmond, Va: 1, 2, 7, 10, 12; Virginia Historical Society, Richmond, Va: 3, 6, 8, 9; Russ Pritchard collection: 4, 5, 11

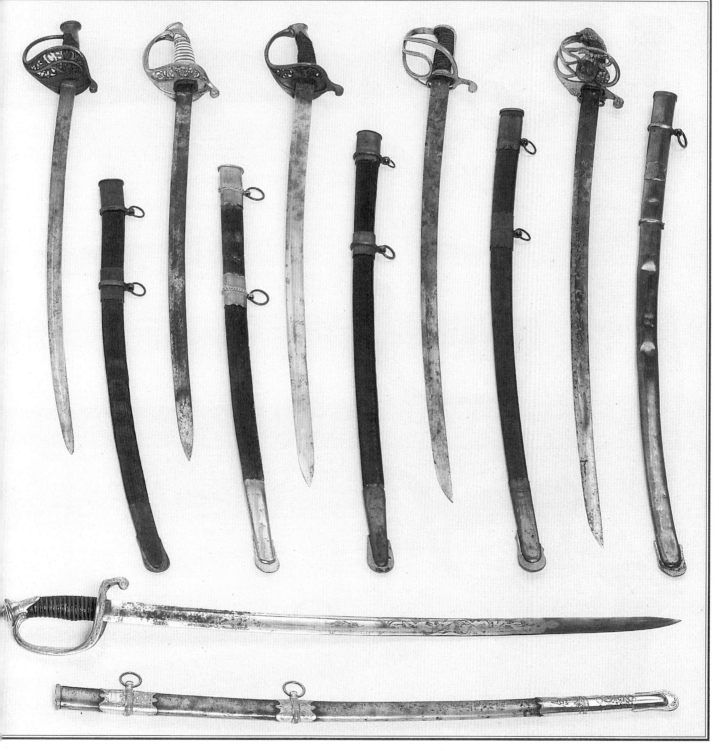

come to his assistance. Only Richmond could do that. Since there was no general-in-chief until 1865, when Robert E. Lee assumed that position, and since there was no chief-of-staff even, only Davis – acting through the secretary of war – could compel one department leader to aid another. This was the way Davis wanted it, and only heavy pressure from his Congress finally forced him to accept a general-in-chief, too late for the move to have any effect.

Because of a greater variation in rank in the Confederate service, there was more variety among army commanders. Grades of general officer ran from full general to lieutenant general, major general, and brigadier. A department and its army, depending upon size, could be commanded by a man of any such grade. In the case of officers who fell out of favor with Davis, such as P.G.T. Beauregard, a man with a very big rank might sometimes find himself in command of a very small department. In Beauregard's case the Georgia and South Carolina coastal defenses in 1863. The armies themselves, as with the Federals, generally took their name from their department, as with the Army of Northern Virginia, Army of the Trans-Mississippi, and so forth. Within those armies, the same organizations such as corps, divisions, and brigades, existed as in the Union forces, and were generally commanded by officers of comparable rank. However, with the high rate of attrition among Rebel officers, it was far more common for men of lesser rank to hold higher commands.

And like the Union, the Confederacy had basically two military organizations, one very large and all-important, and the other negligibly small. On February 28, 1861, the Confederate Congress, then still in Montgomery, Alabama, created the Provisional Army of the Confederate States, abbreviated to P.A.C.S. It was the direct equivalent of the volunteer forces of the North. The legislation allowed the Confederacy to accept regiments of volunteers provided from each of the states, and acknowledged its obligation to feed and pay for them for their term of service.

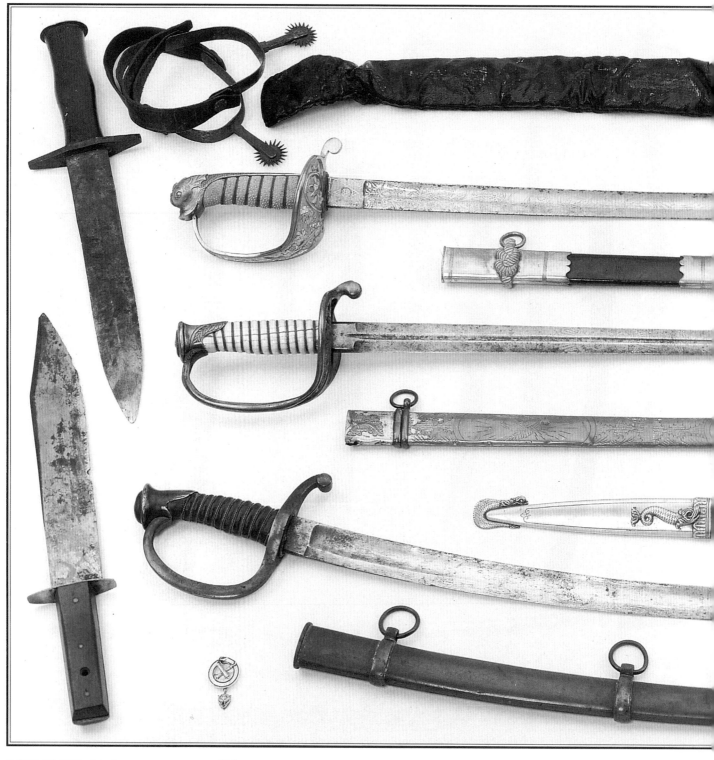

Confederate Officers' Edged Weapons and Memorabilia

1 Spear point side knife
2 Pair of iron spurs of the raker type
3 An oil cloth storage and carrying case for 5 and 6. The case is lined with chamois leather
4 and 15 Burger Brothers side knife and scabbard. Inscription on the blade describes the weapon as a relic of the Battle of Williamsburg, Virginia, May, 1862
5 and 6 Regulation

Confederate States Navy officer's sword and scabbard
7 and 8 Foot officer's sword and scabbard made by Agruider Dufilho of New Orleans
9 Side knife made by Boyle, Gamble and Company, Richmond, Virginia
10 Gold, jeweler-made pin, with artillery insignia
11 and 12 Officer's light artillery saber and

scabbard
13 and 14 Presentation naval dirk with silver mounts: inscribed to John T. Wood
16 and 17 Side knife with etched blade together with leather and brass scabbard, made by Boyle, Gamble and Company, Richmond, Virginia. Inscribed with owner's name on scabbard: Arthur Babcock, 43rd Battalion, Mosby's Command

Artifacts courtesy of: Donald Tharpe Collection

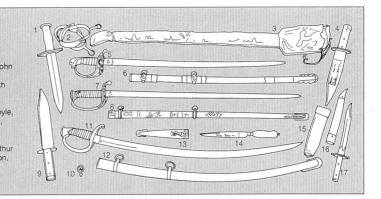

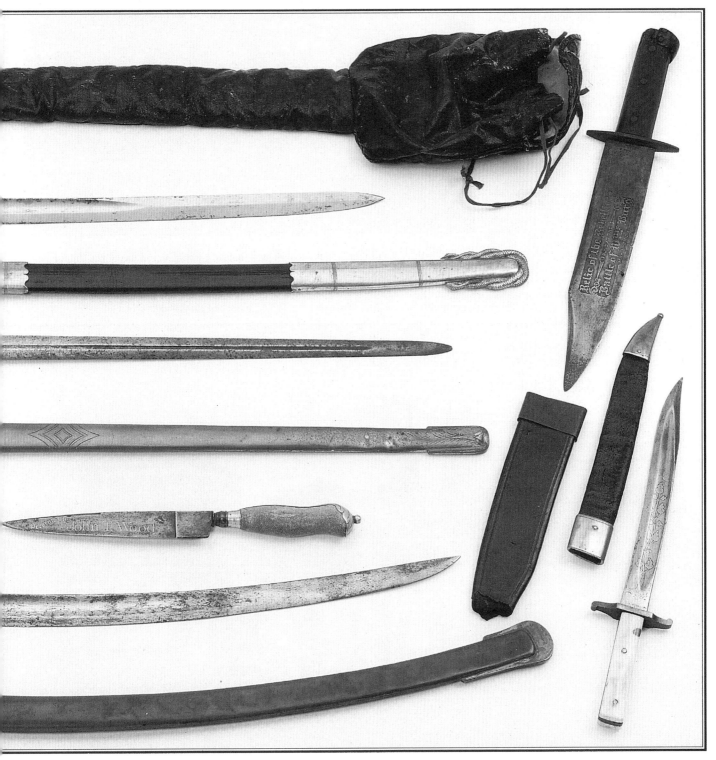

That term, at first, might be only twelve months, but by 1862 only regiments enlisted for three years or the duration were being accepted. Later legislation also provided for the recruiting of more such units, but all were officially a part of the P.A.C.S., and the commissions of almost all officers, even most generals, were provisional. If and when the war should end – successfully, of course – all P.A.C.S. officers and men would return immediately to civil life.[16] Of the 750,000 or more men who served the Confederacy during the war, virtually all were provisional.

But there was another force: the Confederate Regular Army. At least, such a standing professional army was dreamed of. Considering Davis' West Point and Old Army background, it is hardly surprising that – expecting his new nation to survive for a long time – he would want to establish a Regular force of his own. Consequently, on March 6, 1861, the Congress authorized the "Army of the Confederate States of America", calling for one corps of engineers, one corps of artillery, one regiment of cavalry, and six infantry regiments. The War Department staff departments previously authorized were a part of the Regular Army system. Initially only brigadier generals were authorized, but soon that was changed to recognize the full general rank and five were appointed in 1861 – Cooper, A.S. Johnston, Lee, J.E. Johnston, and Beauregard.[17]

Almost from the first, a Confederate Regular Army appeared to be a futile effort. As in the Union, men did not want to enlist for specific mandated periods of time in the Regulars when they could go into the volunteers and leave service as soon as the war was over. Regulars fulfilled an enlistment commitment no matter what happened in the war. Further, because of the very small size of the service, promotion for officers would be just as slow as in the Old Army. While

Above: In the end, the Confederacy somehow managed to come up with almost all that it needed except manpower. At war's end Richmond's Tredegar Iron Works teemed with armament – but too few soldiers.

Below: Inevitably, the flag of the United States flew once more over the Confederate Capitol in Richmond in April 1865. The city, the state, and the Southern people had resisted magnificently.

the legislation called for 15,003 men and officers of the Regulars, in the end only about 1,000 enlisted men and 750 officers and cadets were actually raised, and as the very high proportion of officers would suggest, most were not needed for the few soldiers enlisted, and were instead allowed to serve in the P.A.C.S., where Regular officers with low commissions could often become colonels and generals of volunteers.[18]

In the end, not one single complete regiment was raised. About five companies did serve intact throughout the war, but more often the Regulars enlisted were scattered among other state regiments and only a few dozen Regular officers stayed in the service through the course of the war. A number of other ostensibly "Regular" units did come to life, in all twelve separate regiments and battalions of cavalry, nine regiments and battalions of infantry, and five regiments and battalions of engineers. However, most were simply formed by consolidating the depleted remnants of several volunteer regiments later in the war. Mixing companies from more than one state in such a regiment, the War Department could not decide what state designation to give them, and so called them "Confederate" instead.[19]

Part of the Regulars' problem was confusion in the War Department. With a Provisional Army, a Regular Army, and a shadowy and ill-defined "volunteer" army of state militia that served only within the confines of their native states, cross-purposes abounded in determining where appropriations should go, with the P.A.C.S. consuming so much that there was little left over. Indeed, due to monetary restraints, Regular recruiting stations were closed in July 1861 and never reopened. At one point in 1864, kindly but vague old General Samuel Cooper apologized for being unable to appoint a man into the service, explaining that "there have been no appointments

Above: The last Confederate secretary of war, General John C. Breckinridge, actually improved army supply and organization slightly in the last days. In the end he oversaw the flight of the government.

in the regular army for several years, there being no regular army." The adjutant and inspector general had forgotten the Regulars.[20]

Yet the officers who made up over forty percent of the Confederate Regular Army became, like their Old Army counterparts in the new Union volunteer forces, a major vertebra in the backbone of the P.A.C.S. The Confederacy did not live long enough to build a lasting military tradition, but in its brief, blazing four years of life, its officers, like the men they led, and like the men they fought, built a legend.

References

1 Warner, *Generals in Blue*, p.196-7.
2 Welcher, *Union Army*, p.4.
3 Warner, *Generals in Blue*, p.503.
4 Welcher, *Union Army*, pp.2-4.
5 Davis, *Atlas*, Plates CLXII-CXLXIX.
6 Frederick Dyer, *A Compendium of the War of the Rebellion* (Des Moines, Iowa, 1908), III, pp.1,689-1,716.
7 Boatner, *Dictionary*, pp.495, 673-4.
8 Henry P. Beers, *Guide to the Archives of the Government of the Confederate States of America* (Washington, 1968), p.134.
9 Edward Younger, ed., *Inside the Confederate Government; the Diary of Robert Garlick Hill Kean* (New York, 1957), pp.xxx-xxxi.
10 *Ibid.*, pp.89-90.
11 Warner, *Generals in Gray*, p.225.
12 Beers, *Guide*, p.134.
13 *Ibid.*, pp.152, 210, 233.
14 *Ibid.*, pp.233, 237, 243, 246-7.
15 Davis, *Atlas*, Plates CLXII-CLXXI.
16 Beers, *Guide*, p.301.
17 Richard P. Weinert, "The Confederate Regular Army", *Military Affairs*, XXV (Fall 1962), pp.97-8.
18 *Ibid.*, pp.106-7.
19 *Ibid.*, p.107; Joseph H. Crute, Jr., *Units of the Confederate Army* (Midlothian, Va., 1987), pp.65-72.
20 Weinert, "Regular Army", p.107.

CHAPTER SIX

CLASSROOMS OF CONFLICT

Within weeks after the disaster at Chancellorsville, Union fortunes made an abrupt and astounding recovery. At Gettysburg the Army of the Potomac gave Lee his first crushing defeat, while out in Mississippi, the bastion of Vicksburg surrendered to Grant. Suddenly Union arms seemed victorious everywhere, thanks in no small part to the professionally schooled men leading Lincoln's armies. In the Confederacy, the mounting losses of officers made ever more vital the few trained leaders that were left.

HOWEVER MUCH North and South may have failed to recognize and act upon the need for systematic training of their volunteer officers, both sides never let up in their steady production of professionally trained men to send forth for leadership in their armies. The United States Military Academy at West Point continued its operations without interruption, and so did the United States Naval Academy, though its proximity to danger in secession-sympathizing Maryland necessitated its temporary removal to Newport, Rhode Island. Across the lines, of course, there had never been a Confederate military academy before the war, but the host of Southern military schools, especially Virginia Military Institute and the Citadel, kept right on graduating young cadets who went almost immediately into Southern armies. More than that, Jefferson Davis and his government even created a new floating Confederate Naval Academy, and made some provisions for the appointment and training of cadet infantry officers. Amid the turmoil of a nation torn apart and bleeding, the schools were still teaching young men to be officers.

West Point, of course, led all the rest for the sheer number of graduates that it turned out and for the number that it contributed to the armies, especially the Union. Young men graduating in the early 1860s had been fortunate enough to attend in what many later called West Point's golden years. General Winfield Scott was inordinately fond of the school, meaning that it had his ardent and influential support. The faculty had almost all been trained by Sylvanus Thayer, the man whose vision of the school stamped it and every graduate, practically since its founding. Coming out of a long peace-time era in which many in Washington questioned the need for the Academy, it was now the darling of politicos. "The graduates of that institution contributed in an eminent degree to our unexampled career of success", declared Secretary of War William

Marcy, making West Point an appropriate repository for all the trophies of war taken from the Mexicans. From wanting to see the school torn down, many old opponents now looked to it as a center of Army history and tradition. Even new barracks and class buildings were constructed, and the intellectual cream of the Old Army's officers were sent there to be instructors and administrators.[1]

In the 1850s West Point had enjoyed a series of good superintendents, most notably Robert E. Lee, who took over in 1852. Following him in 1855 came Captain John G. Barnard. Barnard would later achieve distinction as an engineer, and by war's end was chief engineer on Grant's staff. Following him came Major Richard Delafield, who had previously held the superintendency, and who in the war to come would be chief of engineers. By 1861, another new superintendent, Pierre G.T. Beauregard, had taken command, but within only a few days he was relieved because of his decided Southern sympathies, and replaced by Delafield once more. Delafield, his scholarly face rimmed by pure white hair, sideburns, and beard, looked more like a school teacher than an officer anyhow, but he would not remain long in command.

The course of instruction at West Point during the Civil War did not differ substantially from the kinds of classes that cadets had studied for decades. Sciences – natural and physical – mathematics, history and the like made up the liberal arts aspect of the regimen. In military sciences, every cadet was exposed to engineering, infantry, cavalry, and artillery studies and tactics, and for most some studies of French, in order to master the latest European military manuals. Classes continued through fall and spring terms, with a summer encampment a traditional event before the war, and one especially essential once hostilities commenced.

But as the excitement mounted in the later winter of 1860 and spring of 1861, it became more

These young students of West Point's class of 1864 have high expectations of careers ahead. Only one, however, Ranald Mackenzie, standing at left, will see glory, becoming one of the youngest generals in American history.

and more difficult to keep the cadets' attention fixed upon their course of study. War fever seized almost all of them. "'I can think of nothing else", one young man wrote to his girlfriend. It was the same with his classmates. "Everything is cast aside. The professors complain bitterly about the deficiency of cadets in their recitations and the superintendent says that something will have to be done about it. I imagine the only way to prevent it is to stop the war."[2]

When the South Carolina batteries fired on Fort Sumter, all West Point cadets came to a final examination not previously a part of the school's studies. Secretary of War Simon Cameron immediately ordered that all cadets, officers, and faculty at the Military Academy should swear an oath of allegiance. It was essential to weed out at once the disloyal and the wavering. The new plebe class, the first year cadets, were the first required to so swear, and it was an affecting scene. Under the assumption that there would be some who would refuse the oath, causing some drama, most of the Academy's upper classmen were present as well, to witness what happened. The plebes gathered in the chapel before the assembled military and academic staff, all in full uniform. Their names were read aloud, and each of the plebes stepped forward to swear his oath. The first time a Southern boy refused, fellow Southerners stamped their feet in applause, while the rest of the assembly of spectators began a loud hissing. Ten young men could not take that oath, and were soon dismissed. The Civil War had begun to split "the corps".[3]

Of course, the decision of whether to go or stay had been faced by men at the Academy as far back as January 1861, a few days after South Carolina seceded in December. One young man actually asked Beauregard during his brief tenure if he should resign. Still hoping to stay himself, the superintendent counselled the boy, "Watch me, and when I jump, you jump. What's the use of jumping too soon?"[4]

Some had already "jumped". On November 19, 1860, Henry S. Farley of South Carolina became the first cadet to resign. Another South Carolinian followed him four days later, then a Mississippian, and an Alabama boy who had risen to first sergeant and who wept when he said goodbye. As the resignations continued into 1861, the lame-duck president James Buchanan ordered that all cadets suspend studies on February 22, George Washington's birthday, to go to the chapel and hear read to them Washington's farewell address, and to think upon his admonitions of "the immense value of your national union." Later that evening, cadets of opposing viewpoints began to shout cheers for the Union or for Southern rights from their windows. A few weeks later, when the war began, the first shot – a signal shell – was fired by a West Point graduate, Lieutenant Wade Hampton Gibbes, class of 1860. And the second shot came from a new Confederate lieutenant who never quite graduated, Henry S. Farley.[5]

The Academy was in a turmoil for a few days after the outbreak of war, cadets ignoring regulations, missing classes. Then came the oath, and the forcing of resignations from those who would not support the Union. As a result, March and April were bitter months of heart-wrenching partings of close friends, many of whom would never meet again except in battle.

In the end, out of 278 cadets at the Academy at the beginning of November, 65 left either by resignation or from being discharged for refusing to

take the oath. More annoying to Federal authorities were the six cadets who graduated in the accelerated classs of May 1861, and then resigned a few days later, obviously having waited to get their diploma at United States expense. This brought on yet another oath, this one specifically stating that the cadet held the law and authority of the Union above that of any state. This precipitated two more dismissals. As evidence of how agonizing such a fateful decision could be for a man of 21 who had only recently been a boy, one of the last two cadets to refuse later changed his mind and went into the Union army.[6]

Both the departure of so many ungraduated cadets, and the growing needs of the burgeoning army in the field, impelled the War Department to accelerate the rate of graduation of cadets. There was resistance at first, for Secretary of War Cameron thought he saw in the large number of West Pointers – 306 in all – who either resigned from the Academy or from service in the army, "an extraordinary treachery displayed", and asked if it "may not be traced to a radical defect in the system of education itself." The criticism did not last for long, especially when supporters of the Academy reminded critics that at least 66

Above: Cadet John S. Marmaduke of Missouri looks the typical Military Academy student of the late 1850s, and was one of many who had to choose between state and country when crisis came.

Below: Pierre Gustave Toutant Beauregard, in the uniform of a Confederate general, was the last pre-war superintendent of the Military Academy. He counselled young cadets not to be hasty in deciding for the South.

U.S. Midshipman in Service Dress, 1862, and West Point Cadet

Representing long-held traditions when the Civil War broke out, the United States Military Academy at West Point, New York, and the United States Naval Academy at Annapolis, Maryland, both offered a small but steady supply of educated and trained young officers for the Union war effort. The midshipman at left displays the traditional Naval Academy dress of short blue jacket and blue trousers. Next to him stands a cadet sergeant from West Point, considerably more resplendent in black shako with pom-pom, cadet gray short jacket with "frogging" in black, white gloves and crossbelt, and gray pants with black stripe. On certain occasions white trousers were optional. For all but a very few of these young men who graduated after the war commenced, there would not be time to achieve the rank and reputation that went to the prewar-graduates of the academies.

Southern-born graduates had not resigned but remained firm to the Union.[7]

Indeed, soon the War Department was singing the tune that accelerated graduation was a necessity, for there were not enough officers for all the places to be filled – exactly the opposite of the pre-war Old Army experience. In his annual report for December, Cameron recommended "that immediate provision should be made for increasing the corps of cadets to the greatest capacity of the Military Academy." Whereas there were only 142 students at that time, Cameron urged that the number be raised to 400, and that funds be spent to increase that to 500. "It is not necessary at this late day to speak of the value of educated soldiers", he said, forgetting his earlier calumnies on the Academy.[8]

By the end of 1861, two classes had been graduated ahead of time: the class of May 6, with 45 cadets, and the class of June 24, with another 34. Those first two wartime classes would leave their mark. Standing first in the May class was Henry A. DuPont, later a distinguished artilleryman. Ranking third was Orville E. Babcock, who served as Grant's aide by the end of the war and won a brigadier's brevet. Adelbert Ames, fifth ranking, became a leading division commander, and Emory Upton, eighth, achieved a single star and proved to be one of the most distinguished soldiers of the post-war army. Number seventeen was Judson Kilpatrick, much disliked and troublesome, but eventually a major general of cavalry with Sherman in Georgia. Seven of the forty-five would be killed in battle, one of them having later become a Confederate officer.[9]

The June class achieved no less distinction. Alonzo Cushing won immortality by his defense

Above: Fresh from the Academy at the outbreak of the war, many young lieutenants found positions on the staffs of new generals. General Andrew Porter's staff included George Custer, lying at far right.

Below: Here at a school storied in tradition, where legendary names had their first training as soldiers, the young professional officers of the Union were trained: West Point on the Hudson.

of Cemetery Hill on July 3, 1863, at Gettysburg, where he gave his life. Six others of his class met their deaths in the war, and the man who ranked at the very bottom, thirty-fourth, courted death time and time again, but would only find it at the hands of the Sioux eleven years after the war ceased. George A. Custer would become the youngest major general in his nation's history.[10]

Thereafter the classes continued to turn men out for the hungry regiments. The class of 1862 gave twenty-eight, including Ranald S. MacKenzie who would become a brigadier when only twenty-four and later one of the greatest Indian fighters of the West. The next class brought forth twenty-five graduates, and the class of 1864 another twenty-seven. They were the last to see Civil War service, for the 1865 class graduated on June 23, 1865, after all of the hostilities had ended.[11]

Thus the United States Military Academy actually graduated just 159 officers during the war, though the total student body at any time was well over 200; never close to Cameron's hoped-for 500. Far from reducing its appropriations, as might have been inferred from remarks made in 1861, Congress augmented funds earmarked for the institution, to the point that during the last year of the war its expenditures exceeded $200,000, a twenty-five percent increase over its annual average expenditures for the previous twenty years. Maintenance and upkeep were expanded due to the demands of the real practical instruction being given. The library holdings were increased, the officers' quarters dressed up, and even gas pipes and fireplaces repaired. For targets for artillery practice, instructors spent $100, and another $1,000 for

Above: Several members of the West Point class of 1864 pose while still cadets. Only Ranald Mackenzie, seated at left, will have a chance to make a name for himself before the war is over.

Below: Two typical cadets of the class of 1864 assume a casual pose in the Military Academy grounds: William Ludlow at left and Vanderbilt Allen at right. War's end will stunt the growth of most.

new mounts for cavalry and artillery practice. By the end of the war, Secretary of War Stanton was also trying assiduously to get Congress to change the 1843 authorization that limited the number of appointments to the Academy. "Military science and art cannot be disseminated throughout the country", he complained, when the number of graduating cadets was so limited. And, he urged, the standard for admission should be raised, after seeing "the difficulties that have been experienced for years past in training the minds and bodies of the young gentlemen sent to the Academy" who were not equal to its demands.[12]

Thus it was that the United States Military Academy emerged from the Civil War with en-hanced prestige, and a considerable momentum for growth in the last half of the century. Though the total number of its graduates that made up the Union Army's officer corps might have been small as a percentage, their influence went far beyond their numbers. Every one of the major army commanders would be a West Point man, and most of the corps and department leaders as well. Grant, Sherman, Sheridan, Thomas, and more, the men who won the war, all learned much of their craft at the Academy, and so did that small legion of lesser officers like Cushing, who served them so well. And Lee, both Johnstons, Beauregard, Bragg, and the rest of the Confederate high command owed their schooling to the same institution. Indeed, the story of West Pointers in the war could be taken for the story of the war itself, for they were never out of the big action.

Perhaps because so many leading Rebels were graduates, and certainly because of the long-standing military tradition in the South, the new Confederacy was not yet even established before leading secessionists began to call for a Southern military academy. On January 26, 1861, the Mississippi secession convention passed a resolution calling on its representatives in any new confederation "to use their influence to have a military academy similar to that of the United States at West Point." Once the Confederacy was

Union Army Manuals

1 Various instructional manuals for Army and Navy, including *Scott's Infantry Tactics, Army Regulations, 1861*, and Halleck's *Laws of War*
2 Instructional manual for the Model 1863 Springfield rifle-musket
3 Advertisement or broadside for *Baxter's Volunteer Manual*
4 *Patten's Infantry Tactics*, published New York,

1861. The manual features a personal endorsement by Major General George McClellan on the cover
5 Manual and drill book for enlisted men, written by an anonymous officer
6 Manual of U.S. Army cavalry tactics
7 Illustrated edition of *Hardee's Tactics*, published in New York
8 Congdon's version of cavalry tactics

9 Handbook of artillery, inscribed, with owner's name
10 Illustrated infantry drill manual, showing the movements for shoulder arms
11 Pair of spectacles
12 *Baxter's Volunteer's Manual* for company evolutions, as advertised on broadside *3*. Manual published in Philadelphia, by King & Baird, 1861

Artifacts courtesy of: The Civil War Library and Museum, Philadelphia, Pa: 1, 2, 4, 5, 6, 7, 9, 10, 11, 12;
C. Paul Loane Collection: 3, 8

formed, its Congress waited only until May 16, 1861, to approve an act providing that cadets could be appointed by the president on an interim basis, "until a military school shall be established for the elementary instruction of officers for the Army." Not long thereafter, on October 7, 1861, in a treaty concluded with the Cherokee Indians, one of the inducements used to woo the tribe into an alliance with the Confederacy was the promise that one Cherokee youth would be selected every year "to be educated at any military school that may be established by the Confederate States."[13]

For all the good intentions, certainly heartily approved by old West Pointer and now President Jefferson Davis, the South simply never had the time or the wherewithal to set up its own military academy. The act allowing Davis to appoint cadets was as far as Congress got, and he did, indeed, appoint quite a few. They were attached as supernumeraries to existing volunteer or Regular companies, where the cadets, presumably, learned as much of the art of war as would allow them to be commissioned into active service. Several of them became second lieutenants in the Regular Army, and probably more took commissions in the P.A.C.S.[14]

Fortunately for Davis and his cause, he had other sources of excellent trained young officers. The South literally teemed with private and state military schools. Furthermore, a number of colleges and universities offered intensive courses of military instruction, meaning that there were actually thousands of non-West Point-trained men in the Confederate reservoir of potential officers. Indeed, looking just at the field officers – regimental men of colonel's, lieutenant colonel's, or major's rank – in Lee's Army of Northern Virginia, it appears that out of a total of 1,965, some 208 or ten percent were graduates of such schools. Adding to that the 73 West Point field officers gave Lee a very respectable nucleus of trained leaders.

They came from everywhere. In Lee's command there was one from the La Grange Military

Confederate Army Manuals

1 *Cavalry Tactics, Second Part,* published Philadelphia, 1856
2 *Uniform and Dress of the Army of the Confederate States,* Richmond, 1861
3 Record Book of Capt. B.F. Howard, Co.I, 1st Virginia Infantry, Kemper's Brigade, Pickett's Division, 1st Corps A.N.V., open at page dated for the years 1863 to 1864, with references to prisoner exchanges,

desertions and casualties of Gettysburg
4 *Regulations for the Army of the Confederate States,* various editions
5 Confederate ledger book
6 *Uniform and Dress of the Army of the Confederate States,* published Richmond, 1861
7 Account book
8 Payroll book
9 Pine bookrest used by John F. Mayer in the office of the Adjutant

General and Inspector General, C.S.A.
10 Embroidered felt eyeglass polisher used by President Jefferson Davis
11 Confederate cavalry roll book
12 Silver reading glass
13 Letter book of Col. William B. Wood, 16th Alabama Infantry
14 Spectacles and case, possibly used by President Jefferson Davis

Artifacts courtesy of: The Museum of the Confederacy. Richmond. Va

Academy, 14 from the Georgia Military Institute, 37 from the Citadel (formally known as the South Carolina Military Academy), and 156 from another institution that caused the Union an especial degree of discontent. Indeed, when asked why the war was taking so long, one unsubstantiated account says that Lincoln replied that he could win the conflict a lot faster, "were it not for a certain military school they have which supplies them with trained officers." Lincoln may not have said it at all, but even if he did not, certainly he and everyone else knew what school he would have been talking about: the Virginia Military Institute.[15]

Founded in 1839 at the picturesque Shenandoah Valley town of Lexington, it was referred to by locals and graduates as "the V.M.I.", and it rather quickly acquired a sense of tradition and *esprit* rivaling that of West Point. In its 22 years of operation before the outbreak of war, almost 1,000 young men entered its ranks, and 455 actually graduated. At the same time, the 523 who dropped out before graduating had almost all stayed in school from six months up to two years or more, thus acquiring much of the basic training and knowledge of the graduates. Furthermore, all but 35 of the 978 cadets who entered prior to the war came from Virginia, thus ensuring that their loyalties would take them into the Confederacy almost to a man.

Most of them did not stay in the military after graduation. Indeed, perhaps as few as two dozen were all that made careers in uniform, while the rest returned to civil life. Many stayed active in local militia organizations, however, and all remained a part of an "old school" network just as powerful as West Point's. It was certain that if a war came, and any V.M.I. men achieved high

Above: The "West Point of the Confederacy", the Virginia Military Institute at Lexington, had traditions almost as old as those at the Military Academy. Standing orders required a guard at Washington's statue.

Below: From the host of small private state military schools came men trained at arms who went back to civilian life, but who remained members of militia units like the Kentucky State Guard.

position, they would call upon a host of fellow graduates.

In 1861, after Virginia seceded, there was a host of them ready to be called. Out of 882 alumni of the V.M.I. living in July of that year, at least 740 took arms for the South, a staggering eighty-four percent. The impact of their service can be determined just by looking at the commands they held. Of sixty-four units of all arms that Virginia gave to the war in its first year, twenty-two – more than a third – were commanded by V.M.I. graduates. Those not commanded by V.M.I. men

often had a number of former cadets in their ranks. Beyond doubt, such alumni proved to be the dominant force in the officer corps of the Army of Northern Virginia, where all but a few of them served. When Major General George Pickett's Virginia division of fifteen regiments charged across the Pennsylvania fields to their high water mark at Gettysburg on July 3, 1863, thirteen of those regiments were taking orders from graduates of the V.M.I. No wonder then that V.M.I. came to be called "the West Point of the Confederacy."

Above: The V.M.I. as it appeared when the war broke out. The cadet barracks stands at right, with quarters for the faculty and superintendent to the left. Later the big building will be named for Jackson.

Below: These Confederate enlisted men, lean, raw-boned, tough and independent, are the sort of soldiers that fresh young officers from the V.M.I. had to learn to control and command – no easy task.

corps of cadets. There were marches, field exercises, all of the usual forms of guard mounting and details, and practical exercises in the evolutions of each of the infantry and artillery branches. Hardiness and fortitude being requisite to a good officer, the cadets at artillery drill actually had to harness themselves to the cannon instead of horses, though the Institute did relent to the point that it had special lightweight cannon cast for them to pull. In time the boys would dub the guns "Matthew and Mark".

In the fall, the boys went into the picturesque turreted and crenellated Institute barracks for their classroom studies in science and mathematics, natural and experimental philosophy, engineering, and foreign language, especially French. At the same time, active military exercise continued, with at least weekly parades that were a popular event for the townspeople of Lexington to view. The corps even received some practical military exercise by being designated to stand guard at the state arsenal prior to the war.

When the war did come, there was a lot more practical experience in store for the cadets and alumni. For the latter, immediate commissions awaited most. Confident that a V.M.I. training had equipped the graduate with the necessary essentials to exercise firm command, to train raw volunteers into effective soldiers, and to lead them in camp, field and battle, Jefferson Davis and Virginia's Governor John Letcher commissioned hundreds. Even alumni returning from far-flung places like Tennessee and Alabama, found themselves receiving ready commissions from other states' governors, for the V.M.I.'s education was recognized throughout the South.[16]

All told, some eighteen men of the Institute became generals in the war. At least 95 commanded regiments as colonels, another 65 served as lieutenant colonels, 110 became majors, 310 held captaincies, and among both grades of lieutenant there were 221 alumni. Many more served in the ranks without commissions, leading to one informed estimate that as many as 1,796 former cadets or alumni of the Virginia school fought for the Confederacy.

Since there were only 978 former cadets and alumni at the beginning of the war, this staggering figure of 1,796 reveals something else about the school. Unlike West Point, which thanks to Congressional legislation limiting appointees had a restricted class size, the V.M.I. turned out a huge increase in cadets and graduates. Between 1861 and 1865, as many cadets entered the school as had gone there in all the previous twenty-two years.

Training at V.M.I. was much the same as at other military schools before the war. It was a four year course, commencing in July of every year for a summer encampment of the entire

As for the cadets currently enrolled when war broke out, that first summer proved an active one. Classes traditionally graduated on July 4 every year, though that quickly changed since Confederates were uneasy about observance of what had been a national holiday before the conflict. Even before their graduation, however, the class of 1861 got a taste of the war when, on April 21, 1861, the whole corps left for Richmond to undertake duty drilling Confederate volunteers. The leader who rode at their head was their professor of philosophy and artillery tactics, Major Thomas J. Jackson. Once in Richmond, the corps effectively disbanded, as the young men expecting to graduate in a few weeks took service with the Confederacy. As a result, on July 4, though they were no longer at the Institute, the V.M.I.

declared the class of 1861 officially graduated as of that date. On December 6, 1861, the Institute did the same thing for the men who would normally have gotten their degrees as the class of 1862.

In fact, the Institute was not able to reopen until January 1, 1862. Those cadets not already enlisted or graduated returned, and a number of new "rats", as first year cadets were called, entered. Almost immediately their continuing association with Jackson re-asserted itself. When he was a professor he had not been well-liked. One cadet challenged him to a duel. Another reportedly attempted to assassinate him, and most of the boys ridiculed his queer ways by calling him

"Tom Fool", or mocked his eyes with the nickname "Old Blue Light". But by May 1862 he was no longer either of those things, but had a new sobriquet. As "Stonewall" Jackson, bearing the name he had won at the first Battle of Bull Run or Manassas, he was ordered off into the Shenandoah to drive out three separate Federal armies. He did it, in part with the assistance of the corps of cadets. They accompanied him on the march to the Battle of McDowell, though they saw no actual combat, much to their chagrin.

That campaign was also the last time they saw Jackson. A year later, on May 15, 1863, the corps turned out once more as the formal escort to take Jackson's body to his resting place in Lexington's

Confederate Artillery Officers' Uniforms and Equipment

1 Frock coat of Second Lt. George E. Saville, Parker's Light Artillery, (Va)
2 Forage cap of Col. W.J. Saunders, Chief of Artillery, Gen. J.E. Johnston's staff
3 Uniform jacket of Maj. Robert Stiles
4 Shirt of Lt. John Selden 2nd Co. Richmond Howitzers
5 Selden's frock coat
6 Leather gauntlets of

Capt. G. Gaston Otey Co. A, 13th Btn, Virginia Light Artillery
7 Otey's uniform jacket
8 Otey's forage cape
9 Selden's underclothing
10 Sword belt of Second Lt. Charles E. Munford, Letcher Battery
11 1840 U.S. Artillery sword of Maj. Gen. J.L. Kemper
12 Selden's trousers
13 Officer's sash
14 Otey's belt and holster

15 Field glasses of First Lt. W.T.Mumford, Co.G, Louisiana Artillery
16 Sword belt
17 Selden's uniform vest
18-19 Field glasses of Maj. Gen. S. Jones
20 Wooden canteen
21 Canteen of C. Palfrey
22 Campaign chest of Lt. William T. Mumford
23 1840 U.S. Artillery sword of Brig. Gen. Richard Brooke Garnett

Artifacts courtesy of: The Museum of the Confederacy, Richmond, Va: 1-15, 17-23; Russ Pritchard Collection: 16

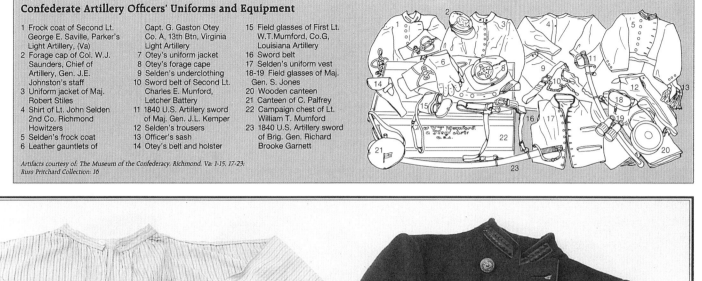

cemetery, after his mortal wounding at Chancellorsville. Six weeks later, on July 3, the Institute graduated its class of 1863.

Three more times the boys and young men were called out for emergencies, once in August when Federal raiders threatened and again in November and December for two more Yankee raids. Yet neither time did they see action. But then came May 1864, and what would ever-after be for the V.M.I. its most treasured tradition and legend.[17]

A Federal expedition commanded by Major General Franz Sigel set out to wrest the Shenandoah from the Confederates, destroy its crops, and use the Valley as a back door into the heartland of Virginia, at the same time as U.S. Grant and the Army of the Potomac were launching a major overland thrust at Lee and Richmond. The Shenandoah, known to Virginians simply as "the Valley", lay almost entirely undefended. As a result, except for harrassing by Rebel cavalrymen, his march south was almost unimpeded. Still thanks to Sigel's timidity and questionable competence, it was a leisurely advance. That gave the Confederate department commander in faraway southwest Virginia, Major General John C. Breckinridge, time to assemble a small scratch force to meet Sigel. It was vitally important to stop the Yankees before they got to Staunton, a major supply and rail connection, and also an avenue to Lee's rear while he faced Grant's forces.

Rapidly Breckinridge forced his small command of a few thousand Confederates toward Staunton. Knowing himself badly outnumbered, he sent orders to the superintendent of the Virginia Military Institute, General Francis H. Smith, to turn out the entire corps of cadets. He hoped that he would not have to use them, but if necessary, use them he would. On May 11, 1864, jubilant at the prospect of seeing action, the 258 cadets and their instructor-officers left for Staunton, where they met Breckinridge the next day. Two more days of marching brought them to the vicinity of New Market, a sleepy Valley farming community just then occupied by the advance

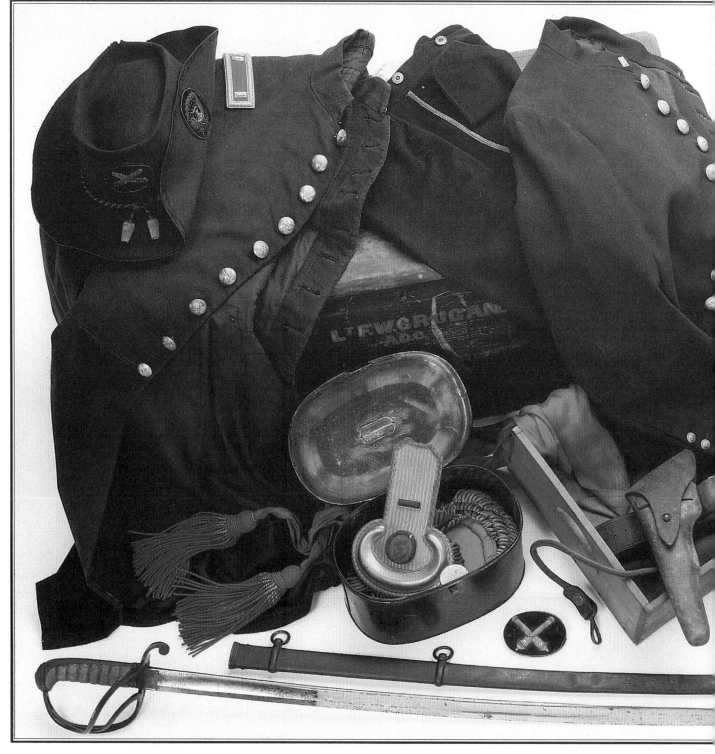

Union Artillery Officers' Uniforms and Equipment

1 Slouch hat of Second Lt. Levi J. Homan, Ermentrout's Independent Company of Pennsylvania Artillery
2 Frock coat of First Lt. Florance Grugan, 2nd Pennsylvania Artillery
3 Grugan's trousers
4 Grugan's short jacket
5 Forage cap of Capt. J. Henry Sleeper, 10th Massachusetts Battery
6 Forage cap of Second Lt.

George W. Webb, Battery F, Independent Pennsylvania Artillery
7 Webb's frock coat
8 Webb's vest
9 Unidentified forage cap
10 Grugan's brass spurs
11 Grugan's field chest
12 Top shelf of 10
13 Grugan's sash
14 and 15 Tin box with epaulettes for 3rd Regt
16 Grugan's holster belt
17 and 18 1840 officer's light

artillery saber
19 Saddle valise of Lt. George W. Taylor
20 1862 Colt revolver
21 Officer's haversack
22 and 23 German sword of Edwin A. Evans
24 Embroidered insignia
25 Strap insignia of Capt. Josiah Meigs, 2nd U.S. Colored Artillery
26 Insignia of Lt. G.W. Taylor, 4th MA Battery
27 Metal variant insignia

Artifacts courtesy of: The Civil War Library and Museum, Philadelphia, Pa: 2-4, 10, 11, 12, 16, 20-23; C. Paul Loane Collection: 5, 9, 14, 15, 19, 21, 24, 25, 26, 27; Gary Leisster Collection: 1, 6-8, 17, 18

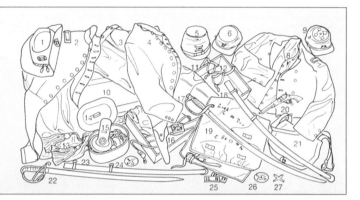

elements of Sigel's army of 6,200. Breckinridge, with less than 5,000, including the cadets and some elderly reserves, decided to attack.

The next morning the Confederates seized the initiative and never let it go. Breckinridge formed his men in line and pushed north, driving back Sigel's outposts, and then elements of his main army. That morning the general had posted the cadets in reserve, stating his intention to keep them out of the battle if at all possible. All through the morning and early afternoon he lived up to his intent.

But then late in the afternoon, as he pushed toward the main Yankee line atop Bushong's Hill, a hole opened in the left center of his line just as the enemy was about to mount a countercharge. Frantically Breckinridge looked for some other unit to fill the gap. There was none available but the corps of cadets. His adjutant Charles Semple saw tears in Breckinridge's eyes. "Put the boys in," said the Kentuckian, "and may God forgive me for the order."

The "boys" went in, and some were no more than boys. The oldest cadet in the battle was 25; the youngest was a bare 28 days past his fifteenth birthday. Bravely they moved into the gap in time to help repulse the Yankee assault. Then, in company with the rest of Breckinridge's line, they swept up the slope in front of them, through mud so sticky it sucked the shoes from their feet, and moved straight toward an enemy battery. In the face of the charge, the whole Federal line retreated so quickly that one gun from that battery was abandoned just as the cadets reached it. The jubilant cadets swarmed all over the fieldpiece,

Above: The Bushong house on the battlefield at New Market. Here was the weak point in Breckinridge's line, and here the V.M.I. cadets went into action, swarming off to the right in the rush to victory.

Below: The Keystone Battery from Pennsylvania. It was against such batteries as this that the disciplined young cadets from the V.M.I. advanced in their legendary battle at New Market.

exulting in their trophy as Breckinridge rode up to them crying, "Well done, Virginians! Well done, men!" Then he immediately took them out of the line again to act as reserve, while his army continued the pursuit of the beaten Sigel.

It was one of the most significant small battles of the war for the Confederacy, and the corps of cadets had played a prominent part in it. Quickly legend would enlarge that part, to the point that it was not a single cannon, but the whole battery that they captured. In time the presence of

several thousand other Confederates would be forgotten as the exploits of this small band of officers-to-be were exaggerated to the point where they and they alone were credited with winning the battle. That they did not, but they held an important post at a crucial time. Breckinridge may indeed have called them "boys" when he ordered them into the line, but after their charge he called them "men".

They suffered like men, too. Five fell dead outright, and five more would soon die of their wounds, while forty-seven others felt the enemy's lead and steel. In all, the corps suffered almost twenty-two percent losses, comparable to many a veteran regiment in a major battle. A week later, when the corps arrived in Richmond to aid in its defense, President Davis himself addressed the cadets and paid tribute to their valor.

Still, the war was not done with the men from V.M.I. In late May the governor assigned them to duty with local defense troops in and around Richmond. Then came word that another raid had struck the Shenandoah, and this time there had been no Breckinridge to turn it back. On June 7 the cadets were ordered back to the Valley to defend Lynchburg, and by the ninth they reached Lexington where, two days later, they took part in the feeble defense of the city against the advancing Federals under Major General David Hunter. Overpowered, the Confederates abandoned Lexington, and Hunter wreaked vengeance for New Market. He burned the barracks at the V.M.I. almost to the ground, so that only its masonry walls still stood.

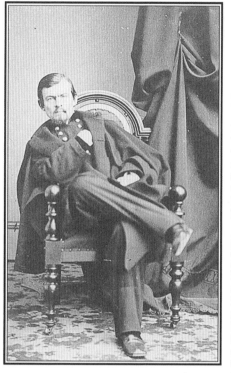

Above: The absolute epitome of a political general, Major General Franz Sigel had not a single attribute of a real leader. He bungled the New Market campaign from first to last, and lost his command.

Their school destroyed, the corps went back to Lynchburg to take post in its defenses, and then late in June returned to the burned-out ruin of their school. Undaunted by war's visitations, there on June 27, 1864, fourteen members of the class of 1864 – all New Market veterans – were graduated while the rest of the cadets were furloughed. Reassembled in October, the corps spent the rest of the war in and around Richmond, where they took temporary quarters for the Institute at the city almshouse. Studies continued until March 1865, when again authorities ordered them out into the field, though they saw no action. On the night of April 2, as Richmond was being evacuated, the Institute's faculty disbanded the corps at the almshouse and sent the boys home.

Yet with incredible resilience, the Virginia Military Institute could not be held down for long. In October of 1865 classes resumed in Lexington, and the work of rebuilding the Institute began. On July 4, 1866, having returned to its traditional graduation day, ten cadets of the class of 1866, all New Market veterans, took their diplomas. As late as 1870, the last of the New Market boys to finish their education at the V.M.I. got their degrees. And on January 16, 1875, by an act of the governing board of the Institute, diplomas were awarded to all remaining New Market cadets who, for whatever reason, had not been able to complete their studies. Many of them had left the corps to take commissions in the Confederate Army.[18]

Just the afternoon of the day of his fatal wounding, Stonewall Jackson had been talking of

the Institute, and his expectation that in the Battle of Chancellorsville, then under way, the influence of his old school would be substantial. "The Virginia Military Institute will be heard from today", he told a friend, and indeed it was. The V.M.I. was heard from on every battlefield of the Army of Northern Virginia, and with many of the other field armies of the Confederacy as well. But for all the generals and colonels and other field officers who would take their training at Lexington with them on those immortal fields, the Institute's place in the Civil War would always be remembered most for what its 258 cadets did at New Market. No class at West Point during the war came even close to the kind of real training by experience as that acquired by the cadets at the V.M.I.[19]

No one was more aware of that than the faculty and students of the Institute itself. In May 1866 the five cadets killed and buried at New Market were brought to the parade ground in front of the burned out barracks for re-burial. Thereafter every year on that site and on the anniversary of the battle, May 15, an affecting ceremony was to take place. Before the assembled corps of cadets, standing at attention, the roll of the corps was called. On that date ten additional names were called with the roll, but those ten, the killed and mortally wounded from New Market, were represented by a living cadet. As the names were called out, the corps and a large audience of civilian onlookers remained hushed.

"Sergeant Cabell."
"Corporal Atwill."
"Private Crockett."
"Private Hartsfield."
"Private Haynes."
"Private Jefferson."
"Private Jones."
"Private McDowell."
"Private Standard."
"Private Wheelwright."

Above: Cadet Private Gaylord B. Clark, Company D, V.M.I. Corps of Cadets. He and over 200 others became to history the "New Market Cadets", and showed that bravery knows no age limits.

Below: The V.M.I. itself paid a terrible price for its contribution to the Confederacy. In 1864 another Yankee raid left the barracks a burnt-out shell, but the spirit of the institution lived on.

With each name called, the designated cadet stepped forward and reported. "Died on the field of honor."[20]

Every year for generations, the corps retraced the march to New Market in May, and on the field of that memorable battle called out the names of the dead, as a living reminder of an era when schoolboys both North and South studied in the shadow of war, a reminder of boys who quickly became men, and who rose through their bravery and devotion to duty to cast a shadow of their own in that great conflict.

References

1 Thomas J. Fleming, *West Point, The Men and Times of the United States Military Academy* (New York, 1969), p.126.
2 *Ibid.*, p.154.
3 *Ibid.*, p.155.
4 *Ibid.*, p.148.
5 Cullum, *Officers*, II, p.513.
6 Fleming, *West Point*, pp.156-7.
7 U.S. War Department, *War of the Rebellion: Official Records of the Union and Confederate Armies* (Washington, 1880-1901), Series III, Volume 1, p.309.
8 *Ibid.*, p.703.
9 Cullum, *Officers*, pp.520-48.
10 *Ibid.*, pp.548-69.
11 *Ibid.*, pp.570-609.
12 War Department, *Official Records*, Series III, Volume 4, pp.213-4, Series III, Volume 5, pp.171-2.
13 War Department, *Official Records*, Series IV, Volume 1, pp.81, 327, 685.
14 Weinert, "Regular Army," p.98.
15 Richard M. McMurry, *Two Great Rebel Armies* (Chapel Hill, N.C., 1989), p.99.
16 *Ibid.*, pp.100-3.
17 William Couper, *The V.M.I. New Market Cadets* (Charlottesville, Va., 1933), p.ix.
18 William C. Davis, *The Battle of New Market* (New York, 1975), pp.122, 147, 195, 197; Couper, *Cadets*, pp.x-xi, 6-7, 254.
19 Douglas S. Freeman, *Lee's Lieutenants* (New York, 1943), II, p.554.
20 Couper, *Cadets*, pp.6-7.

—————— CHAPTER SEVEN ——————

LEADERS AT SEA

While the armies captured most of the attention, the men and ships of the warring navies continued their special kind of conflict on the rivers, harbors and oceans. It was a tale of blockade and boredom, relieved by the occasional battle between the smoke-belching ironclads, or the depredations of the dashing commerce raiders like the Rebel Alabama.

THERE HAS always been a forgotten Civil War, a realm of endeavor in which the services of officers and men are little known and more often ignored. Perhaps it should not be much of a surprise, considering that the role of the navies, North and South alike, was very much a passive one through the bulk of the conflict. Only one or two so-called "fleet" engagements occurred in the entire war, all on the Mississippi River, and there were only a handful of individual ship-to-ship combats. Most of the hostile actions of Union and Confederate warships were against unarmed merchantmen or blockade runners. Certainly the blockade of the Southern coastline made a significant contribution to eventual Rebel defeat, just as the activities of Confederate commerce raiders on the high seas distracted enemy vessels from the blockade while Rebel gunboats on the rivers and harbors of the South helped impede the advance of Lincoln's armies. Nevertheless, this was a war fought and won and lost primarily on the land. As a result, even in their own time, the men who led the navies of North and South found themselves often ignored or forgotten. To posterity and history they are, for the most part, all but lost.

Certainly when the war clouds formed in December 1860, those men were as much in the minds of the political leaders as the officers of the Old Army. There was as yet no Confederate navy, and that of the United States looked even more pitifully small and scattered than its military. When South Carolina seceded in December, President-elect Abraham Lincoln could look to a mere forty-two vessels actually in commission, only twelve of which made up the Home Squadron in American waters. Worse still, of these twelve, only a scant four were berthed in secure Northern ports. Only 7,600 men of all ranks made up the rolls, and of their number, 1,554 were commissioned officers.[1]

Even as a few warships began to return to home ports with the rising of the crisis, the Navy felt the same strains of loyalty that tore apart the Old Army. There were naval bases all around the South, from Norfolk, Virginia, with its vital navy yard, down the Atlantic coast to Key West, and along the Gulf of Mexico at Mobile, Alabama, Pensacola, Florida, and elsewhere. The security of all, when and if war came, would depend upon the loyalty of the officers in command, and of those loyalties the government in Washington could not be entirely sanguine.

While not as popular a vocation as the military, still the naval service enjoyed considerable prestige in the old South, and a sizeable proportion of those 1,554 serving officers when secession commenced were natives of the seceding states. Which way they would "jump", as Beauregard had put it, became a primary concern of the Navy Department in Washington. It needed these trained and experienced men to command its ships; at the same time it recognized that, as with the army, the U.S. Navy would be regarded as a prime resource of officers for any new Confederate navy that might emerge.

Just as the strains on loyalties and oaths taken severely demoralized the Old Army, so it very quickly began to break down the naval officer corps. In January 1861, Captain Samuel F.I. DuPont wrote of being "sick at heart" as he witnessed the scene in Washington. He was "astounded to see the extent of the demoralization, not only in every department of the government, but among the officers of the Navy."[2] Already the resignations were coming in at an alarming pace. In the month of December 1860 eleven resignations arrived, almost all lieutenants and midshipmen, and all but four from the just seceded state of South Carolina. Nine of that eleven would later take commissions in the future Confederate Navy. As more states voted to leave the Union, that initial trickle became a seeming flood. In January 1861 another forty resigned. Twenty left in February, and another thirty-seven in March. With April, the firing on Fort Sumter, the secession of Virginia, and the certain outbreak of war, 114 officers left the service, followed by another 120 in the next three months. All told, by the end of 1861 at least 373 naval officers gave up their commissions.[3]

The decision whether to go or to stay in the old service proved to be every bit as hard for the old Navy men as for their brothers in the Army. Promotion had been even slower in the old Navy, and many an ambitious young officer of Southern blood or sympathy might look for speedy advancement to the new Confederacy. That very December 1860, as the news of the secession of South Carolina reached Washington, forty-

---

The war at sea created the need for some highly specialized fighting ships. The proud commander of the mortar schooner U.S.S. *Para*, surrounded by its crew, poses on the base of its main armament.

seven-year-old Lieutenant David D. Porter of Pennsylvania first heard it from the wife of a prominent Southern politician. "We will have a glorious monarchy," she declared of the expected Southern nation, "and you must join us!" Teasingly, Porter mused that such treason might earn him a title like "Duke of Benedict Arnold". But the lady was serious. "Nonsense," she answered, "but we will make you an admiral."[4]

Porter, having no sympathy with the South or its cause, was not tempted, but certainly others were. Even his own stepbrother, Captain David G. Farragut, felt to some degree the conflicting tugs of nativity versus loyalty. Farragut had been born in Tennessee, yet lived much of his life in Virginia and married a woman from the Old Dominion. Politically conservative, he had near relatives living in the Deep South and almost all of his in-laws were Southern sympathizers by birth and inclination. But he had also spent nearly fifty years in the old Navy. He honored its traditions and had participated in some of the stirring events that had become those traditions. In the end, though suspected of being pro-Confederate both North and South, and even in his own Navy Department in Washington, he emphatically took his stand with his uniform.[5] In time he would become the Union's premier seaman, and its first admiral.

But there were others who could not stay. Indeed, Lieutenant J. R. Hamilton of South Carolina was the very first to submit his resignation, doing so on December 1, 1860, even before his own state seceded. His very next act was to publish in several newspapers a call to other officers of Southern birth to resign. Going even further, he suggested that officers commanding vessels should bring their ships to Southern ports and surrender them to local secessionist authorities. A few weeks later, Captain V.M. Randolph of Alabama, a man with nearly fifty years of service,

Above: The typical midshipman at the United States Naval Academy in 1861 was a jaunty lad of less than twenty, his head crammed with navigation and theoretical seamanship, and looking forward to putting it all to use.

Below: The operating center of all Union sea operations was the Navy Department here in Washington, D.C. Every officer in the service received his assignments, promotions, pay, and subsistence from its administrators.

showed up at the Pensacola Navy Yard in command of a band of secessionists and forced its surrender. He had only submitted his resignation two days before, and since it had not yet been accepted by the Navy Department, he was still a commissioned United States officer when he took arms against his service.[6]

In the end, the old Navy would find itself particularly hard hit exactly where it hurt the most, among the younger mid-level officers who would be expected to take the bulk of the warship commands in the coming war. While there were 93 serving captains – then the Navy's highest rank – only 15 eventually left, and of them twelve joined the Confederate Navy. Certainly they were missed, but most were elderly, and several too feeble ever to take shipboard commands. From the next level, however, 34 out of 127 commanders resigned, 29 of them taking Rebel commissions. Even worse, out of the 351 lieutenants then serving, 89 departed. Of the 123 commanders and lieutenants who turned in their commissions, only 15 did not don the Confederate gray, and it was those who did that formed the overwhelming majority of those who would one day command their own ships in service of the South. For the Union, which would commission hundreds of ships before war's end, the loss of this pool of potential captains was the biggest blow of all.[7]

Among those who left were some of the finest talents of the old Navy. Matthew F. Maury had achieved international reputation as an oceanographer. Franklin Buchanan, after years of distinguished service, was commanding the Washington Navy Yard. Commander Raphael Semmes, though 52, was one of the brighter lights in the Navy's constellation. All went south with their states. With them went a host of others who would win fame in the years ahead: Catesby ap R. Jones, John N. Maffitt, John Taylor

Lieutenant U.S.N. and First Lieutenant U.S. Marine Corps

Officers of the Union Navy looked very smart indeed in their crisp blue uniforms. The lieutenant at left wears the optional white trousers with his dark blue tunic, capped with a white service hat. As was common among the lower officer ranks, his insignia matched — unfortunately for him, as slow as promotion was for the Navy in the Civil War, these are probably the same insignia he will be wearing at war's end.

His friend at right, a lieutenant of Marines, shows the considerable similarities between Marine and Army uniforms. The differences exist chiefly in the insignia and in the gold lace around the collar. With as few positions as there were in the Marine Corps, opportunities for advancement for this officer will be even more scarce than for the naval lieutenant on the left.

Few of these officers will stay in the service after the war's close.

Wood, John McI. Kell, and more. Had they remained in the old Navy, their services to the Union would have proved invaluable.

Unfortunately for Lincoln, much of the damage had already been done before he even entered office, and before his new Secretary of the Navy, Gideon Welles, could do anything about the flow of officers out of the service. When Welles did take office, he was shocked. "I found great demoralization and defection among the officers," he wrote. "It was difficult to ascertain who could and who were not to be trusted." Worse than that, he saw many good officers still undecided who were being assiduously courted by secessionist friends. As a result, Welles remained suspicious even of staunchly loyal men like Porter and Farragut for some time after all doubt of their position had disappeared.

Warnings constantly came to Welles – many anonymously – questioning the loyalty of this officer or that. Then, when the firing on Fort Sumter accelerated the rate of resignations, he finally took positive action. Prior to that time, the Navy Department had routinely accepted resignations without comment or castigation. After Sumter, however, almost every officer ranked lieutenant or above who submitted his resignation did not have it accepted. Instead, the Navy Department formally dismissed him, a treatment that carried with it an ages-old stigma to any career navy man. In short, while the department could not prevent a resignation, it could make it as painful as possible to do so. Further, Welles virtually forced the resignations and dismissals of many, by requiring that all naval officers take an oath of allegiance, just as the army had done. Those who could not in conscience take that oath had little choice but to leave the service.[8]

Above: For most new naval officers, active service began with a trip to the Washington Navy Yard, either to receive assignments, or actually to board their new posting. All war long these wharfs teemed with warships.

Below: The South's naval facilities all had to be captured, like the Pensacola Navy Yard in Florida. Captured with it was the steamer U.S.S. *Fulton*, an unfinished vessel which would be vital to the Confederates.

Only in the last month of 1861 did the bloodletting in the officer corps come to an end with the resignation and dismissal of five lieutenants and one assistant surgeon. Apparently the last resignation as a result of Southern sympathy was that of Assistant Surgeon James W. Herty of Georgia, who submitted his resignation on December 12, 1861, and two months later took a Confederate commission in its place. His act brought to an end the most divisive and painful upheaval in the history of the United States Navy.[9]

For those who stayed loyal to the Union, a huge task remained ahead of them. From its pitiful beginnings in 1861, the Union Navy would grow by the end of the war to include 51,500 men and officers and nearly 700 ships of all classes. Just the civilian employees maintained by the Navy Department in 1865 equalled more than double the entire 1861 manpower of the whole Navy. Lincoln's ships would ply every navigable river on the continent, and every ocean of the world. All of this required a degree of organization previously unthought of, as well as a host of officers to make it all work.[10]

Welles stood at the top of the organization. A Connecticut newspaperman with no prior naval experience, Welles proved to be an able administrator. With fourteen clerks and messengers, he oversaw the work of his office and of four suboffices, those of the Assistant Secretary of the Navy, a Solicitor and Naval Judge Advocate

General, a Commissioner of the Naval Code – essentially a codifier of naval law – and an Office of Naval Records and Library.

Of far more importance to the men out on ships and shore stations, however, were the thirteen bureaus in the department that directly influenced the lives and careers of naval officers. The Bureau of Construction, Equipment, and Repairs did exactly what its title implied until July 1862 when it was broken up into several smaller bureaus for greater efficiency. One of those was the Bureau of Construction and Repair, another the Bureau of Steam Engineering, and a third the Bureau of Equipment and Recruiting. A Bureau of Medicine and Surgery did as its name would suggest, and was the only bureau not commanded by an officer of commander's rank or higher, being led instead by surgeons.

The Bureau of Navigation oversaw five suboffices, partly scientific and partly catch-all, including the Naval Observatory, the Naval Almanac Office, the Chaplain Corps, and the Naval Academy. Its most conspicuous operation was the Office of Detail, which oversaw the assignment of officers to their posts. All naval cannon were handled by the Bureau of Ordnance, and another bureau dealt with Provisions and Clothing. The technology of the age mandated the creation of the Bureau of Steam Engineering, and the developments of the Civil War itself led directly to the establishment of the Office of the General Superintendent of Ironclads, which oversaw construction of all of the behemoth warships built, except for a few serving on the Mississippi that were laid down by the separate Office of the Superintendent of Ironclad Gunboats.

Finally there were other bureaus to administer, such as those of Yards and Docks, Naval Boards

Above: One of the Rebels' first successes was against Rear Admiral Hiram Paulding, who in April 1861 was forced to surrender Norfolk Navy Yard together with its tons of equipment and ordnance.

Below: The officers of the Bureau of Steam Engineering, one of the new departments dictated by the "new" Navy. Chief Engineer B.F. Isherwood sits at center, surrounded by his staff and civilian clerks.

and Commissions, and the Marine Corps, which was then, as later, a part of the Navy. The men in charge of all these several bureaus varied widely in rank and service. Yards and Docks was commanded by Rear Admiral Joseph Smith, a veteran of decades of service. Commanders of the Bureau of Ordnance included two captains, a commodore, and a rear admiral. Thus it went throughout these branches of the Navy Department, though in general its department heads were not quite as superannuated as those in the War Department at the beginning of the war.[11]

Of course, the Navy's real front line was comprised of those officers and men on squadron and station duty. As with the Army, the naval forces of the Union were organized geographically, though instead of departments and divisions, Lincoln's seamen served in squadrons and flotillas. As a general rule, the squadrons patrolled the coastlines and high seas, enforcing the blockade, while the flotillas operated on the rivers, chiefly in cooperation with the army in joint operations. The first of the squadrons was the Atlantic Blockading Squadron, covering the Atlantic coast from Virginia to Florida. In September 1861, however, in response to the increased activity on this line, it was divided into North Atlantic and South Atlantic Blockading Squadrons. Similarly, the whole line of the Gulf of Mexico was originally the assignment of the Gulf Blockading Squadron,

but soon that too was divided, into East Gulf and West Gulf squadrons. Out on the broader oceans, the West India Squadron patrolled the West Indies protecting Yankee commerce from raiders. The Pacific Squadron, the African Squadron, ships in the Mediterranean and off South America and elsewhere, all did similar duty. Of the flotillas, these were more informal, including the Potomac and James River Flotillas. Unlike the actual geographical squadrons, which remained permanent throughout the war, the flotillas sometimes came and disappeared according to need and circumstance. What started as a Mississippi flotilla came in time to be designated the Mississippi River Squadron.[12]

Union Naval Officers' Uniforms and Equipment

1 Blue wool frock coat of Asst. Engineer William A. Dripps
2 White Linen sack coat of Asst. Surgeon Jacob Solis-Cohen
3 Solis-Cohen's wool vest
4 Solis-Cohen's wool frock coat
5 Solis-Cohen's rubberized foul-weather leggings
6 Solis-Cohen's canvas sea bag
7 Monocular glass

8 Naval ordnance instructions manual of Lt. Eli D. Edmunds
9 Model 1852 naval officer's sword of Asst. Engineer George W. Melville
10 Sword belt and plate of Asst. Paymaster George A. Lyon
11 Solis-Cohen's wool vest
12 Octant – a navigational instrument
13 Shoulder straps of a First

Asst. Engineer
14 Non-regulation naval officer's sword
15 Folding scalpel from *16*
16 Solis-Cohen's medical case
17 Oil cloth foul weather leggings of Asst. Surgeon Solis-Cohen
18 Naval medal for service on the U.S.S. *Brooklyn*
19 Regulation Model 1841 Eaglehead naval officer's sword

Artifacts courtesy of: The Civil War Library and Museum, Philadelphia, Pa: 1-6, 8-11, 13, 15-18; William Le Pard Collection: 14, 9; Mort Sork Collection: 7, 12

To an Old Army man, the number of commissioned officers serving at all these posts would have been bewildering. Indeed, in the Navy a far greater number of positions were treated as commissioned ranks than in the military. About one man in every twenty held a commission in the land forces. In the Navy that could be one man in every six. The Army recognized eight gradations of rank from second lieutenant up to major general (excluding the single instance of Grant's lieutenant generalcy). By contrast, the Navy countenanced eight commissioned grades within itself, and an additional six in the Marines. Unlike the land forces, officers in the webfoot service often had very specialized tasks. Instead of being expected to lead a company into battle, many naval officers supervised only a few seamen specialists in particular functions such as operating a steam engine, maintaining sails and rigging, or deck gunnery.

The highest rank at the time of the outbreak of the war was rear admiral, most of them elderly men with forty years or more of service. Just below them came captains, then commanders, then lieutenant commanders, and then lieutenants. Surgeons, passed assistant surgeons, and assistant surgeons came next, followed by paymasters, masters in line of promotion, chaplains, engineers, and professors of mathematics, all of whom were either masters or ensigns. Then came midshipmen and acting midshipmen. The Marine Corps ran the same ratings as the Army, from second lieutenant up to the commandant, a colonel. The degree of specialization is evident.

Just as bewildering to an army man would be figuring out a naval officer's rank by looking at his insignia. They wore both shoulder strap and sleeve markings on their dark blue uniform coats. A rear admiral showed eight gold stripes circling each cuff, with a star above the topmost stripe, and two stars on his shoulder strap, showing him the equivalent in rank to a major general. When the Civil War began, there was no official rank of commodore, it having been simply used as an honorary title for any officer of whatever rank commanding a flotilla of ships. But in 1862 it was recognized as a fixed rank immediately below that of rear admiral, to be recognized by seven cuff stripes and a single star on the shoulder. The captain wore six stripes and a silver spread eagle on his shoulder strap. Each of the succeeding ranks wore successively one sleeve stripe fewer, and the correspondingly lower shoulder insignia the same as that of equivalent army officers, right down to the level of the ensign, whose one stripe and shoulder strap showed him to be the equal in

Above: Men and officers of the tiny United States Marine Corps stand at attention in the grounds of the Washington Navy Yard in April 1864. Unsung, and largely unused in this war, their glory had to wait for later conflicts.

Below: Rear Admiral Silas H. Stringham wears the two stars of his rank on his shoulder straps, but only six stripes on his cuffs – a good example of the informality observed in uniform regulations.

Above: Officers in the Confederate Navy had to face the challenge of mastering whole new classes of vessels like the ironclad C.S.S. *Atlanta*. Worse, those ships often barely functioned adequately.

Below: Yankee officers fared far better, thanks to well-built and maintained vessels like the U.S.S. *Maratanza*, shown here on July 4, 1862, in the James River, her protective stern bulwarks down to show her aft guns.

The men wearing those uniforms and insignia were in a very large measure amateurs so far as naval service went. Of the 1,554 commissioned officers in uniform in December 1860, 353 had left the service either by resignation or dismissal. That left just 1,181. Eliminating the petty officers and midshipmen, that left only 876, including chaplains and paymasters, and other staff officers not really trained or in line to take line commands.[14] And of those remaining, many were under suspicion for, while 373 men, mostly Southerners, had resigned or been dismissed, another 350 of Southern birth had chosen to remain in the Navy. In the higher ranks, from lieutenant upward, from which vessel commanders could be expected to come, Southerners in the old Navy split almost man for man, 126 leaving while 127 stayed.[15]

What this meant was that every commissioned line officer who was loyal would be needed, and promoted midshipmen and Naval Academy graduates would have to fill the places of those lost in the war. The Navy could ill afford to waste a trained or experienced commander on staff duty. As a result, a host of civilians would be commissioned into the Navy as ensigns and masters to fill those posts as paymasters, chaplains, and surgeons of all grades. Such men, like their counterparts in the military, were volunteers as opposed to regular Navy. Their commissions were to be for the term of the war only. One of them, William Keeler of La Salle, Illinois, had been a watchmaker, a steam engine manufacturer, and a tea wholesaler before the war. Thanks to the good offices of a Congressman, Keeler obtained from the Navy an appointment as paymaster with the rank of lieutenant late in 1861, and was off to serve aboard the ironclad *Monitor*. Keeler knew absolutely nothing of naval ways or life, nor was he expected to. He even thought at first that he would not to have to wear a uniform, but was soon told otherwise.

Just as the Navy was strange to these volunteer officers, so were they an oddity to the old regular men. "We don't get a great many sailors from the prairies," an old commodore told Keeler. For his part, Keeler was pleased with what he found in his fellow officers. "There appeared to be more real earnestness of purpose & less of that swagger & bluster & rowdyism about them than among many of the land officers I have met with," he wrote. As for the new Navy suit he was required to wear, "I felt awkward enough at first in mine, . . . but I am getting used to it now," he wrote. "Bright handsome uniforms are so common here that scarcely any notice is taken of them."[16]

status to the Army's own lowly second lieutenant.

The remainder of the men such as gunners, boatswains and the like, were so-called petty officers, the equivalent to non-commissioned officers such as sergeants in the military. As such, they were not technically officers, and it is just as well, for the confusion was bad enough already. Furthermore, all of the officers in line positions wore a silver foul-anchor either in the center or at each end of their shoulder straps. Staff officers – the paymasters, engineers, etc – wore special insignia indicating their function instead of foul-

anchors. Paymasters wore an oak-sprig, engineers wore a cross made of oak leaves, chaplains a silver cross, professors an oak leaf and an acorn, and surgeons nothing at all. Midshipmen wore shoulder-knots in lieu of straps.[13]

All such insignia were honored for the most part, though officers showed just about as much individuality in their adherence as did their brethren in the Army. Especially confusing would be the sleeve stripes, for their width varied greatly according to the whim of the wearer, and often sleeve ornamentation lagged behind the rank displayed on the shoulder.

The same was not necessarily the case across the lines in the Confederacy. There the sight of men in naval uniform would always be an oddity, only because there were so few officers in the first place, and because uniforms were even more scarce in the second. Of course, when the secession crisis began, there was no Confederacy and no Southern navy. Instead, for a brief time, each of the seceding states that had coastlines and ports had its own state navy. Three days after the inauguration of Jefferson Davis, on February 21, 1861, the new Congress in Montgomery, Alabama, passed an "act to establish the Navy Department," and authorized Davis to appoint a Secretary of the Navy. His choice was Stephen R. Mallory of Florida, a lawyer and former United States Senator who, like his Federal counterpart Welles, had little experience of naval matters other than his chairmanship of the Naval Affairs Committee in the old Senate. Yet he proved to be one of Davis' most fortuitous choices as a cabinet minister, and at once he set about organizing his department along lines very similar to that of the United States Navy.[17]

Instead of bureaus, Mallory's department subdivisions were called "offices", and in the end he set up four basic departments: Orders and Detail, Ordnance and Hydrography, Provisions and Clothing, and Medicine and Surgery. Each was headed by a resigned U.S. Navy officer, the first two by captains. Their functions are self-evident. Orders and Detail performed exactly the same duties as the Office of Detail in Welles' navy. Ordnance and Hydrography handled cannon, the construction and placement of "torpedoes", or underwater mines, the collection of navigational information, and for the want of anywhere else to place it, the supervision of the Confederate Naval Academy. Provisions and Clothing dealt with uniforms, provisions and stores, and pay, while Medicine and Surgery oversaw the appointment and assignment of ships' doctors and the acquisition of supplies. Additionally, and in response to the need for the Confederacy to build its own ships, Mallory later created an office for a Chief

Confederate Naval Officers' Uniforms and Equipment

1 Midshipman's cap
2 Signal flag
3 Frock coat of Lt. R. Dabney Minor
4 Officer's belt plate
5 Midshipman's holster
6 Adams revolver for 5
7 Presentation sword of Capt. J. Tattnall, U.S.N.
8 Sword case for 7, belonging to Tattnall
9 Captain's sword
10 Captain's sword
11 Scabbard for 10

12 As 6
13 As 5
14 Lt. Minor's vest
15 Hailing trumpet
16 Frock coat
17 Cap of Raphael Semmes
18 Sword belt of master's mate of C.S.S. *Shenandoah*
19 Signal flag
20 Epaulettes of Commodore Forrest
21 Semmes' fieldglass

22 Naval cap
23 Minor's uniform jacket
24 Uniform frock coat
25 Sword from C.S.S. *Alabama*
26 Master's mate's sword
27 Forrest's sword
28 Log board
29 Compass
30 Minor's field glasses
31 Captain's insignia
32 Semmes' holster
33 Semmes' revolver
34 Clothes bag

Artifacts courtesy of: The Museum of the Confederacy, Richmond, Va: 1-3, 5-23, 25-30;
Virginia Historical Society, Richmond, Va: 4, 24, 31.

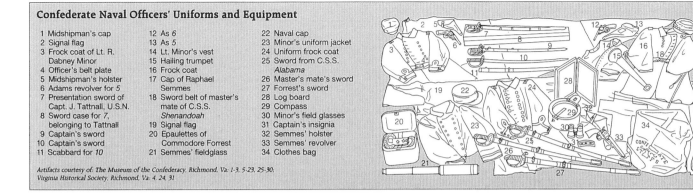

Constructor and of an Engineer in Chief to acquire machinery. Finally, the fledgling Marine Corps was also placed under Mallory's control. Further, in response to the crying need for warships, Mallory was also authorized to maintain naval representation in Europe, where his agents could purchase ships.[18]

Like Welles, Mallory divided his new navy into geographical commands, calling them squadrons. There would eventually be squadrons assigned to the James River in Virginia, a North Carolina Squadron, a Charleston Squadron, a Savannah River Squadron, Mobile, Mississippi River, Galveston, and Red River Squadrons, and several informal lesser commands of no permanence. Since commerce raiders on the high seas operated almost entirely independently, they had no specific designation as commands, roaming where they chose in search of Yankee shipping. The squadrons, meanwhile, had the task of protecting rivers and harbors, and of breaking the blockade when possible. In almost every case, a captain commanded a squadron.[19]

The subject of officers arrived on Mallory's desk as soon as he took office. On March 16, 1861, Congress authorized him to appoint four captains, four commodores, thirty lieutenants, ten surgeons and assistant surgeons, six paymasters, and two chief engineers. Very quickly, however, it became evident that there would be a greater need for officers, and a greater supply thanks to

resignations from the Union Navy. Many, of course, were too old to be useful on the line. "A number of old officers, past service, disdaining to eat the bread of ignoble pensioners upon the bounty of the United States," wrote Captain Raphael Semmes, "came South, bringing with them nothing but their patriotism and their gray hairs." However much they might have been useful in a fully staffed and equipped modern navy, these old gentlemen were for the most part unsuited to the sort of hardship and improvisation that Confederate service would require.[20]

Mallory dealt with the problem by creating two navies, as did the Union. The Regular Confederate Navy accepted all resigned U.S. officers at equivalent rank and gave them assignments, most of the older officers becoming Office heads. Then in May 1863 Congress established the Provisional Navy, and Mallory then selected from the Regular Navy list those younger and more vigorous officers for active commands, at the same time being able to give them increased rank in the Provisional list. In effect, the Regular Confederate Navy became, as Semmes called it, "a kind of retired list."[21]

Below: Officers and men of the U.S.S. *Agawam* on the James River, shared a small deck and below-decks area, and had to get along in tight quarters smoothly and without controversy.

Above: The war was a family business for some. Lieutenant Commander Richard W. Meade, Jr., was the nephew of Army of the Potomac commander Major General George G. Meade.

Above: Captain French Forrest shows that observance of uniform regulations was just as haphazard in the Confederate service. He wears a flag officer's four gold cuff stripes, but a captain's three shoulder stars.

In the end, well over a thousand men served the Confederate Navy as officers, though there were never more on duty at a single time than in April 1864, when the rolls listed 727 active officers and twenty-six others shown absent from duty. All told, perhaps 500 vessels of all description flew the Rebel flag during the war, but only a few dozen were really major ships requiring a full complement of ship's officers. Most were converted ferry boats and river steamers, of small size, with small crews, and as a result, there were always more senior grade officers than there were commands.[22]

The order of rankings in the Confederate Navy for officers very closely paralleled that of the old U.S. Navy, and officers moved up, if at all, very slowly, and only through the death, resignation or dismissal of superior officers. The number of positions at each grade was set by act of Congress, and the maximum of 798 of all grades above petty officers was set in April 1862. Not all of those posts would be filled, however. Congress authorized four admirals, for instance, yet only one, Franklin Buchanan, was ever so appointed. Of ten captains authorized, nine were appointed, and only one of them had resigned as a captain from the U.S. Navy. Confederate regulations did not allow for commodores, but an honorary rank of flag officer filled the same purpose for men commanding fleets or squadrons. Below the captains came the commanders, then the lieutenants, and unlike the Federal service they were broken down into first and second lieutenants. There was no lieutenant commander nor were there to be ensigns, but there were the same masters, engineers, surgeons, paymasters as in the Yankee service.[23]

Regulations called for all these officers to wear steel gray uniforms with rank indicated by shoulder straps and sleeve stripes, cap insignia, and buttons on the front of the frock coat. Since the rank of admiral was created after the clothing regulations were set, and since they were not later amended, there was no specification for an admiral, but presumably it would have been the same as that of a flag officer, with four gold stars on the shoulder and on the front of the cap, and four gold stripes on the cuff, the topmost having a loop. Two rows of nine buttons ran down the front of the coat. A captain wore the same coat, except that there were three stripes on the cuff, the top one looped, and three stars on cap and shoulder strap. A commander wore two stripes of gold lace and two stars on cap and shoulder, and a lieutenant one stripe together with one star. A master wore a stripe of lace with no loop and no

Below: Though most blockade runners were civilian owned and operated, they frequently carried Confederate officers, and some were actually fitted out and operated by the Rebels. The *Giraffe* fitting out at Glasgow.

stars, while a passed midshipman had no stripe at all but three buttons on his cuff and his shoulder strap consisted of a strip of gold lace, while a foul-anchor adorned his cap.

Among the staff ranks the officers wore the same uniform as a master, excepting only that a single stripe of varying widths or else cuff buttons denoted rank of surgeons, paymasters and the like. Surgeons wore black straps with olive sprigs, and so did paymasters except that their straps were green. Engineers wore dark blue straps with oak sprigs denoting rank. Surgeons' caps showed wreaths of olive leaves or stars, depending upon length of service and rank, while paymasters wore exactly the same cap insignia.

Engineers, however, had the letter "E" embroidered on their caps.[24]

Since the Confederacy always had more officers than ships and postings, there was never a shortage of manpower. Of the 798 officers authorized, 281 could be drawn from the resigned U.S. officers who enlisted with the Confederacy. While several of the latter would be on the Regular rolls, and therefore essentially inactive, still it is evident that Mallory had fewer than 500 appointments to make, and the majority of these would be of midshipmen attending the Naval Academy, and therefore not on line duty. For the rest, there was never really a need for an active recruiting effort, as able civilians were brought into

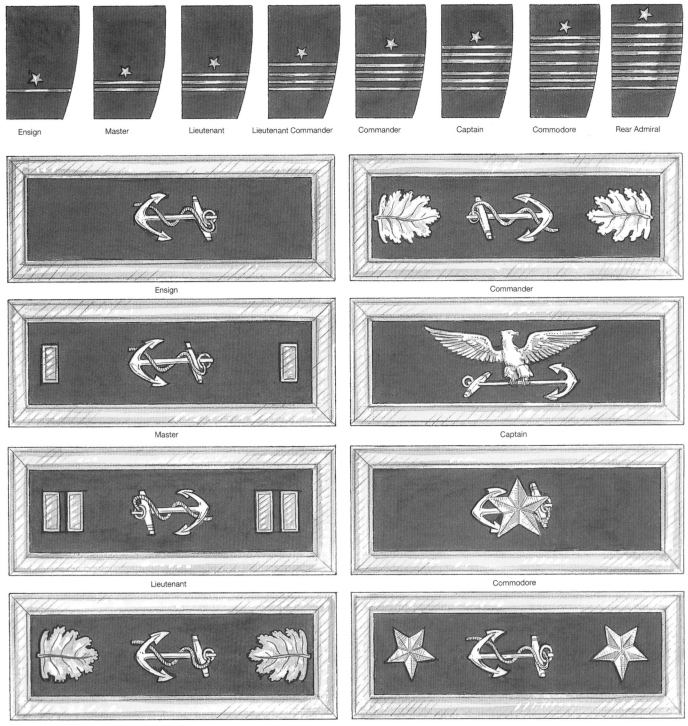

Ensign   Master   Lieutenant   Lieutenant Commander   Commander   Captain   Commodore   Rear Admiral

Ensign

Master

Lieutenant

Lieutenant Commander

Commander

Captain

Commodore

Rear Admiral

Confederate Naval Officers' Insignia

As with their Army insignia, Confederates deliberately designed naval insignia that would be different from that of the old Union. Their shoulder straps particularly made their insignia more in keeping with that of officers of comparable rank in the Confederate Army. The most unusual feature was the creation of a regulation ranking of flag officer, traditionally an honorary position. The Navy also mandated four admirals, though only one was ever appointed, and no insignia for that rank was ever officially prescribed, so we must assume that he wore flag officer insignia. The cuff stripes were a lot simpler and easier to identify than in the Union Navy, while the addition of insignia of rank to the cap gave an added recognition point. Again, as with Union officers, Confederates often observed regulations more in the breach than otherwise. In such a small service, any rank was precious.

the service as and when they were required.

The Confederate Marine Corps, like its Yankee counterpart, never really amounted to much, since there was little need for them. The role of marines in most instances was to help with boarding enemy vessels in battle, but no such action ever took place in the Civil War. Otherwise, they did guard duty, or were detailed to help work guns in battle, or else went ashore on raids and cutting out expeditions. Gideon Welles' U.S. Marines numbered a mere sixty-three officers in December 1860, and twenty of them resigned. All but one became Confederate Marine Corps officers, while the entire complement of Rebel officers in that branch was a mere thirty-three in 1864. Neither service, North or South, grew significantly during the war, and both remain almost totally forgotten.[25]

The only source for replenishing trained officers lost due to battle or resignation were the naval academies. The United States Naval Academy had been established in 1845 at Annapolis, Maryland, and there it continued until May 1861, when the tenuous state of Maryland politics made a move judicious. That month the Navy Department moved the Academy to Fort Adams near Newport, Rhode Island. Five months later it moved again to quarters in the Atlantic House, a hotel, and there it remained until after the close of the war. All of their books, instruments, and

Passed Midshipman

Master

Lieutenant

Commander

Captain

Flag Officer

Passed Midshipman

Master

Lieutenant

Commander

Captain

Flag Officer

Passed Midshipman

Master

Lieutenant

Commander

Captain

Flag Officer

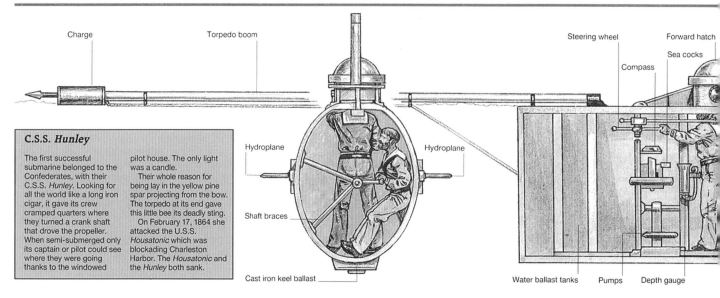

C.S.S. Hunley

The first successful submarine belonged to the Confederates, with their C.S.S. *Hunley*. Looking for all the world like a long iron cigar, it gave its crew cramped quarters where they turned a crank shaft that drove the propeller. When semi-submerged only its captain or pilot could see where they were going thanks to the windowed pilot house. The only light was a candle.

Their whole reason for being lay in the yellow pine spar projecting from the bow. The torpedo at its end gave this little bee its deadly sting.

On February 17, 1864 she attacked the U.S.S. *Housatonic* which was blockading Charleston Harbor. The *Housatonic* and the *Hunley* both sank.

Labels: Charge · Torpedo boom · Steering wheel · Forward hatch · Sea cocks · Compass · Hydroplane · Hydroplane · Shaft braces · Cast iron keel ballast · Water ballast tanks · Pumps · Depth gauge

---

other articles of learning went with them. Upper classmen lived in the Atlantic House, but the first and second year boys had to live aboard the schoolships *Santee* and *Constitution*, anchored off Goat Island. Meanwhile, the Academy's Annapolis grounds were taken over by the Army for the defense of Maryland.[26]

When the outbreak of war came and there was an initial need for more officers to replace those who had resigned, the class scheduled for graduation in 1862 was detached from the Academy for special duty. They never returned and were never graduated, though always thereafter treated as graduates just the same. Those who stayed behind at the Academy studied seamanship, naval construction, tactics, practice exercises, signals, swimming, gymnastics, ordnance and gunnery of both field and naval variety, fencing, algebra, geometry, trigonometry and calculus, steam engineering, astronomy, navigation, surveying, physics and chemistry, mechanics and applied mathematics, English literature, history and law, French and Spanish language, drawing, and chart-making. It was, to say the least, a rigorous program of study. Commodore George S. Blake served as superintendent throughout the war, assisted by a naval and civilian staff and faculty of about 90. The student body itself, like that of West Point, was governed by the Congressionally mandated limit of one cadet per year to be appointed by each senator and congressman, plus ten appointments at large and one

Below: A serious-faced group of midshipmen from the Naval Academy pose in Boston, no doubt uncertain of their service or fate in the war that had come just in time to allow them to show if they had learned their lessons.

from the District of Columbia, all at the discretion of the president.[27] Because of the rigid system of promotion through vacancy only, none of the graduates of the wartime classes had an opportunity to achieve much in the way of distinction, and few even rose above their graduated rank of passed midshipmen by 1865.

The case was a little different to the south. On March 16, 1861, President Davis was authorized to appoint midshipmen, and a month later the limit was set at 106. By 1865 that limit had risen to 150, though through the course of the war a total of nearly 200 young men were so appointed. Many failed to pass the courses, or else left to join the army, accounting for the attrition. However, it was not until later in December 1861 that Congress mandated "some form of education" for midshipmen. The following spring, Congress provided for the appointment of midshipmen

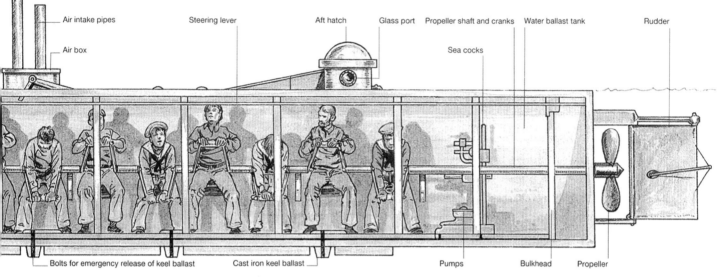

Air intake pipes — Steering lever — Aft hatch — Glass port — Propeller shaft and cranks — Water ballast tank — Rudder

Air box — Sea cocks

Bolts for emergency release of keel ballast — Cast iron keel ballast — Pumps — Bulkhead — Propeller

cadets by representatives and senators, as well as the president, and in May 1862, with no funds or location for a permanent Academy campus, the ship C.S.S. *Patrick Henry* was officially designated as the Confederate Naval Academy. To superintend the new school, Mallory selected Lieutenant William H. Parker, and ordered that the schoolship be moored off Drewry's Bluff on the James River. There the boys could study, while at the same time manning the ship – which was a fully operational sidewheel steamer – in the defense of the James.[28]

At once it became evident that the schoolship was not sufficient to house all the appointees. Extra cabins were constructed ashore at Drewry's Bluff, and alterations were made to the *Patrick Henry* – called simply *Patrick* by the boys – to accommodate more midshipmen. Still only about half of the 106 appointed cadets could live aboard

the ship. As a result, Mallory began to rotate the young men, those on the *Patrick* alternating from time to time with others stationed ashore or out at sea. The boys had to be at least 14 years of age but not more than 18, and were made to pass examinations in reading, writing, spelling, and math. Once admitted as midshipmen cadets, they had to study under the tutelage of the officers commanding their ships or shore stations until the *Patrick* was ready to receive them. In fact, with alterations and other kinds of delays, actual classes aboard the ship did not commence until October 12, 1863.[29]

Below: A few officers served aboard the really powerful prestige ships, like the USS *Wabash*. Several of her officers pose around her 200-pounder rifled forward pivot gun near Charleston in 1863.

The studies of each of the four classes were clearly prescribed, and were essentially the same as the program at the United States Naval Academy, only with the addition of political science. The boys met in two recitation rooms for their classes, working at blackboards with their math problems, or stepping outside for gunnery or small boat drill on the rifled and smooth-bore cannon on deck. They could also engage in sail drill and engine work, or go ashore and practise infantry tactics. "Hard study is the order of the day," Midshipman Hubbard T. Minor confided to his diary. The boys were awakened at 7 a.m., with breakfast an hour later, and then studies until 2 p.m. After a lunch, the boys spent the rest of the day drilling or studying practical applications of their studies. There was little time for recreation, and getting a pass to go ashore was not easy. Poor Minor, after only two weeks at the Academy,

lamented that he walked the deck for hours longing "to be once 'more at home among those who love me so well & who now mourn over my wearisome stay." Homesickness could strike anywhere.[30]

It did not help that the accommodation and fare were pretty miserable. Their uniforms were of coarse and uncomfortable gray cloth. "The food they had to eat," remembered a new midshipman, "was, at first, revolting to me." There was no variety to speak of. "If it was not a tiny lump of fat pork," declared cadet James M. Morgan, "it was a shaving of fresh meat as tough as the hide which had once covered it, with a piece of hardtack and a tin cup of hot water colored by chicory or grains of burned corn, ground up, and brevetted *coffee*." Worse, almost half of the midshipmen at any time seemed to suffer from chills and fever thanks to the cold and damp on the river, but few were excused duty. Instead, they were allowed to lie on deck while the shivers persisted, then stood up and returned to duty. No wonder tempers ran extremely short at times, with at least one challenge for a duel issued but never consummated.[31]

Yet all the frustrations aboard the *Patrick* could be forgotten in an instant when a professor was lecturing in the recitation room and the boom of distant cannon was heard. For as Midshipman James M. Morgan would declare, that ship was "the most realistic war college that ever existed." The boys were literally in the line of fire. With the Union fleet just miles down the James River, threats and alarms were frequent. It was nothing for a professor to interrupt a math lecture by asking a student to "kindly step outside and find out for me which battery it is that has opened up." Indeed even more than the boys at the Virginia Military Institute, the young cadets at the Naval Academy were called upon for active service, and almost everyone volunteered when asked. As a result, the active assignments became rewards, given to the best scholars. Sometimes the boys manned shore batteries near Drewry's Bluff. They laid mines, assisted in boarding parties to capture

Confederate Naval China

1 Deep plate manufactured by E.F. Bodley & Co., Burslem, Staffordshire, England for the Confederate Navy
2 Lid by E.F. Bodley & Co., for the Confederate Navy
3 Cup with insignia, a crown superimposed on an anchor underneath the word 'Marine', probably of English manufacture, belonging to William Augustus Lee,

midshipman serving on the C.S.S. *Patrick Henry*
4 Platter manufactured by E.F. Bodley & Co., belonging to Capt. Michael P. Usina of the C.S.S. *Manassas*
5 Pitcher manufactured by E.F. Bodley & Co.
6 Plate manufactured by E.F. Bodley & Co.
7 Silver butter knife from the Confederate ship C.S.S. *Jamestown*

8 Cup and saucer of Capt. John Maffitt from the C.S.S. *Florida*
9 Cup originally from the C.S.S. *Texas*
10 Saucer manufactured by E.F. Bodley & Co., from the C.S.S. *Texas*
11 Facetted cup and saucer by E.F. Bodley & Co.
12 Cup and saucer manufactured by E.F. Bodley & Co., for the Confederate Navy

Artifacts courtesy of: The Museum of the Confederacy, Richmond, Va: 1-10, 12; Virginia Historical Society, Richmond, Va: 11

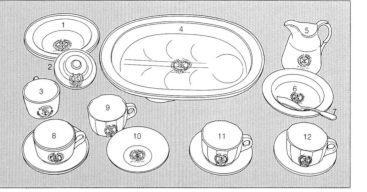

enemy vessels, and even took a hand in defending against Federal land movements. In consequence several midshipmen lost their lives in action.[32]

In the end, their most noted service came in April 1865, when Richmond fell to Grant. Taking part in the evacuation, they burned the old *Patrick Henry* to prevent it falling into enemy hands, then Lieutenant Parker led them off with the fleeing government as a guard for the Treasury and the Confederate archives, which duty they manfully performed until May 2. On that day, at Abbeville, South Carolina, with the Treasury disbursed to the remaining soldiers accompanying the fleeing government, Parker disbanded them and the Confederate Naval Academy came to an end. Parker's last sight of them was as they melted into the shadows, carrying with them bacon and beef, and army bread, to help them get home.[33]

In the end, only two classes graduated, totaling in all a mere forty-eight midshipmen. Many more simply did not have time enough to complete their studies and examinations before the war closed. Much of the cream of Southern youth was here, including the sons of General Breckinridge and Captain Semmes, along with Lee's and Pinckney's and others from the leading families. Theirs had been a noble attempt, under the most adverse conditions possible, and the conduct and training of a number of midshipmen assigned to the various ships and squadrons, as well as the behavior of the boys who escorted the government on its last journey, bears testimony to the caliber of the students and the school they served.[34]

For all of the officers, whether midshipmen or masters, commodores or captains, the life of a serving commissioned leader was governed by his branch of service and posting, and each had its distinctive features. Officers on blockade duty saw a different sort of war from those in the river flotillas and squadrons, officers on ironclads had a more varied existence and routine than those aboard conventional ships, while the men on the cruisers or the men on shore stations lived in yet other environments.

What they all had in common was boredom, for there was little to do when not on duty. Fortunately, therefore, shipboard routine was very well organized and generally followed, so that, at least, the officer knew what to expect from each day and could plan for his free time accordingly. For the most part, that leisure time was occupied with spinning tales, writing letters home, and exactly the same sort of activities that men at war in all times have used to fill their idle hours. Aboard the Confederate warship *Chattahoochee* in Georgia, for instance, things were so quiet that there was but one mail call a week. This ship was a dull assignment, with no action and no prospect of action, so the men were anxious for any diversion. Lieutenant William Whittle undertook to have local cobblers make bargain rate shoes for his friends in Richmond to save them money. Others complained that they had no prospect of promotion, while some idly dreamed of glories that would never materialize. The *Chattahoochee* was still under construction and consequently

Right: An unremembered Rebel, known only as "Captain Smith," commanded the *Old Dominion*, and very probably served both in the Virginia state navy, or else in the forgotten blockade-running fleet.

Above: Admiral John Dahlgren stands at center, thumb in belt, surrounded by his staff aboard the U.S.S. *Pawnee*, flagship of the South Atlantic Blockading Squadron off Charleston. These were the men who starved the South.

her officers lived ashore in temporary quarters, like many Rebel officers in a number of ports when not at sea. At least these men ate well and as one wrote, "have as elegant table as one would wish". Better yet, many officers could visit the nearby plantations and mix into the local social life. And when finally the *Chattahoochee's* officers moved on board their ship, the local belles repaid their visits, finding that the seamen had decorated their quarters with flowers, and even damask cushions upon which the ladies were seated while they all enjoyed strawberries and pound cake and a cream tea.[35]

Others in shore stations, or aboard blockaded Rebel ships that could not leave port, had much the same experience. Indeed, theirs could be an almost leisurely existence. Midshipman Minor, on station aboard the ironclad *Savannah* at

Savannah, Georgia, had little to do but study and go into town to call upon the local ladies. "Enjoyed myself hugely," he would write in his diary in June 1864, having the run of the city, lots of attractive ladies to call upon, and fairly abundant rations.[36]

Across the lines, aboard the U.S.S. *Monitor*, Paymaster Keeler found things a bit different. That was because, being on a Yankee ship in enemy territory, he had to live aboard his vessel. For all who did so on ironclads, North or South, life could be unpleasant. Asked how he liked life on a warship, he replied that, "I have made the discovery that there are some things about it not very romantic." For one thing, aboard an unheated ironclad, on winter mornings he had to arise and eat breakfast in the wardroom with the temperature at 35°F, "shivering so that one can

Below: One of the giant behemoth ironclads of the West, the U.S.S. *Cairo*, off Mound City, Illinois. One of the city-class gunboats, she would be the first to succumb to an underwater "torpedo", or mine.

Above: Officers of the U.S.S. *Monitor* pose in front of their ship's turret on July 9, 1862. Four months earlier to the day, they had shared an epic experience, aboard the first ironclad ship to battle another of its kind.

hardly find the way to his mouth." At night, between cold linen sheets, he shook "till I thought the frame work of my berth would be shaken apart." Relief only came in the morning with hot water in his washbowl, after which he and other officers frequently went to the engine room "to thaw out," it always being warm there. At least eating was not a problem, as "we have the best of food provided." On a ship like an ironclad with a small complement of officers, they all ate together in a single mess in the wardroom, contributing proportionately to the purchase of their victuals out of their own pockets. Eventually steam heaters were installed in the wardroom.[37]

A boatswain's whistle roused the ship at 5 a.m., though off-duty officers could sleep until 8 a.m. or thereabouts when awakened by their servants for breakfast, for many did manage to engage

young Negro boys as valets and the like very cheaply. Then after a day of regular duties, Keeler and others would spend their evenings in reading or conversation or writing, much the same as the men of the *Chattahoochee* and virtually every other warship not cruising.[38]

What few officers did – other than the captain – was spend a lot of time in their quarters, for without fail they were cramped, close, and often unbearably hot or musty. Keeler's room on the *Monitor* was not much over six feet square, his berth occupying half of it, and a desk and stand for washbowl much of the rest. Oilcloth covered the floor, while overhead the ceiling rose to about seven feet, the only illumination being a deck light or window. He had a simple camp stool to sit upon, and yet regarded his quarters as some of the best he had seen of any of the vessels he had served in.[38]

Of privacy there was little on any ship. "As far as sounds are concerned," complained Keeler, "we might as well be in one room." Even as he wrote in his cabin, he could hear every word being spoken in the adjacent wardroom and other cabins. Only the captain had claim to more spacious and private quarters, though on a few vessels other officers enjoyed some elbow room as well. Aboard the Confederate commerce raider *Alabama*, her boarding officer George T. Fullam found the "ward room furnished with a hand-some suite of state rooms." What a far cry that was from the verdict of Lieutenant James Baker of the C.S.S. *Huntsville*. "She is," he said of his ironclad, "terribly disagreeable for men to live on." An officer on another Rebel ironclad, the *Baltic*, despaired of finding comfort. "I begin to think that in our Navy it does not exist", he lamented. Aboard the ironclads especially, in the summers it was oppressively hot and humid, with condensed water dripping from overhead and everything in any way organic mildewing. Ventilation was non-existent, and whenever possible the men and officers slept out on deck, or ashore.[39]

About all the officers could say as a class, North or South, was that their standard of living was

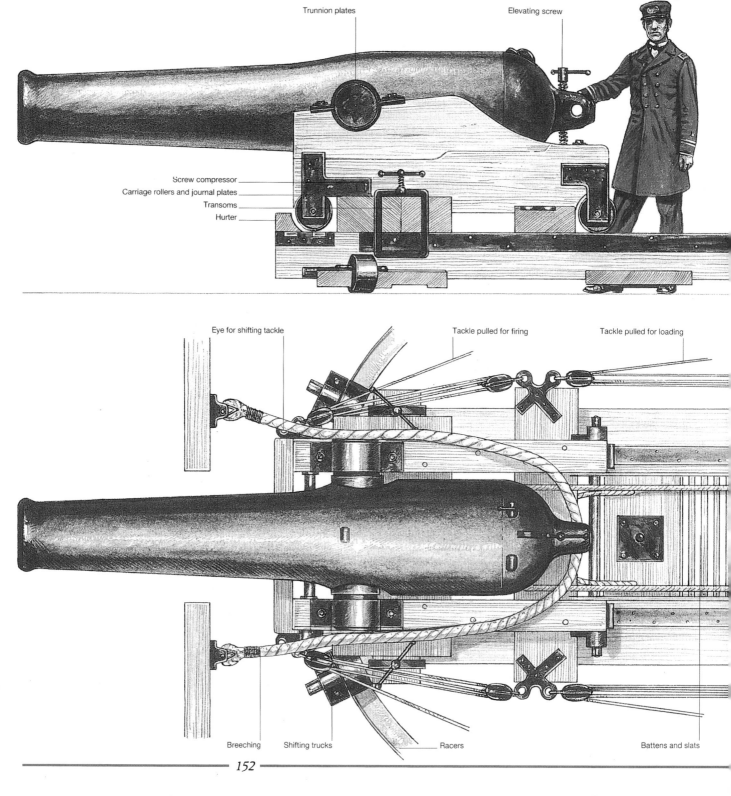

Trunnion plates

Elevating screw

Screw compressor

Carriage rollers and journal plates

Transoms

Hurter

Eye for shifting tackle

Tackle pulled for firing

Tackle pulled for loading

Breeching   Shifting trucks   Racers   Battens and slats

better than that of the lower ranks. The great leveler, when and if it came, was battle, for then all shared the same risks, though here, at least, the ironclad officers had a measure of reward for their otherwise miserable existence. Behind their iron shields, they were far less likely to suffer injury from enemy shot or shell than their comrades aboard wooden gunboats or ocean-going cruisers.

With numerous variations due to size of ship and kind of service, action North and South saw generally the same routine. With battle imminent, the captain stationed himself on his quarterdeck, or wherever the wheel and compass were to be located. Ironclads did not have

quarterdecks, and when Franklin Buchanan took his C.S.S. *Virginia* into battle at Hampton Roads, Virginia, on March 8, 1862, for a time he actually sat atop the casemate on an armchair, fully exposed. On Federal ironclads, the captain stood in the armored pilot house, communicating by messengers or through a speaking tube. The executive officer, a clerk, midshipmen, and a master, were with the captain as well, all to carry out his orders.

Out on the gun decks, or inside the casemate or turrets on ironclads, lieutenants commanded the gun divisions. Depending upon the size of the ship and the number of cannon and lieutenants, a division could be one gun or six or more. The lieu-

tenant saw that the cannon were cast loose from deck moorings and prepared for action. Sometimes marine officers assisted, though usually they commanded smaller deck howitzers or else placed their men in rigging or at gun ports to act as sharpshooters. Another lieutenant commanded the powder magazine and saw to its disbursement to the gun divisions. Meanwhile down in the engine room, the chief engineer and his assistant engineers operated the steam engines if the ship had them. Sail driven vessels had men detailed from the gun divisions to handle changes of sail during combat. The wardroom that normally echoed to the sounds of officers' laughter as they ate and conversed now

Pivot-mounted 11-inch Dahlgren Smoothbore

Perhaps the gravest responsibility a naval officer had was oversight of a gun and its crew. Many different types of gun saw service, but it was on the seagoing sloops and cruisers that the rifles and large caliber smoothbores like this one were more likely to be found. Weighing in at 16,000lb, this pivot gun could hurl a 130lb shell nearly a mile. The favored arrangement called for a fore and aft pivot, with perhaps one or two amidships as well. Its iron-shod wheels or trucks moved along overlapping iron bands fixed to the deck planking, allowing movement over a full 360°, (see diagram at right). The gun crew, at a

lieutenant's command, used rope and tackle to pull it out for firing and back for loading. When not in action, the gun was held firmly in position on the pivot mount by screw-clamp compressors located on both sides. The rate of fire varied from rapid (two minutes per shot) to sustained (three minutes per shot), the gun being aimed by means of a sight bar positioned on the breech and a front sight located between the trunnions. For most gun crews in this war, however, practice constituted most of the firing they were ever called upon to do, for few vessels saw much action, and many never fired a hostile shot during the war at all.

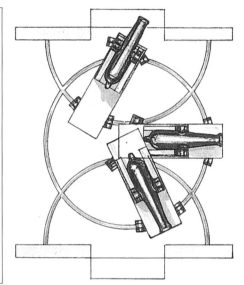

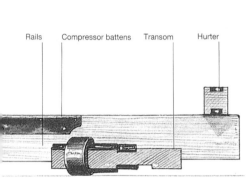

Rails   Compressor battens   Transom   Hurter

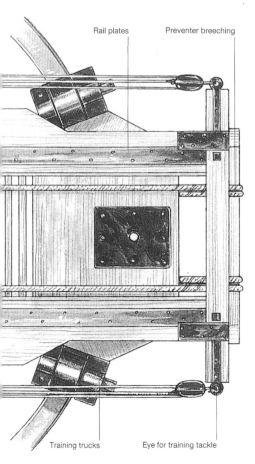

Rail plates   Preventer breeching

Training trucks   Eye for training tackle

Above: The officer commanding a gun aboard ship, like the man standing second from right here aboard the U.S.S. *Mendota*, gave the commands and oversaw the gun crew in every step of loading and firing. It had to be a

very precise operation, for a misstep could see them all injured or killed. In fact, practice like this proved to be the most "action" that many gun crews ever got, for the average warship never saw more than one engagement.

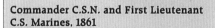

Commander C.S.N. and First Lieutenant C.S. Marines, 1861

The men serving in the Confederate naval forces suffered the greatest obscurity endured by any of those fighting for the South. Such was the nature of life in a war fought almost entirely on land.

Most obscure of all was the Marine, like the first lieutenant of Marines at left. His uniform and his service are patterned largely on that of the old United States Marines, though with a few differences. By the same token, the uniform of the commander in the Confederate Navy, at right, owes much to the U.S. Navy. Significant differences include, or course, the color of the cloth, and the insignia being used.

For the poor marine officer especially, so little is known more than a century later that some aspects of his uniform are still speculative. Service in this war would be frustrating for both officers, with opportunities to see action very few.

Above: The objective for most officers on the blockade service was runners like the *Teaser*, shown in 1864 after her capture, her battered condition offering testimony to the risks a blockade runner took braving Union fire.

Below: Most of the ship-to-ship action in the war fell to the ironclads in the rivers, harbors, and coastal waters. Men and officers like these aboard the U.S.S. *Sangamon* became veterans of shot and shell very quickly.

was happening. The lieutenants at their divisions just kept firing blindly through the gun ports when so ordered.

Happily those scenes were rare in the life of a naval officer. Most Confederate vessels of all classes never fought in more than three engagements in the war, while most Yankee ships chased unarmed blockade runners or bombarded shore positions that often did not return fire. For all its hellish nightmare quality in action, the navy, North and South, was not an inherently dangerous place – just boring.

References

1 William S. Dudley, *Going South: U.S. Navy Officer Resignations & Dismissals On the Eve of the Civil War* (Washington, 1981), pp.7, 19; E.B. Long, *The Civil War Day by Day* (New York, 1971), p.719.
2 Dudley, *Going South*, p.4.
3 *Ibid.*, pp.16-7, 37, 42, 44, 45.
4 David D. Porter, *Incidents and Anecdotes of the Civil War* (New York, 1885), pp.8-9.
5 Charles Lee Lewis, *David Glasgow Farragut* (Annapolis, Md., 1943), I, pp.288-9.
6 Dudley, *Going South*, pp.5-6.
7 *Ibid.*, pp.34-40.
8 *Ibid.*, pp.8-13.
9 *Ibid.*, p.42.
10 Long, *Day by Day*, p.719.
11 Kenneth W. Munden and Henry Putney Beers, *Guide to Federal Archives Relating to the Civil War* (Washington, 1962), pp.453, 458, 461, 484-5.
12 *Ibid.*, pp.486-92.
13 *A Naval Encyclopaedia* (Philadelphia, 1881), pp.155, 826; Francis A. Lord, *Civil War Collector's Encyclopedia* (Harrisburg, Pa., 1963), pp.142-3.
14 Dudley, *Going South*, pp.34-55 passim.
15 J. Thomas Scharf, *History of the Confederate States Navy* (New York, 1887), pp.32-3.
16 Robert W. Daly, ed., *Aboard the USS Monitor: 1862* (Annapolis, Md., 1964), pp.xiv-xv, 4-5, 9.
17 Scharf, *Navy*, p.28.
18 Tom H. Wells, *The Confederate Navy: A Study in Organization* (University, Ala., 1971), pp.13, 46, 74, 91, 95, 107, 118.
19 Beers, *Guide*, pp.345-64.
20 Scharf, *Navy*, p.29; Raphael Semmes, *The Confederate Raider Alabama* (Greenwich, Conn., 1962), p.29.
21 Semmes, *Raider*, pp.29-30, 30-1.
22 Wells, *Confederate Navy*, p.19.
23 *Ibid.*, p.20; Scharf, *Navy*, pp.33-4, 819-20.
24 Wells, *Confederate Navy*, pp.153-8.
25 Dudley, *Going South*, pp.53-5; Scharf, *Navy*, p.820.
26 Munden and Beers, *Federal Archives*, pp.465-6; Mame Warren and Marion E. Warren, *Everybody Works But John Paul Jones* (Annapolis, Md., 1981), p.8.
27 Warren and Warren, *Everybody Works*, p.56; *Naval Encyclopaedia*, pp.14-5.
28 Wells, *Confederate Navy*, pp.67-9; G. Melvin Herndon, "The Confederate States Naval Academy", *Virginia Magazine of History and Biography*, LXIX (July 1961), p.304; William H. Parker, *Recollections of a Naval Officer, 1841-1865* (New York, 1883), p.324.
29 Herndon, "Academy", p.306; Hubbard T. Minor Diary, October 12, 1863, U.S. Army Military History Institute, Carlisle, Pa.
30 Herndon, "Academy", p.309; Minor Diary, October 30, November 10, 1863.
31 James M. Morgan, *Recollections of a Rebel Reefer* (London, 1918), p.205.
32 *Ibid.*, pp.202, 206; Herndon, "Academy", pp.309-10.
33 Parker, *Recollections*, p.365.
34 Herndon, "Academy", p.316.
35 Maxine Turner, *Navy Gray* (University, Ala.,1988), pp.66-7.
36 Minor Diary, June 27, 1864.
37 Daly, *Monitor*, pp.19-20.
38 *Ibid.*, pp.22-3.
39 *Ibid.*, p.26; Charles G. Summersell, ed., *The Journal of George Townley Fullam* (University, Ala., 1973), p.5; William N. Still, *Iron Afloat* (Nashville, 1971), p.100.
40 Wells, *Confederate Navy*, pp.144-8.

became a hospital, with the surgeons setting up their stimulants, and drugs and instruments, ready for the inevitable wounded. The remaining officers posted themselves wherever the captain detailed them.

As was often the case otherwise, the ironclad service had some special features. More officers were free to command gun divisions, since there were no sail parties to lead. The *Virginia* had an officer for every gun in her battle with the *Monitor*. Also these additional officers were thought necessary to command boarding parties, for every ironclad commander expected to batter his opponent with gunfire, then possibly ram him, and in the end board to capture. It never happened in practice.[40]

As for the experience of battle itself, there is little to say. The fear and excitement, exhilaration and depression felt by the officers of the military, were felt in exactly the same way by the commanders at sea. The only substantial differences

were in the setting. An officer aboard a cruiser or open deck gunboat felt very exposed, and saw not enemy soldiers firing at him with rifles, but mighty cannon billowing forth fire and smoke in his direction. It was a mitigating fact that most – though not all – ship-to-ship or shore-to-ship actions took place at some distance, so that the enemy was just a small vision sometimes hundreds of yards or even more than a mile away. It was mostly the ironclads that got to close work, and aboard them the experience was not unlike a 19th century man's concept of hell itself. Deafening roars of his own cannon rang in his ears. His gun deck filled with unventilated smoke that made his eyes tear and his throat parch. The drumming of the engines made the firmament vibrate beneath his feet, while now and then the deafening crash of enemy shells against his iron armor could send him reeling from the concussion. And all the while, only the captain and his pilot could see where they were going or what

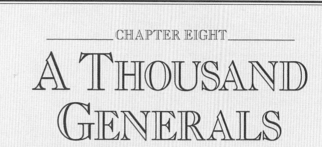

CHAPTER EIGHT

A Thousand Generals

With the war grinding into the spring of 1864, the South was ever-more on the defensive, especially after Grant was called east to take overall command of Union armies. Simultaneous advances on Richmond and Atlanta, the Shenandoah, Petersburg, and Louisiana would overload the Confederacy's power to resist, Grant hoped. For it was certain that the continual fierce fighting would erode the leadership of the beleagured South, as when its *beau sabreur* Jeb Stuart fell at Yellow Tavern in May 1864. Such losses would prove irreplaceable.

ONE OF THE reasons that the naval officers, even in their own time, seemed so overlooked, was the fascination felt then and later with the seemingly more dashing army officers bravely leading their soldiers into battle. No image of the Civil War proved to be more powerful in the American mind, North or South. And for all of their self-proclaimed egalitarian spirit of the "common man", the fact is that most Americans of the era – like Americans of all times – were captivated chiefly by the doings of the high and mighty. There were none who were higher or mightier than the men who carried stars on their shoulders and collars. The generals of Blue and Gray were the true focus of almost universal attention throughout the war, eclipsing all officers of other ranks. The word on everyone's lips after a battle was not what privates or lieutenants did. It was what this or that general did. Indeed, the generals' names became in time synonymous with their commands. To millions of ears, the name "Lee" meant the Army of Northern Virginia, and at every command level down the line, to say that a certain general went into action or was defeated, meant that his brigade or division or corps had done so. To the population at large, and even to many of the private soldiers who served them, the generals *were* the armies.

There would always be a problem, then and later, in simply determining how many generals actually served in the war. The trouble is one of definitions, especially with the Confederates. According to Jefferson Davis' Congress, only officers appointed by the president could be generals, and in most cases those appointments had to be ratified by the Senate. In actual practice, Davis nominated an officer and sent his name to the Senate for affirmation or denial. Sometimes, through oversight, a desire for more information, or simply adjourning before acting, the Senate failed to vote on a nomination. And when the Senate was in adjournment, Davis could appoint generals and hold sending in their nominations until the Senate reconvened.

All of this is simple enough, and the officers so nominated or appointed pending nomination and approval have incontestable claim to having been generals. Yet a host of other claimants appeared during and after the war to considerably confuse the matter. In the far-off Trans-Mississippi Department, where communications with Richmond could be cut off for months, commanding General E. Kirby Smith, through necessity, began to appoint generals on his own in his army, asking Davis and the Senate to approve them later. It was the only way to avoid waiting sometimes months to put a man in a vacancy. Some Davis and the Senate approved, but others were never acted upon, and these latter cannot be deemed genuine general officers.

Finally, there were a number of old Confederates who simply took to calling themselves "general". Often in wartime correspondence a man would be called by that title though he had never been promoted. They may have been so called though confusion, or because they commanded brigades – the usual post of a brigadier general – or perhaps because, as with the old honorary naval rank of commodore, some regarded a man in command of a force as a general regardless of his rank. After the war this confusion became compounded by the tendency of elderly officers to "promote" themselves. In their last years, Major Generals Joseph Wheeler and John B. Gordon both claimed to have been made lieutenant generals. Manifestly, neither was, and Gordon signed his own parole at Appomattox as a major general. Further, a number of colonels, like Charles Crews of Tennessee, wore the wreath and stars collar insignia of a general even though never so promoted. Men seeing them during the war, and their uniformed photographs afterward, naturally assumed that such men had been

Six of the Civil War's premier cavalry generals pose together in 1864: Wesley Merritt at the left, then David Gregg, Philip H. Sheridan, Thomas A. Davies, James H. Wilson, and Alfred T.A. Torbert, each one an outstanding commander.

appointed. Worse yet, the United Confederate Veterans, the influential and universal Rebel veterans organization in the years after the war, had a policy of giving its officers the title of "general", even though few of these veterans had ever been more than lower level officers, and many had been private soldiers. Finally, a number of state militia officers held the rank of general, as with Francis H. Smith of the V.M.I. or M. Jefferson Thompson of Missouri. They, too, wore the uniform of a general, but they were never nominated by Davis and never held any rank in the Regular or Provisional Confederate service.

Out of this mass of confusion, debate can go on interminably. However, after assessing all of the claimants, the best criteria appear to be the fact of appointment, nomination, and confirmation, and officers appointed and nominated but, for whatever reason, not confirmed. Looking at the case in this fashion, there are 425 men who can be said certainly to have held one of the four grades of generalship in the Confederate service.[1]

They were truly a mixed bag of characters. There was a French nobleman, a former vice president of the United States, the son of a president and the grandson of another, alongside farmers and clerks. Many were Northern born, some with brothers in the Union Army. Quite a few had prior military experience of some kind, and at least 146 held diplomas from the United States Military Academy. Three of them had formerly been officers in the U.S. Navy!

In age they ranged widely. The oldest of all was David E. Twiggs, who was seventy-one when commissioned into the Confederate service. Born in 1790 in Georgia, he was the fourth oldest

Above: Standing sixth from the left, Brigadier General Samuel P. Heintzelman typified the early war Union generals — career officers who became commanders because they were available, and not for their talent.

Below: Future Yankee division and corps commanders sit for the camera in 1862. General Henry Slocum sits second from left, then Generals William B. Franklin, William F. Barry, and John Newton, all of the VI Corps.

general officer on either side in the war, and just about the least distinguished of the lot. Suspected even by Confederates after his treasonable surrender of Texas to the Rebels, without bothering to resign his commission, he achieved nothing as a Confederate major general. Indeed, he died of old age less than two months after accepting his commission.[2]

At the other end of the age spectrum was young Brigadier General William P. Roberts of North Carolina. Enlisting at age nineteen, he rose through the ranks to be colonel of his regiment in 1864, and on February 23, 1865, Davis appointed him brigadier. If legend may be believed, so impressed was Robert E. Lee with young Roberts' performance on the battlefield, that he gave the twenty-three-year-old new general his own gauntlets.[3]

They were big men and small. Brigadier General William R. Peck, appointed just five days before Roberts, stood six feet six inches tall and weighed well over 300 pounds. Probably the smallest was young John C.C. Sanders of Alabama. Just past twenty-four when appointed, he apparently stood no more than a few inches above five feet. Ironically, Peck, the biggest target of any Confederate general, came through the war unscathed while Sanders, the smallest, was wounded once in 1862, and again mortally just three months after his promotion.[4]

For some the war was a family affair. Jerome Bonaparte Robertson of Kentucky was forty-seven when he became a brigadier late in 1862. Two years later his twenty-five-year-old son Felix H. Robertson was also appointed a brigadier. Young Felix had another minor claim to fame, in

General R.E. Lee and Lieutenant General T.J. Jackson

Interestingly, the great leaders of the war, though professional soldiers, still tended to take a lackadaisical attitude toward their uniforms and toward uniform regulations in general. Robert E. Lee, though the third highest ranking Confederate general in seniority, rarely appeared in anything other than the uniform of a colonel. While regulations prescribed a wreath around three stars for a general's collar, he wore only the stars, and no cuff braid.

His great subordinate, Stonewall Jackson, was only a little more cognizant of regulations. He often appeared in the field in his old U.S. Army jacket and cap from his Mexican War days. At least, when in Confederate uniform, he did wear the proper insignia. Interestingly, in this war the more concerned a general was about the exactness of his uniform, the less able he usually was on the battlefield.

that when he died on April 20, 1928, he was the last surviving Confederate general officer. He might not have enjoyed that honor if an investigation into his chief claim to infamy had been prosecuted more rigorously, for he was also the only Southern general to be investigated by the War Department for the murder of wounded and captured enemy soldiers, chiefly blacks. Only the end of the war impeded then Secretary of War Breckinridge from concluding the investigation. Obviously no saint, Robertson had also delivered perjured reports on command in 1863 in an effort to discredit then-General Breckinridge, which no doubt added some zest to the war secretary's investigation.[5]

Matt and Robert Ransom were brothers from North Carolina. Robert Garnett of Virginia, the first general killed in the war, was a cousin to Richard Garnett who died leading a charge at Gettysburg. Hugh and Ben McCulloch of Tennessee both became Confederate brigadiers, and so did the Starke brothers, Peter and William of Virginia. Ben McCulloch and William Starke were both killed in battle. Surely the best known close relations to achieve generalships were Robert E. Lee and his two sons William H. F. Lee and George Washington Custis Lee. The latter, Lee's elder son, went to West Point, and served through most of the war on President Davis' staff, where he rose to major general, largely to flatter

Above: Brigadier General John A. Rawlins and his wife at Grant's headquarters at City Point, Virginia, during the Petersburg Campaign. Like many generals, he brought what he could of home to the front with him.

Below: Brigadier General Christopher C. Augur, seated at center, surveys the efforts of his men at Baton Rouge, Louisiana, in 1863 to decorate and appoint their quarters. The servant with the bottle certainly helped.

his father no doubt. The younger son, called "Rooney" by the family, had real field experience becoming the youngest major general in the Confederate service, thanks to his abilities leading a division of Stuart's cavalry.[6]

For others, family connections were less fortunate. John Rogers Cooke of Missouri took at least seven wounds before being promoted to brigadier in November 1862, and was widely acknowledged to be one of the best junior generals in the South. Yet his greatest wound was that his father, Philip St. George Cooke, was even then a major general in the Union Army. Major General James E.B. Stuart felt that same wound, for Philip Cooke was his father-in-law. Also in the Army of Northern Virginia was James B. Terrill of Virginia. On May 30, 1864, he fell killed in battle, the day before his appointment as a brigadier was confirmed by the Senate. Eighteen months earlier his brother, Brigadier General William R. Terrill, was killed at the Battle of Perryville fighting for the Union. Probably best known of all the brothers divided by the war, however, were George and Thomas Crittenden. George, an experienced West Point graduate, became a major general in the army commanded by Albert Sidney Johnston, but resigned under a cloud in late 1862. His brother Thomas became a Yankee major general, and was commanding the XXI Corps at the Battle of Chickamauga when it was routed, effectively

Above: Lieutenant General Thomas Jonathan "Stonewall" Jackson was only one of many Rebel leaders with numerous family connections in his army; his included two brothers-in-law who were also generals.

ending his career. Ironically, their father, Senator John J. Crittenden of Kentucky, had authored and pushed the last attempt at sectional compromise before war broke out. Its failure helped to set the nation on the road to armed conflict, and his sons to opposite sides of the battle-lines.[7]

In their antecedents, the generals were just as varied as in their families and vital statistics. Breckinridge, of course, had been vice president under James Buchanan from 1857 to 1861, and was the highest ranking United States official to take arms with the South. As a result, he was under indictment for treason in the Union. Richard Taylor, the son of President Zachary Taylor, became a lieutenant general, while a grandson of Thomas Jefferson, George Wythe Randolph, became a brigadier after leaving his post as Secretary of War in 1862. There was foreign royalty of a sort in the general called "Pole-cat" by his troops, Camille Armand Jules Marie, Prince de Polignac, of France. And there was native American "royalty" in the person of Stand Watie, a chief of the Cherokee nation, who led many of his followers as Confederate cavalry and won a brigadier's star for his effective efforts.[8]

A Rebel general's nativity could have occurred literally anywhere on the map. While naturally most of the generals came from the Southern states, a score and more hailed from New York, New Jersey, Ohio, Pennsylvania, and even in the

case of Zebulon York, from Avon, Maine. Polignac, of course, came from France, and Ireland contributed in Patrick R. Cleburne and Patrick T. Moore two very distinguished leaders. Devonshire, in England, gave Collett Leventhorpe, who got his appointment as brigadier in February 1865, though for some reason of his own he declined it.[9]

They came from all walks of life. Besides statesmen like Breckinridge, there were former governors such as Henry Wise and William Smith of Virginia, and a host of other lawyers and jurists who, indeed, made up the largest single professional group among the Confederate general officers, some 129. Surprisingly, professional soldiers or men with extensive experience or military training trailed just behind at 125, though in fact, some 272 of the 425 had some sort of military experience, if only of the brief militia sort. But of the remaining 153 men to become generals, they came from a host of professions. A third had been bankers or merchants and manufacturers. Nearly another third had been farmers and planters. Only 24 could be called professional politicians, while the remainder came from such diverse occupations as education, civil engineering, medicine, and clergy, peace officers and Indian agents, the Navy, and the press. There was even one man, Robert C. Tyler, the most mysterious of all the generals, whose only pre-war occupation appeared to be as a soldier of fortune. Certainly the most unique pre-Confederate occupation of any Southern general, however, was that of Frank C. Armstrong, appointed brigadier general on January 20, 1863. Two years earlier he had been an officer in the Old Army, and chose to remain with it through August 1861. As a result, he fought *against* the Confederates at First Bull Run before resigning to become one of them, a living example of the old adage that said "if you can't beat them, join them."[10]

Wherever these men came from, they eventually took appointments into one or more of the four grades of generalship authorized by the Confederate Congress. The most numerous,

Personal Possessions of General Robert E. Lee

1 Field tent. A mock up
2 A saddle blanket, used on General Lee's horse Traveller
3 A scarf sent to the general by an English admirer
4 A frock coat possibly worn at Appomattox
5 A frock coat with Maryland seal buttons given by the ladies of Carroll and Frederick Counties and sent through the lines by Thomas N. Webb of Baltimore
6 Leather haversack
7 Leather gauntlets
8 Sword belt with a Virginia State seal belt plate
9 The camp bed and blanket used by General Lee during the siege of Petersburg
10 Mess gear utensils
11 Leather riding boots
12 Wooden camp chest
13 Mess gear chest
14 Modified Grimsley saddle
15 Field glasses and case
16 Hat given by General Lee to the Reverend J. Clay Stiles
17 Colt Model 1851 Navy revolver, engraved
18 The pen used to sign the surrender at Appomattox
19 A table used at the winter headquarters near Orange Courthouse, 1863-4

Artifacts courtesy of: The Museum of the Confederacy, Richmond, Va: 1-4, 6-19; Virginia Historical Society, Richmond, Va: 5

naturally, was the lowest grade, brigadier general. In all some 328, rose to that grade, ranging from young Roberts all the way to the sixty-year-old John H. Winder, who was made responsible for Union prisoners. Overall they averaged just over thirty-six, though seventy-one were under thirty at the time of their appointments. Many were distinguished, among them John Hunt Morgan, the dashing and colorful – if troublesome – cavalry raider from Kentucky who led numerous raids into Union territory before he was killed in a surprise attack by Federals in 1864. Almost equally as noted was his subordinate and friend, Brigadier General Basil W. Duke, who succeeded to Morgan's command. At the twilight of the war, he commanded the military escort of the fleeing President Davis and cabinet, and after the war became one of the premier writers on the Confederate experience.[11]

At the next level of command, there were seventy-two major generals, of whom Twiggs was the oldest and "Rooney" Lee the youngest. Interestingly they were still a relatively youthful group, average age running thirty-seven, barely a few months older than the brigadiers. Here is where the greatest battlefield reputations of the war may be found. "Jeb" Stuart, John B. Gordon, Joseph Wheeler, Patrick Cleburne, Frank Cheatham, George E. Pickett, Sterling Price, and more and more. These men commanded the divisions, and sometimes the corps, of the mighty armies of the Confederacy. Few who lacked real ability rose to this station.[12]

More rarified still was the fraternity of lieutenant generals, for only seventeen held such rank.

Above: There were all manner of generals, and some of decided idiosyncracies. Grant's engineer and chief of the U.S. Military Railroad, Brigadier General Herman Haupt was often seen surveying a bridge from his raft.

Below: Confederate generals rarely posed in groups. Here in the front row sit, from left, Henry W. Allen, E. Kirby Smith, William R. Boggs, and A.T. Hawthorn. General James Fagan stands at far right.

Here the widest sort of variety showed itself. The oldest was fifty-four-year-old Leonidas Polk, formerly episcopal bishop of the southwest, and a man of almost no military ability at all. Yet he was a West Pointer and, more importantly, an old friend of Jefferson Davis. The youngest was Stephen D. Lee, who was just twenty-seven when appointed. In between there was the cranky and irascible Jubal A. Early, a profane bachelor who apparently detested women yet may have fathered several mulatto children out of wedlock. There was Richard Taylor, who had no military experience other than having been General and President Zachary Taylor's son – and who was also a brother-in-law to President Davis. Nevertheless he showed real talent in a difficult command in Louisiana. Better known were some of Lee's warhorses, men like James Longstreet and Richard S. Ewell and A.P. Hill. Hill being killed in action just as the war was closing, at the same time that he was dying of complications from venereal disease. Out in the western theater there was the capable William J. Hardee and, above all, the incomparable Nathan Bedford Forrest. With no schooling or experience of war at all, Forrest rose from private in the 7th Tennessee Cavalry to become probably the most instinctively talented cavalryman of the war.[13]

At the very top, in the rank of full general, they were all West Point men, all eight of them. Senior in grade, and also the oldest, was sixty-two-year-old Samuel Cooper, who spent his war in Richmond and never saw active service. Of the others, they were a distinguished if flawed lot. Robert E. Lee stood without peer. Albert Sidney Johnston was killed at Shiloh before he could demonstrate if Davis' trust in him was well-placed. Joseph E. Johnston and P.G.T. Beauregard started the war brilliantly, then frittered away much of their time petulantly feuding with an equally argumentative Davis. The great genius of Johnston, widely proclaimed then and later, never appeared on the battlefield, for he rarely risked battle. There was almost no debate on the command merits of Braxton Bragg, however, an absolute disaster as commander of the Army of Tennessee, a man who fought his own subordinates more than he fought the enemy, and who owed his continuation in command to his friendship with Davis.

Far to the west sat Edmund Kirby Smith, another crusty commander who became a virtual king in the Trans-Mississippi domain that was called by some "Kirby Smith-dom". Smith was never an able or experienced battlefield commander, but he ran the administrative nightmare of a province one-third the size of the Confederacy with remarkable success, and was one of the very last to surrender. As for the last and most junior of the full generals, he was John Bell Hood, a daring and bold fighter who simply was not smart enough to command an army, as he demonstrated by nearly destroying the Army of Tennessee when he took its command for a time from Joseph Johnston. Hood owed his position, as much as anything, to his shameless flattery of President Davis, as well as to Davis' own loathing of Johnston.[14]

Certainly within this group as a whole there were all the vices and virtues to be found. Even generals were not immune to temptations and vanities, or worse. They could be a contentious lot, and challenges to duels were occasionally issued. Brigadier General John A. Wharton of Tennessee was killed when a cavalry colonel shot him under strange circumstances, and in a formal

Above: So many of the generals proved to be forgettable, and were indeed forgotten. Brigadier General Francis Patterson made himself a casualty when he shot himself in 1862 rather than face a court of inquiry.

Below: Often they were remembered both for bravery and foolhardiness. No one ever questioned the dashing valor of General John B. Hood – they should have questioned his judgment, however. It killed hundreds.

duel General John S. Marmaduke shot and killed General L.M. Walker. They could be venal, too, as charges of theft and willful dishonesty occasionally attested. Certainly Earl Van Dorn was no saint, invading the sanctity of at least one married woman's bedroom, and losing his life for it.

Van Dorn also suffered another far more common vice, drinking. Alcohol was common enough before the war in the South, and many an officer had developed a taste for it. The pressures and sometimes fears of high command led a few to excess. Breckinridge was accused of drunkenness on two occasions, though his enemy Bragg was the accuser; the charge therefore may be false. But Breckinridge's fellow division commander Major General Frank Cheatham was frequently seen drunk by a number of witnesses. George B. Crittenden resigned his commission in some disgrace after losing first a battle with the enemy at Mill Springs, Kentucky, in January 1862, and then a fight with the bottle that led to his relief from corps command shortly before Shiloh. Perhaps the most noted of all inebriates, however, was Brigadier General Nathan G. Evans of South Carolina. Known as "the most accomplished braggart" in the Confederate Army, he was also a prodigious drinker, having a specially detailed orderly who followed him everywhere carrying a "barrelita" of whiskey for his personal use. Twice he went before courts-martial, once for drinking and again for disobedience, and in 1863 he was finally removed from command, though he was certainly one of the premier fighters in the service.[15]

Worse was cowardice, and certainly there were a few who showed it. Probably best known and most notorious was John Floyd of Virginia, senior commander of Fort Donelson, Tennessee, in February 1862. When surrounded by the enemy,

he turned the command over to a subordinate and effected his own escape, abandoning his command. Worse yet, Floyd's immediate subordinate, General Gideon J. Pillow, proved to be just as cowardly. He, too, turned over the command to the next subordinate, Simon Buckner, and then made good his escape with Floyd. Floyd would be so censured in the Confederacy that he never again held a position, and on March 11, 1862, President Davis summarily relieved him of command. Pillow, an experienced old political

Above: At Pittsburg Landing, Tennessee, where the Battle of Shiloh was fought, the strengths and weaknesses of a host of generals became evident, and legends born: Grant's drunkenness, Sherman's insanity.

Below: Otherwise insignificant spots became notorious thanks to their associations with some generals. Here at Guiney's Station, in this little house, Stonewall Jackson died. It would be a sacred spot for Confederates.

wire-puller, managed to hang on to his commission, though suspect, and at the last minute even got command of a brigade in Breckinridge's division during the Battle of Stones River, Tennessee. But his cowardice there ensured that his field command days would be over for good.[16]

But for every act of cowardice on the part of a Rebel leader, there were scores of individual demonstrations of great bravery and heroism. Armistead's, leading his men right up to the summit of Cemetery Hill at Gettysburg, can never be forgotten, nor can Albert Sidney Johnston's coolness under fire at Shiloh be anything other than bravery, however ill-advised. In an age when leaders were expected to inspire by example, most of these men did just that, though at terrible risk to themselves. Thus fell Johnston and Armistead. Thus was Jeb Stuart lost in 1864, A.P. Hill a year later, Leonidas Polk to a cannon shot in Georgia, and McCulloch and Terrill. Thus fell Stonewall Jackson to shots by his own men in the dark at Chancellorsville.

Indeed, the attrition among the general officers was appalling, and a major source of the weakness in the command structure of Lee's army after Gettysburg. For so many of his experienced brigadiers had been killed or otherwise put out of action due to wounds, that men who had months before been captains were now leading brigades. In all, 77 of the 425 generals were killed or mortally wounded in battle, almost twenty percent. Another nineteen died in service from other causes, yet the true extent of the loss is even greater than it at first appears, for of the total 425 generals, many never held field command and therefore never risked enemy fire. Factoring such officers out of the equation would raise the percentage of field officers killed to fully one quarter

Above: A number of officers achieved their stars only as honorary generals, by brevets. One was Hiram Berdan, commander of the famed 1st United States Sharpshooters, better known as Berdan's Sharpshooters.

Below: This is the room in which Jackson died. Filled now with rubbish and a shaving bench, it had heard those immortal last words, "Let us cross over the river and rest under the shade of the trees."

or more. Unfortunately, the bravest, were the most likely to be hit, and thus many of the best leaders were destined to fall, while several of those not killed suffered disabling wounds. Richard S. Ewell lost a leg as a result of a wound, and was never as effective in corps command again. Hood, bold to rashness, lost a leg at Chickamauga and the use of an arm at Gettysburg. Francis T. Nichols of Louisiana lost his left arm in 1862 and his left foot at Chancellorsville.

Thus their bravery was costly. Forrest, arguably the boldest of all, was wounded several times in the war, yet so fierce was he that he is believed to have personally killed more enemy soldiers than any general of the war. He even killed one of his own officers in a quarrel, though only after the officer had shot him in the hip.

Not so fortunate were many other wearers of the stars. Without doubt, the worst day of the war for the corps of Confederate generals came at Franklin, Tennessee, on November 30, 1864. In a massive frontal attack on the Yankees, Hood at his rashest almost shattered his army, and when the casualties were counted, five of his generals were found slain: Hiram Granbury, States Rights Gist, John Adams, Otto F. Strahl, and worst of all for the Confederacy, Patrick R. Cleburne. That night they were laid out in a row on the porch of a nearby house, while a sixth, Brigadier General John C. Carter lay mortally wounded. Bravery in this war came at a terrible price for leaders.[17]

It was a price paid by both sides, for almost everything suffered by the generals in Gray was felt by their foes in Blue. Indeed, they even shared the initial confusion as to just who really was a general, though from a much different cause. Long before the Civil War, with promotions governed by vacancies at higher levels, and with deserving officers staying in grade seemingly indefinitely, the War Department adopted a system of brevets. Essentially, it meant that conspicuous service, almost always in action, could be recognized with an honorary promotion by brevetting an officer. A captain could be brevetted to major, or even higher, though he only exercised the regular rank of captain unless there were other captains in his command. Then, thanks to his brevet, he would take charge as senior officer.

Unfortunately, when the Civil War got going in earnest, the brevet system got out of control as political and personal influences came to bear while there were thousands of officers hoping to make a record for themselves. No tally of the total number of brevets awarded to officers of all ranks exists, but it would certainly run to 10,000 or more! And just those officers brevetted to brigadier or major general were staggering. Post-war Brigadier General Anson Mills, himself the recipient of a brevet in 1864, wrote after Appomattox that in one or two cases, men who were mere captains – and not in frontline combat units either – wound up holding brevet rank as major generals. Indeed, so invidious did the system become that Congress was eventually forced to enact legislation that prevented brevet officers from holding actual command commensurate with their rank. Thus brevets became almost meaningless militarily, and served only as rewards for outstanding performance.

Just as confusing was the fact that an officer could possibly hold four different ranks simultaneously. A Regular Army captain might have taken a commission as a colonel in the volunteers, though his Regular commission still remained active. Good performance on the battle-

field could lead to a brevet promotion to brigadier general of volunteers and, at the same time, brevet promotion to major in the Regulars. Worse, officers were entitled to wear the insignia of their brevet ranks, which confused everyone. On top of that, two pre-war Regular officers, one subordinate to the other, could find their positions reversed in the volunteer service, and compounded by brevets if they held the same volunteer rank. Thus a brevet brigadier of volunteers would outrank a colonel of volunteers who might, in the Regular Army, be his own superior.[18]

In the end, some 1,367 men received brevet promotions to brigadier or major general of volunteers or Regulars during the war, men who never received actual appointment to those ranks. Thus they do not figure in any tally of true generals. Of those genuinely promoted to wear the stars, however, there were 583.

They represented the same mixed bag as their foes across the lines. Oldest of the lot was John E. Wool, born just a year after the close of the Revolution, and fully seventy-nine when he finally retired in 1863, having done two years' excellent service in the Civil War. Old General Winfield Scott, of course, and Edwin V. Sumner were both born a few years after Wool, Scott in 1786 and Sumner in 1797. Scott never took the field, being too old and corpulent, but Sumner became the oldest active general officer of the war, rising to major general and command of the II Corps of the Army of the Potomac, which he ably commanded in the 1862 Peninsular Campaign. At Fredericksburg that December he commanded Burnside's Left Grand Division, and was on his way to a new command in the West when he died in March 1863, aged sixty-six.

At the other end of the scale was a young man who set a record never yet equalled or exceeded in the United States Army, Galusha Pennypacker – entitled to remembrance if only for his odd name – was elected captain of his company of the 97th Pennsylvania Infantry in August 1861, aged seventeen. Three years later, thanks to able service, and though only twenty, he was colonel of

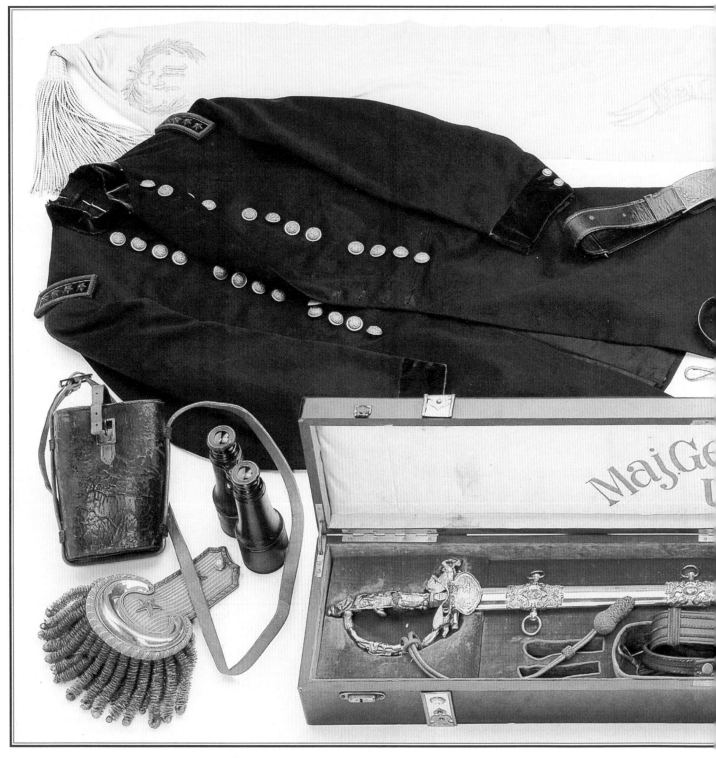

Uniforms and Personal Regalia of General U.S. Grant

1 General's silk sash, embroidered

2 Wool frock coat with insignia of full general, a rank awarded Grant in 1866

3 Leather officer's sword belt with gilt belt plate

4 Wool frock coat made by the John Wanamaker Co., Philadelphia. Button groupings show that it is that of a full general c. 1866

5 Leather binocular case

6 Binoculars from 5

7 See 14

8 Sword in an ivory banded case. The silvered and gilt sword was made by Schuyler, Hartley & Graham, New York, while the gilt and bright blade was made by Collins and Co. in 1862. Also shown are a general officer's sword belt and sash

9 Silver cigar case, engraved with Grant's initials

10 Ivory handled pen commemorating Grant's promotion to lieutenant general in November 1863

11 Shoulder insignia of major general

12 Shoulder insignia of lieutenant general

13 Shoulder insignia of full general of the armies

14 and 7 A pair of major general's dress epaulettes

Artifacts courtesy of: The Civil War Library and Museum. Philadelphia. Pa

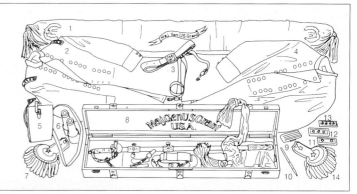

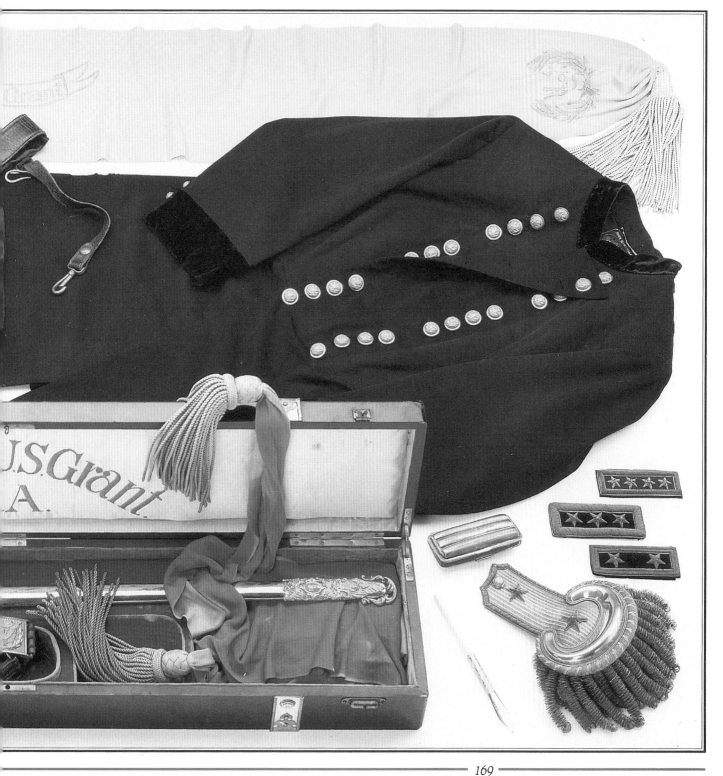

the regiment. He served so well during the Petersburg Campaign that he rose to command of his brigade, took four wounds in battle, and finally felt enemy shot a fifth time in the January 1865 assault on Fort Fisher, North Carolina. "The real hero of Fort Fisher", a superior called him, and his reward came on April 28, 1865, when he received an appointment as brigadier general, thirty-four days before his twenty-first birthday. It made Pennypacker the youngest general in American history, and when he stayed in the Regular Army after the war, he became the youngest regimental colonel in its history.[19]

Overall, as with the Rebels, the Federal generals were young men, as it required the vigor of youth to stand the rigors of field and campaign. The men who became the premier leaders all shared relative youth. U.S. Grant was thirty-nine when he donned his first star. William T. Sherman was forty-one, George H. Thomas forty-four, and Philip H. Sheridan just thirty. On average the brigadiers had passed their thirty-seventh birthday when commissioned, making them just a year older than their Rebel counterparts. Yankee major generals averaged thirty-nine, two years old than Confederates of the same rank, though it must be kept in mind that the advanced years of a very few old men like Scott, Sumner, Wool, and others considerably raised the average.

Largest of all of them was very probably old Winfield Scott himself, who stood six feet five inches and probably weighed in excess of 300 pounds. As for the smallest, figures are uncertain, but "Little Phil" as Sheridan was often called, barely passed five feet in height, and was usually photographed standing alone, or else seated if in a group, no doubt to avoid accentuating his diminutive stature.[20]

Not nearly so many sets of brothers or fathers and sons became Yankee generals as in the Rebel service. John and Napoleon Buford of Kentucky were half-brothers. The former, commanding a cavalry division in 1863, was the first to resist the Confederates at Gettysburg, and may have saved the battle by buying time for infantry to come to the battlefield. His brother served creditably in the western theater of the war. Two other brothers, David and William Birney, had been born in Alabama, but their father, abolitionist James G. Birney, moved them north at an early age. Both became lawyers, yet thanks to their influential father, and their early stand by the Union, each obtained a volunteer commission. By February 1862 David was a brigadier, destined to become a major general with a rather distinguished record until felled by malaria in 1864. Brother William went into the United States Colored Troops, received a brigadier's commission in 1863, and later commanded a division in Grant's army at Appomattox.

However, all families, North or South, were outdone by the McCooks of Ohio. Alexander McCook became a major general and commanded the XX Corps, suffering irreparable damage to his career at Chickamauga, along with Crittenden. His younger brother Daniel McCook led his brigade up the slopes of Kennesaw Mountain, Georgia, on June 27, 1864, and took a mortal wound, dying on July 17, just a day after his appointment as a brigadier. Their oldest brother was Robert L. McCook, made brigadier in March 1862 after a distinguished performance at the Battle of Mill Springs, only to be ambushed and mortally shot under mysterious circumstances by Confederate partisans a few months later. And a cousin of the three brothers, Edward M. McCook, also became a brigadier, serving with Sherman in Georgia in 1864. The stars on the shoulders of this particular family truly made a constellation.[21]

Before the war these men destined for leadership had seen a wide range of experience and circumstances. Quite a number came from Europe, especially from Hungary and the Prussian states, refugees from the political upheavals of 1848 and later. Franz Sigel, Carl Schurz, Julius Stahel, Albin Schoepf, Alexander Schimmelfennig and Wladimir Krzyzanowski were only some of the immigrants who became Yankee generals. Several had genuine military experience. Others were simply appointed out of political expedience, to encourage immigrants to enlist in Union regiments. Few achieved distinction, though that

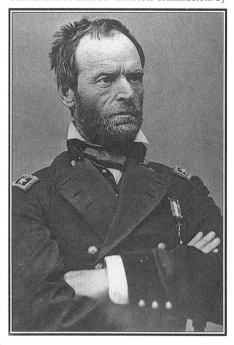

Below: Generalship could show in a host of places, but easiest of all to detect was poor generalship, and that is what the political generals usually displayed. Here at Fort Fisher General Ben Butler showed his ineptitude.

Above: The Civil War proved to be the making of many men, as it was with William T. Sherman. Having resigned from the army and failed in several business ventures, he was at loose ends when war came. It saved him.

Right: Generalship in the Union Army could lead in several directions. For Julius Stahel, a Hungarian who won the Medal of Honor, it led to absolute obscurity thanks to his failures in the Shenandoah Valley in 1864.

Brady N.Y.

had nothing to do with their nativity. Ireland, too, contributed a dozen generals, just as did Germany. Others came from Canada, France, Great Britain, Russia, Spain, Sweden, and even one from Switzerland.

Few of them had quite the distinguished antecedents of Breckinridge or Taylor or the other more aristocratic Rebel generals. None were sons of presidents, though a few would later become presidents – U.S. Grant, Andrew Johnson, Rutherford B. Hayes, Benjamin Harrison and James A. Garfield. Certainly there was a fair share of Senators and Congressmen. Among the most interesting of backgrounds was that of Ivan Vasilovitch Turchinoff, later simplified to John Basil Turchin. Born in Russia in 1822, he attended the Imperial Military School and became a colonel of the Imperial Guard, serving on Crown Prince Alexander II's staff during the Crimean War. Made a colonel and later a brigadier, he brought Russian attitudes toward war to the South, riding roughshod over soldiers and civilians alike, including women. Eventually he was court-martialled and dismissed, but then reinstated by Lincoln, and ended the war with the nickname "Russian Thunderbolt" thanks to his hard-hitting skill in battle.[22]

By and large, the rest of the generals showed much the same profile as their foes. Professional soldiers made up a substantial plurality of 194 out of the 583, while all-told 217 men who attended West Point donned stars. Just behind them ranked the lawyers and jurists, with former merchants and businessmen accounting for almost the same. Far fewer planters and farmers became generals than in the Confederacy, attesting to the generally less rural nature of leading men in the Union. As for the rest, however, almost the same proportions of general occupations occurred North as South of Mason and Dixon's line.

Below: Rutherford B. Hayes began the war as a major in an Ohio regiment. He fought with Sheridan in the Valley and was a major general by 1865. In 1877 as president he was to bring the Reconstruction to an end.

General-in-Chief U.S. Grant and Major General W.T. Sherman

Of all the 1,000 and more generals in this war, few if any emerged from greater obscurity to rise to greater heights than these two men. Each a mystery in his way, they became very close friends without ever truly understanding each other. Grant was a simple man of complex instincts who did one thing, and only one thing, really well, and that was winning a war – but he did it better than anyone else. Sherman, by contrast, was far more intelligent, and perhaps something of an intellectual. Yet he was also erratic, excitable, and needed the steadying influence of Grant, who never faltered and never doubted. Together they were the most invincible team Lincoln had and not unlike the magnificent pairing of Lee and Jackson. Each tended to be careless in his uniform. Grant more often than not appeared in the field in a simple private's blouse, with his insignia of rank sewn on.

Except for the politicians, just over five percent of Confederate generals were professional politicos. In the Union Army that rose to over eight percent, and considering the subsequent military quality of the men as demonstrated in the field, it is apparent that Lincoln's choices were not nearly so good as Davis'. While at least half of the political generals in the South performed creditably, and some like Breckinridge were outstanding, very few in the North rose above mediocrity. Some were absolute disasters. Sigel became a major general, yet lost almost every battle he ever fought, and ran away from at least one. Nathaniel Banks repeatedly showed an almost complete lack of command ability, yet led one army after another until the 1864 failure of his Red River Campaign. Probably most notorious of all was Benjamin F. Butler in the East and the scheming John McClernand in the West. In April 1864, chief of staff Henry Halleck actually wrote to his friend Sherman that "it seems but little better than murder to give important commands to such men as Banks, Butler, McClernand, Sigel, and Lew Wallace, and yet it seems impossible to prevent it." Indeed, it was impossible, and only later in the war, with the Union clearly on the road to victory, and with Grant firmly in command, were the political generals weeded out. Meanwhile, those few who had performed well had nothing to fear. John A. Logan of Illinois distinguished himself repeatedly in the war, rising from prominence as a pre-war Democrat to become a major general commanding the XV Corps. With the death in action of James B. McPherson, Logan was next in line to command the Army of the Tennessee, and for a time did assume temporary leadership. The decision for a permanent commander rested with Sherman, and betraying a

Above: A few general officers took a special interest in what the war had been all about in the first place: the Negro. General Edward A. Wild raised "Wild's African Brigade" in North Carolina in 1863, and led it competently.

Below: A special few officers who rose to generalship showed something beyond what could be expected. Alfred Pleasonton, at right, never did, but his protégé George A. Custer, mounted at left, became a legend.

distrust of politicians, even though he paid high tribute to Logan as a general, Sherman gave the position to a less talented West Pointer.[23]

There were only two grades of generalship, excepting the unique case of Grant's promotion to lieutenant general. Most numerous, as in the Confederacy, were the ranks of the brigadiers, some 450 in all. Youngest, of course, was Pennypacker, while the oldest was probably Daniel Tyler, already a sixty-two-year-old brigadier in the Connecticut state militia when the war began. Many distinguished themselves, especially younger men like the brilliant cavalry raider Benjamin Grierson, who led his 1,700 cavalry on a daring expedition through the heart of Rebel Mississippi in April-May 1863 as a diversion during Grant's Vicksburg Campaign. Others did a different kind of service like John A. Rawlins, who spent the whole war on Grant's staff, constantly watching him for signs of a return to the bottle, advising as friend and fellow officer, becoming in Grant's words "the most nearly indispensible" man on his staff.[24]

Of the major generals there were 132, with Wool the oldest and twenty-five-year-old George A. Custer the youngest – indeed, the youngest in American history. Here were the most storied commanders of the war – men such as Sherman, Sheridan, Thomas, McClellan, Hooker, and more. They were the ones who commanded not only the corps but also the armies, that eventually fought their way to victory.

Of course, not every Yankee general was a hero. Cowardice, intemperance, avarice, perhaps even treason, showed up in their number. Three of them would be court-martialled and dismissed for various offenses. Brigadier General James H. Ledlie commanded a brigade in the IX Corps and

then a division, and was in charge of it at Petersburg when an assault was ordered on July 30, 1864. When his men went forward, with no assistance in preparation for the assault by their general, he sat huddled back in a bomb-proof dugout. He resigned in disgrace a few months later. With him at the time was another division commander of the IX Corps, Edward Ferrero. He, too, cowered in the bomb-proof, sharing a bottle of "Dutch courage" with Ledlie. Irish-born Brigadier General Thomas F. Meagher was a notorious inebriate, who died two years after the war when he got drunk and fell off a steamboat into the Missouri River.

Most ignoble of all, however, was the performance of Brigadier General Justus McKinstry of New York. A career officer, he made brigadier early in the war, and then took charge of the quartermaster's department in Missouri. Quickly he extorted huge sums from contractors dealing with the Army by helping them to sell their goods at highly inflated prices. When his chicanery was finally discovered, he was cashiered in 1863 after a year in jail.[25]

Yet bravery and self-sacrifice they also had aplenty, and the cowards and poltroons were only a fraction of their number. For generations men would tell and read of the exploits of Joshua L. Chamberlain of the 20th Maine. At Gettysburg his performance would win him the Medal of Honor. Six times he felt Rebel lead, and was believed to be mortally wounded at Petersburg when Grant gave him a field promotion to brigadier. Jokingly in later years he would quip that he was "not of Virginia's blood; she is of mine", after having been hit so many times on the state's battlefields. It was no wonder that Grant accorded to him the high honor of formally receiving the surrender of Lee's Army at Appomattox. Ranald Mackenzie, only twenty-four in 1864, led a brigade and then a division of cavalry so magnificently that Grant was moved to remark that he thought the young man, "the most promising young officer in the service."

So many of them were gallant, so many compassionate, so many showed the virtues that all men aspired to, that it is difficult to choose from among them. Even when hostile generals themselves met, they acted like men born to lead, and few episodes illustrate this more than the wartime meetings of two pairs of opposing generals.

At Gettysburg, on the first day of the fight, July 1, 1863, Brigadier General Francis C. Barlow led a brigade of the XI Corps that was driven off Cemetery Ridge by the Confederates. It was his misfortune in the retreat to be struck by a bullet that left him virtually paralyzed for several hours, and he was believed dead or dying and left where he fell. When the advancing Rebels swept over his position, Brigadier General John B. Gordon came upon Barlow. Asking Barlow's name, and thinking him bound to die, Gordon had him put on a litter and carried to the shade, where he promised to send Barlow's letters to his wife and tell her how he died. Showing every tenderness, Gordon fulfilled Barlow's wish. But unknown to Gordon, Barlow eventually recovered. Fifteen years later they met by chance, and formed a friendship that lasted almost twenty years.[26]

Right: Many a reputation expired in the defenses around Petersburg. Here, in 1864, is where men like Ledlie and Ferrero showed their true colors, and where others like Gordon shone by comparison.

Left: Petersburg was the undoing of Ambrose Burnside. A lovable, well-liked officer, he simply had not the stuff of high command, and at Petersburg his bungling of the attack on the Crater eclipsed him.

Below: Major General Erasmus D. Keyes was another sort of general. Starting as a junior officer at the war's outset, he rose by ability to command of the IV Corps of the Army of the Potomac in 1862.

Above: The 1st Rhode Island Cavalry stands at dress parade on Manassas Plain in July 1862. Often it was the dash and gallantry that a cavalry commander could demonstrate that led to a general's stars.

More touching still were the last hours of Major General Stephen D. Ramseur. A West Point cadet in the class of 1860, he took arms with the Confederacy, and at the October 19, 1864, Battle of Cedar Creek in the Shenandoah, was commanding a division in Jubal Early's army. Near the close of the battle, while rallying his troops to hold fast, he felt a Yankee bullet enter his right side and puncture both lungs. His men put him in an ambulance and sent him to the rear, but when the rest of the army began to retreat, Ramseur was stalled, and at nightfall the Yankee cavalry pursuers had caught up with him.

They took him to Union General Sheridan's headquarters, where Sheridan's own physician looked at him and judged the wound mortal. Soon the word that Ramseur was there spread in the Union high command, and his old friends and classmates from West Point came to gather around him. Off and on through the night they say vigil at his bedside. Henry A. DuPont came. So did George Custer and Wesley Merritt, while Sheridan himself frequently looked in on his dying foe. Finally the next morning, when Ramseur breathed his last, he did so made comfortable by the ministrations of an enemy doctor, and surrounded by his old friends. Later that day, while this one dead general was sent off to his family, the other generals who had attended him returned to the business of the war.[27]

References

1 Warner, *Generals in Gray*, pp.xiv-xix.
2 *Ibid.*, p.312
3 *Ibid.*, p.258
4 *Ibid.*, pp.231, 268.
5 *Ibid.*, pp.260-1; Davis, *Breckinridge*, p.460.
6 Warner, *Generals in Gray*, pp.99, 100, 179, 184, 253.
7 *Ibid.*, p.61, 65, 302; Warner, *Generals in Blue*, p.100.
8 Warner, *Generals in Gray*, p.241
9 *Ibid.*, p.185
10 *Ibid.*, pp.xxi-xxii, 13, 313.
11 *Ibid.*, p.xxv.
12 *Ibid.*, p.xxv.
13 *Ibid.*, p.xxv, 92.
14 *Ibid.*, p.xxv.
15 *Ibid.*, p.332; William C. Davis, *Battle at Bull Run* (New York, 1977), p.163.
16 Warner, *Generals in Gray*, p.90; Davis, *Breckinridge*, pp.343-4.
17 Warner, *Generals in Gray*, pp.xviii-xix.
18 Warner, *Generals in Blue*, pp.xvi-xvii.
19 *Ibid.*, pp.xviii, 365-6.
20 *Ibid.*, p.xviii.
21 *Ibid.*, pp.34-5, 53-4, 294-7.
22 *Ibid.*, pp.511-12, 603-4.
23 *Ibid.*, pp.xvi, xix.
24 *Ibid.*, p.342.
25 *Ibid.*, pp.150, 277, 303-4, 318.
26 John B. Gordon, *Reminiscences of the Civil War* (New York, 1903), pp.151-2.
27 Gary Gallagher, *Stephen Dodson Ramseur* (Chapel Hill, N.C., 1985), pp.164-5.

CHAPTER NINE

THEY ALSO SERVED

The months of the spring, summer, and fall of 1864 proved hard on both sides, with no speedy victories. It took Sherman until September to take Atlanta. The Shenandoah was still in Rebel hands, and so was Louisiana, while at best Grant had Lee besieged in Petersburg. With gains sometimes measured now in feet instead of miles, organization and communication became ever more important, placing renewed demands upon the staff organizations of both sides.

ALL TOO often forgotten, then and later, was the fact that few of these generals of the Civil War, or the colonels commanding regiments for that matter, could have functioned as effectively as they did, were it not for the services of the members of their staffs. These men consulted and advised, carried messages and carried out orders, handled almost all of a commander's communications and correspondence, became his friend and confidant, sometimes his alter ego, and in times of dire necessity even replaced the field commander in battle. They saw to his needs and comforts, such as they could, defended him against calumnies and enemies in his own camp if they felt loyal to him, or helped to fan rumor and innuendo if they did not. It would be too much to say that a staff could make or break a commander, but without good men at his side, and without their trust and confidence, even the best of leader's abilities would be seriously impaired.

The whole concept of a staff was dangerously underdeveloped when the Civil War erupted. Because colonels and generals in previous wars had led comparatively few men in camp or battle, often a commander needed no more than a quartermaster and a military secretary to handle his everyday working needs, taking care of much of the work himself, instead of delegating it to others. That was fine in the Mexican War, when a whole field army might number fewer men than in a good-sized Civil War infantry division. When the conflict did erupt in 1861, however, the necessary internal military organization developed just as slowly, and just as much behind the times, as did much of the military technology. Retrospect clearly suggests that in 1861 all soldiers should have been armed with rifled weapons, but they were not, thanks to the conservatism and inertia of entrenched old ranking officers. Similarly, with the prospect of armies that could number 100,000 or more, leaders entrusted with brigade, division, and especially corps and army command, should have had staffs two and three

times the size of those they used. In part they were limited by army regulations specifying the staff officers allowed, and in part by their own inability to delegate or to foresee the needs of their very modern kind of war.

In actual practice, the size of a staff depended upon the level of the commander involved. A colonel commanding a regiment, whether infantry or cavalry, generally had the smallest of all. While there were variations, especially in the Confederate service, the colonel might have an adjutant, a clerk – not a commissioned officer – a surgeon, a quartermaster, and occasionally a chaplain. Sometimes the surgeon had one or two assistants, also commissioned, but that essentially would be all.[1]

At the next level of command – brigade – both war departments recognized the need for more officers, in part because of the nature of most brigades early in the war. A brigadier could expect the same adjutant. With as many as 5,000 rather than 1,000 men on his hands, like a colonel, the brigadier usually also divided the supply functions in two, appointing both a quartermaster to oversee all of the materiel needs of the command, and a commissary officer to see to the feeding of the men and animals. There would also be a surgeon, sometimes a chaplain, and one or two aides-de-camp, often volunteer civilians but frequently commissioned lieutenants, to do whatever tasks came to the general's mind.

When that general rose to division command, he would need all of the above, and also the addition of an ordnance officer, since most divisions contained their own artillery batteries. At this level, too, the general might also find an engineering officer to oversee construction of defenses and battery emplacements, and perhaps even a topographical engineer to help survey landscape and prepare military maps. And should the general rise to corps or army command, then he would have the largest staff to be found in this war: two or three aides, a chief engineer, a chief quartermaster, a chief of ordnance, a medical

More often than they were credited, it was the staff officers, the men who organized the railroads and supplies, who were the ones who made the greatest contribution to the organization of victory.

director or chief of surgeons, a judge advocate general for dealing with military policy and law, a provost marshal for maintaining that law in the army, a chief of artillery who oversaw actual field command of the batteries, whereas the ordnance chief looked after the acquisition and disbursement of the weapons, a chief commissary of subsistence, an adjutant general, an inspector general, and perhaps even others. Often a commander divided his assistants formally or informally into a personal and a general staff, the personal staff consisting of aides, military secretary, and adjutant. Rarely, however, did any officer designate yet another staff member later considered essential – a chief of staff.

Throughout much of the war a well developed prejudice against staff officers flourished in both armies. In part it was well founded, for a considerable number of staff appointments went to men who, like the political generals, had high connections or family ties to thank for their commissions rather than training or ability. Furthermore, there could be an annoying degree of self-importance displayed by some of these men. Attached to headquarters, where food and accommodations and pay were better, without having to suffer the worst rigors of the march and often not called upon to set foot on the battlefield, they sometimes almost flaunted their clean smart uniforms before men whose dress showed the rough wear of the field. They rode while thousands walked. Often they were youngsters still in their teens or early twenties – especially the aides – who showed the immaturity of their years by lording their status over the poor common soldier. Worse, those who had the good fortune to serve a distinguished commander like Lee or Sherman sometimes displayed the puffed-up conceit or pride that more than anything else alienated the common soldier, and even fellow officers. At the same time, commanders often passed along to their staffs their own demeanor and temperament. Bragg's staff could be just as gruff and quarrelsome as he was. The unjustifiably egotistical and pompous Federal major general John C. Frémont, stationed in St. Louis, surrounded himself with a staff that many thought more akin to a palace guard in their high-handedness and finery.

Not because of such men, but in spite of them, did the rest of the staff officers North and South achieve whatever degree of respect and admiration they received, and for many that proved to be considerable. Indeed, a number of them rose to become generals in their own right, and some of note. E. Porter Alexander began the war as a signals officer, and later became chief of artillery for corps commander James Longstreet. His exemplary services were rewarded with a brigadier's commission. John Rawlins, Grant's trusted staff officer, became a brigadier, and so did others of Grant's military family. Several of Lee's officers achieved generalships, including William Pendleton, R.H. Chilton, Armistead L. Long, and Walter H. Stevens. Often, when a staff officer rose to high rank like this, he left staff work to take an active field command, as did Long, but more frequently he remained where he was. Indeed, in some cases the promotion to generalship was a reward for good staff service, and not an indication that higher authorities felt the recipient capable of independent command.

For the overwhelming majority of staff officers, however, theirs was unsung and obscure service. The generals and colonels got the headlines,

Above: Staff service rarely led to generalship, yet for Rufus Ingalls it did, making him chief quartermaster of the Army of the Potomac. If the men in the army were well supplied and fed, it was his doing.

Below: The men who worked for and reported to Ingalls were men like these, the employees of the quartermaster's department, who doled out the bread and beef and hay and forage.

while the field officers on active service received all of the glory and opportunity for speedy advancement. Staff work was tedious for the most part, often involving longer hours than those of the enlisted men and their leaders, and carrying with it the added frustration of having to please many masters at the same time. And perhaps to an even greater degree than field officers, the men of the staff had to suppress their own hurt feelings when their superior overruled their decisions.

In response to their forgotten contributions, some staff men became practically belligerent in their assertions of their worth. None more typified this than the quartermasters, nor with more justification. If there was any staff officer who meant something to the soldier in the ranks, it was the one or ones who fed and clothed him. Asserting that his department was "the most important by far of all the staff", Yankee quartermaster J.F. Rusling neatly summed up what he did for the soldiers. "The Quartermaster's Depart-

ment," he said, "houses and nurses the army; makes its fire and furnishes its bed; shoes and clothes it; follows it up, with its outstretched and sheltering arms, dropping only mercies, wherever it goes; carries, even to its most distant and difficult camps, the food it eats, the clothing it wears, the cartridges it fires, the medicine it consumes; and finally, when 'life's fitful fever' is over, constructs its coffin, digs its grave, conducts its burial, may even erect a head-board to mark the spot where 'sleeps well' the departed hero, and keeps besides, by special Act of Congress, a record of the time and place of his interment, for future references of his friends." A Confederate supply officer, Major Benjamin Bloomfield in Texas, said as much when he wrote of the quartermaster's duty "to ascertain and supply their respective wants, and to treat every soldier with whom he may have business, as some absent one's darling, whose comfort and health are, to a great extent, dependent on his exertions."[2]

Above: Here in a Virginia winter camp scene, the influence of the supply officers is easily seen. The men here would not be cooking or eating, or drinking, but for the efforts of the quartermasters and the commissaries.

Below: Since the dawn of warfare, bread has been the ammunition of soldiers' stomachs. Here army bakers leave the dough out to rise, and mold it into loaves that will fill the hungry bellies of Billy Yank.

Bottom: The loaves are done, and the commisariat at headquarters of the Army of the Potomac, supervised by Captain J.R. Coxe, leaning against the scale, supervises the distribution at Fairfax, Virginia, in July 1863.

In the Confederate Army, he had to deal with more than sixty different forms, sometimes filed singly, and other times in confused combinations, just in order to carry on the routine business of his department. There was a form for forage, another for fuel, one for wagons and harness, and a host of others required every time any sum of money was disbursed. All incidental expenses of an army passed through the quartermaster, even postage.

In the Union, where everything, including manpower, was available in greater abundance, the quartermaster and his counterpart the commissary could carry on their duties in relative security. Their foes to the south, however, faced a distinct challenge in the face of constant shortage, poor transportation, and lack of funds. One typical Rebel quartermaster could speak for all. Captain N.A. Birge, quartermaster at Monroe, Louisiana, from 1862 onward, first of all had to supervise a railhead at Monroe that connected it with Vicksburg to the east, thus making him a transportation officer. Further, he oversaw several steamers on the Ouachita River in order to get his materiel where the railroad did not go, chartering the boats from their civilian owners and paying with government funds. Then he managed 54 wagons in trains that covered the rest of his far-flung territory. All of these arteries of transportation were in constant operation simultaneously, and Birge directed and paid for all of it, using a mountain of those 60-plus forms. Every month he had to file a grand consolidated report of all his department's activities, and frequently he found himself so overtaxed just with management that he did not have time to prepare the lengthy report. His superiors' solution to his problem was to assign him three additional reports to make each month. Truly, an army did move on paperwork, even in those days when already the red ribbon used to wrap folded and docketed official documents in the military had come to be called "red tape".[3]

Above: Staff officers had to administer a number of subordinate services for the troops, including the oversight of sutlers, their wares, and their prices, though inefficiency here raised an almost constant outcry.

Below: Transportation in the occupied South fell to the management of engineers and other staff officers. Prosecuting the war did not just mean fighting – it also meant building, surveying, and moving men.

Above: Intelligence and information services depended upon signal officers, many of whom used observation balloons early in the war. This one is operated by Thaddeus Lowe, working for the military in 1862.

Honesty and character were also an essential element in a good quartermaster or commissary; for as seen in the case of General Justus McKinstry, ample opportunity presented itself for mishandling government funds. Confederate Commissary General Lucius B. Northrop, hardly competent himself, frequently thought he saw signs of dishonesty in others. One supply officer, a Major Lanier, complained to a friend that Northrop had too little confidence in him. "I told him," the friend wrote to Northrop, "that you were probably under the impression that he drove fast horses – gambled occasionally – kept a woman – and drank a quart of whiskey per day – all of which he says is *true*, but nevertheless thinks himself capable of making a good officer and promises to do his duty."[4]

The Confederate quartermaster, especially, also had to suffer the righteous wrath of the citizenry. As rations inevitably became scarce, impressment of civilian foodstuffs became necessary. Though sanctioned by Congress, still it was destined to be a controversial and hated policy, and the staff officer responsible in a department

or an army could become a very unpopular fellow. "The Government has employed an army of barnacles to go out in swarms like the locusts of Egypt", one editor said of the impressment officers. "Many of these agents knew no more of business than a Comanche Indian knew of mathematics."[5] For an officer who might think himself the most important of all in a general's military family, being called a "barnacle" and a "locust" for his efforts seemed a pitiful reward.

Far less disliked – indeed, generally well regarded – was an entirely different staff officer common to both armies, the chief of engineers or topographical engineer. Rarely did an officer below the level of corps or army commander have one, but he could be indispensable, especially for an aggressive commander like Stonewall Jackson, who used geography as a weapon of war just as potent as the rifles of his men. Jackson, in fact, had two such men on his staff, the first being Captain James K. Boswell, and then when Boswell became chief engineer, Jackson found another, Jedediah Hotchkiss. It was on March 26, 1862, as Jackson was planning his legendary Shenandoah

Valley Campaign, that he summoned Hotchkiss to him. "I want you to make me a map of the Valley, from Harper's Ferry to Lexington, showing all the points of offence and defense in those places," Jackson said, thus commencing the career of the most noted military map-maker of the Civil War. He would hold the post as topographical engineer successively on the staffs of Jackson, A.P. Hill, Richard S. Ewell, and Jubal A. Early, almost until the very end of the war, producing maps that were the very model of what a field officer wanted to know of terrain.[6]

Very quickly Hotchkiss and Boswell became best friends, working closely together in their dual role of mapping positions and advising Jackson on the best places for lines of defense. Jackson listened to them time after time, and was rewarded by signal successes, for he had little ability of his own to "read" a landscape for its military merits, but great ability at planning a battle once he understood the terrain. As a result, Hotchkiss developed the habit of taking his maps to Jackson and verbally explaining them. Sometimes his services could extend considerably

Colonel of Engineers, C.S.A.

Whether supervising the construction of a pontoon bridge, a railroad bridge, a corduroy road, or field fortifications and battery emplacements, the engineer officer was uniformly one of the most valued on any general's staff. This colonel of engineers in the Confederate service looked exactly the regulation picture of what he was supposed to be, from special hat insignia (the 'E' in German script) to his otherwise standard blouse, trousers, sash and facings.

Indeed, but for his kepi, he could easily be a Southern field officer of infantry. Regulations required engineers to wear the chapeau, but they never did. In the years before the Civil War, graduates of the U.S. Military Academy at West Point who finished at the top of their class invariably went into the engineers, so prestigious was that service. The war changed that, as it changed so many things, as defenses became less important to peripatetic armies.

afield from topography, as when Hotchkiss asked permission to go into a nearby town to buy himself a hat, and Jackson asked that he buy him one too.[7]

Meanwhile, Boswell, as chief engineer, served yet other staff functions, at the same time as being an indispensable friend to Hotchkiss. The chief engineer constantly rode around his commander's lines, studying positions of troops and batteries, looking for weaknesses or missed opportunities, and suffering with the interference of superior officers who thought they knew better. Once Jackson took command of the II Corps, one of his division commanders was Major General D.H. Hill, always an able general though quarrelsome. Hill insisted on laying out his own defensive lines near Virginia's Rappahannock River in the winter of 1862-3, instead of following Boswell's advice, and only the agreement of Jackson led to an order for a change. As a result, Boswell seemed to spend a great deal of time working with – and being patient with – Hill, "who interferes as usual," the engineer wrote in his diary, "and insists on acting as engineer."

Finally on January 5, 1863, Boswell had taken all he could. "I am disgusted," he declared, "and will let him take his own way." Relenting – and because it was his duty – Boswell tried again to be useful to Hill. One morning he rode around Hill's lines with the general, but later wrote in dismay that "as usual he thinks every point which he visits last the most important to be finished without delay." Other generals could be equally frustrating. A few weeks later Boswell helped General Robert Rodes construct an emplacement for an artillery battery above the Rappahannock. Rodes wanted breastworks eight feet high erected along the river bank. "I think it perfectly useless," complained Boswell, and Jackson agreed with him,

but would not interfere. Surely few of those who scoffed at the easy life of the staff officers ever appreciated the emotional frustrations of men who sought to do the best job possible, only to be thwarted by superior officers who lacked experience, knowledge, or other things but rank.[8]

And staff officers were not entirely immune from danger, either, though Boswell seemed to think so. "Strange as it may seem," he wrote to an aunt on April 21, 1863, "not one of Genl. J's staff has ever been killed, though I doubt not they have been as much exposed as the staff officers of any Major Genl. in the army. I suppose his prayers have shielded us." Perhaps they did, but not for long. Just eleven days later, on the first day

of the Battle of Chancellorsville, Boswell and other staff officers accompanied Jackson on an evening reconnaissance. Confusion in the darkness led to some of their own men firing on the mounted party. Jackson went down with two wounds, one in his hand and the other in his arm, which proved to be fatal. At the same time, three bullets struck young James Boswell. One hit his leg, and might have been of no great danger. But the other two went straight to his heart and killed him instantly. His dear friend Hotchkiss did not know at first of his loss, but when he returned the next morning he found Boswell lying peacefully as if in repose. Hotchkiss took his dead friend to a nearby cemetery and there saw him

Confederate Engineer Officers' Uniforms and Equipment

1 Forage cap of Col. T.M.R. Talcott, 1st Regt. Engineer Troops
2 Frock coat of Maj. Conway R. Howard, Chief of Engineers on A.P. Hill's staff
3 Sash of First Lt. Melcher Mason Long, Co. E, 3rd Regt. Engineers, killed at Cedar Creek, 1864
4 Headquarters flag of the chief engineer, A.N.V.
5 Long's sword belt; of English manufacture
6 Long's 1833 Dragoon saber and scabbard
7 Sword of Maj. Gen. Jeremy Francis Gilmer, chief of the Confederate Army engineers
8 Gilmer's dress sword, of European manufacture
9 Gilmer's prewar collar insignia
10 Gilmer's collar insignia
11 Gilmer's sleeve insignia
12 Non-regulation U.S. foot officer's sword of Maj. Robert M. Sully, 1st Regt. Engineers, manufactured by W. Walscheid, Soligen, in Germany
13 Scabbard of 12
14 A pair of Gilmer's spurs
15 Metal printing cut or block of a map drawn by Gilmer showing the territory between Richmond and Petersburg, Virginia

Artifacts courtesy of: The Museum of the Confederacy, Richmond, VA

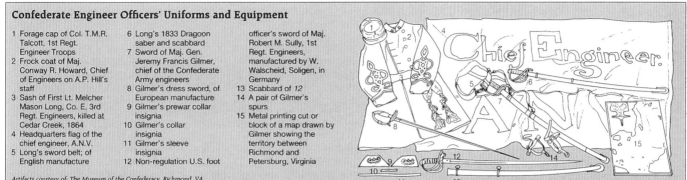

interred. "The charmed circle in which General Jackson and his staff moved," lamented a heart-broken map-maker, "is broken & the break is a heavy one." In the service of a bold battlefield general, staff work was no safe refuge from an enemy ball.[9]

Indeed, staff officers not infrequently found themselves ordered into battle by their general, to take command of a regiment – even a division or more – suddenly deprived of its leader. At the Battle of Baton Rouge, on August 5, 1862, Breck-inridge sent a mere captain of his staff to take command of a brigade after all of his brigadiers and several colonels had been put out of action in the fighting. Certainly there were higher ranking field officers available, but in a command crisis like that, a general needed to have someone whom he understood, and who implicitly understood him, in charge, for he could not take time to get intimately acquainted with some junior field officer he might only have met in passing. More than anyone, Grant would use members of his staff at times to fill temporarily vacant places in high field commands, and some of his staff later went on to command virtual armies of their own.[10]

Surely one of the most frustrating staff assignments in either army was that of a command's policeman, the provost. Usually hated when they did a good job, and generally accused of corrup-tion or favoritism when they wielded a loose rein, the provosts North and South had probably the most thankless staff assignment of all. Most provosts only appeared on the staffs of generals commanding corps and armies, and occasionally at divisional level. Also, wherever there was a stationary command, be it a fort or garrison, or a territorial department, a provost organization emerged. Command confusion sometimes ensued, for the provost might report to his commanding general, or to the general's adjutant, as well as to the provost marshal of the army. When brigades had provosts, they reported to the divisional provost, who reported to the corps provost, and so on. The question of who was in

Union Signal Corps and Engineer Officers' Uniforms and Equipment

1 Binoculars of Captain Elbridge C. Pierce, 19th Maine, Signal Corps
2 Engineer Office map of Southern Mississippi and Alabama
3 Engineer Office map of Arkansas and Northern Louisiana
4 Engineer Office map of Northern Alabama and Georgia
5 Signal Corps flag, 1862

6 Model 1852 staff and field officer's sword of Maj. J.A. Magruder, 15th N.Y. Engineers
7 Magruder's sword belt
8 Officer's haversack
9 Compass case
10 3and 11 Military forms: quarterly returns from ordnance stores
12 Brass hat insignia of the Topographical Engineers
13 Cloth variant of 12

14 Engineer's manual on fortifications
15 Model 1839 topographical engineer's sword of (then) Capt. George Meade
16 Magruder's telescope
17 Map of Virginia
18 Magruder's officer's hat cord
19 Magruder's engineer officer's hat insignia
20 Magruder's shoulder strap insignia

Artifacts courtesy of: The Civil War Library and Museum: Philadelphia, Pa: 1-4, 6-11, 14-20; C. Paul Loane Collection: 5; Gary Leister Collection: 12, 13

charge arose more often for these beleagured policemen than for any other staff officer.[11]

His duties, depending upon the command he was attached to, might range from combatting spying and espionage, maintaining command discipline, looking after transportation, enforcing the draft, providing guards for hospitals, prisoners of war, headquarters, to placing guards over public and private property, overseeing the comings and goings of citizens within the command, running courts-martials, and even sometimes overseeing troop movements. That was not all. He could also be ordered to manage shipping, oversee the impressment of local supplies and, in the case of the Confederates, local labor in the form of slaves. He had to receive and provide escorts for prisoners of a special nature, put down drinking within the command and prostitution near it, act as jailor for soldiers caught breaking camp rules, gather intelligence and manage friendly spies, practise espionage and misinformation campaigns against the enemy, look after men away on furlough to make sure they returned, hunt down deserters, and in the greatest extremity, conduct executions and the resulting burials.[12]

Besides being an onerous load, the nature of the duty was such that few men really cared for it. Lieutenant Charles A. Davidson, of the 1st Virginia Battalion, spoke for a great many when he complained in 1864 that, "I am tired and disgusted with being on Provost duty and should greatly prefer being with the Brigade where there is a chance for promotion and where I could feel I was performing some service." Indeed, sometimes generals actually apologized to officers and commands ordered to perform provost duty, as when Lee offered regrets to one of his generals for imposing "such service" upon him.[13]

To be sure, a provost's position offered some compensations, especially early in the war. Even Davidson admitted that in 1861 he had "quite an easy time" at his post. It was behind the lines, safe from battle, was provided with generally comfortable quarters and good food, and an almost perfect freedom to come and go as the provost officer pleased. Others found it just as pleasant at first, especially the freedom to move about, one provost commenting how he "would have more privileges on the road." Indeed, these extra "privileges" were often a source of the resentment that others felt for the provost officers. In times of scarcity, one Texas provost even boasted of the

Above: Very little loved in any army is the provost, yet keeping thousands of wild and unruly men in order requires a military police. Brigadier General Marsena R. Patrick served well as provost marshal of Meade's army.

Six-Mule Army Wagon

A Civil War army moved on wheels, whether railroad or wagon. Indeed, one of the most familiar sights North or South was that of a train of wagons, miles long, snaking its way along the rough roads of 19th century America. Management of those trains, from acquiring the wagons and the mules, to the harness, fell to staff officers. Indeed, to produce just this one ordnance wagon for the Army of the Potomac's Cavalry Corps, a host of staff officers had to become involved – ordnance, commissary, Cavalry Bureau for the animals, adjutant to produce the orders detailing wagonmasters and teamsters, and more. Once the wagon was produced, however, it became the special province of the division ordnance officer, who looked after it, the mules, the contents, and sometimes even the men.

This box wagon itself was the workhorse conveyance of both sides. It was ten feet long and was pulled by a six-mule team. The driver rode the near pole mule and controlled the team by means of a single rein and voice signals. The brake on the rear wheel was also operated from the saddle. Simple, easily maneuvered over rough ground, and dependable, wagons like this one carried such a variety of goods, from ammunition to generals' baggage, that the unit insignia and contents were usually displayed on the canvas top. This was to aid the easy movement of wagons, because there was a strict rule of precedence on the road. Troops and artillery had priority, while ammunition wagons took precedence over other supply vehicles. Keeping the wagons rolling was a staff priority in every army.

great supply of fresh pork that he could obtain.

But in time all this changed. The resentment of the citizenry soon manifested itself as they encountered provost interference in their lives and mobility. It was a situation made worse by the inevitable fact that the power that provosts had over others sometimes went to their heads. "It seems that instead of these disgraceful, lawless, unfeeling and impolite *men*, not Confederate soldiers in the strict sense, being at the front," complained one citizen to President Davis, "they . . . are running around over town and country insulting even weak unprotected women." Another lamented that the provost officers were an "unnecessary annoyance," and "of no possible benefit to the country."

Soldiers in the ranks were no less cynical. They regarded provost duty as just another way to avoid combat. "Lords ascendant," one man complained of them, "they loll and roll in their glory." Many a commander lamented having to deal with them. A staff officer with Beauregard in Mississippi in 1862 declared that such officers' ineffectiveness was not willful, "they being in most cases men of inferior intelligence." Yet he complained that everywhere he saw "palpable dereliction on the part of police officials." It did not help that some generals looked upon the provost assignment as a place to shelve otherwise deficient officers, in order to get them out of the way. The quarrelsome Major General Rodes felt

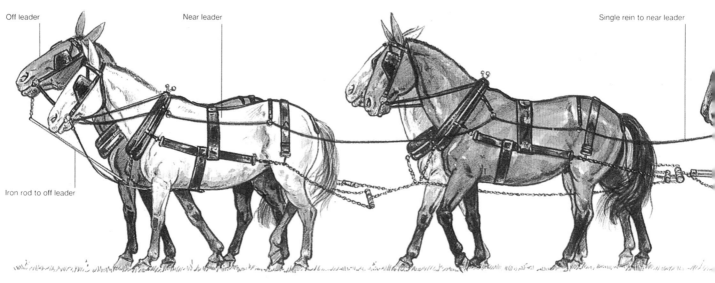

Off leader   Near leader   Single rein to near leader

Iron rod to off leader

Above: A 3.67-inch Parrott rifle and its crew show the best with which Union ordnance officers could equip their batteries. Powerful, accurate, and durable, the Parrott became a workhorse fieldpiece in a host of calibers.

Below: The ordnance officer on an army commander's staff had to look after the guns and animals, like this battery on Morris Island near Charleston, South Carolina. The task demanded good brains and rude muscle.

that Brigadier General Alfred Iverson of his command suffered from a "want of capacity in the field." As a result, Rodes relieved him of his command and assigned him to provost duty.[14]

The general lack of respect that soldiers usually feel for any policeman assigned to curb their behavior showed amply in their attitude toward this maligned officer. "As may be supposed," wrote Brigadier General Arthur Manigault, "they were not regarded with any very kindly feeling by the men, who never lost an opportunity of sneering at them, or letting off some witticism at their expense." Throughout the army, a provost officer and his men would be jeered at and resented, sometimes running a gauntlet of insults. Manigault recalled, "the scorn and contempt with which the Guard passed by, in the most profound silence." By the end of the war, Confederates especially, were displaying sentiments felt throughout the armies of both sides. "A great and growing evil," they said of their provost officers, "a source of almost boundless oppression." Only now and then did a provost, like Lieutenant Colonel John P. Bull of Major General Sterling Price's staff, hear such words of compliment as "able, energetic and efficient discharge of his duties."[15]

No chief ordnance officer or chief of artillery had to suffer the kind of obloquy heaped upon the provost. Indeed, the ordnance man was far more likely himself to be the one complaining for, like the engineer, he was a specialist assigned to perform his duties to the best of his knowledge and ability, and yet always subject to being overruled by a general officer who might know little of artillery tactics and usage, or worse some political general who know nothing about it at all. Major Thomas Ward Osborn served as chief of artillery in the Army of the Tennessee, on the staff of Major General Oliver O. Howard. He took his assignment in August 1864, and a month later wrote that, "since I came to this army I have made a complete revaluation in the artillery organization of this Army and Department." He was appalled. "I found its organization bad, or more exactly I found it without organization." That was sad enough, but when he instituted reforms, he

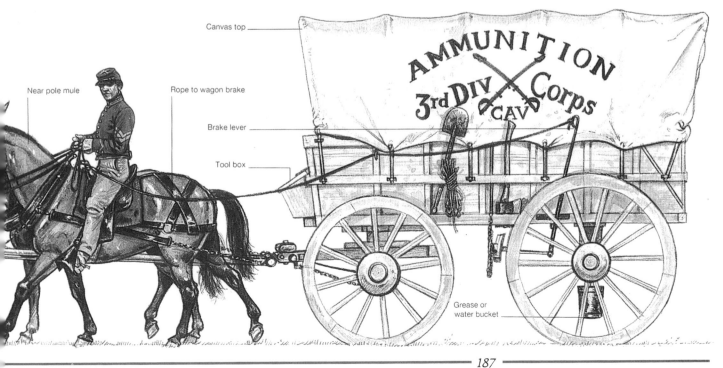

Canvas top

Near pole mule

Rope to wagon brake

Brake lever

Tool box

Grease or water bucket

AMMUNITION
3rd DIV CAV Corps

met constant opposition. "What I have done has been against the wishes of the division and corps commanders." He found batteries scattered about, two or three to each division, and subject to the division commander. Osborn reorganized all of the batteries into a separate brigade within each corps, simplifying command considerably. Yet he only accomplished it because he had Howard's backing. His predecessors had tried the same thing, but been thwarted by Howard's predecessors.[17]

Far worse, though, was what Osborn saw of the way his superiors used the batteries in the field. "The ignorance of some of our general officers in regard to the proper uses of artillery is simply stupendous," he declared that September, echoing the frustration of engineer Boswell with Hill and Rodes. When Osborn complained to an infantry brigadier who had placed his battery several hundred yards in *advance* of his infantry line, with the enemy apparently about to attack, the general replied "What is artillery for if not to protect the infantry?" He had completely missed the essential function of artillery, but poor Osborn could only shake his head. Apparently somewhat super-critical of just about everyone, Osborn concluded that much of the fault lay with other staff officers, those at army high command. With "army staff it has been a dead failure," he declared. "The War Department officers at Washington who have had charge of this part of the work of army organization have fallen very, very far short of being intellectual giants."[17]

The position of chief of artillery was no place for the retiring. The officer was almost constantly in the saddle when on campaign, seeing to the placement and supply of both the field pieces of the army, and the men who served them. He was part quartermaster, part engineer, and at times part field commander. Indeed, in recognition of the responsibility of his position, the ordnance chief or chief of artillery was the staff officer who more often than any other rose to the rank of brigadier general, North and South. "I have this work now on my hands to perform," wrote Major

Confederate Medical Officers' Uniforms and Equipment

1 Lt. Col.'s frock coat of surgeon Lt. Col. Samuel Bemiss
2 Epaulettes of Dr. G.A. Carter, 53rd Va. Inf.
3 Civilian cape of Dr. Alexander Yelverton Garnett, surgeon at Robertson Hospital and physician to Jeff Davis
4 Forage cap of Dr. William B. Wise
5 Surgeon's frock coat of assistant surgeon

Capt. R.H. Parker
6 Spurs of Dr. T. Berry
7 Field plate of Dr. Orlando Fairfax
8 Tourniquet stamped 'J.A. King, Mobile'
9 Brass bell from Jackson Hospital, Richmond, Va.
10-11 Case of surgeon Samuel Hollingsworth Stout, Medical Director of Hospitals, Army of Tennessee
12 Roll of lint bandages

13 Phlebotomy knife found at Gettysburg and carved 'Dr. F. Kempt, 17th Va. Vols.'
14 Officer's sword c. 1820 of surgeon I.C. Habersham, Savannah
15 Medical officer's sash
16-17 Scalpels from 20
18-19 Knives from 20
20 Amputation kit captured at Manassas and used by Dr. James Evans
21 Capt. Parker's sash

Artifacts courtesy of: The Museum of the Confederacy, Richmond, Va: 1-4, 6, 7, 9, 14-20; Virginia Historical Society, Richmond, Va: 5, 8, 10, 11, 12, 13, 21

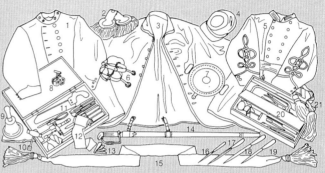

Osborn when he assumed his new assignment in August 1864, "and I will do it regardless of how much there is of it."[18]

Of the rest of the staff members in a general's military family, the surgeon and the judge advocate, and the aides, where there were such, suffered far less in the way of internal frustration or external criticism. The performance of their duties was governed by the resources available to them and the degree of trust and support they received from their commander. Yet of all of the staff officers, there was one who almost invariably stood above the rest in stature if not in rank; the one most turned to, most trusted, most intimately associated with the general in command. That, of course, was his adjutant.

If ever there was a catch-all post, this was it. Definitions were almost impossible. For one thing, his official title was "assistant adjutant general", since there was only one true Adjutant General, and he was on the War Department staff. One former incumbent "A.A.G.", as such staff officers were usually called, did attempt a half serious, half jest description of the requirements for the post. He "should be a man well posted in all arms of the service, know the right flank from the left, and from the front to the rear." "He should be able to tell, without hesitation a jackass battery from one of one-hundred pounder Parrotts; should be able to ride a horse without falling off, and to handle his saber and revolver without wounding himself or killing his horse. He should know how to write both the name of the commanding general and his own; the larger the letters the better. He should be an adept in military correspondence, and be able with Chesterfieldian courtesy to apply the cold steel of official rebuke to subordinate commanders."[19]

This may have been overstating the case a bit, but it was not far from the mark. The adjutant had to understand a great deal in order to intelligibly convey his commander's intentions to subordinates in the myriad orders and circulars that he issued over the general's signature.

Union Medical Officers' Uniforms and Equipment

1 Silvered Model 1840 medical officer's sword of Surgeon P.B. Goddard
2 Wool sack coat of Asst. Surgeon David R. Beaver 191st Pennsylvania Volunteer Infantry
3 Model 1840 medical officer's sword of Surgeon John J. Reese
4 Medical case made by Schively, Philadelphia
5 Brass tourniquet from 4
6 Medical officer's sash of

Asst. Surgeon John Huston, 81st Pa. Volunteer Infantry
7 Pocket case of Asst. Surgeon Joseph K. Corson, 6th Regiment, Pennsylvania Reserves
8 Horse tack box
9 Forage cap of Surgeon Philip Leidy, 119th Pa. Volunteer Infantry
10 Pratt's shoulder straps
11 Wool frock coat of Asst. Surgeon Charles

Archibald McCall
12 Leidy's dress epaulettes
13 Sword belt of Surgeon Pratt
14 Pratt's officer's sash
15 Medical case of Surgeon George L. McCook
16 One of the three trays of instruments from 14
17 Non-regulation sword of Surgeon B.R. Miller, 119th Pa. Inf.
18 Instrument from McCook's medical case

Artifacts courtesy of: The Civil War Library and Museum, Philadelphia, Pa: 1-7, 9-11, 14-17; Don Troiani Collection: 8, 12, 13, 18

Because he needed to be constantly at his commander's side, horsemanship was an important attribute, especially with a commander like Grant. His adjutant, Ely S. Parker, would describe what it was like trying to keep up with his chief. "It has been a matter of universal wonder in this army that General Grant himself was not killed," Parker wrote during the war, "and that no more accidents occurred to his staff, for the General was always in the front (his staff with him of course) . . . he requires no escort beyond his staff, so regardless of danger is he." It could be a killing pace for those officers required to accompany him, and of them all, the adjutant was indispensable. "Now such things come hard upon the staff," Parker confessed, "but they have learned how to bear it."[20]

Like others, the adjutant was denied the luxury of remonstration or gainsaying his commander's instructions or whims. Stonewall Jackson was notorious among his staff for odd and demanding behavior, as his new adjutant Captain Henry Kyd Douglas found out in 1862 soon after taking his assignment. One evening at midnight, Douglas saw Jackson send for Boswell without specifying the nature of his need. Expecting to have to ride off to some threatened point, Boswell dressed for the field at that late hour, only to find on reaching Jackson that the general wanted to know the distance from one point to another, information Boswell could easily have sent by message. Then after Boswell had returned to his quarters and prepared for sleep again, another summons came from Jackson fifteen minutes later, asking for the same information, this time in writing. "I learned afterwards that occasionally his staff officers were subjected to petty ills of that kind."[21]

It could be an exhilarating service at first. When Douglas joined Jackson's staff "and got my first taste of its delightful excitement", Jackson immediately began using him for transmitting important communications. Never thinking of the difficulties he was imposing on Douglas, Jackson one evening handed him a message and instructed him to take it to a detachment "on the other side of the Blue Ridge Mountains, somewhere near Culpepper." "My heart stood still with amazement," Douglas remembered. "For a moment I was stampeded, paralyzed. I had never been over a foot of the country and had only a vague idea that Culpepper was somewhere beyond the mountains; but how to get there I could not imagine." He had already been twenty-five miles in the saddle that day. It was dark, raining heartily. "But a young man soon rallies," the captain declared. "I was being weighed in the balance right there and I determined to throw all my weight on the scales." That was what made a good adjutant. As for Jackson, when Douglas rode off, the general bid him "a successful and pleasant ride!" not devoting an instant's concern to what he was sending the young man into. That, oftentimes, was what made a good general. Douglas successfully completed his mission, riding over 200 miles in four days. Yet when he reported his mission completed to Jackson, expecting some word of praise, all the general said was, "Very good. You did get there in time. Good night." Douglas was outraged. "Refusing to be comforted by the staff, who knew the General better, I threw off my heavy, soggy clothes and retired in grievous disappointment to an uncomfortable bed." The next day, when Jackson made him inspector general, all was forgiven.[22]

Above: Of all the staff officers with whom a soldier came in contact, the surgeons and medical assistants were those most turned to for comfort. These surgeons and assistants served the Army of the Potomac in 1864-5.

In a larger organization, such as a corps or army, the A.A.G. very often served the function of a chief of staff, even if not officially so designated. G. Moxley Sorrel served as such for Longstreet in the I Corps of the Army of Northern Virginia, and the degree of trust that had to arise between general and adjutant is well illustrated in their working relationship. "The General left much to me, both in camp and on the field," wrote Sorrel. "As chief of his staff it was my part to respond to calls for instruction and to anticipate them. The General was kept fully advised after the event, if he was not near by at the time; but action had to be swift and sure, without waiting to hunt him up on a different part of the field." Changing the position of a brigade or a division in battle was a grave responsibility, he knew, "but it often has to be faced by the chief of staff officer if the general happened to be out of reach."[23]

Thus was the adjutant to be seen everywhere his commander went. Often he was an almost comical sight, like Grant's adjutant and military secretary Parker, a Seneca Indian sachem, who stayed glued to Grant's side, carrying a portfolio with the necessary military papers over his shoulder, and a little boxwood inkwell tied to a buttonhole in his jacket. Yet Grant happily paid tribute to the assistance he got from Parker. "The only place I ever found in my life to put a paper so as to find it again was either a side coat-pocket," he said, "or the hands of a clerk or secretary more careful than myself." That was what adjutants – indeed all staff, in the end – were for.[24]

At the topmost levels North and South, the staffs of Grant and Lee present an interesting contrast, not only of the capabilities and functions of the officers assigned, but even more so of the way in which the generals used them.

Back in 1863, during the Vicksburg Campaign, Assistant Secretary of War Charles A. Dana came to Mississippi to inspect Grant's army and, so most believed, to spy on Grant for the War Department. Certainly the snobbish civilian revealed an instant disdain for many of the rough-hewn western characters that served on the general's military family. "A curious mixture of good, bad, and indifferent," he reported of the staff, "a mosaic of accidental elements & family friends." He approved of Rawlins and of Inspector General James H. Wilson, who by war's end

Below: Thanks to disease as well as battle, the general hospitals of the armies sometimes took on the aspect of whole tent cities, like this one at Gettysburg in 1863 in the aftermath of the great battle.

Surgeon, 22nd Massachusetts Infantry

Few otherwise friendly officers could inspire quite the terror in a soldier's heart that came from being approached by a surgeon after wounding, especially if, like this surgeon of the 22nd Massachusetts Infantry, he happened to be carrying his surgical knives or bone saw. Yet considering the damage done by the bullets of the time, a soldier with an amputation still had a better chance of survival than he did with mangled flesh and bone likely to succumb to asepsis. This major, like other officers in staff and support services, wore the regulation uniform for his rank, usually that of major. Only his sash differed, being green, and he wore, when necessary, a special medical officer's sword. His shoulder strap also indicated his branch of service, being the letters 'MS' in silver between two gold leaves which signified his rank. His tools and surroundings marked his trade more than anything else, however. They were largely well-intentioned men.

would command a small army of his own as a lightning cavalry raider. Yet among the others, Dana disparaged one "worthless, whiskey drinking, useless fellow", and another who "violates English grammar at every phrase." "Indeed, illiterateness is a general characteristic of Grant's staff", Dana would assert incorrectly.

What Dana did not immediately see was the way Grant used his staff to relax, all the while testing them and improving them. In the evenings the whole group would sit around a camp fire singing and spinning yarns, while Grant sat quiet, smoking a pipe or cigar, listening but not participating. If Rawlins, notoriously profane, began to swear, the rather straightlaced Grant would "good-naturedly remonstrate with his chief of staff for using too vigorous and sulphurous language," observed Parker. Rawlins would stop, but soon forget himself, and Grant would simply pretend not to hear him. In short, it was an almost typical civilian family scene, with Grant the father, and from that he drew stability when away from home. But he also watched these officers, observed their strengths and failings, and gradually through the war kept the good ones and replaced the others. By war's end, many of his staff officers were in fact brigadier and even major generals, trained specialists at their individual functions, and full participants in his strategic planning. Grant may have made all of the final decisions, but the informed views of his staff were the raw materials from which he fashioned the strategies that took him and the Union forces to victory.[26]

By contrast, Lee was a very different sort of general, and his staff reflected the fact. With only a couple of exceptions, his staff officers were lieutenant colonels or lower ranks, and the size of his staff considerably smaller than Grant's. In many cases, moreover, the men on his staff were not exactly outstanding. His chief of artillery, for instance, William N. Pendleton, had been found unfit for field command of artillery, and consequently promoted to staff command instead, "a well-meaning man," thought Sorrel, "without qualities for the high post he claimed." The situation was much the same on Lee's general staff

throughout the war, perhaps because Lee was loath to pull good men out of active field command where their services were more immediately needed. The trouble with this was that it left Lee himself often having to perform the tasks that abler staff officers should have been doing for him.

On his personal staff, however, Lee had better men, yet the three most close to him – Charles Venable, Charles Marshall, and Walter H. Taylor – were all civilians with no military training. The first two spent the most time with Lee in the

Below: Testimony to the vital importance of capable staff officers is the fact that so many of the leading generals of the war posed for the camera with their military "families". At war's end Grant stands in the center of his.

Above: The fascination with European armies led a number of generals, North and South, to employ French and English officers on their staffs, like these Englishmen at Camp Winfield Scott at Yorktown, in 1862.

Right: One of the premier field commanders of all time, Robert E. Lee kept a very small staff, and did not utilize it well, doing most of his staff work himself, as had generals in past wars. They called him "the tycoon".

field, Marshall being especially useful for handling the paperwork with which Lee never had much patience. Taylor, youngest of all, eventually became Lee's principal aide. Selected more for their personalities and temperaments than their military skills, Lee's staff were congenial and productive, but they were never planners in the way Grant's officers were. Their duties were the performance of details, not the proposal of ideas. Lee relied upon himself for that. Rarely did he have a council of war or a general staff planning session. He carried on his own shoulders the burden of strategic and even tactical thinking, as well as overseeing the myriad other great issues of supply and ordnance and engineering that trained and effective officers should have handled for him. The only real function that Lee's staff had in common with Grant's officers was the use Lee put them to for relaxation. Lee needed them for that far more than Grant, for by doing so much himself, Lee was almost always tired, even exhausted, and very frequently ill, as his overtaxing workload put strains on an already weak heart. Grant, by contrast, was usually rested, relaxed, and able to push himself physically to great limits without impairing his health, because he left the details to his staff.

Worse still, on several battlefields, most notably the Seven Days' Battles and at Gettysburg, Lee suffered reverses largely through terrible staff work, with no one coordinating the execution of orders. Lee tried to manage it all himself, and it was simply too great a task for one man, even one whose staff often referred to him as "the tycoon". Lee looked at running an army the way his predecessors in previous wars had seen it, as the responsibility of the man at the top. Grant looked at the same challenge, and saw it as generations of the future would see it, presaging in his military family the general staffs of the next century.[27]

It is ample proof of the vital role that the staff officers could, and should, have played in the Civil War armies. They may not have been leading troops in battle and winning glory and fame. But properly used and supported by their commanders, they could help ensure that those battleline troops were where they were needed, with the weapons they needed, and in a fit condition, to bring to bear upon an enemy the best an army had to show. And if they were mediocre men, or performed less than ably, then the odium they often received was not undeserved.

Years after the Civil War, a British writer summed up what these men faced, when he wrote that a staff officer was like unto a trouser button. "There are few to praise it while it goes on with its work," he said, "and very few to abstain from cursing it when it comes off."[28]

References

1 Rufus Dawes, *Service with the Sixth Wisconsin Volunteers* (Marietta, Ohio, 1890), p.13n.
2 James L. Nichols, *The Confederate Quartermaster in the Trans-Mississippi* (Austin, Tex., 1964), p.6.
3 *Ibid.*, pp.10-2.
4 Richard D. Goff, *Confederate Supply* (Durham, N.C., 1969), p.127.
5 *Ibid.*, p.54.
6 Archie P. McDonald, ed., *Make Me a Map of the Valley* (Dallas, Tex., 1973), p.11.
7 *Ibid.*, p.xxi.
8 James K. Boswell, "The Diary of a Confederate Staff Officer", *Civil War Times Illustrated*, XV (April 1976), p.31.
9 *Ibid.*, p.38; McDonald, *Make Me a Map*, p.xxiv.
10 Davis, *Breckinridge*, p.321.
11 Kenneth Radley, *Rebel Watchdog, The Confederate States Army Provost Guard* (Baton Rouge, La., 1989), p.11.
12 *Ibid.*, p.336.
13 *Ibid.*, p.241.
14 *Ibid.*, pp.90, 100, 237-8, 241.
15 Tower, *Manigault*, p.166.
16 Radley, *Watchdog*, p.243.
17 Richard Harwell, ed., *The Fiery Trail, A Union Officer's Account of Sherman's Last Campaigns* (Knoxville, 1986), pp.25, 27.
18 *Ibid.*, pp.4, 27, 29.
19 William H. Armstrong, *Warrior in Two Camps: Ely S. Parker* (Syracuse, 1978), p.88.
20 *Ibid.*, p.91
21 Henry Kyd Douglas, *I Rode with Stonewall* (Chapel Hill, N.C., 1940), p.48.
22 *Ibid.*, pp.49-50, 54.
23 Sorrel, *Recollections*, p.129.
24 Armstrong, *Ely Parker*, p.103.
25 *Ibid.*, pp.87, 94-5.
26 T. Harry Williams, *Lincoln and his Generals* (New York, 1963), p.312.
27 Jeffry Wert, "The Tycoon: Lee and His Staff", *Civil War Times Illustrated*, XI (July 1972), pp.11-8; Williams, *Lincoln and His Generals*, p.313.
28 Radley, *Watchdog*, p.233.

CHAPTER TEN

OFFICERS BEHIND BARS

Through the balance of 1864 Grant and Lee glared at each other across the trenches surrounding Petersburg, though the Yankee's grip grew ever-tighter. In Georgia, Sherman advanced from Atlanta toward the Georgia coast, Savannah, and the sea. Along the way, he threatened to take a little spot 100 miles south of Atlanta, forcing its officers to evacuate many of the men held there, Union prisoners of war, in Camp Sumter . . . Andersonville.

ONE DANGER that all officers faced, whether field or staff, was the ever-present possibility of being taken prisoner. Only those posted far, far behind the zones of military activity could be considered safe, and on a few occasions even these men were not immune to capture by daring raiders. The number of officers of both sides actually taken prisoner is undetermined, but at least 13,000 or more Confederates were captured during the war, and the number of Yankees must have been the same or greater. Thus, perhaps 25-30,000 or more men wearing gold on their collars and shoulders soon found themselves thrown into the rude and uncomfortable position of no longer being in command of anything, including their own destinies.

It could be a frightening and unnerving experience, being taken prisoner, though most officers, being used to composure under trying circumstances, seemed to handle it well enough. Major Abner Small and his regiment were a part of Grant's forces besieging Petersburg, and in August 1864 were ordered out on a raid on the Weldon Railroad. Early in the expedition they came face to face with strong Rebel resistance, and when a gap opened in the Yankee line, the enemy poured through it and surrounded Small and his men. "I found myself looking into the muzzle of a gun with a determined face behind it," he recalled.

With a curse on his lips for the Union blunder that got him into such a fix, Small went with his captors to the rear, where first he tried to persuade them to let him go. Then he was taken to talk with Confederate Major General William Mahone, who grilled him for information on Grant's position and numbers. "General," said Small, "you are too good an officer to expect me to give you correct answers," and Mahone only smiled and ordered him taken away. While enlisted men could, and often did give information to the enemy after capture out of guileless innocence, few officers could ever be expected to answer questions.

As he was taken toward Petersburg, Small first hid his watch, knowing that he would likely be stripped of any valuables, as indeed he was later. Once in Petersburg, he was marched down streets lined with old men and women and children "who vied with one another in flinging insults and venom." The women were the worst, he thought; "they spat upon us, laughed at us, and called us vile and filthy names." It was a far cry from the respect and deference an officer had come to expect.

Finally they reached Petersburg's neighbor to the north, Richmond, and marched at once to an old ship chandlery now known as Libby Prison, the most notorious of the Confederacy's prisons for Yankee officers. "We were received at Libby Prison as if at a palatial hotel," Small wrote. Courteously they were asked for their names for the register, then asked if they had any valuables that they wished the commandant to put in his safe for security's sake. Then each man went to a room at the rear, where "a little puppy named Ross went through the clothes of every prisoner", taking whatever money or valuables he could find. They went to that room one by one, and none returned to tell the rest of what to expect, allowing Ross to pillage them freely. Only when they were shown to their quarters in the large second floor rooms did the men compare experiences and learn what had been done to all of them. "We cursed our keepers from that hour."[1]

Robbery of prisoner officers was not official policy North or South, but since in both armies the best men in character were usually at the front, those left behind to act as prison guards were less likely to scruple over the belongings of an enemy. Yet there were exceptions. Confederate Captain William C. Thompson fell into Yankee hands late in 1864 in Tennessee, and early in 1865 found himself transferred to a prison in Nashville. With him he was carrying $4,000 in Confederate currency, a pocket knife, and a fine gold pen with silver appointments. Being ill, he was taken to the prison hospital and hid his

Men and officers of the Rebel armies, captured in battle, soon found themselves the "guests" of their foes, in such places as Camp Douglas outside Chicago, Illinois. For them it was the beginning of months of boredom and danger.

valuables under his pillow. A hospital official came up to him, commented upon the Masonic pin that Thompson wore, and asked if, indeed, he were a Mason, and then inquired if the Rebel had any valuables. "I told him they were under my pillow," said Thompson. "He took these and left, much to my satisfaction, for I knew he would care for them." Indeed he did. True to his fraternal oath to care for a fellow Mason in distress, Phillip Grove of the 92nd Indiana later returned, discussed Masonry awhile, then warned Thompson which guards to beware of, and commenced smuggling little extra bits of food to him. Learning that Thompson's brother was in another prison hospital in Nashville, Grove managed to get Arthur Thompson transferred to be with his brother, and then smuggled in whiskey to help ease the pain of Arthur's recent amputation. Thereafter, "Grove always saw to it that we shared in the food and refreshment that the kind ladies of Nashville brought to the hospital from time to time." Such extraordinary kindness from a jailor was not commonplace, but it happened enough to help ease the otherwise natural hatred of prisoners for their keepers.[2]

Another Confederate, Captain Samuel Foster of Texas, felt absolutely incredulous when captured. A member of the garrison of Fort Hindman, Arkansas, besieged by a Federal gunboat fleet and land troops in January 1863, he wrote in his diary that "there was excitement sure enough." Then, as the bombardment was beginning to cut the defenders to pieces, someone raised a white flag. "It was the only intelligible thing we could do," lamented Foster. The Confederate flag came down, and white sheets, towels, even handkerchiefs were upraised to stop the firing. Soon an enemy officer came among them and ordered them to stack their arms. "No one had ever given us a command in that manner before," said Foster. "The order struck us with awe. We were affronted with the reality that we were prisoners."

Then came a dangerously tense few minutes. The Yankees corraled the prisoners into a group and surrounded them with guards. "The entire Yankee army seemed to be standing around us," thought Foster. Captors and captured began to glare at one another. "Their guards had to fight hard to keep a space between them and us," Foster observed. "The men of both sides began hollering across to each other." Only nightfall relieved the tense moment, but even then it was still difficult for officers who had until a few hours before been men in command to realize their changed status. "Had the sentinels not been so close, with their glistening bayonets," Foster recalled, "we would have been unable to fully realize the situation. One look at them satisfied anybody. Their presence told us that what had happened had not been a joke."[3]

Eventually they reached Columbus, Ohio, which would be their prison home. Late at night, one by one, they were led into a small building where everything of value, money and pocketknives particularly, was taken from them. Then they were released into the prison compound. There was no organization. In the dark men began calling the names of their old friends and messmates, seeking to re-establish their pre-captivity society in some way. "Three hundred men created quite an affair," thought Foster. "We got together, separated, mixed ourselves up, then got together again. The entire situation was humorous." Only when the whole mess was concluded

Above: At the beginning of the war, the armies incarcerated officer prisoners wherever they could find spare room, such as at New York's Governor's Island. Cold, drafty, and damp, such quarters only promoted sickness.

Below: Almost every Northern port city found itself host to Rebel officers. Fort Warren, in Boston Harbor, accommodated scores of Confederate naval officers like these, mostly blockade runners and privateers.

did they finally settle down to start living as prisoners of war. They washed. They ate the rations provided, bread, beef, vegetables, and coffee. "Things suddenly did not seem so bad after all." Then a Federal officer assembled them and returned their knives – unless they were large enough to pose a real threat – and their money. Men with over $100 had their money held for credit for their purchases at the prison's sutler's store. Then he read them the prison rules. Lights out at 8 p.m., and no noise thereafter. No coming within ten feet of the stockade. Assemblies every morning and evening. "We finally began to understand how things were going to be like in this prison," wrote Foster of that moment. "At least, we were getting to know what they expected us to

do. I guessed everybody would do it."[4]

At the beginning of the war, when no one had any concept of its ultimate scope or length, no special provisions were made on either side for handling officer prisoners. They usually just occupied separate quarters in the same prisons with enlisted men, and sometimes with civilian political prisoners as well. Thus it was at Fort Warren in Boston Harbor. It began with some 750 men, most of them Confederates, being transferred from other sites. Many of these were an elite sort of captive, some of the Rebel officers being very wealthy and influential. Officials allowed them to form informal "messes" of half a dozen or so, assigning them to comfortable group quarters, while the private soldiers were crowded

into a large single room. Not long thereafter, officers were allowed to roam free on the island the prison sat upon, giving their parole not to attempt to escape, thus allowing them exercise and fresh air. Some 100 of the less affluent officers from North Carolina contributed some sixteen cents apiece per day to a general fund that purchased luxuries to augment their beef and pork diet.

In general they all had two meals a day, and one wrote that "our closet is never without crackers, cheese, bologna, sausages – fruit cake, plain cake – coffee, tea." None of the private soldiers in Fort Warren ate so grandly, and it proved to be a source of no little resentment. Large contributions of clothing and foodstuffs came from friendly Southern sympathizers in the North, and the officers were allowed to share them. Some officers even had curtains and floor coverings in their quarters. Few Confederate commissioned officers elsewhere in the war would enjoy a standard of prison living to equal that of the Fort Warren occupants. The prisoners even got along merrily with their guards, frequently joining in song and story. One Yankee lieutenant was presented with a gold-headed cane by his prisoners when they finally left the fort. When General Simon Buckner and others arrived at Fort Warren after their capture at Fort Donelson, the commandant actually had tears in his eyes when he explained to Buckner that he had orders to restrict his movements within the fort. In the end, almost all of the officers were exchanged and sent back to their own lines in 1862 and 1863, and no officers were incarcerated there again until after Gettysburg. When new officer prisoners arrived thereafter, they found a strict new commandant and a new set of rules, much at odds with the way the prison had run earlier. Still conditions were better at Fort Warren than at any other prison North or South, as attested by the fact that only twelve prisoners died while being held there.[5]

But Warren was the exception to the much harsher rule that prison, even for officers, was not a pleasant place. Once the Federal War Department appreciated the numbers of prisoners it would have to deal with, it began establishing a host of camps around the country, and decided that all – or virtually all – Rebel officers should be consolidated at one place. For this they selected an island in Lake Erie, opposite Sandusky, Ohio. Johnson's Island was essentially barren when authorities began construction of their new prison on its 300 acres, and by June 1862 its occupants were almost exclusively Confederate officers. In all at least 12,000 prisoners would pass through its gates during the war, from lowly lieutenants all the way to prominent generals like

Brigadier General Joseph William Hoffman

For some reason, both sides picked dour, parsimonious sorts of men to command their prison camp organizations. Though neither inept nor dictatorial, Brigadier General Joseph William Hoffman was an otherwise good match for the South's General John H. Winder. For Hoffman, prison management was a matter of efficiency, reducing the human component of men behind bars and walls, to an accountant's sort of calculation on food and fuel per man ratios.

Proudly at war's end he turned back to the War Department hundreds of thousands of dollars that he had saved at the expense of the health and nourishment and comfort of his prisoners. Like Winder, Hoffman was a regular brigadier general in the volunteer service, and he wore the standard uniform of his rank, with no insignia or other markings to indicate the special nature or responsibilities of his service.

Isaac Trimble and James J. Archer, captured at Gettysburg. Henry Kyd Douglas would wind up there for a time, as would several other generals, and a host of lesser mortals. Their captors confined them in wooden barracks, each room having a wood stove that proved effective except in the bitterly cold winter storms on the lake. They had bunks with straw mattresses, and about three blankets per man. The commissary issued clothing to those who could not buy any from their sutler, or who did not receive gifts from friends at home, and food was both plentiful and of generally good quality. "Our men," wrote one inmate, "live as well in the way of eating as we ever did." Only late in 1864, when Federals began to hear exaggerated stories of the ill treatment of Federal prisoners in the South, did a harsher regime reduce rations in retaliation.[6]

Incarcerated for long periods of time, especially after prisoner exchange was discontinued, the officers found much to occupy their time. They made articles of every description – rings and charms from shells, furniture from available scrap wood, even a violin. One industrious man, having smuggled a glass lens into camp with him, somehow got chemicals and used a tin can lid as a plate, sensitized it with the chemicals, and exposed it in a crude camera that he built, making an ambrotype portrait of a fellow officer. In their evenings, when weather permitted, they played games, chiefly a variant of the still-new baseball. "I don't understand the game," one officer complained, "but those who play it get very much excited over it."

In the winter they had snowball battles, including one memorable contest when General Trimble led one side against another commanded by Missouri militia General M. Jefferson Thompson. Ironically, Thompson was taken prisoner in the fight, giving him the dubious honor of being a prisoner within a prisoner. They read and played cards and chess, received newspapers, and wrote home. Indeed, thanks to the fact that the prison was almost entirely populated with officers, and therefore far more literate than the enlisted men of their army, more prisoner of war letters were written from Johnson's Island than from all the other Confederate prisons in the North. As for reading, in the end they built a lending library of up to 800 books and magazines. They formed a minstrel band and a theatrical group of players. Thanks largely to the quality of their conditions, the officers at Johnson's Island enjoyed a prisoner death rate less than half that of the other camps where enlisted men were kept.[7]

As the war progressed, like most prisons, Johnson's Island's population far outgrew its original intended limits. Expected to house about 1,000, the compound at its peak held over 3,200. Inevitably such overcrowding led to hardships, but on the whole, other than their restricted activity, the officers led lives not materially worse than they would have had had they not been captured. For many, the worst feature of prison life at Johnson's Island was being ordered about by young Yankee enlisted men. "Fall in, boys, I'm in a hurry," an impudent eighteen-year-old sergeant might yell at captains, colonels, and even generals, "his seniors in age, rank, position, and everything that constitutes a man, soldier, and gentleman," complained one indignant officer. It was, however, a small cross to bear.[8]

"As prisoners our days seemed endless," lamented a Rebel at one of Nashville's many prisons. "We were watched, spied upon, and con-

Above: Union authorities built a special prison just to house Confederate officers. Planned as something of a model, Johnson's Island proved to be less than ideal. At best it had one of the lowest death rates.

tinually checked by the guards and watchers," he wrote. "We couldn't get any news of the war. All reports were gloomy." That was very much the usual routine for officer prisoners, North or South. When Captain James Bosang arrived as an inmate of Washington's Old Capitol Prison, he also encountered another of the ever-present enemies of prisoners – lice or bedbugs, sometimes called "chinches" by the prisoners. His first night started comfortably enough, but then "I seemed to have hardly gotten to sleep when I awoke itching and burning with something craw-ling all over me with thousands of hot feet." When he arose, brushing the vermin off himself, he looked about and, by the dim light of a gas jet burning in the room, "could see them by the hundreds, chinches, all over me, all over my bed." The rest of the night he hardly slept, and in the morning gave his clothes and bed a thorough picking over, only to have the same experience the next night. Finally, studying the problem dispassionately, he saw that the only way for the insects to reach him was by crawling up the legs of his bed. Consequently, he obtained four cups, placed one leg of the bed into each of them, then filled them with water. "Oh, the good, undisturbed sleeping I had," he crowed later. "I found but very few that even attempted to swim and they were drowned."[10]

The Confederacy, too, eventually established

prisons intended strictly for officers, the largest and best known being Libby. Unlike Johnson's Island or Fort Warren, Libby afforded absolutely nothing in the way either of comfort or privacy. Most captured Federals had to run the same gauntlet of insults and leering civilians that met Major Small, before they got to Libby. Upon arrival, many found themselves placed in a first floor room with 200 or more crowded into a space 30 feet by 70. "The floor is an inch deep in thick black greasy slime which we cannot remove," Captain William Wilkins wrote in his diary. "A horrible odor pervades the apartment." An open privy stood at one end of the room, while the walls were covered seemingly "with the slops & excretions of the hundreds of men confined over-head." There was almost no ventilation, lice and vermin all over the men, no place to sleep except upon the slimy floor, and no blankets, soap, towels. Meals came twice a day, and drinking water was brought from the nearby James canal, "hot and of a very foul taste."[11]

Daily life very quickly took a dreary and mono-tonous tone. Wilkins started keeping a diary "to divert my mind from constantly dwelling on my sad fate and on the hardships which surround me." Almost immediately the men grew weak from want of exercise in their jammed quarters. "We are so crowded as scarcely to have standing room." Their rations he found reduced to "very greasy soup in the morning & a tainted boiled beef at 4 p.m.; bread at both meals & no more."

Frequently some prisoners were kept incom-municado from the rest, but quickly a system of slipping notes through cracks in the board walls and floors, or bribing guards to carry information, evolved. Different men bore their boredom and trials in very different ways. One sat with his face

buried in his hands all day, day after day. Another walked the floor constantly "like a caged wild beast". General Henry Prince stayed buried in his blankets most of the time, while others played cards. Wilkins, for variety, tried to change his "employments" frequently. He would walk, smoke, play cards or checkers, and sleep, to get through the day. In his diary he would write "Thank god another day is done."[12]

Especially demoralizing was the constant pre-sence of death. Sickness and disease and mal-nutrition killed hundreds, and the room in which they were laid out was directly beneath the first floor that housed Wilkins and many others. Through the crevices in the floor they could look every day on the faces of the deceased. Worse, as Wilkins found, "the sentries stationed around our windows are so anxious to shoot a 'Yankee' that yesterday they kept cocking & aiming their muskets at any of us who even looked out of the window." One captain, washing in the morning, came too near a window and was shot in the wrist and stomach by a guard outside. At times the guards chose to deny delivering to the prison-ers the packages that were sent to them by family and friends at home. Further, officers from the army of the very much detested Federal General John Pope, such as Wilkins, were placed in what he called the "black-hole" on that first floor, while other officers from other generals' commands were assigned to the cleaner and healthier upper floor rooms. "How long, O Lord," Wilkins would supplicate, "how long!"[13]

In fact, Wilkins was one of the lucky ones. With the prisoner exchange system still in oper-ation in late 1862, he was finally "traded" for an officer of equal rank in a Federal prison, and re-leased and sent home on September 24. "It seems

to me like a delightful dream," he wrote that day. Though he had only been in prison for six weeks, it had seemed an eternity. Most other captured officers of either side would spend more time than that behind bars, and many would never leave their prisons alive. Wilkins, ironically, would be recaptured eight months later, only to find himself yet again in the "black-hole".[14]

A year later, in December 1863, Brigadier General Neal Dow became an inmate at Libby, and for generals the treatment could be very dif-ferent. Late in 1863 he noted that he and other ranking officers "continue to receive great num-bers of boxes containing supplies." Dow found himself the recipient of two whole trunks filled with goodies from home – clothes, coffee, tea, sugar, ham, preserved meats, preserves, jellies, nuts, stationery, molasses, and even condensed milk, chocolate, and beef extract for soup. He also received blankets, and was allowed to purchase other commodities from a local market. First he sold United States "greenbacks" to guards and others at a ratio of one dollar for fifteen dollars in Confederate scrip. With some $19,000 of the Rebel "shin-plasters", Dow and others purchased potatoes at $30 a bushel, flour at $200 a barrel, and sugar at $6 a pound.[15]

Then on December 14, 1863, prison officials announced that no more packages from home would be allowed, and the next day purchases from the local markets were prohibited. On a cold Christmas Day soon thereafter, the prison authorities could provide no wood for heat or cooking, so Dow and others broke up their tables and benches for fuel. New Year's Day, 1864, marked six months of captivity for Dow, yet he was not despondent. While others like Wilkins became disheartened by the failure to exchange

Left: Political prisoners and specially suspected Rebel officers were confined in Washington's Old Capitol Prison. Security here was tightest of all. Many who entered its doors abandoned hope.

Below: The Confederates had their own counterpart to Old Capitol Prison, in Richmond's Castle Thunder. Officers from the Union mixed with spies and disloyal Confederates in its dark, desperate cells.

them speedily, Dow wrote that he was "entirely patient, because exchanges are not at present, for the interest of our country or cause." Meanwhile he spent all of his time reading and writing. Somehow he got books like *Tom Brown at Oxford* and Azel Roe's *Like and Unlike*, while other lesser officers were unable to obtain reading matter. One of his difficulties – there were few for Dow compared to the men confined on the lower floor of Libby – was that he was a general, and therefore had to be exchanged for a Rebel officer of like rank. As it happened, in the summer of 1863 Robert E. Lee's son Brigadier General W.H.F. "Rooney" Lee was taken prisoner, and in January 1864 negotiations commenced for a trade of the two brigadiers. It would not take place until March 14, and then only as part of a special exchange. Federal authorities had executed two captured Rebel officers for some reason, and Libby officials were going to kill two Yankee captains in retaliation. Hearing that, the Federals threatened to execute General Lee and another officer. Finally bloodshed was averted by trading Dow and two captains for Lee and two equivalent officers.[16]

Throughout his nine months at Libby, Dow, though very privileged, could still see the sufferings of others like Captain Wilkins, and on his first day of freedom, March 15, he closed his prison diary with words that spoke for the experience of most men kept at Libby. "The imprisonment at Richmond was *close*, severe, and attended by every circumstance of humiliation," he wrote. "Our treatment, in point of food and accommodations, was like that to Negroes – in crowded baracoons, where they are assembled for sale. We experienced nothing from the prison officials but humiliation and contempt."[17]

One of the few differences in the life of Union and Confederate officers was that when captured,

unlike enlisted men who experienced the same horrible conditions North or South, Yankee officers enjoyed very significantly worse treatment than Confederates. It was not in the main intentional, but rather simply a condition of the general shortages of everything in the South, for officers and enlisted men alike. Nowhere was this more evident than in the most hellishly notorious of all Civil War prisons, Camp Sumter, better known by the name of the small town nearby, Andersonville.

Both officers and enlisted men were kept at Andersonville, with no formal differentiation between the quarters or treatment accorded to them. It was simply one rather small stockaded compound, with a sluggish little rivulet flowing through it, no shelters, no sanitary facilities, miserable food, no clothing, and little or no attempt by guards and officials to improve matters. Indeed, they could not, for they lived not much better than their prisoners. As a result, in order to provide some kind of meager enhancement to their execrable rations, the prisoners soon developed an internal system of trade, barter, and commerce. Newly arrived officers could sell their blankets, tobacco – almost anything – in return for food hoarded by others. Some men specialized in buying and selling food. The guards helped a bit, by bringing in tobacco, eggs, and things, concealed on their persons, and "sold" at exorbitant rates when they entered the compound. And the prisoner officers detailed to carry the dead outside every day often had opportunities to effect trade with Southerners they met, bringing their goods back when they returned.

Indeed, such articles were so prized and brought such good "prices" that a subordinate trade appeared inside the prison, selling "chances" to go outside with the dead. "In this way," wrote one colonel, "the dead soon became

articles of merchandise and were bought and sold." Since the daily death rate was up to 100 or more, there were plenty of chances to escort a corpse. The best spot to buy was with one of the first corpses each day, for those escorts got to the traders outside first and acquired the best articles for resale inside the stockade. "It soon became the custom for the price of a corpse to be written on a piece of paper and pinned to the rags of the corpse." The first bodies could bring three dollars each; the last bodies on a busy dead detail day might go for only fifty cents. Worse, those who bought the latter corpses had to sit by them well into the afternoon awaiting their turn to go out for the burial, "and when it did come to your turn to go the stench of your corpse would make you sick and chances for trade would be slim." Prison custom was for a messmate or one who had attended the dead in his last hours to accompany the body, and he was allowed to choose two others to accompany him for the burial detail. These were the men to whom others paid their money for the chance to go out.

Colonel Melvin Grigsby participated in the trade from time to time. He observed others fight with each other sometimes over who should "own" a body and sell the chances. "I often heard it said," he recalled, "that death was sometimes assisted by the would-be mourners that the corpse might reach the dead-line among the first in the morning." The last time Grigsby bought a chance, he carried the end of the stretcher with the deceased's head. "There had been no tender loving hand to close those eyes when the last breath had gone. They were wide open and glaring. The head hung over my end of the stretcher and the eyes glared up at me. They haunted me for weeks. I never bought another corpse."[18]

To their credit, even the prison guards, many of them officers, found Andersonville appalling.

Left: The most infamous of all military prisons would be Camp Sumter, known forever by the name of a tiny nearby town, Andersonville. This image was made August 17, 1864, when the death rate was highest.

Major James Dunwoody Jones of the 8th Georgia Infantry, assigned to Camp Sumter in 1864, put it very simply. "Thirty thousand men in a stockade are apt to suffer more or less," he wrote years later. Only a few of them were officers, but they suffered right along with the rest. Most of the officers sent to the deep South went to a camp near Columbia, South Carolina, that contained some 1,250 of them. Jones was eventually detailed from Andersonville to take the command of the interior of this stockade, and he could not conceal his delight at getting away from Camp Sumter. "To me this was one of the most pleasant episodes of the war," he wrote of his South Carolina service. "I soon made fast friends, I believe, of every officer in the prison."[19]

Undoubtedly Jones' friendships were formed thanks to his humane and friendly treatment of his fellow officers in adversity. He helped one of his prisoners carry on a pre-war love affair with a Columbia lady, even smuggling her photograph into the camp for him. As a result, when the end of the war was approaching, some of his prisoner officers from Illinois urged him to come north with them, offering even to provide him with some land and livestock to get him going. Gratefully Jones declined. Certainly theirs was one of the more unusual relationships between captors and captives, but it was not by any means unique. Officers on both sides returned courtesy for courtesy, and the better of them took neither pleasure nor advantage from seeing fellow officers in adversity.

But still, captivity was captivity, and especially onerous at Libby or Andersonville. Understanding this, Major Jones had told his prisoners at Columbia that "it is your privilege to try to get away, just as it is my business to keep you." "I never punished a man for trying to escape," Jones recalled proudly.[20]

Above: Some officers in prison endured less tragic conditions. Even Fort Delaware, below Philadelphia, could offer some basic comforts, and a local photographer, J.L. Gihon, who could come to make souvenir photos.

And escape they did. From every prison North or South where the officers were kept, some managed to get away. At Fort Warren Lieutenant Charles W. "Savez" Read, a Rebel blockade runner and adventurer, chipped his way up an abandoned chimney in his cell to get free, then stealing a small sailboat to get away. Unfortunately, as soon as he was on the harbor he was recaptured. Another attempt that failed came when Captain Thomas H. Hines sent a special Bible to the

Below: Many of Morgan's captured raiders found themselves housed at Camp Douglas, where another photographer captured many of them in his own way, by camera. The cheerful pose belies their hardships.

mother of his friend Captain John Castleman, then incarcerated in a prison in Indianapolis. The Confederate Hines, an agent operating behind Union lines, took the book to a binder in Chicago, had it unbound, put four small saw blades made of watch spring steel inside the new binding on one side, and $3,000 in Yankee currency inside the other. He marked certain passages in the Book of John, chapter XIV, as hints to Castleman, the most telling being, "Let not your heart be troubled; believe in God, believe also in Me." "Me" in this case meant the Bible but, though he found the money and the saws, Castleman decided not to attempt to break out.[21]

His friend Hines, however, was an old hand at escaping from prison, having taken a leading part in one of the most famous break-outs of the Civil War. In the summer of 1863, Rebel raider John Hunt Morgan led his cavalry across the River Ohio and into Indiana and Ohio. Quickly the Federals were on his trail, and on July 26 they brought Morgan and a few hundred of his men to a halt, forcing them to surrender. On August 1 Morgan, Brigadier General Basil W. Duke, Hines, and sixty-seven other officers were sent to the Ohio State Penitentiary at Columbus. Each found himself searched first, and all pocket knives and other useful articles were taken from them.

At first their captors placed each officer in a separate cell and prevented communication between the Rebels as much as possible. But then, between 7 a.m. and 5 p.m. the jailors released all of Morgan's officers into a single large hall where they could talk. "Many plans for escape, ingenious and desperate, were suggested, discussed, and rejected," wrote Hines. They thought of bribing the civilian guards, but gave up on that and all other schemes until late in October. One day the warden somehow insulted Hines, and the captain retired to his cell, determined not to leave it again until he had devised a plan for escape that would equally humiliate the warden. In a day he had it, aided by having recently read Victor Hugo's Les Misérables. Tunnels and subterranean passages were on his mind, thanks to the book, and while sitting in his cell he noticed that despite its location at ground level, and with no sunlight reaching the floor of his chamber, still the floor was quite dry and free of mold or dampness that might normally be expected if it sat directly above the earth. That meant there had to

be an air chamber or basement of some kind underneath. If he could get through the floor into that chamber, then he and the others could tunnel out through the foundation to the open yard beyond, exit at night, and climb over the penitentiary walls to freedom.

Morgan agreed to the plan the next day, but there was a problem. Only prisoners on the lower floor of cells would have access to that air chamber, and then not even all of them. Thus Morgan and Hines decided to limit the tunnelers and escapers to themselves and five others. To prevent the daily inspection of his cell that was prison routine, Hines so thoroughly cleaned his room himself every day that the prison inspector

no longer bothered to look in. Then associates in the prison hospital managed to smuggle to them some flat table knives. Planning to start excavating on November 4 under the rear end of Hines' cot, the Confederates looked forward to freedom, and Hines to humiliating Warden N. Merion.

When they began, they cut their way through six inches of cement, and then beneath that six layers of brick, before they reached the chamber. It turned out to be four feet high and six feet wide and to run the entire length of the cell block. Then it was time to tunnel. Running at right angles to Hines' cell, they cut through a five foot thick foundation wall, followed by another twelve feet of grouting, then through another six

foot wall, before the tunnel was done. They halted about four feet beneath the surface of the prison yard at a point they calculated to be under a little used section of the compound.

All the while the digging continued, Hines sat on his cot above the hole in his floor, studying French and reading Edward Gibbon's *Decline and Fall of the Roman Empire*. Thus he stood guard. The men digging had reliefs every hour, and all communications were by way of signals, rapping on the floor of the cell. Meanwhile General Morgan's brother, Colonel R.C. Morgan, shredded his bed, ticking and braiding it into a thirty-foot length of rope, and attaching at its end a hook made from their stove poker.

Personal Memorabilia of Brig. Gen. John Hunt Morgan

1 General's frock coat
2 Officer's silk sash
3 Model 1851 Federal officer's sword belt
4 Pair of buckskin gauntlets
5 Confederate First National Pattern Flag
6 Wool blanket
7 and 8 Pair of ivory stocked, engraved Colt Model 1860 Army revolvers
9 Ivory and silver knife and fork carving set
10 Housewife made by the

general's mother in 1861
11 Forage cap
12 Copy of *Hardee's Tactics*
13 Model 1842 Aston pistol given to Morgan by the widow of Brig. Gen. Barnard Elliott Bee
14 Folding pocket knife
15 A pair of silver spurs presented to Morgan by the citizens of Danville, Virginia
16 Tins of percussion caps from pistol set *17*
17 Cased Tranter revolver

with accoutrements for loading and cleaning
18 Colt Model 1860 Army revolver, one of a pair of pistols owned and carried by Brigadier General Morgan and later presented to Captain John Kirkpatrick, 2nd Kentucky Cavalry
19 Custom made silver mounted saddle presented to Morgan by friends from Augusta, Georgia

Artifacts courtesy of: The Museum of the Confederacy, Richmond, Va

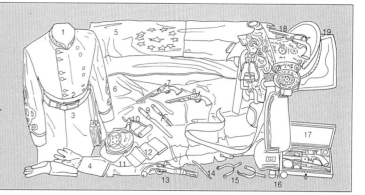

All that remained was to cut holes in the floors of the cells of the other prisoners who were to break out, giving them access to the chamber below. This was necessary since the break had to be made under cover of darkness, when all of the men were locked in their individual cells. To do so, an accurate measurement of the length of the cell block was necessary, else in cutting the escape holes from the chamber *up*, they could end up working in the wrong place. To further his revenge against the warden, Hines tricked him into measuring the block for them. The holes being properly spaced, they were cut almost to each cell surface, with only an inch or two of cement left in place and easily kicked out when the time came.

That time was to be November 27. Having first planned to go to Canada, the Confederates changed their minds. Instead, armed with a newspaper, they saw that they could take a late evening train that would get them to Cincinnati before the cells were opened in the morning, and their absence discovered. When they were locked up that evening, General Morgan, who was kept on the upper level of cells, quietly switched places with his brother on the lower level.

The train to Cincinnati left at 1.15 a.m. The guards checked the cell block every two hours. Consequently the daring Rebels determined to break out immediately after the midnight check. After the guard had left the block, they each arranged their bedclothes to simulate the appearance of the beds being occupied, then broke through the little crust of cement, and hurried out the tunnel and broke through the earth above. Quickly they ran in the rainy darkness to the wall, threw their hook over the top of a gate, and climbed up to the top of the wall. Each wore two sets of clothes, and now they walked atop the wall to an empty sentry box, and inside took off their dirty outer coats and pants. That done, they used their rope to lower themselves to the outside, then separated into groups of two and three and walked the quarter-mile to the railroad depot, bought their tickets, and rode through the night to Cincinnati. A ferry took them across the Ohio to their native Kentucky, and from there they began to thread their various ways south to

Tennessee and friendly lines. Hines was recaptured while crossing the Tennessee River, but Morgan and some of the others reached safety, Morgan writing to Hines' father of the captain's capture, and closing with the promise that "he will certainly escape." Indeed he did, and Hines, too, reached safety. Meanwhile, far behind them all at the Ohio Penitentiary, Warden Merion found on the morning of November 28 a note left behind for him, telling of the digging of the tunnel, the number of hours per day it occupied, the tools used, and a little taunt in French to show that Hines had paid attention to his studies while standing guard.[22]

Federals, too, could escape. Indeed, the majority of successful prison breaks were by Federals, for a variety of reasons not the least of which was

Above: Taken years after the war, this image shows the fireplace where Major Rose commenced digging his tunnel to freedom. Every morning the bricks had to be replaced to conceal the signs of any work going on.

Below: The "Chickamauga Room" on Libby's first floor was named for prisoners kept there who had been captured in the battle in September 1863. This clean post-war view does little justice to the real conditions.

that Southern captives were likely to have more numerous and more able guards than the old men and young boys often detailed to prison staff in the South. Also, Federal prisoners were better supplied with money and other items for bribery, while their guards, living a life of constant scarcity, were more apt to be tempted by a bribe.

John Bray of the 1st New Jersey Cavalry found himself dropped into the Pemberton Factory Prison in Richmond in November 1863, and stood it for a month before deciding that "I had long enough submitted to the hardships of prison life, and that, if possible, I would make my escape." His first step was a disguise, and this he got easily enough by trading his warm new uniform coat to one of his guards for a ragged Rebel blouse, and a few days later traded trousers as well. "I became, to all appearances, a Rebel soldier, having a suit of gray exactly like those of the guards."

The next day when the prisoners were allowed out into the compound yard for rations, Bray meant to make his move, but the opportunity did not present itself. It was January 10, 1864, when finally he broke free. Going out into the yard, he wore his blanket over his uniform and stayed close and under the cover of fellow prisoners who agreed to help him. "Reaching the yard which was filled with Rebel soldiers," he wrote two months later, "I suddenly, upon a favorable opportunity, slipped the blanket from my shoulders to those of my chum, and, stepping quickly into the throng, stood, to all appearances, a Rebel, having precisely their uniform, and looking as dirty and ragged as the worst of them." After that, he simply walked out of the yard, whistling the "Bonnie Blue Flag" as he walked, and passed out of the prison. Two days later he reached the safety of Federal lines.[23]

While most break-outs were performed by single men or small groups like Morgan's, attempts at much larger escapes were made occasionally. One of the most ambitious was a Confederate plan to capture a Lake Erie warship and use it to free the officers on Johnson's Island. The operation actually got started, but fell apart almost at once, with not one prisoner released and the would-be rescuers fleeing back to Canada.[24]

But one massive prison-break did succeed, and it came where one might have expected it – Libby. The miserable conditions made escape an ever-present thought on the inmates' minds. The number of officers crowded together was bound to lead to numerous plans for breaking out, while the flimsy nature of the building itself invited attempts. The one that succeeded was the brainchild of an engineer, Major Thomas E. Rose, who started looking for a way out as soon as he arrived. At once he surveyed the prison. It contained four floors, each 45 feet by 105 feet. The top three were divided into three rooms each, while the ground floor was kept off limits to the men except its middle chamber, used during the day as a kitchen. Rose, looking out a window at the end of the building, saw about seventy feet away two small outbuildings. He believed that if the prisoners could somehow get access to the unused basement floor, which was partially below ground level, they could do as Hines and Morgan had done, break through the foundation, and tunnel under the open lot to the two outbuildings. Once there, they could emerge at night and take their chances on Richmond's streets.

It was easier said than done. The only access to the cellar would have to be by the floor above, yet only the central portion was open to the men for their cooking, and it would be impossible to reach the part of the cellar they needed from that position. Directly above the basement room they wanted was the prison hospital, and they couldn't break through that. Finally they devised a scheme to tunnel through the brick wall of the kitchen fireplace, angling downward so as to miss the hospital on the other side, but reaching the cellar beneath the hospital. They had to work at night, when no one was in the kitchen, using only a jack-knife and a chisel found by Rose. Brick by brick, the tunnel was opened up in silence and darkness. At 4 a.m., with dawn approaching, all of the bricks taken out were carefully replaced and then the back of the fireplace covered with soot to prevent detection. It was incredibly tedious, yet finally they succeeded in reaching the cellar, only to discover that it was a haven for hundreds of vermin. "Rat Hell" they called it.

Once in Rat Hell, Rose and his companions, their number growing rapidly as the scope of the work before them became evident, stumbled for awhile deciding what to do next. After several false starts and missed opportunities, they chiseled through the foundation and started tunneling. The men worked in relays in the dark and foul air. One would chisel the earth, fill a spittoon with it, while another at the tunnel mouth would haul it out by a cord, the tunneler using a cord of his own to pull the empty vessel back in for

Brigadier General John H. Winder

It would have been difficult to find a Confederate general more universally unpopular, North or South, than Brigadier General John H. Winder. Despised not only by Yankees unfortunate enough to be kept in his prisons, he also enjoyed the enmity of Confederate soldiers and civilians alike. Inefficient, unconcerned, and at times dictatorial, he offended almost everybody.

Besides overseeing all prisons for Federal captives, he was also chief provost for Richmond, controlling the issuing of passes into and out of Rebel lines. Though widespread accusations of corruption are probably inaccurate, still he proved so erratic in his regulations for granting passes that even higher Confederate authorities finally curbed his power. As for his administration of the prisons, while never willfully cruel, his mismanagement still led to untold hardships for prisoners. Fortunately for him, he died before the end of the war.

refilling. Another man used a blanket to fan air into the tunnel. To keep the men working all day long, even though there were twice daily roll calls, other off-duty prisoners were instructed to answer to the names of the absent when called. With 1,200 prisoners in all, no guard would note a voice heard a second time answering to a different name. Soon this became too dangerous, and finally they had to work only at night, which slowed progress in the rat-infested darkness.

Finally one of the diggers thought the tunnel had gone far enough, and broke through to the surface, only to find that he was still twenty feet short of the objective. Hastily they filled the opening with a coat and some earth, and pushed on forward. At last, terrified of discovery, Rose himself got back in the tunnel and refused to come out, single-handedly digging much of the rest of the needed distance in a little more than a day. Taking heart, Rose did the same thing again two days later, and after eighteen or more hours of constant digging, fainting from exhaustion, hunger, and lack of air, he rolled over on his back ready to quit. Suffocating, he dropped the chisel and beat his fists against the roof of the tomb-like tunnel. As if in response to his entreaties, the roof suddenly gave way and he broke into the cool night air above.

Rose clambered out and found that he was in a small shed, with good cover for reaching the city streets. He covered the opening with a plank and crawled back through the tunnel to tell his excited compatriots. They agreed to wait until the next night for the escape, as it was by this time almost dawn. The original fifteen tunnelers also decided to take another fifteen into their confidence for the break itself, though the rest of the prison's 1,200 inmates had been kept ignorant of the weeks-long excavations for security.

They started the next evening, February 9, 1864, shortly after sundown. Rose and the first fifteen went through and out of the tunnel without difficulty. But behind them, the word had leaked from someone in the second party, and soon hundreds of prisoners clamored for a chance to go. All order broke down, and in the end scores of men poured through the tunnel, though, incredibly, they retained enough composure to stay quiet when they exited. The prison guards never knew what was happening until the next morning when roll call showed 109 officers missing. After a series of individual adventures too lengthy to tell, sixty-one of the escapees reached friendly lines and freedom. An unlucky forty-eight, sadly including Major Rose, were recaptured and returned to Libby. For Rose, however, liberty had to wait only another few weeks, for he was exchanged on April 30, and soon rejoined his regiment, never to be captured again, and proud of his part in the "great escape" of the Civil War.[25]

For those, the great majority, who could not escape – and most never tried – there was only the long unremitting boredom of endless days and nights that seemed to lead nowhere. Their enemies were tedium, malnutrition, exposure, and disease, as well as the occasional inhumane guard. For a very few, more violent dangers lurked near, in the way of reprisals. When a Federal command murdered – for whatever reason fair or foul – a Confederate officer, the Southerners felt fully justified in executing a prisoner of equal rank as a discouragement of further outrages, and vice versa. It happened very seldom, but it did happen.

More outrageous, however, was the much-touted plan of Confederate authorities in Charleston to place several dozen Federal prisoners directly in the line of fire from their own cannon shelling the city, as a means of coercing the Union to commence exchanging prisoners without restrictions. In fact, there may have been no such intention, but still about fifty Yankee officers suddenly found themselves under their own shells. "We are exposed to the fire of our heavy guns," wrote Lieutenant Edmund Ryan of the 17th Illinois, "but as a general thing the Federal prisoners take great delight in seeing and hearing our shells drop into the heart of this rebellious city." Apparently one officer was wounded.

Soon stories of this reached the Federals, and quickly they took fifty prisoners from various compounds in the North, and sent them to Morris Island, near Charleston, where they were to be kept directly in line of fire of the Confederate cannon. Four of them were generals, including Franklin Gardner, Edward Johnson, and Basil Duke, along with M. Jefferson Thompson. The officers were shipped south but, in the end, they were not placed in harm's way and, instead, were shortly exchanged for the Federal prisoners in Charleston.[26]

But then a few weeks later, on August 15, 1864, Major General John G. Foster commanding Federal forces besieging Charleston, learned that another 600 Federal officer prisoners were being kept in Charleston under fire. Indeed they were, though not intentionally to expose them to hazard, but simply until some other place for their confinement could be found. However, having once experienced the usage of prisoners as a tool to coerce him, Foster was not prepared to believe what was, almost certainly, a genuine explanation of the presence of the 600. Accordingly,

Below: In this house on Broad Street in Charleston, Confederate authorities kept Union prisoner officers under their own fire in an attempt to coerce the Federals into stopping their shelling of the city.

Above: The stockade for Confederate officer prisoners on Morris Island, near Charleston. Here the so-called "Immortal 600" were kept under the fire of their own guns until a threat to Union prisoners was removed.

600 Confederate officer prisoners were soon shipped to him, and placed under fire of their own guns, on Morris Island. They came to be known in the South as the "Immortal Six Hundred." For forty-five days they lived under shelling from Charleston's guns. Miraculously none were killed or seriously injured, though they suffered considerable hardship from exposure and tension.[27]

For all of these men, the happiest day of their lives would be the one on which they were finally exchanged or released. Yet even then their trials might not be over. Confederates especially had a long road home from prison, though the Federals provided most of them some form of transportation to their home states. For Federal prisoners, they were taken care of by their own kind, but that did not always promise safety. On April 25, 1865, almost 2,000 released Federal prisoners from Andersonville and elsewhere boarded the steamer *Sultana* at Vicksburg, bound for the North and home. One of them was Lieutenant William F. Dixon, of the 10th Indiana Cavalry. He was aboard as the boat steamed north, passing Memphis the next day. That night most of the men were asleep. "I was lying on the crowded cabin floor," he wrote later, "I was sound asleep and knew nothing until I was awakened by a sudden jar that threw me across the boat." The *Sultana's* boiler had exploded. Quickly fire spread as the ship started sinking into the cold, dark Mississippi. "The thought rushed through my mind," wrote Dixon, "of the long months that I had struggled for existence in prison . . . , and now that I must die an awful death."

The choice before him and the other survivors of the explosion was simple, "to either burn or drown." All around him he heard screaming, saw others jumping into the inky darkness, and clumps of scrambling men in the water dragging each other under. Only by grabbing a plank and diving in, avoiding all others, did Dixon manage to get away from the inferno. He paddled his way to the bank in the darkness, now illuminated by the fire of the ship and made terrible by the cries and screams behind him. Some even got to shore, clinging to overhanging trees, but were so weakened by the cold water that they could not pull themselves out of the river and drowned. Dixon floated on his plank some eleven miles to Memphis, where he was pulled out of the river the next morning. Behind him lay the greatest maritime disaster in American history. At least 1,238 – and perhaps as many as 1,647 – former prisoners, many of them officers like Dixon, their war and its trials over, going home, had perished. For weeks the bodies continued washing up on the banks down river.[28] There could not have been a more tragic ending to the whole tragic business of being a prisoner in the Civil War.

Above: For those fortunate enough to survive the disease and malnutrition and exposure of Civil War prison life, an end did finally come. These Federal officers of Iowa, kept at Camp Ford in Tyler, Texas, are going home.

Below: The final exchanges of prisoners, the event of which all dreamt, came under flag of truce meetings like this one, probably taken near Vicksburg, Mississippi in 1864-5. For all too many, exchange came too late.

References

1 B.A. Botkin, ed., *A Civil War Treasury of Tales, Legends and Folklore* (New York, 1960), pp.447-50.
2 William C. Thompson, "From the Defenses of Atlanta to a Federal Prison Camp," *Civil War Times Illustrated*, III (February 1965), p.42.
3 Samuel C. Foster, "We are Prisoners of War," *Civil War Times Illustrated*, XVI (May 1977), pp.29-30.
4 *Ibid.*, p.33.
5 Minor H. McLain, "The Military Prison at Fort Warren," *Civil War History*, VIII (June 1962), pp.34-47 *passim.*
6 Edward T. Downer, "Johnson's Island," *Civil War History*, VIII (June 1962), pp.100-3.
7 *Ibid.*, pp.104-5.
8 *Ibid.*, pp.100-12 *passim.*
9 Thompson, "From the Defenses of Atlanta," p.43.
10 Botkin, *Treasury*, pp.445-7.
11 William D. Wilkins, "Forgotten in the 'Black Hole'," *Civil War Times Illustrated*, XV (June 1976), p.37.
12 *Ibid.*, pp.36, 38-9.
13 *Ibid.*, p.40
14 *Ibid.*, p.44.
15 Frank L. Byrne, ed., "A General Behind Bars: Neal Dow in Libby Prison," *Civil War History*, VIII (June 1962), pp.62-3.
16 *Ibid.*, pp.61, 76.
17 *Ibid.*, p.78.
18 Botkin, *Treasury*, pp.451-3.
19 James Dunwoody Jones, "A Guard at Andersonville – Eyewitness to History," *Civil War Times Illustrated*, II (February 1964), pp.24, 28.
20 *Ibid.*, pp.28-9.
21 Richard M. Basoco, "A Sequel: 'Savez' Read's Adventures After His Capture at Portland Harbor," *Civil War Times Illustrated*, II (February 1964), p.32; John B. Castleman, *Active Service* (Louisville, Ky., 1917), pp.176-8.
22 Castleman, *Active Service*, pp.113-22; Philip Van Doren Stern, *Secret Missions of the Civil War* (New York, 1959), pp.164-5.
23 John Bray, "Escape from Richmond," *Civil War Times Illustrated*, V (May 1966), p.30.
24 Downer, "Johnson's Island," pp.108-9.
25 Frank E. Moran, "Escape from Libby Prison, Part I," *Civil War Times Illustrated*, IX (October 1970), pp.28-39 *passim;* Frank E. Moran, "Escape from Libby Prison, Part II," *Civil War Times Illustrated*, IX (November 1970), pp.39-43.
26 William M. Armstrong, ed., "Cahaba to Charleston: The Prison Odyssey of Lt. Edmund E. Ryan," *Civil War History*, VIII (June 1962), p.120; Basil W. Duke, *Reminiscences of General Basil W. Duke* (New York, 1911), p.378; Donald J. Stanton, Goodwin F. Berquist, and Paul C. Bowers, eds., *The Civil War Reminiscences of General M. Jefferson Thompson* (Dayton, Ohio, 1988), p.227.
27 War Department, *Official Records*, Series II, Volume 7, pp.7, 598, 625, 683; Rod Gragg, *The Illustrated Confederate Reader* (New York, 1989), pp.165-6.
28 William F. Dixon, "Aboard the *Sultana*", *Civil War Times Illustrated*, XII (February 1974), pp.38-9.

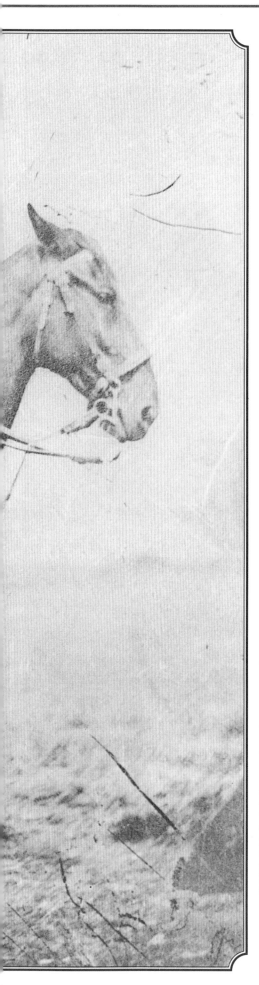

_____ CHAPTER ELEVEN _____

THAT SPECIAL DASH

It was inevitable that greater resources, manpower and organization would get the upper hand eventually. By the late spring of 1865, the South was defeated everywhere but in the mind of Jefferson Davis. Petersburg fell to Grant early in April, and Lee was on the run. All resistance to Sherman had practically vanished, the Shenandoah lay securely in Union hands, and the Far West hardly mattered. All that was left to the Confederacy was to die bravely, and that it did.

WITH ALL those tens of thousands of officers in service, most of them frequently engaged in battle, it was inevitable that some would come to stand out from the rest, men of special gifts, a genius for war, or extraordinary personal bravery. Part of it was the requisite of leadership, of setting an example for the men. Yet a special few truly rose above their brothers in arms to show what genuine heroism and bold leadership could achieve.

Of course, it was different for officers than for enlisted men. Most of the outstanding acts by the men in this war were solitary deeds, by one man alone. Officers, on the other hand, were most often leading men and thus their great deeds depended upon the collaboration of their followers. It made them none the less bold – indeed, it took a special kind of man to get others to follow him into some of the places these intrepid commanders ventured.

Yet there were a few individual officers who took their risks alone. Indeed, as examples of such heroism began to mount, both Union and Confederacy took steps to recognize their heroes. Each authorized the awarding of a medal of honor to such men, though only the North actually went beyond the authorization to present medals, the predecessor to the Congressional Medal of Honor. Authorized on July 12, 1862, the first medals went to enlisted men involved in a daring raid on Rebel railroad facilities in Georgia, but soon officers, too, began to earn them. During the course of the war some 1,520 medals would be awarded: 1,196 in the Army, 307 in the Navy, and 17 in the Marine Corps. While many were awarded indiscriminately for lesser deeds – often to be revoked after the war – the majority were earned for real valor. Most were earned by enlisted men in the Army, yet of that number 301 were awarded to officers, just over a quarter. Of those given in the Navy, all went to petty officers and lower ranks, while in the Marine Corps only non-commissioned officers and enlisted men received the Medal.

Of those officers in the Army to receive the award, every branch and variety of service was represented. There were chaplains and surgeons, staff officers of every description, and men of every rank from second lieutenant up. At least twelve general officers won the award, including Absalom Baird, Daniel Butterfield, Manning Force, John P. Hatch, Oliver O. Howard, and Major General Daniel Sickles, who received the award for great personal bravery amid what most critics regard as a very stupid act – the advance of his III Corps to an exposed position at Gettysburg, where the corps was destroyed and Sickles lost a leg. Some of the awards were certainly politically motivated, but the overwhelming majority, especially among the lower commissioned and staff ranks, were earned the hard way.[1]

Assistant Surgeon Richard Curran of the 33rd New York went into the Battle of Antietam, on September 17, 1862, with no orders as to where to place his field hospital. Left with no choice, when the battle began he started treating his men almost where they fell, right in the line of enemy fire. Though repeatedly ordered to the rear by other ranking officers, Curran stayed where he was needed. Sometime later, when the wounded were removed some distance to the rear, though still in range of Rebel artillery shells, Curran stayed with them, having one poor patient's leg blown away by a cannon ball even while the surgeon treated his other wound. His heroism won him the Medal of Honor.[2]

At Gettysburg there were more officers who distinguished themselves, and not just for stupidity like Sickles. Indeed, others would win the Medal because of Sickles' ill-advised exposure of his corps. Second Lieutenant Edward Knox of the 15th New York Light Artillery received orders to take two field pieces to support the threatened left of Sickles' badly placed line. In his enthusiasm Knox took the guns too far, some 100 yards beyond any support, and just as the Rebels were launching a charge. He fired both pieces into them, then ordered his men to lie down and

Always in this war, the public imagination would be captured by a special few, men braver than the rest, more daring, perhaps just more foolhardy, but who in the end left the mark of their special dash and élan on the course of the war.

pretend to be killed or wounded. As a result, the Confederates charged right over them without stopping, and when their assault was repulsed and they passed back over Knox once more, the rash but daring artilleryman got his men and guns back to relative safety. That same day Captain John Lonergan led his severely reduced company to surround a house filled with Confederate sharpshooters, and boldly bluffed them into surrendering. He captured eighty-three, more men than in his company. Another captain, J. Parke Postles of the 1st Delaware, was already feeling ill that day, but volunteered to ride through a storm of Rebel fire to deliver an order to some Federal sharpshooters in a different building on the battlefield. Boldly riding across the field, Postles figured out that the only reason that he was not hit was that he was a moving target. That was fine so long as he rode, but he would have to stop when he reached the building to deliver his order. Consequently, when he arrived, instead of stopping, he jerked back on his rein, put the spurs to his poor horse, and thus jumped and bucked around the yard while he shouted his message to those inside. He evaded all of the enemy fire, and received a Medal of Honor for his pluck.[3]

There was just as much heroism in the Western theater of the war. Few could compare with the exploits of Captain Patrick M. White of the famed Chicago Mercantile Battery. At Vicksburg, an order came directing him to take one field piece into a shallow ravine and break down a Rebel earthwork. Incredibly, all the while under fire from the foe, White and a few of his men manhandled their gun right up to within a few yards of the fort, and then calmly began battering it with cannon balls, White himself cutting the fuses so that they exploded just moments after leaving his gun. Before long he silenced an enemy cannon in the fort, set the works ablaze, and drove the defenders out, continuing to hold his ground for some time until ordered to withdraw. For their gallantry and devotion to duty, White and five of his brave men would win the Medal that day.[4]

And in the far-away Trans-Mississippi, heroism could still be rewarded. Lieutenant Colonel Frank Hesseltine had just 100 men from his 13th Maine Infantry to reconnoiter the Matagorda Peninsula, off the Texas coast. On December 29, 1863, they landed from a Yankee steamer, and were immediately cut off from the boat by a sudden storm. Then Hesseltine learned that two Rebel cavalry regiments were thundering toward his rear. Overwhelmingly outnumbered, isolated from the safety of the steamboat, and having no supplies but what the men had carried ashore with them, Hesseltine started a retreat. Finally he reached the beach, with nowhere to turn. Ordering his men to build driftwood breastworks, he waited through the stormy night for the inevitable attack. But the assault did not come. Instead a Confederate gunboat arrived to start shelling them. Slowly Hesseltine moved his command along the beach for nearly two days, across twenty miles of sand, through a raging storm, and often under the fire of pursuing cavalry and gunboat. He lost not a single man and got them all back to safety.[5]

Right: Some men simply looked the part of the dashing commander. Regis de Trobriand took a volunteer commission in the Union army and became a brevet brigadier, proving himself an able commander.

Major General G.A. Custer

The "Boy General", they called him, though there were a few generals on either side actually younger than George Armstrong Custer. Still, when he became a major general in 1865 at the age of twenty-five, he set a record yet to be broken. Custer was well known in the Army, and could hardly be mistaken thanks to his theatrically flamboyant manner and dress. He virtually designed his own uniform. He wore a dark blue short jacket, with a blue sailor-collar shirt underneath, a red cravat at the neck, blue trousers tucked into oversized cavalier style black riding boots, and a wide-brimmed hat with his insignia of rank. Easiest to recognize of all was his long, curly blond hair. As a lowly captain, Custer did not stand out from the crowd of officers. With his rise to prominence, he became steadily more theatrical and ostentatious in dress and manner, facts, however, that could not detract from his leadership qualities.

Such heroism and resourcefulness was not limited to Yankee officers. On October 13, 1862, Jefferson Davis signed into law an act passed by the Confederate Congress authorizing him "to bestow medals, with proper devices, upon such officers of the armies of the Confederate States as shall be conspicuous for courage and good conduct on the field of battle." But a year later, indicative of the scarcity of raw materials and services of all kinds in the South, the War Department still had not fixed a design for the medal nor manufactured any. Instead, so as not to postpone any longer recognition of bravery, it created a "roll of honor" to be read before the armies listing the names of the daring. That was as far as the government got.[6]

Yet there was one case of an officer receiving something more tangible, and for one of the most incredible acts of daring of the war. On September 8, 1863, Lieutenant Richard W. Dowling commanded a small garrison of forty-three men, mostly Irishmen, holding a fort guarding Sabine Pass at the mouth of the Sabine River, which flows southward into the Gulf of Mexico, form-

ing the boundary between Texas and Louisiana. Dowling's fort stood on the Texas side overlooking the entrance to a river that would be invaluable to the Federals as a means of invading the interior of Texas. Dowling and his little command were all that stood in the way of such an invasion.

On that September day, 4,000 men of the XIX Corps appeared on transports off the mouth of the Sabine, expecting to steam up the river. To silence little Fort Grigsby, as Dowling's earthwork was called, they were accompanied by four gunboats, the *Clifton*, *Sachem*, *Arizona* and *Granite City*, mounting between them more than twenty guns, versus the four smoothbores and two howitzers in the fort. Well before dawn Dowling's lookouts saw signaling among the Federal ships, and he ordered the fort's cannon loaded and ready for action. When the sun rose, he could see the *Clifton* anchored some distance from the fort, and at 6.30 a.m. she opened fire. For an hour she kept it up, doing no damage. Then the *Sachem* entered the fight by opening fire on the little support steamer *Uncle Ben* moored near the fort. This fire, too, was ineffective, and the gun-

boats did not renew the firing until 3.40 that afternoon, when several of the ships approached again. It was then that Dowling opened fire for the first time, concentrating on the *Sachem*. At once one of his shots penetrated her steam boilers and she raised a white flag, out of action. Then another shot ruined the *Clifton's* steering apparatus, and she ran aground right under Dowling's guns. For twenty minutes he pummeled her until she, too, surrendered. The whole fight lasted about forty-five minutes before Dowling boarded his prizes. The other Yankee gunboats withdrew, for a time abandoning the transports, and the whole operation was cancelled by the Federals.

"This seems to me to be the most extraordinary feat of the war", district commander Major General John B. Magruder wrote two days later. Perhaps it was. With six cannon and forty-two men, Dowling had disabled and captured two gunboats with their thirteen cannon, 340 prisoners, and put the rest of the expedition to flight. A few months later the Confederate Congress would give Dowling and his men an official

Below: Major W.F.M. Arny, United States Indian agent in the New Mexico Territory, added a special bit of color to his duty by adopting Indian dress himself, and later by calling himself a general.

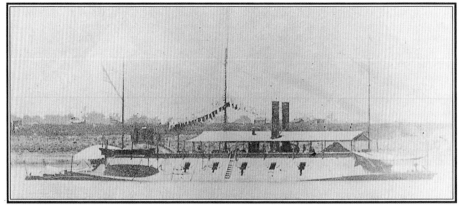

Above: Though far more formidable than the gunboats that attacked Sabine Pass, the U.S.S. *Benton*, shown here off Natchez, Mississippi was still as vulnerable to plunging fire as those Dowling fought.

Below: The U.S. transport *Fulton* as it appeared in June 1864. Though probably larger than those repulsed by Dowling, it fairly represents the sort of vessel used to bring troops to a battle.

vote of thanks. Better yet, in the brief but desperate little battle, not a single one of his command, called the "Davis Guard", was injured in any way. Probably nowhere else in the Civil War was there such a lop-sided disparity of odds going into an action, and conversely such a lopsided list of casualties.[7]

Even in faraway Richmond, President Davis was impressed. "The success of the single company which garrisoned the earthwork is without parallel in ancient or modern war," he would declare, "It was marvellous."[8] But perhaps even more memorable than the words of their president, were the tokens that Dowling and his forty-two defenders received a few days after the fight. They were simple silver medals, made from coins, with the initials "D.G." for Davis Guards inscribed on one side, and "Sabine Pass, September 8, 1863" inscribed on the obverse. Modest though they were, they were the only medals ever issued for valor to Confederate officers and men.

Such desperate stands were not entirely uncommon in this war, though rarely were they as dramatic as at Sabine Pass. For the Confederates particularly, so often outnumbered, the prospect of disparate odds frequently had to be faced. In April 1865, when Richmond and Petersburg were being abandoned and Lee and his Army of Northern Virginia valiantly tried to escape toward Appomattox, one incredibly brave band of men stalled the advance of the pursuing Federal army for hours at two tiny outposts, Forts Gregg and Whitworth. There on April 2, officers of the South discovered the cost of true leadership.

Fort Gregg was nothing more than an earthwork with a six-foot deep trench in front of it, and several piles of cannon ammunition. Semicircular in shape, it could be outflanked on either side. Nearby Fort Whitworth offered some protection, but neither was manned until the desperate hours of April 2 as Lee was starting to pull

Below: Officers of the 96th Pennsylvania Infantry fought in every major campaign from 1862 until late in 1864, achieving an excellent record for that special dash that made some units élite.

out of his lines. Brigadier General Nathaniel Harris had only 400 men, yet he divided them between these two forts, while men of the Washington Artillery of New Orleans dragged three field pieces into Fort Gregg. Other bits and pieces of commands, including Brigadier General James Lane, filtered into the forts. But then Lane had to return to his North Carolina brigade, forming a thin line some distance to the rear of the forts, and that left Gregg and Whitworth all by themselves in front of the advancing enemy. Soon the defenders of Fort Whitworth abandoned it, and only Gregg, now commanded by Lieutenant Colonel James H. Duncan and Captain A.K. Jones, under the general direction of Major General Cadmus Wilcox, remained. They had fewer than 300 troops to effect a defense. "Men, the salvation of this army is in your keep," shouted Wilcox, "Don't surrender this fort."

Soon afterward the enemy opened fire, and for half an hour an artillery barrage plowed the earthworks before the first infantry assault was

Above: No photographs exist of "Dick" Dowling's fort guarding Sabine Pass, but it might have looked something like Fort Barrancas near Pensacola, Florida; only on a smaller scale.

seen forming. Some in the fort thought the bluecoat line three-quarters of a mile wide, numbering 9,000 or more. Then the Yankees advanced. Twice the Federals charged and were repulsed. Duncan coolly watched them reform a third time. Nearby a surgeon urged a gun captain to surrender. "Let it go as it will," replied Captain W.S. Chew, "We'll not give up." Then the third wave came forward. Duncan ordered his men to hold their fire until they could hear the enemy's boots on the hard soil between them. Then the Rebels delivered their last volleys, but the Union line kept coming, over the bodies of the dead and wounded from the earlier assaults, over the ditch, up the parapet, and into the fort. Bayonets and musket butts were the only weapons left to the

defenders now. They threw bricks, even lit fuses to the artillery shells in the fort and threw them like grenades at the enemy.

Captain Jones was one of the few survivors. "The battle flags of the enemy made almost a solid line of bunting around the fort," he recalled. "The noise was fearful, frightful and indescribable. The curses and groaning of frenzied men could be heard over the din of our musketry. Savage men, ravenous beasts! We felt that there was no hope for us unless we could keep them at bay. We were prepared for the worst, and expected no quarter." For ten minutes or more the death struggle continued inside Fort Gregg, officers fighting without distinction of rank

alongside their men. Then at last it was over. Duncan lay unconscious, badly wounded. Miraculously Wilcox, Jones and twenty-eight others were unhurt, out of the few who entered Fort Gregg that morning. Out on the field before them, and in the compound and ditch around Fort Gregg, lay at least 714 Yankee casualties traded for the 57 dead, 129 wounded, and thirty uninjured prisoners taken.[9] Better yet, the bravery of those officers and men had bought enough time for Lee to stabilize Longstreet's corps, time to set up a defensive line that allowed Lee to escape.

There were many definitions of heroism, and some of them might appear otherwise to be little more than pointless exposure and risk. But then,

sometimes, these things had to do with a code of honor and gentlemanly conduct even older than the hatreds that brought on the Civil War, and they could only be observed with wonder.

At Gettysburg on July 2, 1863, most of the Confederate cavalry present was massed on the extreme left of the Rebel line, considerably out of the day's action. Brigadier General Wade Hampton of South Carolina commanded them, and there they sat on their horses awaiting orders. Hampton had enlisted as a private soldier, but soon raised his own command, the Hampton Legion, and rose to generalship through bravery and ability, though he had no prior training or experience. Six feet tall and incredibly muscular,

Confederate Cavalry Officers' Uniforms and Equipment

1 Uniform trousers of Capt. W.H. Cleaver, Steele's Texas Regt.
2 Cleaver's frock coat
3 Frock coat of Maj. James B. Ferguson
4 Militia pattern hat, 6th Btn. Tennessee Cav.
5 Captain's frock coat of Lt. Col. R. Randolph; killed May 1864
6 Randolph's trousers
7 Sword of Lt. Gen. Wade Hampton
8 1851 Federal saber belt

9 and 10 Officers' maroon silk sashes
11 Belt with Virginia plate belonging to Col. Oliver R. Funsten
12 Model 1851 Federal sword belt and plate of Lt. Benjamin M. Parnham
13 Parnham's holster
14 Officer's silk sash
15 Saber of Maj. Heros von Borke, member of J.E.B. Stuart's staff
16 Jacket of Capt. W.H. Cleaver

17 Folding dagger owned by Col. John S. Mosby
18 Saber made by Boyle, Gamble and Macfee
19 Spurs of Capt. William I. Rasin
20 Haversack of Capt. J. Hobson
21 Hobson's tin canteen
22 Hobson's revolver saddle holsters
23 Havelock of Lt. Richard L. Dobie
24 Havelock of Lewis H. Stern

Artifacts courtesy of: The Museum of the Confederacy Richmond, Va: 1-17, 19-24; Russ Pritchard Collection: 18

Hampton was, thought one Rebel, "unquestionably the strongest man in the Confederate service." Certainly he had strength of nerve and character, as he was about to demonstrate.

Hampton was out in front of his troopers, out of supporting distance from them, when he heard a bullet whistle over his head. In a moment, looking at a belt of woods 300 yards away, he saw the muzzle flash of a rifle, and quickly heard another bullet. Instead of retiring, Hampton spurred his horse to a trot and made for the place where he had seen the flash. After going more than half the distance to the woods, he came to a high fence and, looking over it, saw at the edge of the wood a young Federal cavalryman, Frank Pearson of the

6th Michigan Cavalry. Incredibly, rather than standing behind cover, the boy had taken position atop a tree stump, no doubt to give himself a better line of fire on the Confederates. It also made him an outstanding target.

Hampton pulled his revolver, and he and Pearson fired simultaneously. Hampton sent the bark flying from Pearson's stump, while the Federal bullet lodged in a fence rail near the general. Then Hampton did something inexplicable. Clearly having the edge with his revolver, while the Yankee carried a single-shot carbine, Hampton turned his pistol upward and calmly waited for Pearson to reload. Then they fired again. It had become a duel.

This time Hampton missed, but Pearson pierced his coat and grazed the South Carolinian's chest. The Federal's gun then jammed as he tried to load another round. Looking at Hampton, he raised his right hand in a way that seemed to say "Wait a bit, I'll soon be with you." Quickly he cleaned his bore, while Hampton looked on. "The delay sorely taxed the patience of Hampton," wrote a friend, "as it would that of any gentleman who was kept waiting to be shot at." But the general would not fire until the boy was ready. It echoed a day just weeks before at Brandy Station, when Hampton charged a Yankee lieutenant intending to cut him down with his saber, only to find the Federal's sword arm was disabled and he

Union Cavalry Officers' Uniforms and Equipment

1 Forage cap
2 Frock coat of Capt. William P. Wilken, 1st Virginia Cavalry
3 Slough hat of Capt. Alexander H. McHenry, Co. G, 13th Pa. Cav.
4 First lieutenant's shell jacket
5 Forage cap of Capt. William Cunningham, 3rd Massachusetts Cav.
6 Shell jacket of Capt. J. H. Workman, 6th Pa. Cav.

7 Slough hat of 4th U.S. Cavalry
8 Workman's trousers
9 Workman's model 1840 cavalry officer's saber
10 Model 1860 cavalry saber of Capt. Charles R. Suter
11 Officer's sword belt
12 Model 1840 cavalry officer's saber
13 Freeman Army Model

revolver, .44 caliber
14 1853 lefaucheux revolver
15 Captain's straps
16 Major's shoulder straps
17 Officer's sash
18 Dragoon's epaulettes
19 Dress epaulettes
20 Dragoon dress epaulettes of Capt. Alfred Pleasanton, later major general
21 Cavalry hat insignia
22 Officer's high boots

Artifacts courtesy of: West Point Museum, West Point, N.Y.: 6, 8-14, 17-18; First Troop Philadelphia City Cavalry Museum, Philadelphia, Pa: 4; The Civil War Library and Museum, Philadelphia, Pa: 1, 15, 16; Don Troiani Collection: 7, 22; Gary Leister Collection: 3, 21; Bob Walter Collection: 2, 5

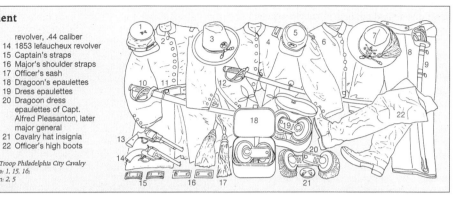

could not defend himself. Hampton saluted him and rode away.'

Now the Yankee cavalryman had his carbine ready, and the two duelists finished their private battle with a final exchange of shots. Hampton felt nothing, but Pearson dropped his weapon, his wrist hit by Hampton's bullet. Picking up his carbine, the young Yankee disappeared into the woods. Just then, Hampton felt a terrible blow on the back of his head. So caught up was he in his duel with Pearson that he did not hear the approach of a lieutenant of Pearson's regiment behind him. It was not a cowardly act. The Yankee approached with the fence between him and Hampton and knew only that here was a Rebel officer firing in the direction of his own men. He would not run the general through from the rear, for it would have been dastardly. Yet he could not risk demanding surrender, for Hampton was a huge man who looked as plucky as he was, and the lieutenant figured the general would most likely just turn around and use the pistol in his hand. So he hit Hampton with his sword blade instead.

The lieutenant reckoned without Hampton's thick hat, thicker hair, and tough skull. Barely dazed, Hampton wheeled around anxious to use his pistol. The lieutenant turned his mount and raced away, Hampton in hot pursuit, repeatedly pulling the trigger on his revolver. Fortunately for the Yankee, every chamber refused to fire. Then the foe wheeled off toward safety through a gap in the fence and Hampton could only hurl his pistol at him, "accompanying it with some words which did not entirely become his character as a vestryman of the Protestant Episcopal Church."

There, seemingly, it ended. But there was to be a postscript. Ten years later, in 1873, Hampton's younger brother Frank met that same Yankee lieutenant in Mobile, Alabama. In fact, the officer sought him out. "Colonel," he said, "I sought your acquaintance in order that through you I might make the *amende honorable* to your brother." He had been troubled by the manner in which he struck Hampton from behind, and sought now to explain and to apologize. In time Hampton wrote to the Yankee expressing his gratification that his pistol had malfunctioned that day, and heartily accepting the Federal's apology. Further, through the Federal, Hampton commenced a correspondence with Frank Pearson, then a successful farmer back in Michigan. Pearson assured Hampton that he was happy now that he had missed him with all those carbine shots, and the general, for his part, replied how sorry he was to have wounded the young private at Gettysburg.[10]

This was individual dash on a grand scale. But most of the generals who achieved a reputation for daring did so as leaders rather than for their own personal deeds. Major General Jeb Stuart, though certainly brave and dashing, won his lasting renown through the bold raids that he led into enemy territory. Twice he rode entirely around Federal General George B. McClellan's Army of the Potomac, once on June 12-15, 1862, and again on October 9-12. Ever the daring raider, Stuart led other similarly bold enterprises against Yankee communications and supply, each one accompanied with the trademarks of his dash – swift movement, lightning strikes, the gathering of considerable plunder, and few if any casualties taken himself. Best of all, he gathered the information that his commander Lee needed in order to thwart repeated Federal campaigns. To be sure, Stuart was a flawed cavalryman at times.

Above: The Cavalry School of Practice at Carlisle Barracks, Carlisle, Pennsylvania. The second oldest Army post in the Union, it was to be raided by Jeb Stuart's cavalry in 1863, during the Gettysburg Campaign.

Below: Most dashing of all the *beaux sabreurs* of the Confederacy, Major General Jeb Stuart set the standards for gallantry by which most others were measured. In the end his example cost him his life.

Above: The outskirts of Richmond in 1865. Several bold raids were aimed at the Confederate capital, most notably the Kilpatrick-Dahlgren raid of 1864, which failed spectacularly.

Below: Harper's Ferry changed hands several times in the war, and was repeatedly the objective of bold plans by North and South. The key to the Shenandoah, it was a prize to the end.

More than once he let the glee of taking and returning with captured goods distract him from his primary mission. At Gettysburg, when he should have been acting as Lee's eyes and ears, he was off on a pointless raid that gained nothing and may have helped cost Lee the battle. But that was an aberration in Stuart. The real man was unfailingly courageous and selfless, and whatever hardships his men suffered, he shared as well. Thus it was that he was in the thick of the fighting with them at Yellow Tavern, Virginia, on May 11, 1864, when a Federal trooper fired a .44 pistol ball into his right side. Twenty-seven hours later he died, having braved every danger to which he had exposed his men. Certainly there was a special kind of bond between such charismatic leaders and the men they led.

Equally dashing and far more productive, though less flamboyant, was another cavalryman, this time a Yankee. Though he led only one cavalry raid, it was, perhaps, the most effective of the war. He was, of course, Colonel Benjamin Grierson, whose drive through the heart of Mississippi during April 17-May 3, 1863, proved to be the greatest – and most dangerous – diversionary action of the war.

The plan grew in the mind of U.S. Grant, who wanted something to distract the attention of the defenders of Vicksburg away from his attempt to move his army below the city on the west bank of the Mississippi, then cross the river below Vicksburg and move against it from the rear. He needed to cut the rail line connecting the city with the rest of Mississippi and the Confederacy, and sufficiently confuse the foe as to what was going on to buy time to move his army. Already Grant had seen promise in Grierson, and on February 13, 1863, Grant suggested that the colonel and 500 picked men might make a raid against the railroad east of Vicksburg. "The undertaking would be a hazardous one," said Grant. "I do not direct that this shall be done, but leave it for a volunteer enterprise." Grant's friend Sherman had already recommended Grierson as "the best cavalry officer I have yet had," and Grant would come to agree.[11]

Left: It took daring on the part of a Yankee naval commander to run his ship past batteries composed of guns like this English 7.44-inch Blakely rifle, mounted on the bluffs protecting Vicksburg.

The plan evolved considerably before it actually went into action. For one thing, Grant suggested that instead of returning from the railroad raid, Grierson should push on to the south and east, into Alabama, but in the end left it to Grierson's discretion. That showed the greatest trust of all, for only the raiding commander on the scene could decide what was best; no one could predict all the variables that might combine against him, and he had to have the latitude to adjust his plans to the circumstances.

Poor Grierson, away on furlough, only reached his command three hours before they departed on April 17. There was no time to rest. Before dawn Grierson led his command, now 1,700 strong, out of their camp at La Grange, Tennessee, and soon crossed the border into Rebelheld Mississippi. For the next sixteen days, they would see no friendly faces, have no support to look to, and nothing but the enemy behind and ahead of them. Daring in the face of a daunting situation, Grierson reduced his command the third day out by sending some 175 men who were unfit for the rest of the expedition back to La Grange, instructing their leader to be as ostentatious as possible, hoping that this party might distract Rebel attention from the main column.

A day later the Confederates had gotten Grierson's trail and were after him. Thereafter it was a chase through Mississippi, with the Federal sending out decoy parties to fool the enemy as to his destination, while the Confederates slowly brought more and more troops to bear on bringing Grierson to bay. On the eighth day out, the raiders took Newton Station, on the railroad to Vicksburg, and effectively cut the line. They burned bridges, tore up rails, and destroyed two locomotives and large stores of ammunition. Then they were off that same afternoon to the southwest towards Natchez. Ahead of them the Rebels were telegraphing to all points to gather troops to cut off any avenue of escape. Traps were laid at most of the major roads. By April 30, Grierson and his men had been in the saddle day and night for two weeks without more than a few

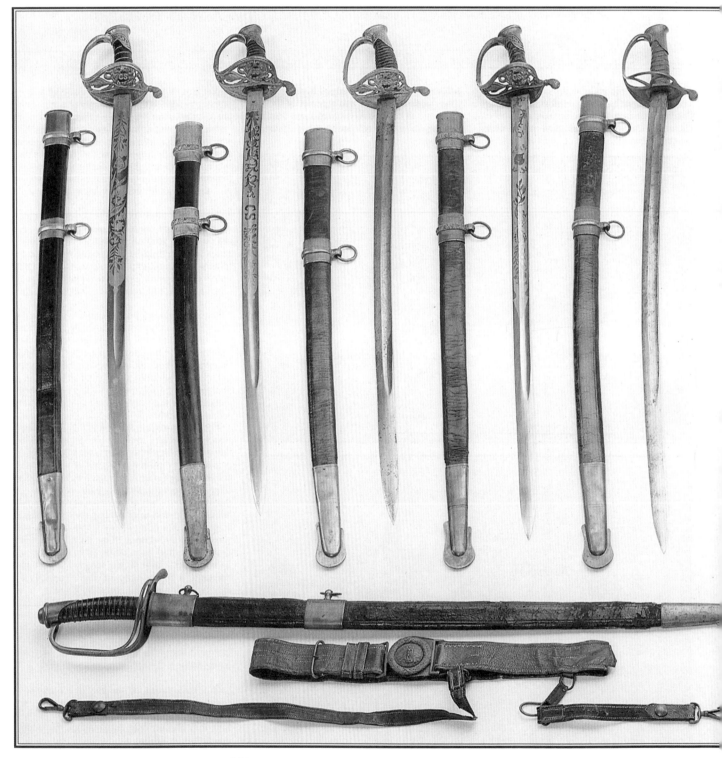

Confederate, Richmond Manufactured, Officers' Edged Weapons

1 Boyle, Gamble and Company staff and field officer's sword
2 Boyle, Gamble and Company staff and field officer's sword
3 Mitchell and Tyler staff and field officer's sword
4 Boyle, Gamble and Company staff and field officer's sword
5 Boyle, Gamble and Company foot officer's sword, variant
6 Boyle, Gamble and Company foot officer's sword
7 Boyle, Gamble and Company foot officer's sword
8 Boyle, Gamble and Company deluxe staff and field officer's sword
9 Boyle, Gamble and Company foot officer's sword
10 Model 1850 U.S. staff and field officer's sword, with blade etched by Boyle, Gamble and Company
11 Boyle, Gamble and Macfee foot officer's sword
12 Belt with two piece, interlocking Virginia state seal plate, belonging to Brigadier General John B. Floyd
13 Belt with two piece, interlocking C S plate accompanying 6
14 Boyle, Gamble and MacFee naval officer's sword

Artifacts courtesy of: Donald Tharpe Collection

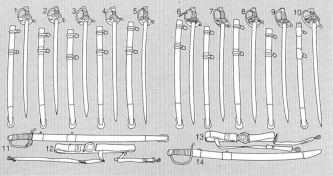

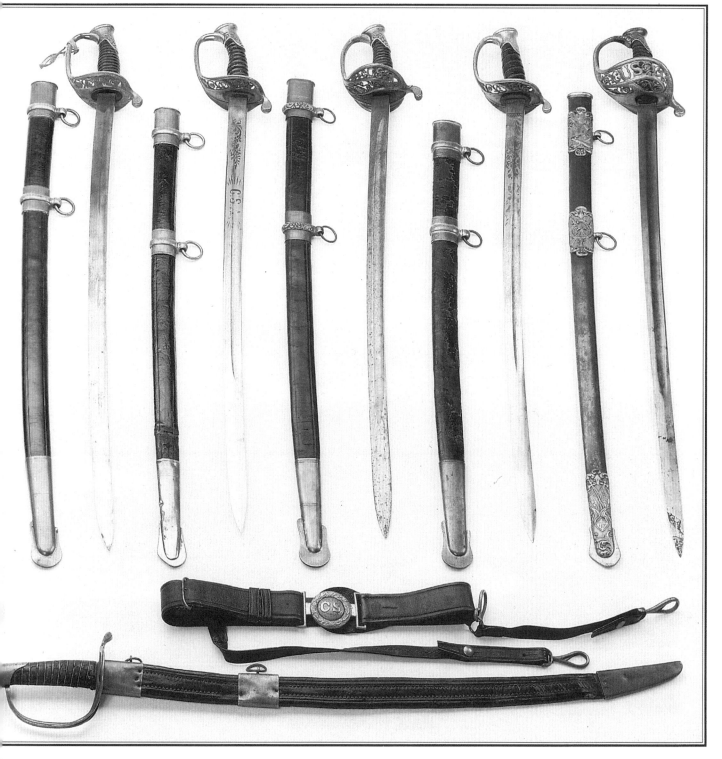

hours' rest at a time. Bone weary, they kept on until May 1, their fifteenth day out, when they came up against a roadblock in their path. At Wall's Bridge, on the Tickfaw River, an ambush had been laid. They had to cross that river or else lose valuable time, time that would allow the converging Confederates in their rear to trap them. With nothing else to be done, Grierson and his exhausted troopers attacked across the bridge and drove its defenders away in the biggest fight of the raid. But then they had to cross Williams' Bridge on the Amite River a few miles further southwest. Confederates knew it too, and began ordering troops there for another trap. But in a frustrating misadventure, the Rebels stopped for

a party on the way, and Grierson's column crossed the bridge two hours before their would-be ambushers arrived. From that point onward, the raiders rode as if possessed. For twelve straight hours through the night of May 1-2, they rode without stopping, racing toward Federal lines at Baton Rouge, Louisiana. With thirty miles still to go, they pressed on again, finally reaching safety late on May 2.

What Grierson had done was phenomenal. He had ridden his command over 600 miles in sixteen days. They killed or wounded more than 100 Confederates, captured and paroled 500 more, tore up fifty or more miles of railroad, destroyed 3,000 stands of arms and considerable other

stores, and captured 1,000 horses and mules. In return, Grierson's losses were three killed and seven wounded, and nine missing. On their final day of the raid they had ridden 76 miles, fought four small engagements, forded a river so deep the horses had to swim, and all without food or rest. "Grierson has knocked the heart out of the State," a friend told Grant. Grant did not have to be told. "Grierson's raid from La Grange through Mississippi has been the most successful thing of the kind since the breaking out of the rebellion," he declared. Years later Grant would be even more effusive. "It was Grierson who first set the example of what might be done in the interior of an enemy's country without any base from which

Personal Possessions and Memorabilia of General J.E.B. Stuart

1 Headquarters flag First National Pattern
2 Stuart's field glasses and case. After his wounding at Yellow Tavern, May 11, 1864, the general gave these to his aide-de-camp Lt. Theodore S. Garnett
3 Stuart's haversack
4 Leather riding boots
5 1858 McClellan saddle
6 Buckskin gauntlets
7 General's silk sash worn by Stuart at Yellow Tavern

8 Stuart's jacket
9 Stuart's wool vest with Federal staff officer's buttons
10 Plumed felt officer's hat, made in Paris
11 Stuart's trousers
12 Field glasses and case
13 Uniform frock coat, possibly Stuart's
14 Whitney revolver carried by Stuart at Yellow Tavern
15 Le Mat 1st Model

revolver
16 English holster for 15
17 Tin wash basin and bowl
18 Tin cup
19 Leather gun case
20 Calisher and Terry carbine
21 Model 1860 cavalry saber, of French make
22 Model 1851 Federal saber belt with plate
23 Federal officer's sword belt and plate worn by Stuart at Yellow Tavern

Artifacts courtesy of: The Museum of the Confederacy, Richmond, Va: 1-6, 10, 12, 13, 15-22;
Virginia Historical Society, Richmond, Va: 7, 8, 9, 11, 14, 23

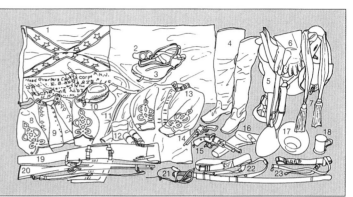

to draw supplies," he wrote. His friend Sherman was more succinct. He called it "The most brilliant expedition of the war."[12]

None of Stuart's celebrated raids came close in their results to Grierson's achievements, perhaps the ultimate combination of dash and daring with positive military objectives and accomplishments. Yet it would be Grierson's only great moment. There was another leader, however, who took personal courage and military accomplishments to practically the same heights again and again throughout the war, perhaps the greatest cavalry leader ever produced in America: General Nathan Bedford Forrest. The feelings of his men said much. "As long as we followed Forrest," said one, "we were heroes."

Given his poor and ignorant background, few would have expected much of this man. Yet he possessed an authentic military genius, along with the drive that also made him a fortune before the war. Having read none of the military manuals, he felt little but disdain for them. He fought by commonsense and keen intuition. "Whenever I ran into one of those fellers who fit by note," he said of the book-learned generals, "I generally whipped hell out of him before he could get his tune pitched." He was only crudely literate, and wrote few letters. One that survives says much of his elemental view of waging war. "I had a small brush with the Enamy on yesterday I Suceded in gaining thir rear," he wrote. "They wair not looking for me I taken them by Suprise they run like Suns of Biches." While he never said that his theory of war was "to git thar fustest with the mostest," as Civil War mythology would suggest, still that elemental philosophy characterized his generalship. Along with it went incredible personal daring. Thirty Federals at least fell by his own hand. Twenty-nine horses were killed under him as he stayed in the thick of the fight time after time. Three times the enemy's bullets

Above: The greatest cavalryman America ever produced was barely literate, untroubled by issues of gallantry, and had a jugular instinct for damaging the foe: Nathan Bedford Forrest in 1864.

Below: The results of one Yankee cavalry raid by General Judson Kilpatrick in 1864. Six grain mills, a saw mill, and six loaded canal boats along the James and Kanawha Canal all succumbed to the raid.

tore into his flesh. Nothing could stop him.[13]

Forrest's brilliance and daring shone on his very first raid, when he was just a new brigadier. In July 1862 he led 1,000 men from Chattanooga into middle Tennessee, and almost at once captured a whole brigade of Yankee infantry, some 1,200 men including General Thomas Crittenden, one million dollars' worth of property, and considerable cavalry stores and four cannon for his command. This done, he moved on toward Nashville, burning railroad bridges along the way, and sending such a fright into Tennessee's Union governor that two infantry divisions of Federals were detailed away from the Army of the Ohio to guard railroads. The result was to cause a serious delay in an offensive campaign that army had planned. All in all, a very successful conclusion for a new general's first independent command.[14]

He did nearly as well a few months later when he led 2,500 men on a three-week raid to cut off Grant's communications between his base at Holly Springs, Mississippi, and Columbus, Kentucky. Though meeting more resistance this time, Forrest still managed to put the Mobile & Ohio Railroad almost completely out of operation. Later that year, after personally threatening to beat General Braxton Bragg if the irascible army commander ever gave him another order, Forrest received an independent command in northern Mississippi and western Tennessee. There for much of the rest of the war he repeatedly outwitted and defeated larger Federal forces, taking time off to lead yet another raid during the Atlanta Campaign. He won victories at Brice's Cross Roads, captured Memphis briefly, then took Athens, Alabama, moved on into Tennessee, captured two vessels on the Tennessee River, then moved against the supply base at Johnsonville and bluffed the garrison into destroying a huge cache of Federal supplies and burning their fleet of supply ships. All told, Forrest took and

Major General J.E.B. Stuart

Though hardly as showy as the Yankee General Custer, Rebel Major General Jeb Stuart represented much of what was most dashing in the bold cavaliers of the South. His short jacket, buttoned back in the Revolutionary War style to show its buff facings, the ostrich plume in his hat, the gleaming black high-topped boots were all the trademark of the officer that friends called "Beauty". Most elegant of all were his whiskers, and the merry twinkle in his eyes that

everyone around him noted.

Carrying his heavy dragoon saber and his French Le Mat pistol, Stuart could always be found in the middle of the action on any field of battle. Only death from a mortal wound at Yellow Tavern could stop him, and his absence left a permanent gap at the once-merry campfires of the cavalry corps of the Army of Northern Virginia. Even his personal banjo player never quite sounded the same after his death.

destroyed four gunboats, fourteen transports, twenty barges, twenty-six cannon, and $6,700,000 in U.S. government property. And everywhere he went, Forrest led the way, absolutely fearless, absolutely confident in himself and his men. Even his enemy Sherman sent him a note congratulating "his dash" in taking Memphis, but then so discomfited was Sherman by the raider's exploits that he later turned the full force of his own cavalry to bear on this genius in the saddle. It was Sherman himself who gave the Confederate his enduring sobriquet, "that devil Forrest."[15]

Of course there were others, especially the cavalrymen, and most of them seemed to be Confederate. John Hunt Morgan led many a daring raid, though like Stuart's they provided less in the way of tangible benefits than Forrest's and, indeed, were often ill-managed grasps for plunder. The Virginian raider John Singleton Mosby made himself a terror as leader of the 43rd Virginia Partisan Rangers. His raids, including the capture of two Yankee generals, became legendary, and right until the end of the war, nothing that the Federals could do could stop him.

Besides the cavalrymen, who had the most opportunity for daring escapades, civilians North and South thrilled to the adventures of the spies and secret agents, very often officers, who operated behind enemy lines. Unfortunately, because they dealt in a business of lies and deception, their own later stories of their adventures are highly embellished and unreliable, as if their habit of deception did not wear off when the war ended. Some even completely invented wartime careers for themselves, and invented their commissions as well. One of the best known was a woman, Loretta Velasquez, who claimed to have operated disguised as a man in Confederate uniform, and even obtained a commission as "Captain Buford". Her whole story was a fabrication.

Quite genuine, however, were many of the daring escapades of officers who rode gallant ships instead of horses. Again, perhaps because of their perpetual underdog status, the Southerners seem somehow to have provided the majority of stirring examples. One officer, Captain Raphael Semmes, made an absolute habit of bold deeds, starting on June 30, 1861, when he steamed his little raider C.S.S. *Sumter* out of Pass à L'Outre at the mouth of the Mississippi and made for the open seas. Outrunning a Yankee warship that pursued him, Semmes embarked on a six-month cruise that saw eighteen Yankee merchantmen captured, seven of which he destroyed. Finally cornered by Federal warships in the neutral port of Gibraltar, the *Sumter* sat idle for a few months, and was later auctioned to a British firm. She was no longer needed, for early in 1863 word reached Semmes from Confederate naval authorities in Britain that a new ship would soon be ready for him, a bigger, more powerful, more formidable vessel altogether. To conceal her intentions, they called her for the moment the "*290*". To the world and posterity, she would soon become known as the C.S.S. *Alabama*.[16]

Here was a commerce raider to challenge the seas; 900 tons burden, 230 feet long and 32 feet wide. "Her model was of the most perfect symmetry," wrote Semmes, "and she sat upon the water with the lightness and grace of a swan." Her engine developed 300 horsepower, and on her decks sat six 32-pounders in broadside, while at her bow a massive 100-pounder Blakely rifle was mounted as a pivot gun, with an 8-inch

Above: Few raiders of the war could even attempt to approach the record of the "Gray Ghost", Colonel John Singleton Mosby of Virginia. He seemed invincible and unstoppable, and indeed he was.

Below: These scouts and guides working for the Army of the Potomac were shadowy, elusive men, of whom little is yet known. Many were officers in civilian garb, and all faced constant peril.

1859 Officer's McClellan Saddle of Major General John Sedgwick

Sedgwick began his Civil War career during the 1862 Peninsula Campaign. Promoted to major general the same year, he was wounded at Antietam, but was fit enough later to command the VI Corps during the Fredericksburg Campaign. His command was in reserve during Gettysburg but fought later at Rappahannock Bridge. In 1864 Sedgwick led his corps at the Wilderness and Spotsylvania, where he was killed. His saddle was presented to him by the officers of the 2nd Division, 2nd Army Corps

1 Pair of saddle revolver holsters mounted in front of the saddle pommel
2 Martingale or breast strap with brass presentation plaque
3 Saddle valise for stowage of personal items and additional articles of clothing
4 Saddle bags for the stowage of various additional items of clothing and equipment
5 General officer's shrabraque or saddle covering, with the insignia of a major general
6 Sweat leathers to prevent soiling of the rider's uniform
7 Stirrups and hoods for the protection of the rider's feet

Artifacts courtesy of: West Point Museum, West Point, NY

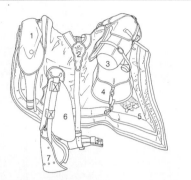

smoothbore pivot aft. With 144 men and officers, she was ready to take on Uncle Sam's shipping.[17]

She did so with a vengeance, in the north and south Atlantic, the Caribbean, the Gulf of Mexico, and around the Cape of Good Hope to the Indian Ocean. She made sixty-six captures, one of them the Yankee warship *Hatteras*, which she met in open battle and sank in action off Galveston. For two years Semmes plied the seas, becoming such a terror that he and the handful of other Rebel commerce raiders eventually tied up some seventy-nine Federal warships assigned to hunt for them; Federal vessels totaling almost eighty thousand tons and mounting 774 guns, all of them vessels that Lincoln would have preferred to keep on blockade duty. Their diversion to the chase for Semmes and the others undoubtedly contributed substantially to the frequent perforations of the blockade that allowed a trickle of much-needed supplies to keep coming into the Confederacy from abroad right up to the end of the war.[18]

Finally, however, for reasons that still baffle students, Semmes took on even more than his daring could handle. Having put into Cherbourg harbor on June 11, 1864, for repairs, he found himself blockaded by the arrival of the Federal warship U.S.S. *Kearsarge*. The Yankee vessel outclassed the *Alabama* in every category; she displaced over 1,000 tons, had better engines, and mounted eight guns, all of them of substantially heavier caliber than Semmes'. He later said that "the disparity was not so great but that I might hope to beat my enemy in a fair fight." Years later Semmes also would claim that it had not been fair that the commander of the *Kearsarge*, Captain John Winslow, hang chains over the sides of

his ship, making of her a sort of "ironclad", in order to protect his engines. Displaying a quaint and very impractical notion of war ethics, Semmes complained that Winslow should have warned him of this, as if a combatant was obliged to reveal his plans to a foe he was about to meet. With the chain protection on the *Kearsarge*, Semmes pouted that the ships were no longer evenly matched and that he would not have given

battle. (Semmes never seemed to think it unfair that the *Alabama* completely outclassed the *Hatteras*, the only warship he defeated, or that none of the merchantmen he captured had been armed at all. For all their daring, men who lost battles in this war could find some pretty silly excuses to explain away their defeats.)[19]

On June 19, Semmes steamed out of Cherbourg to give battle. Almost immediately it became

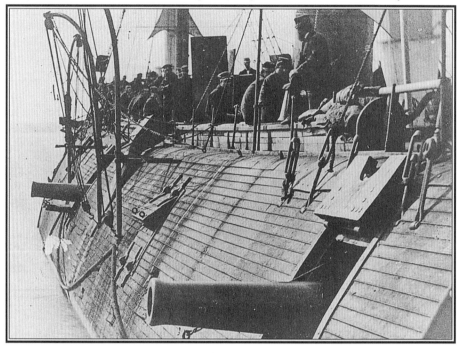

Below: The U.S.S. *Kearsarge* took on one of the most formidable opponents of the war in 1864 when she engaged in battle the Confederate cruiser *Alabama*. It proved to be an entirely one-sided contest.

Above: The U.S.S. *Galena*, one of the early experimental ironclad designs, served through most of the war though early proven to be a poor concept. Bravery was all that kept officers and men aboard.

Right: Midshipman Henry H. Marmaduke looked danger square in the face when he manned a gun on the ironclad C.S.S. *Virginia* in her battle with the *Monitor*. He took a wound when his gun was destroyed.

apparent that the *Alabama* was outclassed. Seven times the ships circled around each other, firing away as best they could. Semmes did next to no damage to the *Kearsarge*, but Winslow's superior gunnery gradually made a wreck of the *Alabama*. Finally, after an hour and ten minutes, Semmes saw that his ship was sinking. Sadly he ordered her abandoned, and a short while later she sank to the bottom where she still rests today.[20] What-

ever may be said for Semmes' apparent poor judgment in going out to meet the *Kearsarge*, once he steamed out for battle he did so with a daring that would have done credit to Stuart or Grierson.

In the end, however, it probably belonged to an obscure gunboat captain on the Mississippi to show daring at its zenith. Isaac Brown commanded a hastily built and still incomplete Rebel ironclad, the C.S.S. *Arkansas*. She had been

"completed" up the Yazoo River, a tributary of the Mississippi above Vicksburg, and in July 1862 was desperately needed to help defend the city against an assault by two combined Yankee fleets. His vessel was almost comical, an iron sheathed shed atop a hull, three guns protruding on either broadside, and one gun each fore and aft. Her armor was forged from railroad iron, and there lay her strength. On July 14 she began her journey, ready as she would ever be, down the Yazoo toward Vicksburg. Ahead of Brown there were at least thirty-seven Yankee vessels that he knew of.

The next morning Brown saw three Federal ships: one ironclad and two heavy gunboats. As he opened fire, the Yankee ships returned a few shots then turned and fled, fearing the much-rumored ironclad. As Brown pursued, he disabled the ironclad *Carondelet*, then raced on down toward the mouth of the Yazoo. When he got there he saw "a forest of masts and smokestacks." "It seemed at a glance as if a whole navy had come to keep me away from the heroic city," he wrote. Ahead of him were seven rams, five ironclads, and a fleet of heavy wooden gunboats and cruisers. He was all by himself. What he decided to do was to steam into the very center of the enemy squadrons, hugging them close so they would have to watch their fire for fear of hitting one another.

He later said he felt as if in the middle of a volcano, guns blazing all around him, smoke everywhere. He could only keep firing and steam straight towards the safety of the Confederate lines at Vicksburg. Along the way, the *Arkansas* inflicted serious injuries on at least four of the enemy ships. Steaming through a solid wall of flame and iron, Brown left the Yankee fleet behind, dazed and reeling, and brought his battered ship into the safety of Vicksburg. Later that day he would say simply that "it was a little hot this morning all around."[21] That is surely the epitomy of officers' dash and daring.

References

1 Editors of Boston Publishing Company, *Above and Beyond* (Boston, 1985), pp.316-24.
2 *Ibid.*, p.25.
3 *Ibid.*, pp.28-31.
4 *Ibid.*, pp.34-5.
5 *Ibid.*, pp.45-6.
6 *Ibid.*, p.53.
7 U.S. Navy Department, *Official Records of the Union and Confederate Navies in the War of the Rebellion* (Washington, 1894-1927), Series I, Volume 20, pp.559, 561, 562-3.
8 Jefferson Davis, *Rise and Fall of the Confederate Government* (New York, 1881), II, p.238.
9 Burke Davis, *To Appomattox* (New York, 1959), pp.74-9; Douglas S. Freeman, *Lee's Lieutenants* (New York, 1942-1944), III, pp.681-2.
10 T.J. Mackey, "Hampton's Duel", *Southern Historical Society Papers*, XXII (1894), pp.122-6.
11 Dee Brown, *Grierson's Raid* (Urbana, Ill., 1954), p.8n.
12 *Ibid.*, pp.219-23.
13 Robert S. Henry, *"First With The Most" Forrest* (Indianapolis, 1944), pp.7-8.
14 *Ibid.*, p.90.
15 *Ibid.*, pp.342, 381.
16 Harpur A. Gosnell, ed., *Rebel Raider* (Chapel Hill, N.C., 1948), p.209; Charles G. Summersell, *The Cruise of the CSS Sumter* (Tuscaloosa, Ala., 1965), p.161.
17 Semmes, *Raider*, pp.33-4.
18 *Ibid.*, p.xix; Summersell, *Cruise*, p.177.
19 Semmes, *Raider*, pp.369-70.
20 *Ibid.*, p.373.
21 Samuel C. Carter, *The Final Fortress: The Campaign for Vicksburg, 1862-1863* (New York, 1980), pp.69-71.

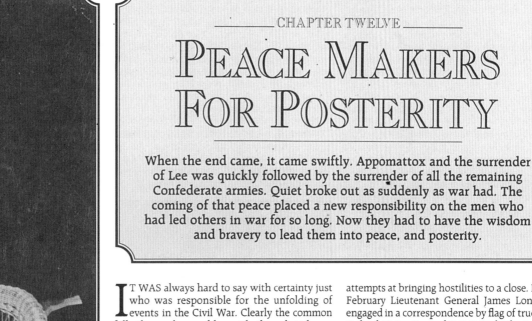

CHAPTER TWELVE

PEACE MAKERS FOR POSTERITY

When the end came, it came swiftly. Appomattox and the surrender of Lee was quickly followed by the surrender of all the remaining Confederate armies. Quiet broke out as suddenly as war had. The coming of that peace placed a new responsibility on the men who had led others in war for so long. Now they had to have the wisdom and bravery to lead them into peace, and posterity.

IT WAS always hard to say with certainty just who was responsible for the unfolding of events in the Civil War. Clearly the common folk, those who would provide the enlisted men of both sides, could be held little responsible for bringing about the conflict. That guilt lay with the leaders of North and South, largely the same men and class that would provide so much of the military leadership of the armies. Yet, once they went to war, the fate of battles most often rested in the end with the common soldiers. Generals and lesser officers could plan as they would, but if the men did not fight, then the contest was lost. Sometimes, as at Missionary Ridge on November 25, 1863, the foot soldiers could go beyond their officers' commands and take control of the battle on their own.

But there had to come a time when, once again, it was all out of the hands of the common soldiers, a time when they had fought the best they could and one side or the other could fight no more. When that day came, the war would be all but over. Then, again, it would be time for the officers to take over in earnest, for only they could put an end to the marching and fighting, only they could officially admit victory or defeat. To them would fall the first step in making peace.

In Virginia that day came on April 9, 1865, at Appomattox Court House. The soldiers he still had were full of fight, but Robert E. Lee simply no longer had enough of them. His once mighty Army of Northern Virginia was reduced to barely a good-sized army corps of previous days. A week before he had had about 50,000 men in the trenches around Richmond and Petersburg, facing Grant's combined armies totaling 112,000. But then after being forced out of his lines on April 2, Lee made a forlorn attempt to escape to the southwest to join forces with the remnant of Joseph E. Johnston's Army of Tennessee in North Carolina. All along that trail of tears to Appomattox, Lee lost more men until, by the morning of that Palm Sunday, April 9, he had only 26,600. And Grant had him surrounded.[1]

In fact, even before the evacuation of the Confederate capital, some officers had made fleeting attempts at bringing hostilities to a close. Back in February Lieutenant General James Longstreet engaged in a correspondence by flag of truce with Federal Major General E.O.C. Ord. The two foes met on February 21, and agreed that if a cease fire were called, and if Grant and Lee could meet, then perhaps the two generals might work out a way of ending it all. Longstreet even suggested making it sort of a social occasion, with the wives of generals on opposing sides paying calls to their counterparts, to ease tensions while negotiations went on. It was the sort of thing that Old Army men would think of, reminiscent of the part played by officers' wives on the frontier posts in putting an end to petty disputes. When Longstreet suggested this to President Davis, the idea was approved but nothing came of it.[2]

Still, in the end, it fell to Grant and Lee. Indeed, two days before that Palm Sunday, on the afternoon of April 7, Grant sent a note to Lee through the lines. "The results of the last week must convince you of the hopelessness of further resistance," Grant said. "I feel that it is so, and regard it as my duty to shift from myself the responsibility of any further effusion of blood, by asking of you the surrender of that portion of the C.S. army known as the Army of Northern Virginia." Lee received the note when Longstreet was with him and the two were almost ready to sleep for the night. "Not yet," was Longstreet's laconic reply when Lee showed him the note. Their situation was desperate, but on April 7 there was still slim hope.[3]

Still hoping to find some accommodation short of surrender, and wishing to keep communication open with Grant, Lee replied asking what terms Grant would offer. The next morning (April 8) came Grant's response. "Peace being my great desire," he said, he would ask only that Lee's men put down their arms and give their parole not to take them up again until and unless properly exchanged. Struggling to avoid facing actual surrender, Lee replied that same day that his situation was not yet that desperate. Still, he wished that the two generals might meet to discuss the "restoration of peace." What Lee could

It was remarkable how quickly the men who made war could turn their hands to making peace. None surpassed Grant, though in peace he would never shine as he had in war. In old age he wrote one of America's finest military memoirs.

have meant by that is a mystery, though it may be that he wanted to talk of something broader. Now that he was general-in-chief of all Confederate armies, he might have hoped to call a war-wide armistice. But all that could have done would have been to buy a little time. With the South so clearly on its knees on all fronts, the Union would hardly accept any conclusion to the war other than total victory.

Whatever Lee meant, Grant declined the interview, but his reply did not reach Lee until the morning of April 9. By then, Grant's hard-riding cavalry under Sheridan had gotten ahead of Lee's retreating columns, cutting off their escape from the van of the Union army. Now Lee was trapped, the situation changed irretrievably, and he had no choice but to send Grant a final note asking for a meeting specifically to discuss surrender. "I would rather die a thousand deaths," said the proud Lee.[4]

Their meeting itself came in the home of Wilmer McLean in the village of Appomattox Court House. Lee arrived first and was shown into a plain front parlor, where Grant joined him shortly afterward. The staff officers of the two – Lee had only Marshall with him, Grant had Parker and several other officers, including Sheridan – noticed the marked contrast between the two commanders. Lee arrived in his best and most fully appointed uniform; Grant, who had come in haste, was dusty from the ride and wearing only his customary private's blouse with insignia of his rank sewn on.

They shook hands, then each sat at a separate table. An uncomfortable Grant tried to make small talk and asked if Lee remembered their meeting once during the Mexican War. It was Lee who turned the conversation to the point. Grant repeated his simple terms, and Lee agreed. "This will have a very happy effect on my army," Lee said as he read Grant's generous terms after they

were put down on paper. As a further gesture, Grant allowed that any man claiming to own a horse or mule in Lee's army would be permitted to take it home with him. There would be spring planting to do. Lee would always be grateful for Grant's magnanimity, so much so that in later years, when president of Washington College in Lexington, Virginia, Lee threatened with dismissal any faculty member who should speak disrespectfully of Grant in his presence.[5]

There was something remarkable in the way that these men who had made war like no others so instinctively embraced peace. Grant even fed Lee's starving army from his own commissary. The victor felt depressed at the humiliation of his noble foe, and ordered that the firing of any

Right: Lieutenant Colonel Charles Marshall accompanied Lee to his Appomattox meeting with Grant, one of only two officers present with the great gray chieftain. Like his commander, he was proud in defeat.

salutes in celebration be stopped immediately. "The war is over," he said. "The Rebels are our countrymen again."[6]

It was left to their subordinates to work out the details of the surrender itself. Longstreet, Gordon, and Pendleton represented Lee, meeting with Grant's men Charles Griffin, Wesley Merritt, and John Gibbon. While they deliberated, the officers of the two armies crossed the lines to look for old friends from before the war. Almost at once, the Old Army fraternity reappeared. Sheridan found Longstreet, Wilcox, and Heth, and brought them to see Grant. Major General George G. Meade, commanding the Army of the Potomac, went over to see his old friend Lee. "What are you doing with all that gray in your beard?" teased Lee. Looking back on two years of commanding his army in the frustrating attempt to bring Lee to this pass, Meade responded, "You have to answer for most of it!"

Grant, tender toward Lee's feelings to the last, left for Washington before the formal surrender ceremony took place on April 12. He gave to Brigadier General Joshua L. Chamberlain the honor of formally receiving the stacked arms and furled flags of the proud Army of Northern Virginia. It is good that he did, not only for the acknowledgement of Chamberlain's outstanding record, but even more because it put Chamberlain in a place to see and record, as no other pen could have, the moving last moments of Lee's army.

Chamberlain formed his command on either side of the road leading into Appomattox Court House, and toward the village Lee's men slowly marched. Gordon, commanding the II Corps led the way, followed by the remnants of Richard H. Anderson's and Henry Heth's commands, and then Longstreet's I Corps. In total silence they slowly marched forward along the road, heads hanging in sadness, feet dragging the dust. And then something almost magical happened. See-

Below: The fall of Richmond in April 1865 brought a flood of blue uniforms to the Confederate capital: Major General Godfrey Weitzel, standing on the steps at left with his hand on the rail, and staff.

ing Gordon approach, Chamberlain ordered a bugler to call his men to attention, then to shift their position from "order arms" to "carry arms". To a civilian it meant nothing; to a soldier it meant the marching salute. Chamberlain was honoring Gordon's men as they approached.

And now Gordon was seized by some similar inspiration of the moment, some instinct of nobility greater than the sadness burdening him. "Gordon at the head of the column," wrote Chamberlain, "riding with heavy spirit and down-cast face, catches the sound of shifting arms, looks up, and, taking the meaning, wheels superbly, making with himself and his horse one uplifted figure, with profound salutation as he drops the point of his sword to the boot toe; then

facing to his own command, gives word for his successive brigades to pass us with the same position of the manual – honor answering honor."

Only men made of stone escaped with dry eyes. "Memories that bound us together as no other bond," said Chamberlain, "thronged as we looked into each other's eyes." No victor cheered. There was, in fact, "not a sound of trumpet more, nor roll of drum; not a cheer, nor word nor whisper of vain-glorying, nor motion of man standing again at the order, but an awed stillness rather, and breath-holding, as if it were the pass-ing of the dead!"[7]

Events seemed to pile on top of one another after that, as the whole Confederacy crumbled.

Captain, 9th Texas Cavalry

This captain of the 9th Texas Cavalry ably depicts what many of the mounted men from the western Confederacy looked like. Even more than their eastern counterparts, they carried a wide variety of weaponry depending upon what was available, and not according to regulations. This officer holds an English-made percussion shotgun, double-barrelled. In his other hand he wields a Confederate-made Dance revolver, a close copy of the pre-war heavy Colt .44 caliber dragoon percussion revolver. Distinctive to several Texas regiments was the "lone star" inside a circle badge on his hat and his belt plate, while the slouch hat, too, is of the type generally worn by western Rebel cavalrymen. His jacket is gray, trimmed in gold, over brown trousers and brown leather boots. On these last he wears a distinctive Mexican style of spur with spiked rowels. His war-making, like his uniform and weapons, was rough and ready.

Charleston was finally taken by Federal authorities, and on April 14, four years to the day from the sad moment when he had hauled down Fort Sumter's flag in surrender, Brigadier General Robert Anderson returned to Sumter and raised that same flag once again. That night Union jubilation suffered a severe blow when President Lincoln made a trip to the theater from which he never returned, yet despite this the Union victory train kept on moving.

The next great meeting of the officers would come in North Carolina, and here again it was old antagonists coming together to begin peace and a life-long friendship. Joseph E. Johnston had been brought almost to a standstill by Sherman's advancing host in North Carolina. He was not trapped as Lee had been, but desperately outnumbered, and with nowhere really to go, he asked President Davis – himself in flight through North Carolina with his cabinet – to allow him to ask Sherman for an armistice to discuss surrender. Reluctantly Davis assented.

The two generals met on April 17 at the Bennett farmhouse near Durham Station. Neither had met the other previously, despite their mutual Old Army service, but, said Sherman, "we knew enough of each other to be well acquainted at once." Alone in Bennett's place, they talked. Sherman – after telling Johnston the news of Lincoln's assassination – said frankly that further resistance was pointless, and his old foe agreed. But Johnston suggested that they should go farther than the surrender of just his own army. Thinking he could get authority from Davis to surrender all Rebel forces still in the field, Johnston proposed that this form the line of their discussion. Sherman agreed, and after several minutes of open and pleasant conversation, they agreed to meet again the next day, when Johnston hoped to return with Davis' authorization.

In fact, Johnston did not get Davis' explicit agreement, but he did get Secretary of War Breckinridge to come and meet Sherman with him on April 18. First he counted on Breckinridge's well-known eloquence as a weapon in persuading

Union and Confederate Presentation Swords and Spurs

1 Presentation grade sword of Major William Norbonne Starke presented to him by the men of Co. E, Louisiana Infantry Regt., 1861

2 Silver spurs given to Lt. Gen. A.P. Hill

3 Silk sash of Brig. Gen. Nathan George Evans

4 Cased sword presented to Evans by South Carolina, when he was a captain in the Federal Army

5 Prewar non-regulation militia staff and field officer's sword of Brig. Gen. Patrick Theodore Moore

6 Cased Model 1852 US naval officer's sword and two scabbards, presented to Lieutenant Robert B. Pegram by the state of Virginia

7 Cased silver spurs engraved to Colonel Robert A. Crawford

8 Snuff box of Maj. Gen. Sterling Price

9 Price's presentation grade sword given by the women of New Orleans

10 Price's gold medal, presented by the St. Louis Grays

11 Model 1840 cavalry officer's silver mounted saber engraved to Captain George H. Thomas

Artifacts courtesy of: The Museum of the Confederacy, Richmond, Va: 1-6, 8-10; Virginia Historical Society, Richmond, Va: 7, 11

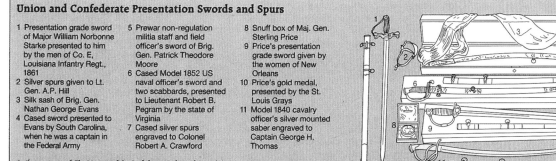

Sherman to grant the best possible terms. Beyond that, Breckinridge was the only remaining cabinet member with any real influence on Davis, and might be able to persuade the president to abandon hope and accept terms embracing all Confederate forces. At first Sherman declined to meet with the Kentuckian, since he was a civil officer of a government that the Union did not recognize. However, he was also a major general, and as a military officer Sherman agreed to allow him into the conference.

The three generals talked for some time, Breckinridge speaking eloquently in favor of recognition of political and property rights for former Confederate men and officers. In the end,

they agreed upon a settlement that would disband all Rebel military forces. Federal authority was to be recognized, Southern state governments were to be reorganized as soon as their members took an oath of allegiance, Federal courts would be re-established, and former Confederates would have restored to them full constitutional rights so long as they obeyed the law.

The agreement went far beyond what Grant had proposed to Lee, and reflected the war-weariness of the generals who framed it. Indeed, it was probably the most far-reaching agreement ever concluded by generals commanding armies, going way beyond the limits of their military authority. The presence of Breckinridge – in

whatever capacity – gave it some measure of civil Confederate approval, but Sherman had no such power, and a few days later Washington would reject the terms entirely, starting a feud between Sherman and Secretary of War Stanton that made headlines. Given no choice, Johnston then surrendered his own army alone to Sherman on April 26, with the same terms given to Lee. Some 30,000 Confederates turned in their arms and were soldiers no more. Sherman graciously provided transportation to help most of them to get home again. Still though their attempt at being universal peacemakers had failed, Sherman and Johnston forged a personal friendship that lasted until the great Federal general's death in 1891.

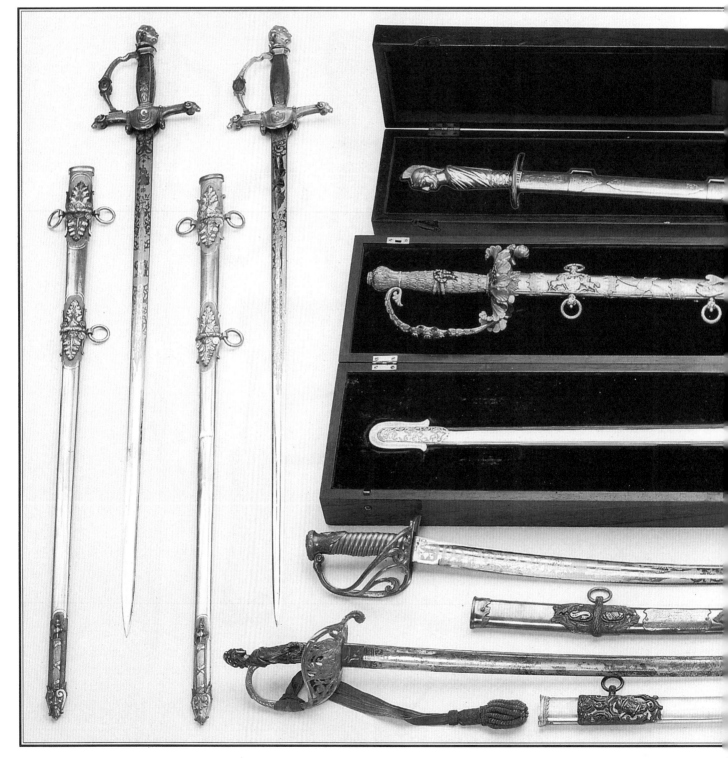

Union Officers' Presentation Swords

1 Deluxe sword made by Tiffany, New York and presented to Brig. Gen Godfrey Weitzel
2 Deluxe sword made by Tiffany, New York and presented to Maj. Gen. John M. Schofield
3 Cased deluxe sword given to Brig. Gen. John Cook for gallantry at the capture of Fort Donelson, 1862
4 Eaglehead sword sold by Spies, New York and owned by Colonel Sylvanus Thayer, ''Father of the U.S. Military Academy''
5 Militia staff and field officer's sword presented to Thayer by graduates of the West Point class of 1820
6 Deluxe sword made by George W. Simmons and Brother, Philadelphia, Pa, and presented to Brig. Gen. Charles Ferguson Smith
7 Cavalry saber made by Clauberg, Soligen, Germany, and given to Maj. I. Townsend Daniel
8 Cavalry saber made by Sauerbier, Newark, New Jersey, and given to Brig. Gen. Judson Kilpatrick
9 High quality sword made by Frederick Horster, Soligen, Germany, retailed by Tomes Son and McLvain, New York, given to Colonel H.F. Clarke

Artifacts courtesy of: West Point Museum, West Point, N.Y.: 2, 4-7, 9; Donald Tharpe Collection: 1, 3, 8

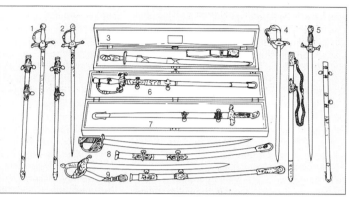

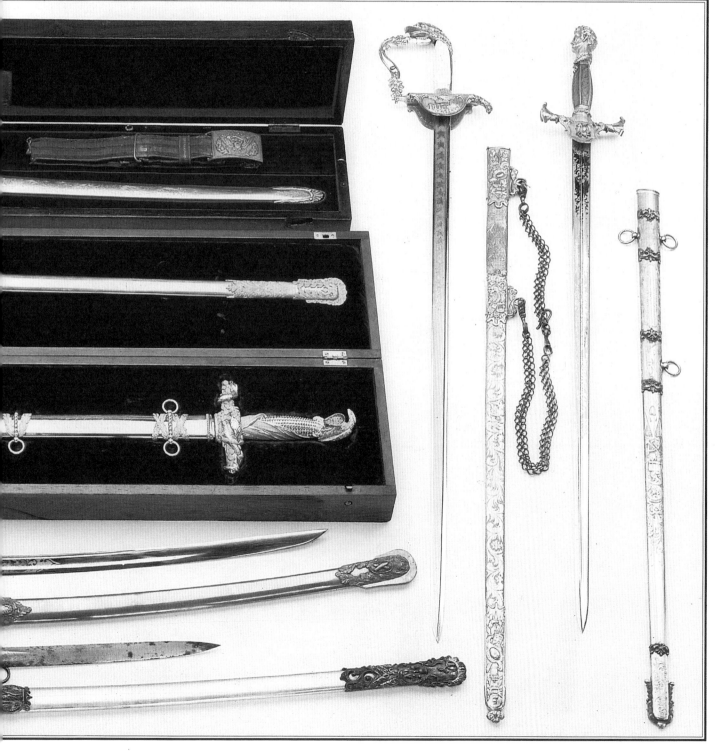

Present at his funeral was his old foe Johnston, who stood bare-headed in the rain as Sherman's bier passed by. Five weeks later Johnston, too, died, reportedly from a cold he took by refusing to wear his hat at Sherman's funeral.[8]

Just as they were so often forgotten during the war, so were the far western armies forgotten in their surrenders, In fact, the combined forces of Lieutenant General Richard Taylor's 12,000 men in Alabama and the 43,000 that General Kirby Smith had in the Trans-Mississippi were almost exactly equal to the numbers surrendered by Lee and Johnston. Both, as it happened, made terms with an almost unknown major general, E.R.S. Canby, a forty-seven-year-old Kentuckian whose

highly creditable service had been spent almost entirely in these regions. Taylor met with him on May 2 at Citronelle, Alabama, receiving terms similar to those given Lee and Johnston. Kirby Smith never did meet Canby himself, sending instead a poor man destined to repeat an earlier experience in surrendering for timorous superiors, Lieutenant General Simon B. Buckner. Buckner met with Canby's representative in New Orleans on May 26. By this time all vestiges of the Confederate government had disappeared, Jefferson Davis and most of his cabinet were prisoners, and fighting on was nothing more than pointless. Nearly a month later, at Doaksville in the Indian Territory, General Stand Watie surrendered what

remained of his Confederate Indian regiments, and in so doing made the last capitulation of a formal Rebel command. It was all over.

At least, it was all over for the overwhelming majority of the officers who had followed the blue and the gray. For a very few, however, the danger was not entirely past. Some military officers of the Confederacy had been indicted for treason in Federal courts during the war, but their surrender and parole virtually quashed any possibility of further prosecution. But for Breckinridge, who as vice president had been a very important civil official of the old Union, those indictments were still active, as they were for several of Davis' cabinet. Consequently, he felt it

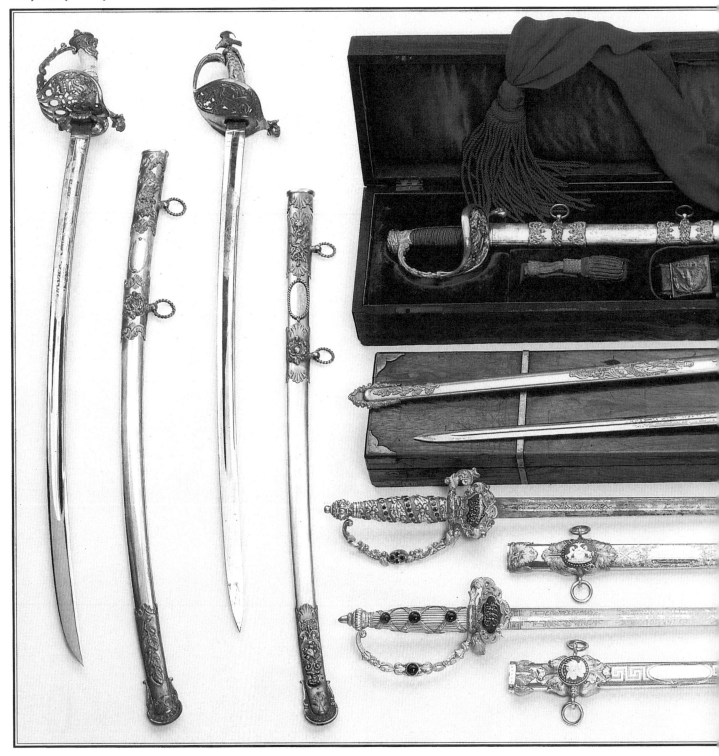

Union Presentation Edged Weapons

1 Presentation cavalry saber of Lt. Col. Gabriel Middleton, 20th Pennsylvania Cavalry
2 Presentation officer's sword of Major William Sterling Moorhead, 76th Pennsylvania Veteran Volunteer Infantry
3 Cased presentation foot officer's sword, maroon silk sash, buff leather gauntlets and officer's sword belt of Captain Poinsett Cooper,

42nd New York Volunteer Infantry
4 Presentation Model 1850 staff and field officer's sword of First Lt. Isaac Seesholtz, 118th Pennsylvania Volunteer Infantry
5 Presentation Model 1850 staff and field officer's sword of Col. Thomas E. Barker, 12th New Hampshire Volunteer Infantry
6 Cased presentation

militia staff and field officer's sword belonging to Colonel Peter Fritz, 99th Pennsylvania Volunteer Infantry
7 Deluxe presentation sword belonging to Major General George Gordon Meade, commander, Army of the Potomac
8 Deluxe presentation sword of Major General Francis P. Blair

Artifacts courtesy of: The Civil War Library and Museum. Philadelphia. Pa

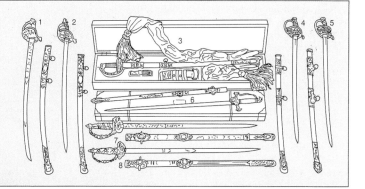

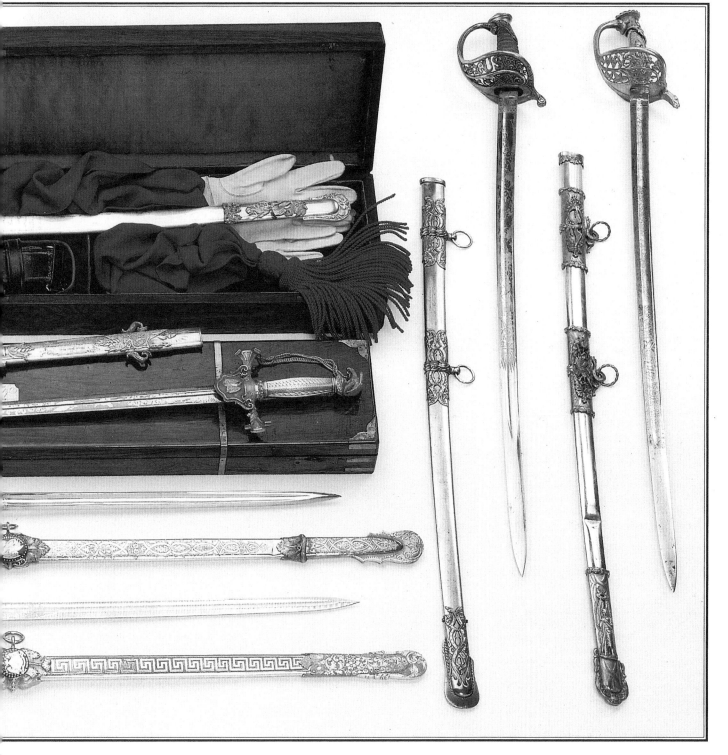

in his best interest not to be captured. First, after consulting with Sherman and Johnston, Breckinridge finished his primary mission, which was to see Confederate armies surrendered and to oversee the escape of Davis and the government. He did so as best he could, finally parting with Davis in South Carolina on May 2 and riding off with a small party of followers, hoping to decoy pursuing Federals from Davis' trail. It did not work, and Davis was taken in Georgia on May 10. When he learned of that, Breckinridge was free to make his own escape, and set off for the coast of Florida. Along the way he picked up others, including the daring Confederate commerce raider John Taylor Wood. Together they rode as far as Fort Butler, on the St. Johns River. Then loading their small party of three officers and three Confederate enlisted men and Breckinridge's servant Tom Ferguson into a small boat, they sailed the St.Johns to the Indian River, then all along the Indian – a part of the inland waterway – to its mouth. Along the way they engaged in a running gun battle with renegades living near present-day Miami, and turned pirate by commandeering at gunpoint a larger sailing boat from the hands of Federal deserters. Having tried unsuccessfully to reach the Bahamas, they now decided instead to sail out across the Gulf Stream to Cuba. They chose to do so amid one of the worst storms of the decade, and then only after eluding one Federal patrol boat, and boldly trading for supplies from another Yankee steamer. For four days they braved near-hurricane winds and seas, almost going under at least twice, before in the end they saw the coast of Cuba ahead. On June 12, 1865, they landed at Cardenas, and Breckinridge began what would be a three-and-one-half-year exile until the Universal Amnesty of Christmas 1868 allowed him to return to Kentucky without fear of molestation.[9]

While Breckinridge was the only high-ranking officer who might genuinely have feared for his life, there were many others who simply could not accept defeat, nor the prospect of life under Yankee rule. In the months after the surrenders, somewhere between 5,000 and 10,000 Confederates and their families left the South in the largest expatriation movement in American history. Almost 5,000 went to Mexico to start new lives in the settlement of Carlotta. Among them were several generals, including Sterling Price, John B. Magruder, Thomas C. Hindman, Joseph O. Shelby, and others. Several took service in the army of the Emperor Maximilian in his war against the Juarista insurgents. One of them, Brigadier General Mosby M. Parsons, along with his former adjutant, were killed by the Mexican rebels. Unfortunately for them, their attempt to start a new colony in Mexico failed, and most eventually returned to the South to try to pick up their old lives.

Elsewhere, old Confederates, again largely ex-officers, moved to settlements in Central America, and even South America, especially in Brazil, where their descendants still live. Some stayed in Cuba, while even more went to Canada. There, especially in Toronto and at Niagara, a virtual little Confederate community arose. For a time Breckinridge was their leading citizen, soon joined by Jubal Early and a host of lesser officers. Breckinridge stayed only as long as he had to, purposely living just across the Niagara River from United States soil so he could see the Stars and Stripes flying over Fort Niagara, a flag and a country he had never wanted to fight against.

Above: In the waning days of the war, with the Confederacy in shambles and its government in flight, final acts achieved notoriety. Colonel Benjamin Pritchard, third from left seated, captured Jeff Davis.

Below: Once the peacemakers did their tasks, the army establishment quickly demobilized, leaving only occupation troops during Reconstruction. General Meade set up headquarters here in Atlanta.

Early and others were there out of pure bitterness, though almost all of them, in time, would return to the South.

More of these men, almost entirely officers, crossed the Atlantic to Europe and the Near East. In the late 1860s, when the Khedive of Egypt needed trained soldiers, several men including Brigadier Generals Charles W. Field and William W. Loring took commissions in his army. There, ironically, they found themselves serving side by side with other soldiers of fortune, former officers of the Union Army.

More still went to Europe, and especially to England and France. These men were truly exiles, not there to stay but simply wandering until they

could go home. Breckinridge also turned up here, and again was the leading figure for a time. His society often included men like Longstreet's old staff officer Osmun Latrobe and General Louis T. Wigfall. The Confederates, for the most part, were well accepted into European society. Prominent politicians and socialites paid them attentions and sought their friendship. Breckinridge became acquainted with Thomas Carlyle and the Archbishop of Canterbury, while others married into European society. There had been considerable sympathy in Europe for the Confederate cause, and many of the former officers were just as flattered and indulged as any exiled royalty, of which there was always a surfeit. Yet almost all of these officers, too, wanted only to go home. By 1869, most of them had.[10]

What so many of them feared when they left the South, especially those under indictments, was trial and perhaps even execution. Since there had never been an insurrection in the United States before, no one could predict what the victorious Union would do with its former enemies. The terms of Grant and Sherman, and the well-known attitude of Lincoln toward leniency, would have seemed to bode well. But then a madman killed Lincoln just in the moment of triumph, and a bitter vengeful mood swept much of the North. In such a climate, many might logically fear for their lives.

Yet they needed have no fear. Even Davis and his leading officers of government suffered no more than imprisonment for a time. None were ever brought to trial, all were released, and some even sought and obtained their full rights of citizenship again. Several officers, most of them generals, were also imprisoned for a time, most because of suspected war crimes or else because they had been involved in espionage. All of them, too, were eventually released.

In fact, after all this terrible, bloody war, with the deaths of 620,000 and untold devastation of property and civilian lives behind them, the Union, even in its vindictive mood after Lincoln's death, took as reprisal the life of only one man. He was an officer; Major Henry Wirz, the commandant of Camp Sumter, the infamous Andersonville. In what was unquestionably a miscarriage of justice, he was brought before a military tribunal some months after the surrenders and charged with intentionally starving and mistreating thousands of Union prisoners to death. Perjured testimony appeared to prosecute him, attempts were made to link his crimes with Jefferson Davis, and he was denied many of the safeguards that would have been available to him in a civil court. Worse, he spoke with a thick Swiss accent that only further aroused the xenophobic prejudices of the officers on his court. Not a particularly likeable man, still he was no war criminal, but in this court he never had a chance. The court convicted him and sentenced him to death. On November 10, 1865, while the soldiers stationed around him chanted "Andersonville" over and over again, he was hanged, the sole Confederate executed as a result of the Civil War. For Wirz it was a personal tragedy. For the reunited Union, it was evidence of the most incredible restraint ever shown in history by a victor dealing with a defeated separatist movement.

Such restraint would be needed through the dark days of Reconstruction ahead. Though its horrors have been greatly magnified by Southern writers since, still the years from 1865 to 1877 were hard ones for the South. Only with the passage of time would passions die and the men who had led the armies of the Confederacy rebuild their lives. Yet most of them did. Indeed, within two decades after Appomattox, almost all of the once-Confederate states were again firmly under the control of the men who had been captains and colonels and generals in the armies of the gray. Gordon would become a United States Senator and later governor of Georgia. Francis Nichols became governor of Louisiana, and John S. Marmaduke won the governorship of Missouri. No-one has counted the total number of former Rebel officers who became governors, senators and congressmen, or elected and appointed state officials, but surely it runs into

Above: It was amazing how little vindictiveness there was on the part of the victors. But with the commander of Andersonville it was another matter. Reporters gathered to view his execution.

the thousands. Several even became Republicans, like Longstreet and William Mahone, earning no little criticism from their old comrades in arms. And one, the oft-imposed-upon Simon Buckner, finally had a measure of repayment for the surrenders forced upon him during the war by being nominated for the vice presidency in 1896. His running-mate was one-time Union major general John M. Palmer, and though they lost, still their candidacy truly represented the unity of the reunited states. Buckner's own son and namesake would become a lieutenant general in the United States Army, dying on Okinawa in 1945.[11]

As evidence of the degree to which the officers of the Confederacy assimilated themselves into the Union once again, several of them later reentered the U.S. Army during the Indian campaigns of the 1870s and 1880s, and most notably during the Spanish-American War. Both Joseph Wheeler and Fitzhugh Lee, major generals in the Confederacy became major generals of volunteers in 1898, and were retired, respectively, in 1900 and 1901, as brigadiers in the Regular Army. Ironically, this made them and all the other ex-Confederate officers who returned to the military

Below: The death of Henry Wirz, with the Capitol dome in the background providing an ironic picture of an unjust trial's result, in sight of the symbol of American justice. It was a sacrifice to public outrage.

eligible to receive a pension from the government they once had fought to overthrow. Only in America.

The Confederates also became active in their own veterans' organization, the United Confederate Veterans, and for decades the old officers once again held sway as the leaders of the local "camps" of the U.C.V. A succession of them acted as grand commanders, their purpose being the care and comfort of aged and infirm former soldiers, and the preservation of the story of the Confederate epic. Indeed, that preservation was on the minds of veterans of both sides. Immediately after Lincoln's assassination, a group of Union officers formed the Military Order of the

Loyal Legion of the United States, generally known by its much less cumbersome acronym "MOLLUS". Originally intended as a sort of guard to protect against chaos in the wake of Lincoln's murder, it quickly turned to more peaceful pursuits. State commanderies were established in every Union state, and not many years passed before they began a systematic program of publishing papers by officers recounting their Civil War experiences. While many officers also belonged to the much larger Grand Army of the Republic, or G.A.R., only officers were allowed MOLLUS membership, and the contribution of their collection and publication of memoirs and reminiscences of the war would prove to be a

major boon to historians, just as the museums they established in their commanderies kept alive for visitors the exciting years they had shared.

In other spheres, their influence was equally profound. Even more so than their former foes, the officers of the old Union virtually took hold of American politics for two generations. Indeed, in the years following the war, service in that war became almost a prerequisite for winning political office. Only two of the presidents elected during the remainder of the century were not veterans. Andrew Johnson, U.S. Grant, Rutherford B. Hayes, James A. Garfield and Benjamin Harrison had all been generals, and William McKinley,

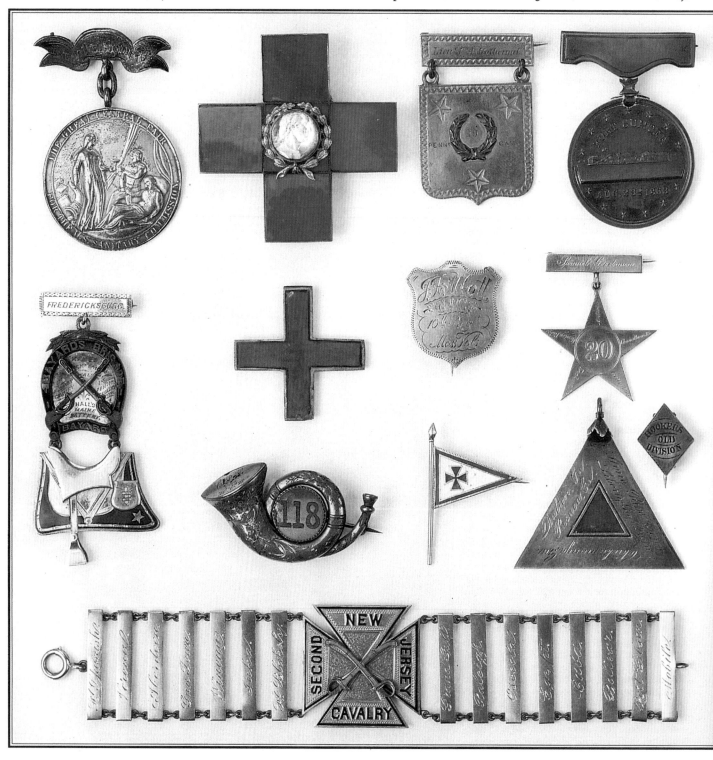

Union Officers' Corps Badges, Medallions and Insignia

1 Sanitary Commission Fair, 1864, medal of Col. C.P. Herring
2 1st Div., 6th Corps badge of Brevet Major James W. Latta
3 Identification badge of Lt. J.A. Rothermel
4 Gillmore Medal of Honor
5 Identification badge of Col. P.J. Yorke
6 1st Div., 6th Corps badge
7 Identification pin
8 20th Corps badge of Lt. Samuel Goodman
9 Identification badge of Col. C.P. Herring
10 1st Div. 5th Corps pin of Capt. N. Bayne
11 1st Div., 4th Corps badge
12 2nd Div., 3rd Corps badge
13 Colonel Yorke's 5th Corps badge
14 Sheridan's Cavalry Corps badge of Major John Cassals
15 3rd Div., 9th Corps badge of Lt. William Goodrich
16 5th Corps badge of Brevet Brig. Gen. C.P. Herring
17 Devin's 1st Div., Sheridan's Cavalry Medallion
18 Badge of Lt. Daniel Layton
19 Pin of Co. A, 132nd Pa Inf., 3rd Div., 3rd Corps
20 3rd Brigade, 1st Div., 5th Corps watch fob of General C.P. Herring
21 Silver Meade Medal
22 Gold Meade Medal

Artifacts courtesy of: The Civil War Library and Museum, Philadelphia, Pa

who took office in 1897 and served until his death in 1901, had been a lieutenant in Hayes' regiment. Untold governors and senators and congressmen, ambassadors, state legislators, and others sprang from the ranks of the veteran officers of the Union. The United States as a whole was in the firm grip of the men who had led its companies and regiments and armies in the great war for the Union.

Yet the years after the war were not glorious for all of them. When the Union armies demobilized and the nation returned to its old Regular Army establishment, men who had been major generals of volunteers reverted to their old Regular ranks. George Custer, youngest major general in American history in 1865, was a lieutenant colonel of the 7th Cavalry a year later, and in 1876 would die with it at the Little Big Horn. Mackenzie was also destined to become a famed Indian fighter, but the rigors of a lifetime of campaigning finally exacted a toll, and he died in an asylum for the insane. Poor Canby, destined to receive obscure surrenders, suffered an obscure death when three Modoc Indians attacked and murdered him during an 1873 peace negotiation. Rawlins would die in 1871 of tuberculosis, while alcoholism, hard times, or just boredom would kill others. For many of those who had suffered wounds, especially amputations, there were ahead lifetimes of addiction to morphia that started with its use as a pain killer. For every officer who parlayed his service into post-war personal and career success, there were the tragedies of men who, having tasted excitement and responsibility, could never find it again and suffered the inexorable and debilitating gradual descent back into obscurity.

Just as the veteran Yankee officers who did well, rose to greater heights than their old foes after the war, so did the Confederate officers who fared badly, do so more than the Federals. Raphael Semmes and Richard Taylor would die penniless. Forrest never rebuilt the considerable fortune he had when the war started. Bragg was living a hardscrabble existence when he fell dead on a Galveston street in 1876. Buckner did only a little better though he lived a long time and was much honored. Hindman was assassinated in his Helena, Arkansas, home in 1868, and poor Brigadier General Thomas Benton Smith suffered perhaps the worst fate of all. Captured at the Battle of Nashville in December 1864, he was being taken to the rear when, for reasons unknown, Colonel William L. McMillen of the 95th Ohio drew his sword and repeatedly hacked at Smith's head before he could be restrained. The assault left Smith's brain partially exposed, yet miraculously he lived – if it could be called living.

Captain U.S.A. Veteran Reserve

As the war progressed and casualties mounted, both sides faced the twin problems of reduced manpower and the growing number of convalescent men able to perform light duty but not up to the rigors of active campaigning. To many it appeared that a solution might lie in outfitting such men for light work such as acting as guards, recruiting officers, and behind-the-lines garrisons, thus freeing able-bodied men for service with the armies in the field.

Thus was born the Veteran Reserve Corps, often referred to as the Invalid Corps. Men with infirmities that did not disable them but which made them unsuitable for the field were allowed to wear the sky blue uniform of the corps, as does this captain. For men whose answer to their country's call still rang in their ears, here was an honorable way to keep serving their cause. The Confederacy never successfully created a counterpart organization.

Troubled constantly by the wound, he eventually lost his reason and spent forty-seven years in an insane asylum before dying in 1923.[12]

Whereas poor Smith died in obscurity, the already tragic John Bell Hood was under the eyes of the whole South when on August 30, 1879, already bankrupt, he died of yellow fever, along with his wife and one child.

For the officers of lower ranks, the share of success and tragedy proved much the same. Yet one thing they had completely in common with their old foes of the North, and here perhaps the former Confederate officers managed to emerge pre-eminent. Having lost the war, they almost immediately took possession of its presentation to posterity. A flood of memoirs and histories began to emerge from Northern and Southern officers alike almost as soon as the war ended. Captain Ed Porter Thompson of the old 1st Kentucky Brigade actually started writing his history of his unit in 1864, before the war was over, and hundreds more would follow. Having lost the contest by the sword, the old Confederates quickly won it with the pen. In 1876 former officers who had formed the Southern Historical Society began publishing an annual series of "Papers" that would eventually run to more than fifty volumes, providing one of the most reliable and authoritative sources of first-person accounts of the Confederate side of the conflict. Much later, in 1892, former captain Samuel Cunningham started the publication of the *Confederate Veteran* which for forty years would publish articles about the war and veterans' affairs. Jubal Early and a few other officers of the Army of Northern Virginia virtually controlled the Southern Historical Society, presenting an almost official revealed version of Lee and his campaigns that remained influential for more than a century in Civil War historiography. Indeed, other Confederate officers who dared to write or say anything contradictory – as Longstreet did in his own memoirs – quickly found the Society's *Papers* used as a powerful weapon against them.

The flood of individual recollections was staggering. Hood, Johnston, Beauregard, Longstreet, Early, and dozens of other generals – and hundreds of lower grade officers – wrote their memoirs. The generals were often, like those above, still fighting their old internal battles in their books. One, however, Richard Taylor's *Destruction and Reconstruction*, was of a different stripe, quickly coming to be recognized as perhaps the finest of all Confederate memoirs. For all that their old foes might publish, the portrait of the war presented in these old officers' books still remains the most persuasive version.

The Federal officers were not idle, of course. McClellan, Custer, Sheridan, and dozens of others left behind important books telling their sides of the war. Sherman wrote an unfailingly interesting autobiography, and U.S. Grant, even while dying of cancer, wrote what some regard as the finest American memoir of all time, and certainly one of the greatest books ever written by a soldier. The Federals, too, formed their societies, and more than just the MOLLUS published extensively on the Union side of the war. In the end, nearly 50,000 books and articles would be published on the conflict, perhaps a fifth of them coming from the pens of former officers of blue or gray. It was as if the event of their youth had been so great that they could not rid themselves of it, but had to tell and retell again the stories of those days when they all faced death.

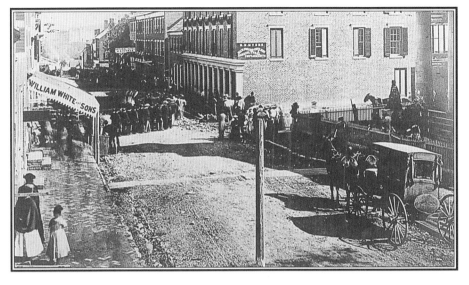

Above: As the years wore onward, the officers and leaders of both sides gradually disappeared. Here in Lexington, Virginia, in 1870, the funeral of Robert E. Lee lays to rest a living legend.

Below: The victors aged as well, getting together from time to time to remember their glory days. Sheridan sits at center, with Admiral Farragut just to the right, and General Heintzelman to the left.

A few years after the war's conclusion, ex-Confederate Carlton McCarthy would lament that "the historian who essays to write the grand movements will hardly stop to tell how the hungry private fried his bacon, baked his biscuit, and smoked his pipe." Indeed, for many years the story of the common soldier's war was almost completely ignored. Yet ironically, for all the voluminous memoirs they left behind, the officers of North and South, however well remembered *individually*, have been equally forgotten *collectively*. Perhaps in the flood of books about the generals, people lost sight of the contribution made by the *whole* officer corps of both sides. How the raw young lieutenant learned his drill, led his men, and bore his heavy responsibility, was just as important in determining the course of the war. By all that they left behind, the officers of blue and gray showed how much they believed that what they had suffered and done deserved to be kept alive in memory's shrine.[13]

References

1 William C. Davis, "The Campaign to Appomattox," *Civil War Times Illustrated*, XIV (April 1975), pp.5, 48.
2 Longstreet, *Manassas to Appomattox*, p.584.
3 Davis, "Appomattox", p.27
4 Ibid., pp.32-3.
5 Ibid., pp.36-8.
6 Ibid., p.41.
7 Ibid., pp.42-8.
8 William T. Sherman, *Memoirs* (New York, 1875), II, pp.349-54; Davis, *Breckinridge*, pp.512-3.
9 Davis, *Breckinridge*, pp.521-40 passim.
10 William C. Davis, "Confederate Exiles", *American History Illustrated*, V (June 1970), pp.30-43.
11 Warner, *Generals in Gray*, p.368.
12 "Confederate Generals", *Southern Historical Society Papers*, XXII (1894), pp.65-6; Warner, *Generals in Gray*, p.284.
13 Philip Van Doren Stern, ed., *Soldier Life in the Union and Confederate Armies* (Bloomington, Ind., 1961), p.293.

APPENDIX

The specially commissioned color photographs of Civil War weapons, uniforms and personal belongings which have appeared throughout this book, represent perhaps one of the finest collections of contemporary artifacts brought together under one cover. As an additional source of information on each photograph's content and origin, Russ A. Pritchard, Director of The Civil War Library and Museum and technical advisor to the book has compiled this Appendix. Further information can also be obtained from the Bibliography and list of museums and societies on page 256.

Personal Memorabilia of General Thomas Jonathan Jackson pp.14-15

Jackson graduated from West Point in the class of 1846, and went on to distinguish himself in the Mexican War. He resigned from the Army in 1852 to become an instructor at V.M.I. At the beginning of the war he was appointed a colonel in the Virginia militia and thereafter his rise was uninterrupted. His sobriquet "Stonewall" was earned at First Manassas, and came from a comment from General Bee. He was promoted major general in August 1861, and the following year waged a campaign in the Shenandoah that is still a text book study to this day. With the exception of the Seven Days Battles Jackson performed incredibly well during his career. He saved Lee at Sharpsburg and was made lieutenant general, commanding 2nd Corps. His flank march at Chancellorsville was brilliantly executed, but he was mortally wounded by his own forces while making a night reconnaissance, dying May 10, 1863.

Uniform and Personal Belongings of Major General George G. Meade pp. 18-19

George Meade graduated from West Point in 1835 near the top of his class. He resigned almost immediately to seek a career in civil engineering. Returning to the Army in 1842, he was breveted first lieutenant during the Mexican War. As a captain in 1861, he was given command of one of the Pennsylvania brigades and promoted brigadier general. He fought under General McClellan during the Peninsula Campaign and was severely wounded at the Battle of Glendale (June 30, 1862). Barely recovered, he fought at Second Manassas, South Mountain and Antietam. Meade commanded a division during the failure at Fredericksburg, performed well at Chancellorsville the following spring and literally was placed in charge of the Army of the Potomac while on the march to Gettysburg. Meade held the Federal forces together and forced the retreat of General Lee, but was severely criticised for not mounting an aggressive pursuit. The general offered his resignation, but was refused, and was promoted to brigadier general in the Regular Army in January 1864. Meade led the army through the Wilderness, Spotsylvania, Cold Harbor and the seige of Petersburg, though always under the shadow of Grant. He was finally promoted major general

near the end of the war. His post-war years were spent in command of military districts, and he was in command of the Division of the Atlantic headquartered in Philadelphia when he died of pneumonia on November 6, 1872.

Confederate Headgear and Epaulettes pp.30-31

While regulations were quite specific, the Confederate officer wore whatever hat was available at the time. Replacements were difficult to obtain, so many pieces of equipment were used until they were little more than rags. Surviving material was used up after the war due to the desperate economic situation in the South during Reconstruction. Extant specimans of Confederate hats are very scarce.

Union Officers' Headgear and Insignia pp.32-33

Figure 2 was the hat of Lt. Henry M. Brewster, 57th New York Infantry. Figure 3 belonged to Lt. George W. Taylor, 4th Massachusetts Battery. Figure 4 was the cap of Maj. Samuel S. Linton, 38th Illinois Infantry. Figure 5 belonged to First Lt. Peter Palen, 143rd New York Infantry. Figure 6 belonged to Capt. Charles P. Pierce, on the staff of Brig. Gen. Henry M. Judah. Figure 7 was the cap of Capt. Selleck L. White, 10th Connecticut Infantry. Figure 8 belonged to Capt. Lindley M. Coleman, 19th Maine Infantry. Figures 9 and 10 are insignia from the hat of Capt. Langhorne Wister, 13th Regt. Pennsylvania Reserves. Figures 17 and 18 are insignia from the hat of Col. Richard Biddle Roberts, 1st Regt. Pennsylvania Reserves.

Union Zouave and Rifle Officers' Uniforms and Equipment pp.36-37

Zouave uniforms originated from French colonial troops in North Africa. American officers, acting as observers, were greatly impressed by the quality of these troops, and their reports caused considerable effort to emulate them.

Rifle uniforms were almost the opposite in color and concept. Designed to be as inconspicuous as possible, the color of the uniforms was usually green. The branch insignia has a green background, and piping was green also. These elite units were few in number and surviving equipment is very rare.

The Potter or Ponder house in Atlanta pays ample evidence to the ferocity of the shelling during the Battle of Atlanta. Nowhere else in the war did civilians feel so fully the costs of warfare.

Confederate Officers' Camp Equipment
pp.52-53

The Confederate officer was no different from his Federal counterpart when it came to comfort. In the early months of the war, he too tried to be prepared for any situation. The first hard campaign usually convinced him that he needed only the bare essentials, and many of the luxuries were discarded or sent home.

Union Officers' Camp Equipment
pp.56-57

Indicative of the lavish lifestyle of some officers in camp is the silver service and liquor set of Maj. John Cassals (Figs. 1, 2, 20, 21 and 28); the service is engraved: 'To "Our Captain", Major John Cassals, 11th Pennsylvania Cavalry, from Company C, Bermuda Hundred, Virginia, November 4, 1864'. The field desk (Fig. 16) belonged to Lt. Col. Joseph Fulton Boyd.

Confederate Infantry Officers' Uniforms and Equipment pp.68-69

Like the Federals, the Confederate infantry officer had considerable latitude selecting his uniform and accoutrements, although the basic branch identification color was blue for infantry, the same as that in the Federal Army. Confederate officers of all branches did use strikingly different rank insignia, but their swords were, in many cases, copies of current Federal models, as were their handguns.

Union Infantry Officers' Uniforms and Equipment pp.70-71

Regulations concerning officers' uniforms allowed considerable latitude and therefore articles of uniform, accoutrements and accessories depended more on the individual officer's taste and financial resources than on military requirements. While Regular Army officer's were issued many regulation articles of uniform and equipage, the volunteer officer was left to his own resources. There were, however, several regulations that were observed with some consistency by everyone. The insignia for infantry was the curled horn, and the branch color was blue.

Union and Confederate Officers' Handguns pp.74-75

Figures 1 and 2: each of these pistols is silvered with ivory grips. The butts of each are engraved: 'Presented to Maj. Gen. John M. Schofield, Comd. Dept. of the MO by his Friends in St. Louis, Augt. 1863'. Figure 3: pistol engraved: 'Presented to Adjt. Charles C. Knight 119th Regt. P. V. by H. G. Leisenring, August 1862'. Figure 12: Adams was colonel of the 67th New York Volunteer Infantry, the pistol's ivory grips bear battle honors on both sides. Figure 13 engraved: 'Capt. James Starr'. Starr commanded Co.E, 6th Pennsylvania Cavalry.

Confederate Officers' Edged Weapons pp.78-79

Figure 1 is patterned after the Model 1839 topographical engineer's saber. Figure 2: Leech and Rigdon was also known as the Memphis Novelty Works. They also made revolvers, spurs, bayonets and knives. At least six major types of Leech and Rigdon swords have been identified. Figure 5: Boyle, Gamble and Co. was the premier sword maker of the Confederacy. Figure 6: W. J. McElroy of Macon, Georgia manufactured sturdy but unrefined edged weapons; the metal scabbard is etched with Gothic CS between the ring mounts, a feature peculiar to this maker. Figure 8: etched blade with Georgia state seal on obverse and CS within a wreath on the reverse. Figure 12: scabbard is engraved: 'Capt. Jno. L. Saffarrans From his Friends In Honor of his services at the battle of Belmont, Memphis, Feby. 22, 1862'.

Union Officers' Edged Weapons pp.80-81

Although it was an official badge of rank, the sword as a weapon was obsolete. Many veterans sent swords home or relegated them to the wagons, preferring instead a reliable revolver or a rifle-musket in some instances.

Union General Officers' Uniforms and Equipment pp.94-95

A general's rank was designated by stars on shoulder straps which were normally worn. Another consistent device was the black velvet cuffs and collar. Although regulations specified a buff sash, many maroon sashes were utilized, and swords and sword belts were a matter of personal choice.

Confederate General Officers' Uniforms and Equipment pp.100-101

A major difference is noticeable when comparing Union and Confederate general officers, besides basic color. The Confederate general officers rank is indicated by collar insignia and sleeve braid rather than the shoulder straps of his Federal counterpart. This is a major deviation from the Old Army regulations in form, yet both armed forces still recognized the star insignia and the buff sash as indicative of a general officer.

Confederate Officers' Edged Weapons pp.104-105

Figure 6. The College Hill sword was made in Nashville, Tennessee. Figure 8. Dawson was captain and later major in the Terrell Light Artillery of Georgia. Figure 12. A foot officer's sword made by Boyle & Gamble of Richmond.

Confederate Officers' Edged Weapons and Memorabilia pp.106-107

Figures 1 and 2: these belonged to John Boston Hill, brother of Maj. Gen. A. P. Hill. Figures 5 and 6: the Sword belonged to Capt. William Maury, C.S.S. Georgia, and was retailed by Firmin and Sons, London. Figure 10, engraved: '2nd Co., Washington Artillery, Try Us, Capt. T. L. Rosser, 7th June 1862'. Figures 13 and 14: dirk has pillow pommel with shark skin grip, silver mounts and silver scabbard. Obverse of blade is inscribed: 'From his shipmates aboard CSS Virginia March 9, 1862'.

Union Army Manuals pp.116-117

The majority of manuals were published by the Government Printing Office in Washington D.C., followed closely by J. B. Lippincott & Co., Philadelphia. Other major publishers were Harpers & Brothers and D. Van Nostrand, both of New York. Manuals with owners names, rank and unit are particularly collectable and eagerly sought.

Confederate Army Manuals pp.118-119

In almost every case, Confederate manuals are an exact copy of the then existing Federal manuals, with the insertion of the letters CS wherever US appeared in the original. With exception of uniform regulations, there is little difference in the publications of either side.

Confederate Artillery Officers' Uniforms and Equipment pp.122-123

The branch designating color for the artillery in both armies was red. Red forage caps topped with gold braid added to the aura of the artilleryman. They are among the most colorful uniforms of the Confederate forces.

Union Artillery Officers' Uniforms and Equipment pp.124-125

The artillery branch of service color was used as background for shoulder straps, piping for coats and trousers. Crossed cannon insignia, both embroidered and stamped metal, was used to indicate the branch on headgear. There does not appear to be any distinction made between light and heavy artillery insignia.

Union Naval Officers' Uniforms and Equipment pp. 136-137

Naval artifacts in general are quite scarce, due primarily to the fact that the Navy was small in comparison to the Army. Much naval material was also quite functional, and post war changes in regulations did not necessarily make uniforms obsolete; so they were worn until worn out.

Confederate Naval Officers' Uniforms and Equipment pp.140-141

Confederate naval material is exceedingly rare. The dolphin head naval sword (Figs. 25, 26, 27) is one of the most desirable objects in the whole field of Civil War collectibles.

Confederate Naval China pp.148-149

The majority of this rare service exists in two institutional collections with scattered pieces in less than a half a dozen private collections. There is considerable speculation concerning the presence of such china on C.S.S. Alabama, discovered in the English Channel during the mid-1980s.

Personal Possessions of General Robert E. Lee pp.162-163

Lee's military and civilian career was exceptional. A West Point graduate of the class of 1829, Lee served as an engineer during the years preceeding the Mexican War. He won three brevets for gallantry, serving well after the war to become superintendent of West Point in 1852. Assigned to a line command in the cavalry in 1857 he was at home on leave when John Brown and his insurrectionists stormed the arsenal at Harper's Ferry. Lee was placed in command of the detachment of Marines that captured Brown. General Winfield Scott recalled Lee when the lower southern states seceded in 1861, and offered him command of the Federal forces which he declined, instead going with his state of Virginia. At first appointed brigadier general of Virginia's forces, he later received a regular Confederate commission. By 1862 he was military advisor to President Davis, and after the wounding of General Joseph E. Johnson in May 1862, took command of the Army of Northern Virginia. Lee fought aggressively and was immensely successful at Second Manassas, Fredericksburg and Chancellorsville. Then, after the repulse at Gettysburg, he was forced to turn to the defensive. He did well through 1864 in the Wilderness and into 1865 around Petersburg, but the situation became critical. After a last effort to break away from the encircling Federal forces, Lee and the remains of the Army of Northern Virginia surrendered at Appomattox Court House, April 9 1865. Lee returned to

Richmond and began to be a roll model for all ex-Confederates. He assumed the presidency of Washington College in Lexington, Virginia and spent the remainder of his life 'binding up the wounds' caused by the war. A symbol in the South, he became a living example of honor and decency. He died on October 12, 1870, already a legend.

Uniforms and Personal Regalia of General U. S. Grant pp.168-169

Born at Point Pleasant, Ohio on April 27, 1822, Grant attended West Point. As a student, Grant was less than mediocre, but he was noted as an excellent horseman. He served with distinction during the Mexican War being breveted first lieutenant and then captain. Post war assignments found him far from home in the Northwest territories. After reprimands from superiors about his excessive drinking, he resigned from the Army to pursue civilian occupations at which he failed repeatedly. At the outbreak of war, he sought reinstatement into the Regulars with no success. Finally, he was appointed colonel of the 21st Illinois Infantry and his abilities began to be noticed. Promoted to brigadier general, Grant led the successful assaults on Forts Henry and Donelson, and which resulted in his promotion to major general. The battles of Shiloh and the campaign and capture of Vicksburg followed. Then, the relief of Chattanooga and the rout of Confederate General Bragg earned Grant the rank of lieutenant general. Grant came east and received the command of all U.S. armies early in 1864. The battles of the Wilderness, Spotsylvania Court House, Cold Harbor and finally Petersburg brought the Confederates to bay. Spring 1865 saw Grant drive Lee west to Appomattox Court House where he accepted the surrender of the Army of Northern Virginia. In 1866, he was appointed general of the army and, in 1868, became the republican candidate for president. Winning easily, Grant stepped into an arena that was totally foreign to him, and easily managed to surround himself with corruption and disaster. His own basic honesty saved his reputation, and he retired to private life in 1876. Again, all his business ventures failed and he found himself destitute and dying. The last years were spent writing his memoirs which were published by Mark Twain. He died July 23, 1885 at Mount McGregor, New York.

The cased Grant sword by Schuyler, Hartley & Graham, with accessories, was presented to the general by the officers of the Army of Tennessee in recognition of the capture of Vicksburg, July 4, 1863. The name 'Vicksburg' is engraved between the two ring mounts on the scabbard. All Grant material from the Civil War Library and Museum was placed in the museum by Major General U. S. Grant, III.

Confederate Engineer Officers' Uniforms and Equipment pp.182-183

The Confederate engineer, like his Federal counterpart, used the castle insignia as a branch designating device. In addition though, the Confederate engineer adopted an E in Gothic script as a button and headgear device.

Union Signal Corps and Engineer Officers' Uniforms and Equipment pp.184-185

The Signal Corps originated in the early days of the Civil War as a special unit. While their uniforms and equipment were basically the same as other Federal units, their mission was that of setting up and maintaining communications.

Engineer officers were the elite of the graduating class of West Point each year. Their branch insignia, the castle, was distinctive. Within this branch were the Topographical Engineers who wore the distinctive Model 1839 saber which is very rare today.

Confederate Medical Officers' Uniforms and Equipment pp.188-189

The Confederate Medical Corps was much the same as its Federal counterpart. Ranks were the same, as were the facings and the green sash. Most surgeon's kits were made in the North or imported, and many southern doctors had been trained in Baltimore, Philadelphia and New York. The major difference was the lack of drugs and supplies faced as the war continued.

Union Medical Officers' Uniforms and Equipment pp.190-191

Union medical officers did not have a branch color in the manner of the combat branches, but did wear the distinctive letters MS (Medical Service) surrounded by a wreath as an insignia on headgear. In addition, dress epaulettes also bore the letters MS, together with a green silk sash worn with a distinctive Model 1840 medical officer's sword. Surgeons usually were accorded the rank of major, and assistant surgeons that of first lieutenant.

Personal Memorabilia of Brigadier General John Hunt Morgan pp.204-205

General Morgan was born in Huntsville, Alabama on June 1, 1825. He was educated at Transylvania College in Lexington, Kentucky and saw service during the Mexican War. After discharge from the Army, he returned to Lexington and entered the family business, becoming active in the local militia unit, the Lexington Rifles. At the outbreak of war he took his small unit to Bowling Green and offered his services to General Buckner. He was soon promoted to colonel of the 2nd Kentucky Cavalry and proceeded to establish himself as one of the most feared Confederate Cavalry leaders. His raids into Kentucky, Tennessee, Ohio and Indiana caused great concern. He was once captured and interned in the Ohio State Prison but escaped. In September 1864 while enroute to attack Federal units at Knoxville, he was surprised by Federal cavalry and killed. He is buried in Lexington, Kentucky.

Confederate Cavalry Officers' Uniforms and Equipment pp.216-217

The branch of service color in the Confederate cavalry was yellow, as in the old cavalry before the war, and was the same as its Federal counterpart. The same insignia, the crossed sabers was also utilized. With the exception of rank device and color, there was a striking similarity in uniforms.

Union Cavalry Officers' Uniforms and Equipment pp.218-219

The cavalry branch of service color was used as background for shoulder straps, piping for coats and trousers. A predecessor branch, dragoons, utilized the color orange in the same manner until discontinued in favour of cavalry in 1861. Crossed sabers insignia, both embroidered and stamped metal, was used on headgear.

Confederate, Richmond Manufactured, Officers' Edged Weapons pp.222-223

Richmond was one of the primary ordnance manufacturing locations within the Confederacy.

The most prolific edged weapons fabricator, the form of Boyle, Gamble and Company, also known as Boyle, Gamble and McFee, operated there throughout most of the war. The firm made swords copied after Federal models, swords of its own design, as well as embellished captured swords or blades.

Personal Possessions and Memorabilia of Maj. Gen. J. E. B. Stuart pp.224-225

A West Point graduate of 1854, Stuart served in the U.S. Cavalry until his resignation and appointment as colonel of the 1st Virginia Cavalry in 1861. By mid 1862 Stuart had risen to become a major general and commander of the cavalry of the Army of Northern Virginia. It seemed as if he led a charmed life and could not fail, until the Battle of Brandy Station (June 1863), where Confederate cavalry realized that the Federal cavalry had become a force to be reckoned with. From that point on, Stuart and his men were hard pressed by Federal horsemen at every encounter. Stuart's absence during the initial stages of the Battle of Gettysburg has always been controversial. Stuart was mortally wounded at Yellow Tavern May 11, 1864 and died in Richmond the next day.

1859 Officer's McClellan Saddle of Major General John Sedgwick p.229

After a brave career that had taken him from the Peninsula Campaign to the Wilderness, Sedgwick died in one of the most ironic of ways. At Spotsylvania on May 9, 1864, he was shot through the head by a Confederate sharpshooter after having just stated "they couldn't hit an elephant from that distance". Sedgwick was known as a fearless, talented commander.

Union and Confederate Presentation Swords and Spurs pp.236-237, 238-239

The presentation of ornate, deluxe edged weapons to prominent politicians, war heroes and local favorite sons was a recognized tribute in the 1860s. The majority of these presentation edged weapons were enhanced models of those swords then in current issue to the Army. There were exceptions where no expense was spared, and the result was a sword of exquisite quality and craftsmanship such as those shown here. Some were jeweler – made by Tiffany of New York, or Bailey and Co., of Philadelphia, with gold, silver and semi-precious stone embellishment. Such pieces were not made to be carried in the field. Swords of this quality are prime collector's pieces and rarely seen for sale today.

Union Presentation Edged Weapons pp.240-241

The two swords (Figs. 7 and 8), presented to Generals Meade and Blair are truly spectacular, and were made by Bailey and Company of Philadelphia, with semi-precious stones and enamel decoration. Few edged weapons of this quality are in private hands, the majority of them residing in institutional collections.

Union Officers' Corps Badges, Medallions and Insignia pp.244-245

Figure 21 bears the motto: 'the Victor of Gettysburg, The Deliverer of Our State, The Faithful Soldier of Our Country'. Presented to dignitaries at the time of the presentation of the gold medal to General Meade (Fig. 22). Figure 22 bears the legend: 'Presented July 4th 1866 to Maj. Gen. George G. Meade by the Union League of Philadelphia as a token of the gratitude of this country',

INDEX

Ranks shown are the latest recorded in the text
Page references for illustrations are listed in *italics*

Viewed from one-time Confederate fortifications, a veritable jungle of man-made obstacles litters the ground over which Yankees would have to attack Atlanta. Only the best of officers could get men to follow them across ground like that.

BIBLIOGRAPHY

Further reading to the Appendix subjects

Albaugh, William A., Benet, Hugh Jr., Simmons, Edward N., *Confederate Handguns*

Albaugh, William A., *Confederate Arms*

Albaugh, William A., *Confederate Edged Weapons*

Albert, Alphaeus H., *Buttons of the Confederacy*

Allen, Glenn C. and Piper, Wayne C., *The Battle Flags of the Confederacy*

Bailey, D. W., *British Military Longarms 1815-1865*

Belden, Bauman L., *War Medals of the Confederacy*

Brown, Rodney Hilton, *American Polearms 1526-1865*

Brown, Stuart E. Jr., *The Guns of Harpers Ferry*

Burns, Z. H., *Confederate Forts*

Caba, G. Craig, *United States Military Drums*

Cannon, Deveraux, D., Jr., *The Flags of the Confederacy*

Criswell, Grover C., *Confederate and Southern State Bonds*

Criswell, Grover C., *Confederate Currency*

Cromwell, Giles, *The Virginia Manufactory of Arms*

Crown, Francis J. Jr., *Confederate Postal History*

Daniel, Larry J. and Hunter, Riley W., *Confederate Cannon Foundries*

Davis, Rollin V. Jr., *U.S. Sword Bayonets, 1847-1865*

Davis, William C., *The Image of War*, Vols. 1-6

Dickey, Thomas S., and George, Peter C., *Field Artillery Projectiles of the American Civil War*

Dorsey, R. Stephen, *American Military Belts and Related Equipment*

Elting, John R. (ed.), *Military Uniforms in America*

Fuller, Claud E. and Stewart, Richard D., *Firearms of the Confederacy*

Fuller, Claud E., *Confederate Currency and Stamps*

Fuller, Claud E., *Springfield Shoulder Arms 1795-1865*

Fuller, Claud E., *The Whitney Firearms*

Garofalo, Robert and Elrod, Mark, *A Pictorial History of Civil War Era Musical Instruments and Bands*

Gary, William A., *Confederate Revolvers*

Gluckman, Arcadi, *United States Muskets, Rifles and Carbines*

Govt. Printing Office, *Uniform Regulations for the Army of the United States, 1861*

Hardin, Albert N. Jrs., *The American Bayonet, 1776-1964*

Hazlett, James C., Olmstead, Edwin and Parks, M. Hume, *Field Artillery Weapons of the Civil War*

Hopkins, Richard E., *Military Sharps Rifles and Carbines*

Huntingdon, R.T., *Hall's Breechloaders*

Jangen, Jerry L., *Bayonets*

Keim, Lon W., *Confederate General Service Accoutrement Plates*

Kerksis, Sydney C., *Field Artillery Projectiles of the Civil War, 1861-1865*

Kerksis, Sydney C., *Heavy Artillery Projectiles of the Civil War, 1861-1865*

Kerksis, Sydney C., *Plates and Buckles of the American Military 1795-1874*

Laframboise, Leon W., *History of the Artillery, Cavalry and Infantry Branch of Service Insignia*

Lord, Francis A., *Civil War Collector's Encyclopedia*, Vols. 1, 2, 3 & 4

Madaus, H. Michael and Needham, Robert D., *Battleflags of the Confederate Army of Tennessee*

Madaus, H. Michael, *Rebel Flags Afloat*

Marcot, Roy, *Spencer Repeating Firearms*

McAfee, Michael J., *Zouaves . . . The First and The Bravest*

McKee, W. Reid and Mason, M. W., Jr., *Civil War Projectiles*

McKee, W. Reid and Mason, M. W. Jr., *Civil War Projectiles, Small Arms and Field Artillery*

Miller, Francis Trevelyan, (ed.), *The Photographic History of the Civil War*, 10 Vols.

Murphy, John M., *Confederate Carbines and Musketoons*

Phillips, Stanley S., *Bullets Used in the Civil War, 1861-1865*

Phillips, Stanley S., *Civil War Corps Badges and Other Related Awards, Badges, Medals of the Period*

Phillips, Stanley S., *Excavated Artifacts from Battlefields and Camp Sites of the Civil War*

Pitman, John, *Breech-Loading Carbines of the United States Civil War Period*

Rankin, Robert H., *Small Arms of the Sea Service*

Reilly, Robert M., *United States Military Small Arms 1816-1865*

Riling, Ray (ed.), *Uniforms and Dress of the Army and Navy of the Confederate States*

Ripley, Warren, *Artillery and Ammunition of the Civil War*

Sellers, Frank M. and Smith, Samuel E., *American Percussion Revolvers*

Smith, Winston O., *The Sharps Rifle*

Stamatelos, James, *Notes on the Uniform and Equipments of the United States Cavalry, 1861-1865*

Steffen, Randy, *United States Military Saddles, 1812-1943*

Thomas, Dean S., *Cannons*

Thomas, Dean S., *Ready . . . Aim . . . Fire! Small Arms Ammunition in the Battle of Gettysburg*

Todd, Frederick P., *American Military Equipage, 1851-1872*, 4 Vols.

Wise, Arthur and Lord, Francis A., *Bands and Drummer Boys of the Civil War*

Wise, Arthur and Lord, Francis A., *Uniforms of the Civil War*

LOCATIONS OF MAJOR CIVIL WAR COLLECTIONS

Ancient and Honorable Artillery Company Armory
Faneuil Hall
Boston, MA 02109

Atlanta Historical Society
3101 Andrews Drive, N.W.
Atlanta, Ga 30305

Augusta-Richmond County Museum
540 Telfair Street,
Augusta, Ga 30901

Casemate Museum
Fort Monroe, Va 23651

Chicago Historical Society
Clark Street at North
Avenue, Chicago, Il 60614

Chickamauga-Chattanooga National Military Park
Fort Oglethorpe, Ga 30742

Civil War Library and Museum
1805 Pine Street
Philadelphia, Pa 19103

Confederate Museum
Alexander Street,
Crawfordville, Ga 30631

Confederate Museum
929 Camp Street,
New Orleans, La 70130

Confederate Naval Museum
201 4th Street
Columbus, Ga 31902

Fredericksburg and Spotsylvania National Military Park
120 Chatham Lane,
Fredericksburg, Va 22405

Fort Ward Museum and Historic Site
4301 W. Braddock Road,
Alexandria, Va 22304

Gettysburg National Military Park
Gettysburg, Pa 17325

Grand Army of the Republic Memorial Hall Museum
State Capitol 419 N.
Madison, WI 53702

Kentucky Military History Museum
Old State Arsenal
East Main Street
Frankfort, Ky 40602

Milwaukee Public Museum
800 W. Wells Street,
Milwaukee, WI 53233

Smithsonian Institution
National Museum of American History, 900 Jefferson Drive, S.W.
Washington, DC 20560

South Carolina Confederate Relic Room and Museum
World War memorial Building, 920 Sumter Street, Columbia, SC 29201

Springfield Armory National Historic Site
1 Armory Square,
Springfield, MA 01105

State Historical Museum of Wisconsin
30 North Carroll Street,
Madison, WI 53703

The Confederate Museum
188 Meeting Street,
Charleston, SC 29401

The Museum of the Confederacy
1201 E. Clay Street,
Richmond, Va 23219

U.S. Army Military History Institute
Carlisle Barracks, Pa 17013

Virginia Historical Society
428 North Boulevard,
Richmond, Va 23221

V.M.I. Museum
Virginia Military Institute,
Jackson Memorial Hall,
Lexington, Va 24450

Warren Rifles Confederate Museum
95 Chester Street, Front Royal, Va 22630

War Memorial Museum of Virginia
9285 Warwick Blvd.
Huntingdon Park
Newport News, Va 23607

West Point Museum
United States Military Acadmy, West Point, NY 10996

PICTURE CREDITS